THE ASTROTWINS'

2021 HOROSCOPE

Contributing Editors: Felicia Bender, Matthew Swann
Managing Editor: Lisa M. Sundry
Copy Editors: Amy Anthony, Jess Garcia
Researchers: Ember Ashford, Stephanie Gailing, Jasmmine Ramgotra

Cover Illustrations © 2020 by Bodil Jane. www.bodiljane.com
Book Design: Rosie Dienhart
Interior Illustrations: Bodil Jane, Gabriel Stromberg

ASTROSTYLE

2021 *Contents*

The AstroTwins' 2021 Horoscope   2

A MESSAGE *from*
The AstroTwins

Dear Reader,

As astrologers, one of our jobs is to ask—and answer—the question "Why?"

After all, we have a metaphysical magnifying glass, or maybe it's a microscope, that allows us to translate the tableau that this cosmic lens reveals.

At a time when nothing seems to make sense anymore, it's easy to feel like the universe that once "had our backs" has now turned its back on us. Is this the end of civilization, the twilight hour of the human race?

It would be perfectly legitimate to ask such things. A simple scan of 2020's headlines reveals a dismal year-in-review that would never earn a passing grade. Corruption, deception and disinformation ran rampant. Humanity couldn't seem to catch a break, and neither could our planet. This new year couldn't come fast enough.

Luckily, the stars pattern themselves into a bigger story—a story that explains how, like Bridget Jones on steroids, we now find ourselves at "the edge of reason." Sometimes, just knowing a little more of the "why" can reboot our engines and, frankly, get us through the hour.

In this eighth edition of our annual horoscope guide, we'll give it to you straight, but we'll also serve up a substantial spoonful of hope. You won't be sold false optimism, but you'll hear a (hopefully) balanced view. We can't erase the collective chaos that's left us all scarred and sapped. But we can put it into context for you, giving you a reason to brush your hair or get out of bed, a concrete milestone to work toward, and a glimpse of the happiness that awaits every sign in 2021, even if it's not at bucket-list peak level.

Moving into the second year of the decade, many of us have lowered our expectations, resigning ourselves to "more of same." But we invite you to join us in not allowing this self-protective buffer to become a self-fulfilling prophecy.

As ever, we believe in the power of the human spirit and our ability to co-create destiny with the planets. In these pages, may you reclaim your magic and find a guiding light through these transitional times.

Ophi & Tali
The AstroTwins

2021 FORECAST

What's in the Stars for All of Us?

As we examined the stars for 2021, looking in earnest for signs of stability, a story began to unfold. There's no denying it: We are in the middle of a great historical change that we believe will truly start taking shape in 2022. In many ways, the cosmic lineup of both 2020 and 2021 are a prelude—a Star Wars prequel for some, a Hunger Games for others—designed to prepare us for shifts in world power, economic systems, weather patterns and the way we live.

The prospect of change can seem upsetting and scary when it's ahead of us. But what really drives our angst is the idea of navigating the unknown without a map. As astrologers, it's our job to provide that galactic GPS.

Here's a simplified strategy: To navigate through 2021, you must keep your eye on both the here-and-now and the fast-approaching future.

In other words, live in the moment and "one day at a time." But simultaneously play the long game by saving money, being resourceful and investing in things that may not pay returns for five to ten years or longer. Build and plan…but also let go and be flexible. If 2020 taught us anything, it was that the best-laid plans must sometimes pivot on a moment's notice.

Hey, we made it through 2020, didn't we? The losses and challenges may have left us battle-weary, our "cars" in need of bodywork and repair. But here we are, with another year stretching in front of us—and the bewildering prospect of trying to plan in the face of massive global uncertainty.

In 2021, both expansive Jupiter and structured Saturn will travel through Aquarius, the sign of society, technology and revolution. This is a huge change from their stalwart march through Capricorn in 2020, which emphasized themes of government (historic election much?), business and hierarchy. Now, our sights are set on innovation and massive changes that will reform the way society is organized, governed and serviced. Will all the technological advances set us free…or limit our freedom and privacy?

Here are some things that will remain in a state of flux, if not continue to undergo seismic shifts, in 2021:

Our relationship to time will change.

While Jupiter, Pluto and Saturn all circuited through Capricorn in close proximity for most of 2020, our sense of time warped, flattened or outright disintegrated. Before the discovery of Uranus in 1781, Saturn (aka Chronos the timelord) was the ruler of both Capricorn and Aquarius. This year, as Saturn darts into three shape-shifting squares (90-degree angles) with disruptor Uranus, we can expect to dance the Time Warp again, a la the song from oh-so-Aquarian cult musical, *The Rocky Horror Picture Show*.

When Jupiter dips into Pisces, which is associated with non-linear time, from May 13 to July 28, things could get even more "quantum." Interestingly, the European Union has voted to end Daylight Savings Time in March 2021.

Gathering and communing remain socially distanced.

We got a sneak preview of "social distancing" when restrictive Saturn made a short visit to Aquarius, the zodiac sign that rules group gatherings, from March 21 to July 1, 2020. Now, Saturn is hunkered down in Aquarius until March 2023 for a celestial winter.

That doesn't necessarily mean that we'll have to cancel every wedding, industry conference or music festival until then. But we can certainly expect to see modified versions of these assemblages, perhaps with some technological help from pioneering Aquarius.

Saturn-Uranus squares: Old-school meets new.

Three times in 2021, stalwart Saturn and disruptive Uranus will get into cosmic clashes, locking into 90-degree angles (squares). Old-school Saturn is in innovative Aquarius, while scientific Uranus (the ruler of Aquarius) is hunkered in traditional Taurus. Talk about a double, or quadruple, paradox. Our digitized

> **"One ticket to...the supermarket? Since June 2020, eclipses have overturned our relationship to travel and community."**

reality could drive what experts are calling the Fourth Industrial Revolution, transforming everything from money to manufacturing, banking to government.

Revolutions, banned protests and government suppression.

In the United States, dealing with voter suppression, police-protestor clashes and the 2020 election's COVID-spreading campaign trail was bad enough. Worldwide, governments helmed by dictators were able to use unchecked means of controlling their populations and maintaining their ironclad grip on power. From Internet blackouts to protest clashes and shutdowns, standing up for individual rights has grown exponentially complicated. During the COVID crisis, some countries even issued false reports about their population's health and economic progress, arresting and torturing activist leaders who attempted to deliver resources to their stricken citizens.

With authoritarian Saturn and freedom-seeking Jupiter both in Aquarius, the sign of society and human rights, we can expect much more of this. We've written extensively about these transits, both past and future, in the pages ahead.

Jupiter in Aquarius and Pisces: Finding hope again?

As expansive Jupiter darts between idealistic Aquarius and compassionate Pisces (which it ruled in classical astrology), at least some of our focus is on crafting a more hopeful future worldwide. But with restrictive Saturn also in Aquarius this year, it won't be an overnight job. Truth-teller Jupiter reveals what's been hidden. We'll be patching up, if not gut renovating, the very infrastructure that's needed to make these lofty Jupiter visions into reality.

Gemini/Sagittarius Eclipses: Global transformation.

One ticket to…the supermarket? Since June 2020, a series of eclipses on the Gemini/Sagittarius axis has overturned our relationship to long-distance travel (Sagittarius) and local community (Gemini).

As the karmic north node moves through Gemini from May 5, 2020, until January 18, 2022, our relationship with mobility, community and communication gets an overhaul. This cycle, which happens roughly every 19 years, disrupts all themes associated with Gemini and Sagittarius. With the south node submerged in Sagittarius, which rules global travel and relations, it's no surprise that countries have banned foreign travelers and "sheltering in place" has become part of our lexicon.

Taurus/Scorpio Eclipses: Economic revolution.

A new eclipse series will transform the economy starting on November 19, 2021, as these lunar shape-shifters begin sweeping through the "money signs" of Taurus and Scorpio. For the next year, these eclipses will be interspersed with those on the Gemini/Sagittarius axis, altering commerce and community at once.

This is the first time we've had Taurus/Scorpio eclipses since November 2012 to October 2014, which was a time of economic turnaround in the United States and turmoil in other parts of the world, such as Greece, Venezuela and Russia.

The first eclipse is in Taurus, the sign of finances and material security, and it may be a sneak preview of the fiscal reforms ahead. We have our sights set on April 30, 2022, when a Taurus solar eclipse makes close contact with Uranus, the planet of technology and upheaval. The global economy could make a major pivot, perhaps a larger leap from government-backed currency (coins and bills) to blockchain and cryptocurrency.

Is the world ready for a new monetary system? Well, a prior Taurus/Scorpio eclipse series brought us the Euro, which began to officially circulate as coins and notes in 2002. Just like in 2021, this was a year when eclipses also fell on the Gemini/Sagittarius and Taurus/Scorpio axes, shifting global and economic policies. The next round is certain to bring a new wave, and perhaps, as we've predicted for several years now, the "Internet of the economy" will be fully born.

Lunar Year of the Metal Ox

Chop wood, carry water? Stability and hard work will be strong themes under the endurance-obsessed Ox year, which begins mid-February. In a year ruled by the organized Metal element, our shaky infrastructures will demand repair. Persistence will pay off, and so will preparation.

Numerology: 5 Universal Year

In 2021, the 5 Universal Year will bring creativity and energy to all we do. But things can take a turn for the dramatic under this influence, too. In our Numerology section at the end of the book, you'll learn what's ahead. Wishing you a happy, healthy 2021. ✳

NEW & FULL MOONS

Learn when to plan and produce by the monthly lunar phases.

Following moon cycles is a great way to set goals and reap their benefits. Energy awakens at the new moon, then peaks two weeks later at the full moon. In many cultures, farmers have planted by the new moon and harvested by the full moon. Why not get a little lunar boost for your own life?

Every month, the new moon begins a two-week initiating phase that builds up to a full moon, when we reap what we've planted. There is a six-month buildup between new and full moons. Each new moon falls in a specific zodiac sign. Six months later, a full moon occurs in that same zodiac sign.

New moons mark beginnings and are the perfect time to kick off any new projects or ideas. Lay the groundwork for what you want to manifest in the coming six months. Set intentions or initiate plans and tend to them for a half year.

Full moons are ideal times for completions, emotional outpourings, and reaping results. They're also your cue to cash in on anything you started at the corresponding new moon six months earlier. What have you been building toward? Full moons act as cosmic spotlights, illuminating what's been hidden. Take stock of your efforts and change course at the full moon. ✳

2021 New Moons

2021 Full Moons

	New Moons			Full Moons
1/13	(12:00am): Capricorn		1/28	(2:16pm): Leo
2/11	(2:05pm): Aquarius		2/27	(3:17am): Virgo
3/13	(5:21am): Pisces		3/28	(2:48pm): Libra
4/11	(10:30pm): Aries		4/26	(11:31pm): Scorpio
5/11	(2:59pm): Taurus		5/26	(7:13am): Sagittarius
6/10	(6:52am): Gemini		6/24	(2:39pm): Capricorn
7/9	(9:16pm): Cancer		7/23	(10:36pm): Aquarius #1
8/8	(9:49am): Leo		8/22	(8:01am): Aquarius #2
9/6	(8:51pm): Virgo		9/20	(7:54pm): Pisces
10/6	(7:05pm): Libra		10/20	(10:56am): Aries
11/4	(5:14pm) Scorpio		11/19	(3:57pm): Taurus
12/4	(2:42am) Sagittarius		12/18	(11:35pm): Gemini

Based on Eastern Time (ET) in New York, NY.

ECLIPSES IN 2021

At solar and lunar eclipses, expect the unexpected.

Eclipses happen four to six times a year, bringing sudden changes and turning points to our lives. If you've been stuck in indecision about an issue, an eclipse forces you to act. Unexpected circumstances can arise and demand a radical change of plans.

Truths and secrets explode into the open. Things that aren't "meant to be" are swept away without notice. Shocking as their delivery can be, eclipses help open up space for the new.

The ancients used to hide from eclipses and viewed them as omens or bearers of disruptive change. And who could blame them? They planted, hunted, fished and moved by the cycles of nature and the stars. While the modern astrological approach is not fear-based, we must still respect the eclipses' power.

Solar vs. Lunar Eclipses

There are two types of eclipses—solar and lunar. Lunar eclipses fall at full moons. The earth passes directly between the Sun and the moon, cutting off their communication and casting a shadow on the earth, which often appears in dramatic red and brown shades. A solar eclipse takes place when the new moon passes between the Sun and the earth, shadowing the Sun. The effect is like a spiritual power outage—a solar eclipse either makes you feel wildly off-center, or your mind becomes crystal-clear.

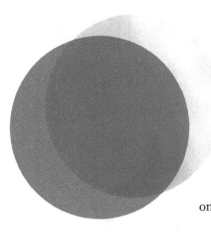

The effects of an eclipse can usually be felt for three to five days before and after the event (some astrologers say eclipses can announce themselves a month before or after, too). Expect the unexpected, and wait for the dust to settle before you act on any eclipse-fueled impulses.

Eclipse Calendar for 2021

May 26: Sagittarius (Total Lunar Eclipse - 7:13am)

June 10: Gemini (Annular Solar Eclipse - 6:52am)

November 19: Taurus (Partial Lunar Eclipse - 3:57pm)

December 4: Sagittarius (Total Solar Eclipse - 2:42am)

In 2021, there will be four eclipses. We'll complete a series on the communicative Gemini/Sagittarius axis that began on June 5, 2020. Themes of travel, community, neighborhoods, schools and socializing have been shaken and stirred since these eclipses arrived shortly after the COVID-19 global pandemic caused countries to close their borders and governments to mandate lockdowns and shelter-in-place orders. In 2021, these lunar events will bring more of Gemini's "hybrid" style to the way we commune and commute, learn and earn.

Economic reform is afoot later in the year, when November sparks up a new Taurus/Scorpio eclipse series, spanning until October 2023. Show me the...crypto? The birth of a new financial system could appear, along with new ways of balancing our material and spiritual realities. ✳

RETROGRADES IN 2021

When planets reverse their course, delays and disruptions can happen.

You've heard the hype about retrogrades—but what are they, really? When a planet passes the Earth in its journey around the Sun, it's said to be going retrograde. From our vantage point on Earth, it is almost as if the planet is moving in reverse. This is an illusion, but it's a bit like two trains passing at different speeds—one appears to be going backward. When a planet goes retrograde (for a few weeks, or sometimes even months), everything that falls under its jurisdiction can go a bit haywire. Survival tip: Think of the prefix "re-" and review, reunite, reconnect, research. Retrogrades aren't the best times to begin something new, but they can be stellar phases for tying up loose ends or giving a stalled mission a second chance. ✷

2021 Retrograde Planets & Dates

MERCURY
January 30–February 20 (Aquarius)
May 29–June 22 (Gemini)
September 27–October 18 (Libra)

VENUS
December 19, 2021–
January 29, 2022 (Capricorn)

JUPITER
June 20–July 28 (Pisces)
July 28–October 18 (Aquarius)

SATURN
May 23–October 10 (Aquarius)

URANUS
January 1–14 (Taurus)
August 19, 2021–
January 18, 2022 (Taurus)

NEPTUNE
June 25–December 1 (Pisces)

PLUTO
April 27–October 6 (Capricorn)

CHIRON
July 15–December 19 (Aries)

Visit the

ASTROTWINS **SHOP**

For books, charts, courses, gifts & more!

JUPITER IN AQUARIUS & PISCES

The celestial supersizer does an unusual dance in 2021 as it weaves between Aquarius and Pisces all year.

Jupiter in Aquarius: December 19, 2020–May 13, 2021

Jupiter in Pisces: May 13–July 28, 2021

Jupiter in Aquarius: July 28–December 28, 2021

Keep hope alive! While sober Saturn weighs anchor in Aquarius, other planetary forces draw our energy up to the surface. Buoyant, optimistic Jupiter spends most of 2021 in Aquarius, co-piloting alongside Saturn through the sign of wishes and the future. Amidst legitimate concerns about "what's next for humanity," Jupiter in Aquarius throws open the shades, directing our attention to the bright side of things.

Jupiter's trajectory is an unusual one in 2021. Generally, the heavenly titan orbits through a single zodiac sign for a steady 12-to-13-month circuit. This year, however, Jupiter weaves in and out of innovative, scientific Aquarius and enchanting, esoteric Pisces.

Jupiter already landed in the Water Bearer's realm on December 19, 2020, so it starts 2021 in this wishful sign. From May 13 to July 28, Jupiter spills out of the Water Bearer's jug and takes a splash through the Fish's seas.

Pay attention! This "preview tour" will reveal the course we'll set sail on again at the year's end, when the red-spotted planet plunges back into Pisces for two more laps: December 28, 2021, to May 10, 2022, and again from October 28 to December 20, 2022.

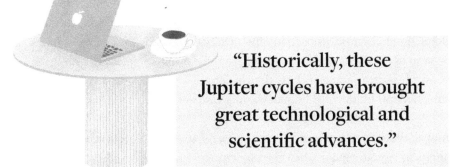

"Historically, these Jupiter cycles have brought great technological and scientific advances."

Historically, these Jupiter cycles have brought great technological and scientific advances, political revolutions and distinct achievements with flight and space travel. That's not a huge surprise, considering that no-limits Jupiter exposes, expands and amplifies whatever it touches. In the final two signs of the zodiac, Aquarius and Pisces, neither the ceiling nor the g-force can hold us!

Science and Ethics

Do all scientific advancements truly benefit humanity? That depends on how they're used. While philosophical Jupiter tours Aquarius, global conversations around ethics are bound to arise.

In 2020, scientist Jennifer Doudna (born February 19, on the Aquarius-Pisces cusp) won the Nobel Prize for her CRISPR technology. This system of gene editing, described as "DNA scissors," allows researchers to interrupt mutations by cutting a viral genome out of a DNA strand, which in turn enables cells to naturally repair themselves. Doudna imagines using CRISPR to cure diseases like sickle-cell anemia and multiple sclerosis. But in a TED talk given in 2015, she warned of the dangers of its potential misuse. To wit, in late 2019, Chinese scientist He Jiankui was sentenced to three years in jail after using CRISPR to implant gene-edited embryos into two women.

While the world may not ready for "designer babies," we can ostensibly imagine a sci-fi future where parents select the eye color and other features of their unborn children. Jupiter in Aquarius may expedite eugenics developments for livestock and crops. This is already a hot-button issue as activists continue to fight for genetically modified food to be labeled as GMO.

Previous Jupiter in Aquarius cycles brought similar developments. After 30 embryos were injected with the genetic material of a third person, the first child of three parents was born in 1997. Dolly the Sheep also made headlines that year as the first mammal cloned from an adult somatic cell using the process of nuclear transfer. Less than a month later, President Bill Clinton banned federal funding for human cloning research.

Rational thought may temper our eagerness to share developments when Jupiter's in Aquarius, but when the planet moves on to boundary-challenged Pisces, all bets are off. Jupiter is the ancient ruler of Pisces (Neptune is this sign's modern ruler), which can drop some serious rose-colored glasses over our eyes. Fantasy may outweigh the "restrictions" of reality as we push developments to market before they've been thoroughly tested. Between May 13 and July 28, this could be the case—a cause for concern in a year where coronavirus vaccines are going through clinical trials.

When Jupiter toured Pisces in 1998, former physician Andrew Wakefield published a (later discredited) paper in *The Lancet* linking measles, mumps and rubella (MMR) vaccinations to autism. Flaws in the study led to him being struck from the medical register, but the widespread fear it created was linked to a drop in MMR vaccinations and gave rise to the modern-day "anti-vax" movement. Public health professionals are now concerned that this same phenomenon will find people refusing COVID vaccines in 2021.

With a global pandemic still plunging every world nation into a public health crisis, we need Jupiter in Aquarius' scientific developments—and ethical standards—more than ever! In 2009-10 (Jupiter's last sweep through Aquarius and Pisces), we were plagued by the swine flu/H1N1 pandemic, which is reported to have caused around 284,000 deaths worldwide. Issues of public misinformation, medical shortages and concerns about the side effects of the vaccine are eerily similar to the circumstances surrounding our current COVID-19 crisis. Will we learn from the past or repeat the lessons?

Power Plays

Aquarius rules electricity, science and energy. Pisces governs water and the unseen. While Jupiter orbited through these two signs between 1938-39, German scientist Otto Hahn discovered nuclear fission, which is used in modern nuclear power plants to heat water and produce steam (Pisces). The steam is then used to spin large turbines, generating electricity (Aquarius). Fascinating!

Sadly, Jupiter in Aquarius and Pisces transits have brought abuses of this power throughout history. In 1986, the Chernobyl disaster at a Ukrainian nuclear power plant killed 31 people and rendered the area uninhabitable for 20,000 years. Radiation that spread from the (preventable) accident is still pegged as the cause of rare forms of cancer and birth defects today.

Use of nuclear arms can also be traced to past Jupiter in Aquarius and Pisces phases. In 1938, Albert Einstein (a Pisces) penned a letter to U.S. President Franklin Delano Roosevelt (an Aquarius), explaining how the power of fission chain reactions utilizing uranium could be used to construct "extremely powerful bombs." Einstein, who believed that the German government was already busy researching this, urged the United States to follow suit. One year later, in 1939, FDR met with his unofficial advisor, Alexander Sachs, to discuss the letter.

Subsequent Jupiter in Aquarius/Pisces cycles brought more developments. In response to the Soviets, the U.S. engineered its first hydrogen bomb in the early 1950s. The Cuban Missile crisis created a huge scare in 1962, when a 13-day confrontation between the United States and the Soviet Union was sparked by a Soviet ballistic missile deployment in Cuba. In 1974, India detonated a weapon and became the sixth nation in the world to declare itself a nuclear state.

On February 5, 2021, when Jupiter will again be in Aquarius, the New Start Treaty between the U.S. and Russia is set to expire. (At this writing in October 2020, negotiations are underway to extend it.) With the clock ticking on this nuclear arms reduction deal, election politics have already complicated negotiations. As we enter the new year, Iran continues to expand its nuclear program with threats from the Saudis to follow suit. Currently, nine nations have nuclear weapons: Britain, Russia, the U.S., China, France, India, Pakistan, Israel and North Korea. Scary as it sounds, Jupiter in fair-minded Aquarius may foster greater cooperation for nations in the year ahead.

Changes in Government and the Ruling Class

Power to the people! When outspoken Jupiter sweeps through communal Aquarius, the cry for equity gets louder. From social justice movements to populist pushback, these periods in history give voice to the underrepresented masses. Part of the reason for this? Aquarius sits directly opposite Leo on the zodiac wheel, a diametric force opposing the regal Lion. Mass rebellions could transform governments and transfer power.

The protests of 2020 were a prelude to what's likely to come in 2021. Last year, (Gemini) Breonna Taylor and (Libra) George Floyd became tragic figures of the Black Lives Matter movement, and the global protests against unjust treatment of African Americans by law enforcement. With Jupiter in anarchistic Aquarius, the growing call to "defund the police" may amplify in 2021.

Historically, many major uprisings and peace accords have occurred when Jupiter was in Aquarius and Pisces. In late 2020, as Jupiter advanced toward Aquarius, tens of thousands of Thai protestors assembled on the streets of Bangkok to decry government abuses. Risking riot police and harsh jail sentences, the student-led crowds called for the king-approved prime minister to step down, a new constitution to be drafted and a massive reduction to the Thai monarchy's power.

Will more people get down on the English crown? In 2021, Harry and Meghan's groundbreaking exit from their palace duties could continue to boost their iconic status in North America. Last year, the Duchess of Sussex spoke out on a number of Aquarian-ruled issues from Black Lives Matter to the pitfalls of social media. Eschewing class-based privilege, this pair could pave the way for further unraveling of obsolete monarchies and questionable oligarchic strongholds. (In a sad synchronicity, Princess Diana died in a paparazzi-fueled car crash while Jupiter was in Aquarius in 1997.)

The Arab Spring rocked many Middle Eastern nations while Jupiter was in Pisces in early 2010. Armed rebellions and anti-government protests sprang up first in Tunisia, then spread across five other Arab nations. Between 1998 and 1999, The Good Friday Agreement was signed in Ireland, bringing an end to much of the violence of the Troubles, a political conflict that had been waging in Northern Ireland since the 1960s.

During that same Jupiter in Aquarius and Pisces period, the Truth and Reconciliation Commission was formed in South Africa to investigate and heal the wounds caused by apartheid. A prior Jupiter in Aquarius and Pisces circuit from 1986-87 saw Mikhail Gorbachev introducing Perestroika and Glasnost to the Soviet Union. At the time, this was a revolutionary concept that included "restructuring" of policies and "openness" to express opinions without fear of being turned in to the KGB. In 1987, the First Palestinian Intifada erupted in response to Israeli occupation of the West Bank, a clash that went on for over five years. The People Power Revolution restored democracy to the Phillipines after a long reign by Ferdinand Marcos.

Under Jupiter's last Aquarian tour in January 2009, Barack Obama was inaugurated as the first African American president of the United States. Later that year, the Tea Party movement was formed by a group of fiscally conversative Republicans calling for lower taxes and decreased government spending.

Central banks, which tend to thrive under Jupiter in budget-conscious Capricorn, may be challenged when the enterprising planet orbits through utopian Aquarius. On January 3, 2009, one week before Jupiter transited from Capricorn to Aquarius, a decentralizing currency was born: the genesis block, the first block of Bitcoin ever mined.

As we enter 2021, the pandemic-wrecked economy is widening class divisions and pushing millions more below the poverty line. Jupiter's entrance into Aquarius leaves us poised for social reform. Will governments lead the way, or will people be forced to continue assembling to fight for their rights? In the U.S. many are embracing—and vilifying with equal fervor—progressive platforms like Democratic Socialism. No matter your political views, it's impossible to ignore that the world is facing unprecedented challenges around providing resources to its vulnerable populations.

Little known astro-fact: Jupiter is also associated with the law. Legal disruptions and scandalous exposures within government have occurred during prior cycles. Back in 2010, WikiLeaks released a collection of more than 250,000 American diplomatic cables, laying bare confidential disclosures and brutally honest views of world leaders. In 1998, the U.S. House of Representatives voted to impeach President Clinton. And…you can't make this up, folks, the Watergate scandal, which led to Nixon's resignation, all went down while Jupiter was in Pisces in 1974!

Will we finally get the truth on Trump's tax returns in 2021? Uncover more back-channel dealings and nefarious plotlines involving global administrations? Hang on to your Swarovski-embellished masks, people, because jaws could hit the ground.

Water, Water Everywhere?

As galactic gambler Jupiter rolls the dice on the zodiac's Water Bearer and Fish, we may become more enterprising about H2O. Currently, investors are looking to water as a viable commodity, much like oil or gold. It's a matter of supply and demand. Although 70 percent of the Earth is covered in water, 97 percent of it is saltwater, which cannot be utilized for much without treatment and processing. Pollution, rapid industrialization, the agricultural industry, the growing population—all of these contribute to an even greater scarcity of clean, fresh water. United Nations projections predict that more than half of the world's population will live in highly water-stressed areas by 2030.

Blue-chip and small-cap companies alike are all getting in on these "liquid assets." Despite the environmental impacts of plastic waste, the bottled water industry continues to grow due to increased global demand. Water-based ETFs and mutual funds are now available, which may contain stocks from water utility companies, treatment plants and more.

Will water barons become the new Rockefellers? Rumors continue to swirl about the Bush family's holdings in Paraguay, one of the four countries (along with Uruguay, Argentina and Brazil) that cover the Guarani Aquifer. This freshwater reserve, which is the size of Texas and California combined, contains enough drinkable, potable H2O to sustain the world's population for

200 years —definitely a valuable lifeline for human sustenance! Some activists view the Bush family's Paraguayan land purchase as a modern-day imperialist threat to South America's sovereignty.

Meanwhile, enterprising Jupiter may pave the way for radical developments in desalination, the process of extracting the harmful hypersaline brines to create safe drinking water. Current iterations of this treatment tend to be both expensive and environmentally harmful. But in the past year researchers have been refining their processes. A team of engineers at Columbia University led by Ngai Yin Yip created TSSE (Temperature Swing Solvent Extraction),

"Will water barons become the new Rockefellers?"

a separation method that doesn't require costly, high-impact evaporation. We anticipate more developments from labs in 2021.

Climate change is occurring: Polar ice caps are melting, and global weather patterns appear to be shifting. Will rapid-moving Jupiter amplify this trend while in Aquarius and Pisces? Bring clock-slowing breakthroughs? Or both? Scientists are finding evidence that the East Antarctic ice sheet, which holds 70 percent of the world's ice, is far more vulnerable to melting that we previously thought. But this might not be entirely due to greenhouse gases which appear to be the culprits behind the disappearing ice in other regions. Naturally accumulating deposits of uranium—released from decaying rocks and gravel trapped under the East Antarctic ice sheet—may be contributing to the cause of this phenomenon. It's also worth mentioning that Antarctica is home to at least 138 newly discovered volcanoes, making this frozen continent the most volcanic of the planet, no doubt playing a subterranean role in any long view of the continents' glaciation, or lack thereof.

And what of electric storms arcing across our skies? Jupiter is the god of lightning and Aquarius is an air sign. With our planet a mere 93 million miles away from the Sun, it's not hard to envision some kind of electromagnetic disturbance descending upon us again, hopefully one that doesn't impact our fragile lives. To wit, the largest geomagnetic storm in recorded history, known as a coronal mass ejection (CME), disrupted our planet in the not-so-recent past on September 2, 1849. Named the Carrington Event for British astronomer Richard Carrington, who observed and recorded it, this CME caused telegraph systems across the U.S. and Europe to fail, giving operators electric shocks. A similar CME today would create widespread power outages and blackouts with extensive damage to our electrical grid.

One ticket to Mars, please? We're not trying to spin up doomsday scenarios here, but admittedly, the statistics are making us wonder what advancements to space travel Jupiter in cosmonaut Aquarius will bring. Certainly there will be some interesting overlaps between the air and water elements in 2021. Jupiter's last spin through Aquarius coincided with the "Miracle on the Hudson," when a US Airways pilot skillfully navigated an emergency water landing on the Hudson River after the plane struck a flock of Canadian geese and subsequently lost thrust of both engines.

Always Be Prepared

Once again, we're not trying to churn up fear, but we'd be remiss if we didn't make note of the storms that have occurred during cycles of Jupiter in Aquarius and Pisces. On January 12, 2010, a magnitude 7.0 earthquake had devastating effects on the population of Haiti. In April 2010, Mount Eyjafjallajökull erupted in Iceland, snarling air traffic in Europe for days. As of this writing, we are aware of numerous geologic disturbances, many of which locate upon ancient fault zones. With Yellowstone National Park also issuing warning signals of rising magma levels, we must look to previous cycles that have coincided with calamitous volcanos, earthquakes and tsunamis to be responsible dwellers of an active planet.

While we pray for a 2021 free from weather-related issues, it never hurts to have an emergency preparedness plan in place. Stock up the pantry, obtain clean, storable water, take note of the evacuation routes. Understand the emergency precautions necessary for whatever risks are posed in your region, from earthquakes to tornados. An ounce of prevention is worth a magnitude of meteorological cure.

The AstroTwins' 2021 Horoscope   24

And Don't Forget to Fantasize...

When it gets too crazy out there, we can always rely on the powers of our imagination during these Jupiter cycles. With people isolated indoors due to the virus, reality-simulating digital experiences will be more in-demand than ever. Where will machine learning take VR and AI technologies in 2021? These markets could get even hotter with venturesome Jupiter in the mix.

Media-savvy Jupiter's journeys through special-effects master Aquarius and cinematic Pisces have often dovetailed with epic developments in the arts. In 2009, James Cameron's blockbuster *Avatar* brought groundbreaking advances in 3D technology to the screens. The first DVDs were announced at the Academy Awards while Jupiter toured Aquarius in 1997. That same year, *Harry Potter and the Philosopher's Stone* was published, the first book in the wildly popular series which is rife with Aquarius-themed wizardry and Piscean enchantment.

Even the types of programming we consume may be guided by Jupiter. We could practically roll our eyes at this "coincidence," but here goes. *Titanic,* which treated us to the iceberg-melting onscreen romance between Leonardo DiCaprio and Kate Winslet, won Best Picture days after Jupiter flowed into Pisces in 1998. Fantasy crept into our modern-day bedrooms that very same year with the premiere of Candace Bushnell's *Sex and the City* on HBO. Aquarian sexual liberation blended with the envelope-pushing emotionality of Pisces (not to mention this foot-ruling sign's fetish for Manolo Blahniks) made this show instantly iconic.

Escapism or empathy? In addition to shows that take us away from reality, compassionate programming could rise exponentially in this era of amplified anxiety. Prior Jupiter in Pisces cycles brought the first national broadcast of *The Oprah Winfrey Show* (1986) and the soap opera *General Hospital* (1963).

Now for the part where some Aquarius innovation could really come in handy: How to get the casts together safely in the coronavirus era? While studios are still figuring it out, the ongoing pandemic could give rise to groundbreaking broadcasting techniques that we've yet to imagine. ✳

SATURN IN AQUARIUS

Revolutions in technology, finance and citizens' rights will change the structures of our lives for the next two years and beyond.

March 21–July 1, 2020

December 17, 2020–March 7, 2023

Back by unpopular demand, it's border cop Saturn patrolling the graffiti-lined streets of Aquarius Land. From March 21 to July 1, 2020, we got a glimpse of what happens when the planet of restrictions tours one of the zodiac's most social and revolutionary signs.

Humans distanced. We sheltered in place. We quarantined. And yes (no drumroll needed), we socially restricted ourselves—a synonym for "Saturn in Aquarius" if ever there were!

We found new ways to connect through technology. We signed up for webinars. We kicked ourselves for not buying stock in Zoom. We picked up Chromebooks from the school district and played amateur teachers while our education professionals struggled with the limitations of Google Classroom. We enrolled in TikTok University and made awkward attempts to crush the "Savage" challenge led by Aquarius Megan Thee Stallion.

We marched for social justice. We protested. We wore our masks or rebelled against them. We parsed through conspiracy theories (or were they?) about germ warfare, 5G networks, deep state Satanic cults, and oligarch-funded vaccines. We set up Autonomous Zones and encampments in major cities. We jumped in our trucks and showed up with our guns.

We empathized. We militarized. We polarized.

And, here we are...entering 2021 with global societies so fractured that "all the King's horses and all the King's men" ain't putting this beast back together again. And maybe that's the point of this exercise. Aquarius is the utopian idealist of the zodiac, a sign that thrives on equity, community and the principles of "One Love" espoused by Bob Marley, a legendary Water Bearer. Kings have no place when Aquarius is at the helm...unless they're being moved across the chessboard of an outdoor street match. Besides, grandfather Saturn in Aquarius doesn't do chess. In 2021, he'd rather play Go, the world's oldest strategy game, which was invented in China 2,500 years ago and remains popular today.

Over the past five years, planets strengthened the powers of the billionaire class, a trend that we see continuing. From 2017-18, the lunar North Node took a royal processional down Leo's red carpet. Along with a series of eclipses—including the sky-darkening Leo solar eclipse of August 21, 2017—this powered up the palace intrigue. Staunch Saturn floated through its own homecoming parade in its native sign of Capricorn, from December 19, 2017, to December 17, 2020. All systems ruled by Saturn and Capricorn were fortified for much of this journey: the patriarchy, governments, corporations and the economy.

Then along came 2020. (Crash! Boom!) As evolutionary underlord Pluto and expansive overlord Jupiter caught up to Saturn in the sky, the three planets commingled in Capricorn for the first time since 1285 AD. Everything systemic that fell under this reign seemed to go off the rails in 2020. Our own forecast of a "Black Swan event," which appeared in last year's edition of this book, came hauntingly true. (Special thanks to Astrostyle in-house astrologer Matthew Swann for that prediction!) And here we are.

While Saturn tours Aquarius until March 7, 2023, we will all be navigating its paradox. How can we smash through the rules while adhering to time-tested principles? Unleash our rebellious individualism while fostering communities based on equity and accessibility? We have two years to unpack this riddle— which is bound to bring more incendiary uprising and backlash than we've already seen.

Saturn-Uranus Squares: Global Disruption and the Digitization of Reality

February 17, June 14, December 24

If there's palpable tension in 2021, much of it will be supplied by a standoff between structured Saturn and changemaker Uranus—the co-rulers of Aquarius. These planets may be next-door neighbors, but they're the Hatfield and McCoy of the solar system. Each possesses a valid claim over the Water Bearer's realm while enforcing contrary agendas (think "square peg, round hole") providing for many of our most vexing, intractable problems. And three times in 2021, they'll lock into a stressful square (a 90-degree angle), grappling for the upper hand.

Before Uranus was discovered by telescope in 1781, Saturn was considered the galactic guardian of Aquarius (Uranus is its "modern ruler"). That means Water Bearers have two celestial sentinels: quirky, side-spinning Uranus and disciplined Saturn. Quite the contrasting energies! Perhaps that's why Aquarians possess such range, flipping from metaphysical wizards to science-bound empiricists.

This year, the contradictory push-pull will express itself in every zodiac sign's life and also in world events. Can change happen without a collapse of key infrastructures? Can order be kept without suppressing the voice of "the people"? Saturn and Uranus square each other roughly every 14 years. Historically, these tumultuous standoffs can force deep structural changes in society, often involving widespread disruption and destruction.

As suppressive Saturn tightens its authoritarian grip on freedom-fighter Uranus, a war between chaos and control erupts. Like an earthquake, the stable ground beneath us is left shaken. Later, we must rebuild from the rubble. Put plainly, Saturn wants law and order; Uranus wants change at any cost. We've been feeling this since the two planets began their dance in January 2020, bringing everything from economic shakeups to the global COVID-19 pandemic to sweeping Black Lives Matter protests. As the Saturn-Uranus tension reaches a head in 2021, society is embroiled in heated efforts to change "the system" (Saturn) through (Uranian) protests, citizen uprisings and attempts to redistribute rights and resources through the greater population.

The Economy: America 2.0

Disclaimer: The information in this book should not be considered professional financial advice. All writings on this site are purely based on the authors' opinions and are intended for entertainment purposes only. Please consult a certified professional financial advisor when considering any investment or financial decision.

Saturn and Uranus were square from 1929-31, during the initial stages of the Great Depression. Shortly after the 1929 U.S. Stock Market crash, when stocks lost 90 percent of their value, Saturn and Uranus began squaring each other in lockstep for two years. At the 2008 Great Recession, another time of profound economic turbulence, these two outer planets were embroiled in an opposition.

As 2021 begins, Saturn and Uranus are back in a square aspect, a conflict intensified by their positions in the staunch "fixed" signs of Aquarius and Taurus. It's conceivable that an avalanche of negative events and sentiment could pierce the current Wall Street "Everything Bubble," echoing the great '29 crash by eventually consuming every index and currency market on the planet.

When Pluto makes its grand return to 27 degrees Capricorn in the U.S. natal chart on February 21, 2022, Saturn and Uranus will still be square—a double impact we'll feel through all of next year. As Lord Pluto completes a 246-year revolution around the Sun, his arrival could catalyze this domino-like collapse, unleashing a national disaster that includes armed civil conflict between various polarized social groups vying for social dominance.

Interestingly, the word "disaster" originates from the 16th-century Italian word *disastro*, which means an "ill-starred event." *Dis-* "apart from" and *astro* "star" (from Latin *astrum*). The etymological omen: To prevent a crisis, align with the patterns of the stars.

In this cosmic unfolding, which will extend through 2022 and accelerate into 2024, dynamical and mathematical forces will likely compound overlooked stress points in the economy. These could include municipal bond downturns, unavailable shipping containers, declining commercial real estate values (including REITs), corporate insolvencies and eventually, unfunded government liabilities—plus a wave of sovereign "bad actors" taking full advantage of the dystopic atmosphere.

The AstroTwins' 2021 Horoscope   29

The Saturnian deleveraging of the economy, set against the Uranian volatile conditions, will impact the growth of the country well beyond 2024. There's also the likelihood of largescale populist strikes emerging by 2025, protesting the liquidation of America. This continued Plutonic deterioration will be able to trace its origins to three unambiguous signals in the autumn of 2019: the October outbreak of the coronavirus in Wuhan, the Wall Street repo market collapse and the death of the WeWork unicorn, all of which provided for the initial "Minsky Moment" shockwave of March 23, 2020, when the Dow index fell from 29,568 to 18,213, an event that Astrostyle reported upon at that time, given the gravity of the collapse. The retesting of this March 2020 low would parallel the 1929-31 second-year crash.

If markets follow the patterns of 2008 and 2019-20, a crisis in 2022-24 will result in the U.S. Federal Reserve again pumping trillions of stimulus dollars into the economy in an attempt to keep it buoyant. Into this inequity, new, questionable concepts about the utility of money will be circulated, in economic circles what's known as MMT (Modern Monetary Theory). Essentially, MMT aims to replace the role of the Federal Reserve central bank to control inflation and employment with a fiscal policy steered by the government, in all likelihood featuring UBI (Universal Basic Income) to maintain money velocity for our economy.

Can we have faith that the U.S. Congress will do any better than the Fed or disengage from its endless, polarized strife to responsibly lead the global economy? MMT's many critics point out that it's a fiscal policy for inflating our already unmanageable national debts past the event horizon of a debt blackhole into fiscal oblivion with no hope for recovery.

Will foreign nations accept the U.S. saving itself while their countries, unable to print dollars, sink into depression? From the rest of the world's perspective, the U.S. economy is a Frankenstein monster being kept alive by Federal Reserve stimulus and corporate stock market buybacks—an illegal practice until 1982.

In such a scenario, which will extend from the present to 2022 then accelerate into 2024-25, margin call trading requirements will force many investors to sell off all their assets in a scramble to raise cash before the market hits bottom. Deep-pocketed investors and large institutional players, watching from the sidelines, will no doubt wait for the bottom of the market before moving in, reconfirming the ancient Wall Street adage, "Buy low, sell high." From there, we'll see Bitcoin skyrocket, along with safe haven assets like gold and silver.

Since Pluto is associated with generational wealth, especially as it transits through Capricorn, the sign of long-held family assets, vast fortunes will be made. The take-all winners? Those who are positioned to capture the largest wealth transfer in global economic history after a massive deleveraging of the U.S. economy.

The disconnect between the stock market and the rest of the economy has been a feature of the U.S. economy since at least the 2008 financial crisis, promoting calls for a reevaluation of the role between the Federal Reserve central bank and the markets, which have diverged with such force that it can prompt us to question whether we have free markets at all. Nonetheless, the Fed pumping the markets with stimulus could—incredibly—cause a rising stock market, perhaps surpassing the psychological barrier of 30,000-plus Dow points before eventually succumbing to a market contraction.

It's likely that this "melt up" would bring no-growth, stagflating forces to bear on the U.S. economy with inflationary pressures exerting more destabilization on the lives of consumers before a reordering of the economic system is mandated. Remember, previous market highs were the order of the day before each catastrophic crash. Is there hope for America ahead? Perhaps our future is also guided by Uranus, the planet of "electric" genius and the estimated $100 trillion electric vehicle market? No doubt your purchase will be transacted with a digital currency, itself ruled by Uranus, too.

It should be no surprise that the eventual preeminent reserve asset will be governed by hardy Capricorn. Bitcoin, which minted its genesis block on January 3, 2009, is a tough, decentralized Goat while also being ruled by the shrewd Rat, the first of the Chinese zodiac signs. Bitcoin, unlike government-issued fiat currency, is a digital currency that is not subject to central bank manipulation or devaluation. In financial parlance, Bitcoin is "hard," which is why it's poised to be coveted by individuals, companies and countries alike as the ultimate reserve asset in any portfolio when we find ourselves deep in the Aquarian financial winter.

In this charged financial environment, stalwart, must-have commodities plus a basket of rare earth elements, to name a few, may be so difficult to come by that they increase in price due to supply chain disruption. The term "supply and demand" will make itself known again, taking on foreboding meaning with every new lockdown from continued seasonal waves of the COVID-19 virus. This volatility could easily send fragile nation states into regional warfare, per Astrostyle's March 2020 prediction. The current war between Armenia and

Azerbaijan is one such hot zone that will typify impending conflicts spurred by the ongoing global fracturing.

As the world teeters at the precipice of imminent change, we again forecast a restructured global financial system, one that's on par with the 1944 formation of the Bretton-Woods monetary system and incorporates emerging blockchain technology. The question: Will it be administered by the U.S. Federal Reserve... or a larger global entity, such as the IMF?

Of course, there's a probability that an extended no-growth period lasting a decade is our financial lot, too, one that mirrors the perpetual flatline of Japan and its 30-year balance sheet recession. A long period of "stagflation"—persistent high inflation paired with high unemployment rates and low or stagnant demand—is a grim possibility after the dust settles, given our catastrophic debt levels and global encumbrances.

In the second half of this decade, after the U.S. completes its Plutonic restructuring and the icy dwarf planet enters Aquarius from 2024 to 2043 (yep, nearly 20 years), changes can occur in a zeptosecond. The United States will have the opportunity to revisit and determine its core values, as we move into our high-tech future, prompted by the deglobalization occurring now. In this view, it's likely that technology and sciences will lead us into the Age of Aquarius, where the material becomes immaterial, and technological and transcendental revolutions await.

Just as when we wrote about 2020 back in 2019, when we could not foresee how the dynamics would exactly play out (COVID, protests, lockdowns) only time will tell how these historic patterns will specifically unfold in 2021 and beyond.

Preparation is the best antidote when outer planets clash, which is why we've chosen to include these stark predictions. As 17th-century Enlightenment philosopher Baruch Spinoza said, "If you want the present to be different from the past, study the past." Accurate astrology is not only about seeing the future; it demands that we understand history and its cycles as well.

Planetary history also teaches us that the American Civil War erupted when Saturn was similarly squaring Uranus in 1861, troubling to note in a year where this seems like a distinct possibility. Complicating matters, Saturn is in rebellious Aquarius until March 7, 2023—the zodiac sign that's ruled by Uranus!

Meantime, destabilizing Uranus is in its weakened "fall" sign as it occupies Taurus, the sign of security and finance, which, as we shared above, has already caused major fluctuations in the global markets. Certainly, this won't make for an easy moment in history, but the changes we see in 2021 will likely bring awe-inspiring developments in many sectors. With Saturn in Aquarius, a "Great Reset" is undoubtedly in the stars for all of us. We expect the commercial banking sector to implode with the arrival of negative interest rates during Saturn's wintry transit through Aquarius as everyday account holders will refuse to pay banks to hold their money.

Is this why Virgo billionaire investor Warren Buffet (aka "the oracle of Omaha") sold his bank stocks earlier this year and exchanged them for gold stocks? Who is the real beneficiary to these momentous changes? The Federal Reserve central bank may see the utility in this NIRP (negative interest rate policy) landscape, as it will allow the consolidation of power among a select group of survivor banks, eventually allowing the Federal Reserve to hold the existing notes of an entire economy, thereby making it easier to issue a new financial system, one that is cashless and controlled directly by the Fed in a blockchain offering as the world's non-dollar currencies collapse. Are you ready to download your Fed wallet app?

With this monetary transition descending below the zero threshold into negative territory, along with yield rate control and the rise of digital currencies, the time-value of money is being inverted in ways never witnessed in history. This state of "neganomics" (negative economics) will give rise to a virtually controlled monetary system, one where the public good of money is rendered inaccessible from behind a cryptographic veil. In the mounting battle for control of the world's reserve currency, likely between the dollar and the Chinese *yuan* (and Bitcoin?) will the very technology designed to free money from state control create a techno-totalitarian grip on humanity?

This "Minsky Moment" morality play will bring a more centralized control of the economy and the ability to tax private citizens as all consumer transactions will be observable on the blockchain ledger. A Big Brother Bank by any other meme, this is a harbinger of Saturn's de-democratization of our common goods and a radical expression of Saturnian self-interest blended with high-tech Uranian genius. If the charter between the Fed and the government is modified, expect this scenario to play out over the ensuing years as a digital moral hazard is stepped over. Astrostyle predicts that during the Age of Aquarius, the next great political revolution, among many, will be the separation of money from the state.

A New Relationship with Hopes and Dreams

Wishful thinking: interrupted? Future-minder Aquarius is the sign of hopes and dreams. But how do we keep optimism alive while dour Saturn curbs collective enthusiasm? The answer may lie in changing our perception of time, which is clock-watching Saturn's domain. Rather than fixating on the long game, the next two years could deliver a master class in mindfulness and presence.

When Saturn last orbited through his sign in the early 1990s, Aquarius Eckhart Tolle was planted on a park bench, contemplating the nature of time, which he subsequently recorded in his first *New York Times* bestselling book, *The Power of Now*, a universal paean to both lords of Aquarius, Saturn and Uranus. While Tolle's popularity has hardly waned over the past 30 years, this topic is due for a resurgence. From his perspective, "As soon as you honor the present moment, all unhappiness and struggle dissolve, and life begins to flow with joy and ease."

These could be words to live by in 2021. In recent years, the Uranus (and Aquarius) ruled technology community of Silicon Valley has embraced stoicism—an ancient philosophy that sits in sharp contrast to the embarrassment of riches this group enjoys. CEOs slipped off to Joshua Tree for plant-medicine ceremonies, plunged into cold pools, fasted on liquid-only diets, or followed former American Apparel marketing exec turned stoicism guru, Ryan Holiday (a Gemini), who authored books in both categories, including *The Ego Is the Enemy* and *Trust Me, I'm Lying*.

In a nod to wise Saturn, it's worth mentioning that some of the wealthiest men of ancient Rome also practiced stoicism, disabusing themselves of many bodily pleasures exactly as our Silicon Valley overlords do today, including the second wealthiest Roman in history, author of the play *Medea* and chief counsel to infamous emperor Nero 2,000 years ago. That was none other than the great Seneca who, tragically, was ordered by Nero to take his own life shortly after the Great Fire of 64 A.D. consumed Rome.

Whether you care to become a modern-day stoic like Holiday or not, self-disciplined Saturn in idealistic Aquarius could raise the bar on this "pain and punishment as social currency" trend. And with Uranus squaring Saturn, we expect people may go to great lengths to prove their mettle. Scary schemes could gain cultish followings, like the 2003 "Spiritual Warrior" retreat led by James Arthur Ray, which ended in the death of three participants in an overheated sweat lodge. For others, the Saturn time warp will initiate a profound social awakening. When Saturn toured Aquarius in 2020, the death of George Floyd sparked a worldwide reckoning over the inhumane treatment of Black citizens.

In June 2020, Aquarian attempts to ease the racial disconnect included the rising popularity of *White Fragility*, a 2018 book that occupied the number-one spot on *USA Today's* bestselling book list last summer. Other books on anti-racism also soared to the top ten in sales, including *So, You Want to Talk About Race* by Ijeoma Oluo and *Me and White Supremacy* by Layla F. Saad. We anticipate more movement in this woke direction as Saturn takes up residence in Aquarius again until March 7, 2023.

No matter what philosophies you subscribe to, there will be an undeniable period of time when this Aquarian mind shift between future-tripping and here-and-now presence will feel like a buzzkill. Prior to moving into Aquarius, Saturn took a three-year lap through ambitious Capricorn (December 19, 2017, to December 17, 2020). High achievers bounded ahead of the pack, inspiring the world as supercoaches, influencers and masters of the expert industry—with the TEDx talks and YouTube channels to prove it.

Then along came the COVID-19 pandemic, imperiling the world's markets and our dreams with every lockdown, highlighting that none of us afflicted were experts on real viruses as our deepest cultural fragilities were exposed and found to be as invisible as the virus, yet located right under our proverbial noses.

Of course, Saturn was in Aquarius for the initial pandemic shock, ushering in the viral devastation on a global scale, taking its preview lap through Aquarius from March 21 to July 1, 2020. Uncertainty, fear and safety concerns dominated our moment-to-moment thinking as the virus impacted the simplest decisions on how to thwart its rampage through our bodies and cities. The newly arrived burden of sheer survival blurred our thought processes, leveling each consideration to the maddening logic of the pandemic. All flights were cancelled, whether flights of fancy or flights to remote locations to escape each other. Could there be any more socially impoverished condition to typify Saturn's oppressive effect on neighborly Aquarius?

As we raced to take advantage of low interest rates, grace periods and remote work arrangements, the impending sense of doom created its own kind of depression—an emotional one. Without a bright future to dream about, we were deprived of one of the major drivers of human survival: the neurochemical dopamine.

In his book, *The Molecule of More*, Harvard University professor Daniel Lieberman writes how this single molecule "not only allows you to move beyond the realm of what's at your fingertips, but also motivates you to pursue, to control, and to possess the world beyond your immediate grasp. It drives you to seek out those things far away, both physical things and things you cannot see, such as knowledge, love, and power. Whether it's reaching across the table for the saltshaker, flying to the moon in a spaceship or worshipping a god beyond space and time, this chemical gives us command over every distance, whether geographical or intellectual."

With technology advancing exponentially since Saturn's last lap through Aquarius from 1991-94, doors opened to unforeseen possibilities. No wonder we're all such excitement junkies! Yet, even before we had this much opportunity within swiping range of our fingertips, humans have been on an eternal quest for inspiration. Martin Luther King, Jr.'s "I Have A Dream" speech, given while Saturn was in Aquarius, has spanned the decades as a timeless call to action.

So how do we find our flow in 2021? For the Gen Z crowd, this crushing moment is a particularly heart-wrenching entry into adulthood. With university classes relegated to Zoom, internships cancelled and the job market dwindling in many sectors, there's hardly a world of options awaiting. This generation has already inherited a climate crisis and, in most countries, a monetary policy that has perpetually saddled them with colossal, non-repayable national debts. It's little wonder that studies are showing an ongoing increase in opioid use among the Millennial and Gen Z age groups, drugs which flood the brain's reward circuit with (you guessed it) dopamine. They are starved of hope and dreams, and they know it. Again, it's a neurochemical signature of Saturn's obdurate presence.

Clearly, we need some sunshine during this long Aquarian winter, whether from safe amounts of dopamine or Vitamin D3. Our bodies thirst for a surge of health. Good news: There are ways to nourish dopamine that don't require a Percocet prescription. Brain-boosting nootropics have become the latest, er, buzz, in performance enhancement, some of which amplify dopamine production. With scientific Saturn squaring high-tech Uranus in earthy Taurus, there could be an upward trend in the "natural" versions of these, like the amino acid L-theanine that's found in green tea and certain mushrooms.

Speaking of mushrooms, psychonaut Uranus in earthy Taurus could bring a revolution in mental health. At time of writing, Measure 109, which would legalize the use of psylocibin in therapeutic settings, garnered enough signatures to make it on the Oregon ballot in November 2020. Who knows? Tripping out on the therapist's couch could be the new substitute for those pandemic-foiled ayahuasca ceremonies in Peru.

Calling all mycologists! Legal 'shrooms, like chaga, reishi, and ashwagandha are also making headlines for their adaptogenic properties. While nootropics boost brain function, adaptogens literally help us adjust to things like stress, harsh weather conditions and noise pollution.

With sage Saturn in Aquarius, the sign that rules the technical mind, squaring eureka-seeking Uranus in Taurus, taking care of mental wellbeing will be more important than ever this year. Remember, the ecology of the inner self is maintained in homeostatic ways no different than the green outer world. Let "balance" be your mantra for optimal health in 2021, which also includes a message from Neptune, ruler of REM and currently transiting its home sign of Pisces. Turning off your devices and sleeping on a regular schedule in a dark room is proven to protect your body's immune system and any precious existing dopamine stores.

And when you're not sleeping? Perhaps this is the year to start a new meditation practice: Doing breathwork and yoga and, of course, embracing the power of now, are all associated with restorative Neptune and feeling better. And please, talk to your health care provider if you're feeling overwhelmed, or before taking any sort of supplement. There are people who care about you, we promise.

A New Wave in Energy

The glyph for Aquarius is a set of two waves representing the flow of energy. Aquarius is an air sign that is represented by the Water Bearer—spanning two elements is just another one of this nimble zodiac sign's gifts. Timelord Saturn in Aquarius could sound a louder alarm about the relationship between air, water, and human survival. As greenhouse gases trapped in the air from carbon emissions warm the earth, many climate scientists are telling us that waters are heating up, promoting animal species to migrate with the temperature changes. Glacier retreat is being documented, too, allowing comparisons with earlier periods in Earth's history in an effort to determine exact causes. Although we've only had weather satellites since 1960, other terrestrial data suggests climates are shifting with unknown storm patterns and frequent flooding in some areas, and prolonged fires and droughts in others.

No surprise, renewable energy is a crucial topic as we enter 2021. Our modern lives require power. Solar and wind could potentially solve the crisis. But a viable green solution for producing those panels and windmills has yet to be obtained. Will the Saturn-Uranus squares yield the scientific breakthroughs we need to get to net-zero emissions by 2050? Uranian conversations about the Green New Deal are sure to resurface in the year ahead while Saturn could bring funding from big business to support developments.

Auto manufacturers are already in a high-speed chase with Tesla in 2021, with a fresh fleet of electric vehicles (EVs) coming to market. The 2021 Mustang Mach-E bears more resemblance to an SUV than a sports car but boasts an ability to hit speeds of 60mph faster than a Porsche 911 GTS. Want to roll through town in a Hummer? Better find a charging station. In 2021, these military-inspired vehicles, which went out of production in 2010, will be back on the market with an SUV, a pickup truck, and LeBron James as the spokesman.

Not to be outdone, Cancer Elon Musk (who shares a zodiac sign with Nikola Tesla) has been beta-testing the Full Self Driving software on his vehicles, with plans to offer a monthly subscription plan for this feature in 2021.

UFOs, Aliens and Mega-Constellations: Are We the New Sky Gods?

The technological revolution occurring at warp speed suggests that maybe we'll skip this whole automotive thing and board a spaceship...or voluntarily follow the aliens onto their UFOs like many abductees self-report. When Saturn buzzed Aquarius in 1962, M.I.T. sent TV signal by satellite for the first time. Astronaut John Glenn became the first American to orbit Earth, and Project Apollo—NASA's lunar landing program—was being developed in earnest. Glenn called upon mathematician Katherine Johnson, a pioneering African American woman and the subject of the movie *Hidden Figures*, to hand-calculate the computer-generated orbital equations that ensured the safety of his missions. In 1992, Mae Jemison was the first African American woman to go into space aboard the Endeavor STS-47.

Similarly, Saturn's squares to "Father Sky" Uranus have dovetailed with developments in flight, both for airplanes and spaceships. The Saturn-Uranus squares of the mid-70s were particularly active! In 1975, the U.S. and Soviet Union had their first joint space mission. NASA unveiled the first space shuttle, Enterprise, in 1976. That same year, the Viking 1 had its first successful mission to Mars while the high-speed Concorde hosted its first commercial flight. Fun factoid: Chiron, a small, comet-like solar system body known as a "centaur" that orbits between Saturn and Uranus, was discovered in 1977 while the two planets were assembled in this dynamic break dance.

In recent years, Amazon and SpaceX have launched "mega-constellations" of satellites into orbit. While these fleets provide much-needed broadband Internet to the wired masses, they're creating disruptions for astronomers. Since satellites can reflect sunlight, they appear as bright streaks when viewed or photographed through a telescope, mimicking the appearance of stars, potentially confounding our view and understanding of the constellations and the zodiac itself.

In the coming years, tens of thousands of these satellite stacks are expected to be photobombing the sky, impacting cosmic observations from Earth. The fiercest space race of 2021 could take place between Capricorn Jeff Bezos and Cancer Elon Musk—or scientists versus the oligarchs!

That is, if the aliens don't get in on this Aquarian/Uranian party first. Will the Pentagon release more videos of UFOs in 2021 like the astounding Tic-Tac UFO imaged by a U.S. Navy fighter jet's radar camera? Interest on the topic is bound to rise under this year's cosmic influence. Esteemed ufologists like Jacques Vallée have been advancing the "interdimensional hypothesis" for decades, an idea that some UFOs could actually be visitations from coexisting dimensions, or more shocking, these UFOs are ourselves, humanity returning from a future time as ETs, confirming our latent intuitions that we, in fact, are the Promethean sky gods. With clock-ruling Saturn, a fascination with time travel and time dilation could emerge.

In recent years, Simulation Theory, a contemporary idea with ancient roots extending back to Greek philosopher Plato in the 4th century B.C.E., has been gaining interest as our computational powers have increased. Sometimes called matrix theory, its various iterations propose that the universe and all of reality within it, including humans, are expressions of a vast digital construct loosely

39

akin to an advanced computer program that allows the laws of nature, including evolution and the biological creatures animating it, to unfold.

As of 2020, the cognitive scientist Donald D. Hoffman has expanded upon his alternative view of human consciousness, speculating that we don't know the actual truth of our cosmic condition since it's not in our best evolutionary interests to do so. He states that we are limited by our human perceptions, casting doubt on whether our theories of space-time and quantum mechanics can ever grant us a total understanding of the cosmos. His ontological pessimism posits that we're biological "interfaces" at the behest of selective pressures in which to support our genetic fitness to propagate the species.

Big Brother is Pixeling You

Complex technology often becomes accessible to the masses when business-minded Saturn gets in a dynamic dustup with technocrat Uranus every 14 years. Both Microsoft and Apple formed during the Saturn-Uranus squares of the mid-1970s, making home computing a groundbreaking reality. Currently, the Internet of Things (IoT) is revolutionizing the ways we use technology. As thumb-sized computers with tiny sensors are being programmed to make our devices "smart" and our homes totally automated, we don't need Rosie the Robot to push any on/off buttons for us. But Alexa, where did I leave my mask?

Quantum computing is also revolutionizing digital capabilities. In October 2019, Google announced that it had achieved "quantum supremacy" with its qubit technology. Bounding beyond the binary "0 or 1" coding model of classic computing, the qubit has the capability to exist in both states of 0 and 1 simultaneously.

The qubit allows computers to handle vastly higher operational speeds while consuming far less energy, and this technology is poised to revolutionize the industry in years ahead. The drawback? Quantum computing puts at risk present-day encryption. That computational hard reality will demand that a new processing arms race will ensue as superpowers and leading companies attempt to protect themselves from the onslaught of quantum computing hackers in a race for global dominance.

As we step into 2021, Google is embroiled in a major antitrust lawsuit, battling claims by the U.S. Department of Justice that it maintained a monopoly and impeded the growth of other search engines. During the Saturn-Uranus squares of 1999-2000, Microsoft (who owns rival Bing) was embroiled in its own trust-busting case. After being ruled a monopoly, the DOJ ordered the company to split into two entities. Bill Gates appealed the case and won after agreeing to share computing interfaces with other companies.

The Atari 2600 console dropped during the Saturn-Uranus squares of 1977, bringing gaming to our living rooms. Today, the struggle to separate kids from screens has only intensified with classes being taught via Zoom. Parents juggling work with their newly minted roles as co-teachers are often too busy to notice their kids "multitasking" with multiplayer games. Livestreaming on Twitch and TikTok while listening in on their English Lit class? Taking an extended recess because...Roblox? We've heard countless stories of parents taking away phones during class time for this very reason. ("Ahem," to Ophira's daughter Cybele, whose gaming livestream went viral while her mom was writing this book!)

How much power are we handing over to the tech lords of our times? Thanks to the pandemic, most people can't work or go to school without a wi-fi connection, which, in turn, elevates anyone who controls our Internet into dangerously empowered deities. While Saturn briefly toured Aquarius last year, Human Rights Watch issued a warning about government-imposed Internet blackouts. As countries including Ethiopia, Myanmar and Bangladesh shut down online access to citizens, HRW alerted the world to the grave impact of limiting access to health information during the pandemic.

With disruptive Uranus in his zodiac sign since 2018, Taurus Mark Zuckerberg has become something of a Silicon Valley villain, as people delete their Facebook accounts to protest the company's policies. Yet the human need to "tend and befriend" during stressful times has prevented a mass exodus from his Facebook and Instagram apps. While we scroll through envy-inducing #TBT posts from the days when we could group hug or dance at a festival, we ignore the knowledge that our behaviors are being tracked, our profiles "pixeled" by ad servers and our privacy sacrificed as the cost of admission. Somehow, it seems harder to step away from this social machine than to rebuild what has become, for many of us, the ultimate contact database.

And let's be honest: For many, social media has become a sanity-saving lifeline. It's a place for cathartic #WineTime confessions, a resonant respite from the uncertain modern world. As news outlets become increasingly biased, we log in to these apps to share realtime videos of real-world events, many which are brutal, shocking and revelatory. Conversely, it's also home to much of the fake news and doctored memes that have spawned legions of misinformed citizens.

Marching into the new year, Saturn in Aquarius may bring stricter regulations on how individual data is protected and shared across platforms. During this brief cycle last year, Seattle imposed its controversial JumpStart payroll tax. This directly impacted Amazon, which had flexed its power to avoid such expenses in recent years. But with many small businesses relying on Facebook ads to boost sales and Amazon.com as a virtual storefront for products (not to mention a safer way to acquire goods during the pandemic), there's no easy solution.

Balancing Technology and Biology

Artificial intelligence, augmented reality, virtual everything...while Saturn's in tech-savvy Aquarius until March 7, 2023, the geeks (not the meek) shall inherit the Earth. In fact, the World Wide Web came to life during the prior Saturn in Aquarius cycle. On April 30, 1993, the www source code was released by CERN, making the software free and available to anyone. A year before that, in 1992, futurist (and Aquarius!) Ray Kurzweil's book *The Age of Intelligent Machines*, essentially forecasted the wild popularity of the 'net as we know it!

While many people worry that A.I. developments could make human labor obsolete, pragmatic Saturn cautions against spiraling into doomsday thinking. Nevertheless, the ringed planet wants us to hustle and bring our skills up to snuff. Train on the software, apps, social media and whatever technological advances are happening in your industry.

When Saturn orbited through Aquarius back in 1962, ABC premiered its first animated color TV series, *The Jetsons*, about a family living in the Space Age. The Hanna-Barbera producers imagined an "impossible" world where people could talk to each other on video screens, food could be programmed to come from a machine and robots worked as household servants. In 2021, we're suffering from Zoom fatigue, much like George Jetson taking calls from his boss Cosmo Spacely on a giant screen in the family room while his son whizzed by in a jetpack.

But seriously Siri...does everything need to be upgraded to 5G? For some, the crush of apps, social media and rapidly developing technology has spurred a move in the extreme opposite direction. The Japanese practice of *Shinrin-Yoku,* or forest bathing, involves spending time immersed among trees. A study from the U.S. National Library of Medicine showed that a walk in the woods supported both subjects' immune systems by raising Natural Killer (NK) cell activity, an effect that lasted for more than seven days.

The #CottageCore movement is another of many analog uprisings that is sure to gain even more popularity as Saturn squares Uranus in terrestrial Taurus. Defining this ethos is a love for simplicity, with home-baked, hand-sewn, woodsy wonderland everything. It's a bit like living in a 1970s dollhouse. Or make that a tiny house...or a Scamp trailer with gingham curtains parked on a patch of land. (A Sagittarius astrologer can dream!) High tea on the lawn replaces the high anxiety of modern life. Both Instagram and TikTok offer a rabbit-hole of #CottageCore videos with upcycling projects, mushroom foraging tips, salvage decorating and much, much more. (Trust us.)

Agricultural updates have also been big in the news since Uranus began its seven-year tour of earth sign Taurus in May 2018. We've literally been reinventing the cow since innovative Uranus moved into the sign of the Bull. To wit, Beyond Meat is now available at fast food chains. Rival company Impossible Foods is busy developing a plant-based milk that mirrors the creamy texture of cow milk, can be frothed and won't curdle in your coffee. (Barista, we'll take one venti Caramel Impossiccino, please!)

With water shortages around the world, agricultural products that don't require copious amounts of hydration will grow in demand. And while gene-editing software like CRISPR could produce crops of pesticide-free super-plants, this is sure to engender more backlash from the non-GMO activists as science develops rapidly in the coming years. Recent scientific studies are even tracking electrophysiology—currents sent between plants to signal to each other! With Uranus, planet of electricity, in earthen Taurus, germinating more data about the secret language of plants and crops seems inevitable. In the meanwhile, don't feel guilty for pulling those carrots out of the ground, okay?

The Revolution Will Be Hashtagged

Saturn's tour through idealistic, humanitarian Aquarius is sure to shift society. But how? Major divisions between left and right continue to grow, while also getting hacked by technology in head-spinning ways. Agreeing on the perfect utopia? One nation under a groove? That seems like the most far-fetched notion from our current view. Through the Internet and encrypted message apps, people are fracturing into micro-societies, mobilizing around their ideals. With righteous indignation and Twitter accounts as the common threads, we expect to see every incarnation of Aquarian/Uranian energy spin up in 2021: sci-fi conspiracists, one-love bohemians, metaphysical interdimensional travelers, and anti-government radicals...plus some new unicorns who will emerge in the high-tech kaleidoscopic herd.

Prior Saturn-Uranus squares have been associated with unrest, uprisings and new parties being born. The American Civil War erupted during this cosmic configuration in 1861. In 1930, Mohandas Gandhi led The Salt March, an act of non-violent civil disobedience protesting British rule in India. South African riots, thought to be the beginning of the end for Apartheid, exploded during this disruptive transit in 1976.

The NAACP was founded during the Saturn-Uranus square in 1909. In 1930, during another dust-up between these two planets, the Communist Party of Vietnam was established, while in Detroit, Wallace Fard Muhammad founded The Nation of Islam. That same year, the International Left Opposition (ILO) was formed in Paris, France. While Saturn squared Uranus in 2009, the Tea Party movement emerged.

With many U.S. citizens fed up with the two-party system, will the government convulse and go through a revolution in 2021? Democratic socialists like Bernie Sanders and Alexandria Ocasio-Cortez may be polarizing to both the left and right, but are undeniably popular among younger voters ready for a dramatic change. For years, Pacific Northwesterners—spanning Washington, Oregon, British Columbia, parts of California and Idaho—have snarked about seceding from the union to form the independent nation of Cascadia. Those "jokes" have gotten louder since Trump came to office, and with the X-factor of a Saturn-Uranus square, it's anyone's guess what could erupt in 2021.

Simultaneously, this very area of the U.S. has given rise to anti-government, anti-police militia groups like the Boogaloo Boys. With a passion for libertarian politics, Hawaiian shirts, body armor and Second Amendment Rights, some members call for the collapse of the American government while others claim to be preparing for a race war—both as white nationalists and as supporters of Black Lives Matter.

Are you confused yet? Don't expect the Aquarian air to clear in 2021. In fact, life could take a further turn for the sci-fi. In 2020, the far-right network QAnon surged in popularity, spreading conspiracies about the "deep state" and Satan-worshipping pedophiles across social media and 8kun forums. The ANTIFA (anti-fascist) ideology was hacked by trolls, setting off hysteria about busloads of non-existent protesters showing up to loot suburban towns.

Hashtag wars are likely to intensify under the technology-fueled battles of Saturn and side-spinning Uranus—and not just with fringe groups. Last year, the K-Pop stans called upon their loyal legions to get involved. When police departments urged citizens to send videos of "illegal protest activity," users flooded the feeds with short "fancam" videos of their favorite performers and overwhelmed the #WhiteLivesMatter hashtag with K-Pop clips.

It's noteworthy that the K-Pop phenomenon came to life with support and special protection from the South Korean government. During a financial crisis in Asia in the late 1990s—near the time of a Saturn-Uranus square, incidentally—a fundraising idea was born. The Ministry of Culture was formed in South Korea with a department focused on K-Pop. While the karaoke bars may be closed due to COVID-19, the hologram technology and hashtagging fans will wage on.

Will music lead the revolution in 2021? Music is in large part ruled by the eleventh house, home of Aquarius and its co-ruling planet, Uranus. We can't say for certain, but prior Saturn-Uranus squares gave birth to renegade genres that shape movements to this day. The 100 Club Punk Festival of 1976 is thought to be the moment that mainstream culture was introduced to this form of music. The Clash released their first album during the squares of 1977. During that same mid-1970s period, another revolution was brewing in the South Bronx. DJ Grand Wizard Theodore invented the record scratch in 1975—a quirky Uranian twist on music if ever there were. One year later, DJ Afrika Bambaataa and Disco King Mario had the first DJ battle on record. In 2021, new forms of electronic music could emerge, along with a slew of special effects and revolutionary ideals.

45

With this anarchic footnote, it's likely that songs of insurrection and suffrage will continue in the digital airwaves for the foreseeable future. So grab a Moog and a Fender Stratocaster guitar and let it rip. Uranus will amp your efforts!

New Waves of Social Justice

Saturn in Aquarius has historically brought developments for gender rights. During a prior cycle in 1993, Justice Ruth Bader Ginsburg took her oath of office as the second woman to serve on the U.S. Supreme Court. Her 27 years on the bench earned her the title of "The Great Dissenter" due to her fierce stance for women, the LGBTQ community, undocumented immigrants and voters.

The "Notorious RBG" lived through the 2020 pass of Saturn in Aquarius. Her fierce resolve kept her going to age 87, but she lost her battle to pancreatic cancer in September 2020. Justice Ginsburg's "fervent" dying wish was that she would "not be replaced until a new president is installed." Despite this, hearings began within the week for conservative-endorsed Justice Amy Coney Barrett, provoking fears about women's reproductive rights being overturned.

When Saturn was in Aquarius in 1963, President John F. Kennedy signed the U.S. Equal Pay Act into law to "prohibit discrimination on account of sex in the payment of wages by employers." Later that year, Dorothy Hodgkin was the first British woman to be awarded the Nobel Prize in Chemistry for her work on penicillin and Vitamin B12. Carol Moseley Braun, the first African American woman to be elected to the U.S. Senate, claimed her seat in November 1993, when Saturn cycled back to Aquarius. Saturn-Uranus squares have brought developments for women on both sides of the aisle. In 1975, Margaret Thatcher was the first woman chosen to lead the British conservative party. In 1976, the first class of women was inducted into the U.S. Naval Academy.

Aquarius' "one love" mantra puts the A in androgyny (and LGBTQIA). With Saturn here, we may add more gender checkboxes to the list—or do away with the category altogether on many forms. Some states are now allowing "X" to be checked as a third gender option on drivers' license. In 2021, gender rights activism will continue to expand beyond the binary male versus female categories. Notably, in the summer of 2020, Black Trans Lives Matter marches called attention to the murders of this population by police. The Brooklyn Liberation March drew 15,000 people in support of the cause. Tragically, two more black transgender women were slain within 24 hours of the event, Dominique Rem'Mie Fells, 27, and Riah Milton, 25.

In June of 2020, a historic decision by the U.S. Supreme Court ruled 6-3 that the 1964 Civil Rights Act would hereby protect lesbian, gay and transgender employees from discrimination based on sex. Two conservative judges, including Justice Neil Gorsuch, who was appointed by Trump, joined the four liberal justices in this landmark decision.

Three days prior to this ruling, however, the Department of Health and Human Services erased provisions in the Affordable Care Act protecting the rights of transgender patients against discrimination. The changes now narrowly define gender as the biological male-female binary assigned at birth. This new language makes it easier for providers to deny coverage and treatments to trans patients. At time of writing, two transgender women in New York have brought a lawsuit against the DHHS to contest this change as illegal in light of the Supreme Court's decision.

Gender rights reformation may intersect with religion in new ways under the Saturn-Uranus squares. In a documentary that aired in late 2020, Pope Francis expressed support for same-sex civil unions. While he has not endorsed gay marriage, this is a major admission, and some believe that this is a step in a proactive direction for LGBTQ rights within the Catholic Church.

Cyber-Communing and Co-Sharing

As the world adapts to climate change, pandemic-spurred population decline in major cities and shifting economies, we may need to pool more of our resources. But how to do so fairly without destroying the vibrancy of free will that is so essential to an Aquarian or Uranian transit? At a time when we need to share more than ever, Saturn is restricting our ability to gather in person. That said, in future-minder Aquarius, Saturn is pushing us to find new ways to commune. Tapping into technology has allowed us to connect in unprecedented ways, at times from remote regions that were previously denied access.

Silver linings like these are sure to emerge during 2021, perhaps in a more organized fashion, thanks to Uranus in super-planner Taurus. Some school districts are testing out the "neighbor helping neighbor" concept of timebanking to lend support with educating kids. For example, a small pod forms of 5-10 parents. They select a leader and agree upon their currency structure. In many timebanks, individuals receive one "time credit" for each hour of service given. But it's conceivable that a pod could assign values like "five credits for preparing and dropping off lunches" or "two credits for an after-school study hall." At some point, these credits could be traded for services from other parents in the educational pod, like afterschool care or morning dropoffs.

While successful timebanks require structure (and adulting!), that's where Saturn comes in. Community Weaver software already exists to help organize and track credits for timebanks.

The first Israeli kibbutz was formed during a Saturn-Uranus square in 1909. Residents were given food and housing in exchange for service, which often involved farming, schooling the children, or production of goods that were sold to fund the community. We may see collective land purchases become a new trend in 2021—perhaps out of necessity! Job losses from the virus have plunged millions below the poverty line, spurring many to think in this communal, Aquarian way. Cities like New York and San Francisco are reportedly depopulating, with record vacancies both in residential and commercial buildings.

Another novel example? Tenants may pool funds to buy a building from their landlord, turning it into a co-op. And hey, if they're really on the Saturn-Uranus bandwagon, they'll install solar panels and other clean energy upgrades. Let's keep going with this vision: These modernistic Meccas could offer childcare, Zoom rooms for students, WFH office pods, and a co-op grocery store for tenants only. Heck, why not throw in an urgent care clinic with COVID testing and flu shots? With residents abiding by distancing regulations, safety could be far more ensured. Utopian mini-societies like these require agreement and integrity, but that's not impossible to imagine with Saturn in idealistic Aquarius.

The nuclear family is no longer considered the ideal option for many. According to Greek mythology, the Water Bearer was a young man named Ganymede who was the object of Zeus' affections. He served cups of life-giving H2O to the gods in exchange for eternal youth. While adulting is never overrated with wise, maturing Saturn in town, communal living could extend the dormitory vibes into old age—especially once a safe, successful vaccine is available. ✳

Aries

HOROSCOPE

2021 HIGHLIGHTS

LOVE

Cupid launches a crowdsourcing campaign on your behalf as lucky Jupiter and stable Saturn unite in your communal eleventh house. Although you're not naturally a "joiner," love may be found through your participation in groups, organizations and online communities. Digital dating brings luckier swipes for single Rams, but a fateful introduction could just as easily come via mutual friends. No matter your relationship status, this is a year to be experimental and open. Need to let go of a past love? Grieve and heal while Jupiter in Pisces loosens the ties that bind from May 13 to July 28. Long-term goals come to the fore November 5, as Venus embarks on an extended, four-month tour through Capricorn, but ease off the throttle while the love planet's retrograde from December 19, 2021, to January 29, 2022.

MONEY

Innovative Aries will thrive in 2021, as enterprising Jupiter fistbumps industrious Saturn in your futuristic, tech-savvy eleventh house. As the zodiac's trailblazer, you love being part of whatever is new and next! Good news: In 2021, emerging industries call your name. From alternative energy to plant medicine that treats trauma, you could find yourself submerged in a cutting-edge field. Learn whatever new technology is involved. Studying and learning will be as enjoyable as reaching the end goal, thanks to a pair of Sagittarius eclipses on May 26 and December 4. Under 2021's team-spirited skies, who you work with matters as much as what you're doing. Surround yourself with thought leaders who aren't afraid to question the status quo—and challenge you on your assumptions. A new revenue stream flows in near the November 19 lunar eclipse, the first in a profit-boosting series that lasts for two years.

HEALTH & WELLNESS

Log on to that fitness app and rally friends for a 30-day challenge. Wellness goals get a motivating boost when you track them with tech and tackle them with a team. Holistic healing, alternative medicine and anything involving the mind-body connection will be your greatest form of prevention in 2021. Thinking of a detox? Jupiter's brief tour through Pisces (May 13 to July 28) is ideal for that and may involve taking a mental health sabbatical from work. Support your knees and stretch your calves! These body parts are under weighty Saturn's strain in 2021. Simultaneously, Jupiter's influence could cause you to overextend, so curb competitive urges and take time to learn the correct postures before trying a new sport.

FRIENDS & FAMILY

The Aries soul squad is shaping up! As Jupiter expands your social reach, you'll attract new friends both online and IRL. Simultaneously, Saturn draws well-connected people in your realms of interest, from activism to entrepreneurship. Family may take a backseat to your friend group this year, but take care not to neglect your clan. On June 10, the Gemini solar eclipse could reconfigure your inner circle, shifting people's roles and changing your priorities. Siblings, neighbors and close friends could be part of this evolution. You won't take kindly to anyone clipping your wings or demanding 24/7 participation. At the same, time, membership has its privileges in 2021, so if you've found a crew that speaks your language, stop being a stubborn holdout, Aries. Sign up and pledge your allegiance!

Aries
POWER DATES

ARIES NEW MOON
April 11 (10:30 PM ET)

ARIES FULL MOON
October 20 (10:56 AM ET)

SUN IN ARIES
March 20 – April 19

Although you're the zodiac's solo star, in 2021, you'll thrive when you team up with kindred spirits and fellow disruptors for a common cause.

Saturn in Aquarius: Level up your social circle.
December 17, 2020–March 7, 2023

Welcome back to the collaboration station, Aries! After a preview stint from March 21 to July 1, 2020, serious Saturn returns to Aquarius, activating your communal, consciousness-raising eleventh house. Unleash your *esprit de corps!* For a change, you're not chomping at the bit to be in charge. Pass the captain's hat

The AstroTwins' 2021 Horoscope   52

to a capable colleague (you can always consult from the sidelines), or experiment with the idea of a "leaderless" organization based on trust and agreement. Idealistic as it sounds, if you're working with the right people, you could pull this off beautifully while Saturn plays in Aquarius' lab from December 17, 2020, to March 7, 2023.

Because of Saturn's weighty influence, the impact of your decisions will reverberate through your environment. Observe and you'll see: When you slip up, Team Ram starts slacking. When you hold yourself to impeccable standards, your crew crushes it. People will act as your mirrors this year. Yes, Aries, that's a lot of responsibility to bear…and power to wield!

Nonetheless, this won't prevent you from going "renegade Ram" on certain days. Aquarius and the eleventh house are the "autonomy zones" of the zodiac. Planets passing through this district can incite a rabble-rousing instinct that is all too familiar to your iconoclastic sign. You want to challenge every bankrupt system, protest the patriarchy on the steps of City Hall, and even set fire to corrupt ideals on a scorching Twitter feed.

But should you? Tough love Saturn won't give you much wiggle room to do things by the Book of Aries—no matter how badly you want to steer the ship… or should we say, rock the boat. The medium is as important as the message while sophisticated Saturn is in the mix. Bellicose behavior may alienate supporters. By lighting your own short fuse, you could hand over a victory to your opponents.

If you truly want to be an agent of change, you must follow Saturn's prescription. The cautious planet rewards authority, integrity and experience. Think strategically, like a decorated general instead of a rogue bounty hunter. Map out your five-point plan before you start recruiting your army, making certain that you work out all the Saturnian details involving time and budget. With a rock-solid game plan, you can raise a utopian vision from the dust like the trailblazer you were born to be. And sure…have that last laugh, Aries, because the haters who insisted your idea was impossible will bow down.

No matter where you direct your prodigious energy in 2021, assembling the right squad is essential to your success. Rather than dazzle crowds with your genius moves, empower people to "do for self." Show them the ropes, then step back and allow them struggle, trusting that this is the best way for them to learn (with some gentle guidance along the way, of course). Need support for your missions? Join mastermind groups where you can mingle with people whose credentials and connections can elevate your plans. Scour your existing contact database, because there's gold in them hills! Whatever you need could be right there, within a degree or two of separation. But before you start pinging people for favors, hang on! Has a glowing endorsement been earned? Show and prove your worthiness first by lending support to one of their missions. Gaining allegiance won't take long, whether you're playing Zoom M.C. for their livestreamed event or spreading the word of their work on social media. Thanks to Saturn's staying power, this could evolve from mutual backscratching into a lasting camaraderie.

Innovative Rams will thrive during this Saturn cycle, so get serious about building one of your "mad scientist" dreams into a bona fide business. Aquarius and the eleventh house rule science and technology. Start prototyping that mobile app, downloadable curriculum or even a motorized tool that makes life more convenient or luxurious for people (maybe both). Have any of your "weird" hobbies morphed into a profitable hustle? Show the world how it's done. Broadcasting as a YouTube expert could make you Internet famous, bringing sponsorship and advertising dollars once you build your audience. Call the I.P. lawyers to discuss trademarks or patents! Five years from now, your "crazy little invention" could be in demand by major manufacturers, or your proprietary methodology embraced by practitioners globally. You never know, Aries. But if your intuition is whispering, "This could be huge," invest in upfront protection. That $500 legal fee could multiply exponentially in future wealth. Bring on the passive income!

With Saturn parked in your tech-sector, you could make a serious connection online. Confident Rams are rarely shy about DM-ing people who pique their interest. From style bloggers to thought leaders to prospective project partners, pitch away, Aries. Post evocative comments on people's timelines and feeds. The discussions you spark could open up powerful dialogues about all kinds of opportunities, including business collaborations.

Are you still using your pet's name as your password? Change it to something stronger, ASAP! With tough-teacher Saturn in your tech house there's greater risk of data breaches, identity thefts or other digital disasters caused by careless sharing. Check the settings on every app installed on your phone. If you don't switch off certain features, photos you upload could be tagged with metadata, location information and other trackable intel that leaves you at the mercy of predatory marketers who purchase your info for their "lists." (And let's not even start talking about the random trolls…) As convenient as cloud storage may be, take the added step of encrypting data. Texting apps like Signal can also add

> ## "For many Rams, the past two years have felt like professional boot camp."

a layer of privacy protection to the messages you send. In 2021, this is more important than ever, Ram!

When it comes to your interpersonal affairs, Saturn tests your commitments, especially relationships that seem to be restricting your evolution. But does that mean you should break up with your long-term, monogamous partner who you stopped sleeping with five months ago? Not necessarily! While Saturn plays ringmaster in Aquarius' three-ring circus, you could get serious about exploring edgier romantic terrain. As long as you're doing so with integrity (think: safewords, barriers and clear agreements) this can be a sexy exploration.

As the planet of repression, Saturn can bear down so hard that you have no choice but to rebel. After three years of hosting Saturn in Capricorn and your tenth house of public prestige, Rams have had enough! Saturn in Aquarius can churn up a desire to get naughty and push back against "restrictions." Fantasies involving bondage and restraint could be fun to play out while Officer Saturn wields the heavenly handcuffs. Other Rams could find themselves elevated to "sapiosexual" status, turned on by intellectual chemistry above all else.

Single Rams could fully embrace that status while Saturn hovers in Aquarius, the sign of universal love. A Pew Research study released in August 2020 showed that only 14 percent of "socially single" people (those who are not partnered) actually wanted to get married, or even date. Whether you care to walk down the aisle or not, Saturn's tour through rational, liberated Aquarius can open your mind to unconventional relationship structures, such as L.A.T. (Living Apart Together), long distance or an open marriage.

Footnote: The cosmic Lord of the Rings only visits this part of your chart every 29 years. Its last extended tour through Aquarius was from February 6, 1991, to January 28, 1994. Scan your archives, if you're old enough. Clues of similar patterns and lessons from that time period could crop up again. Born between 1991 and 1994? You may be having your Saturn return this year, a time of major maturity and growth.

Saturn in Aquarius Square Uranus in Taurus: Simplify.

February 17, June 14 & December 24

While Saturn is teaching you a master class on community activism, another revolution will take place for Rams in 2021. But this one's far more personal and even mundane, impacting your day-to-day affairs. Open your calendar app and take a look at your schedule. (If you're saying, "What schedule?" right now, you might just be…an Aries.)

All year long changemaker Uranus is stirring the pot in Taurus and your second house of daily routines. The way you "do life"—from your workflow to time management—is undergoing a massive, seven-year reorganization that began in May 2018. With liberated Uranus here until April 2026, breaking away from the nine-to-five grind is practically a must. Since Uranus is the planet that rules technology and the future, many Rams were already well-versed in Zoom (and plenty of other platforms) long before COVID-19 made videoconferencing essential.

Three times this year—February 17, June 14 and December 24—rule-obsessed Saturn and rule-breaker Uranus will challenge each other, crashing into a trio of 90° squares. This dynamic mashup can provoke sudden change, waking you up to your power and impact, but potentially redirecting your moneymaking plans.

The ebb and flow of money that Uranus in Taurus has caused may have taken a toll on your sense of stability. (And if you lost income due to the pandemic, you may really need to tap into your innovative nature to reboot your revenue.)

First and foremost, look at how you do your work. With Saturn in your collaborative eleventh house, you may realize that your independent, impulsive fire sign flow is driving Team Aries crazy! As much as you hate to regulate yourself, not adhering to some sort of consistency could be blocking progress and killing off cooperation. Maybe it's time to use project management software or pick one group messaging app, like Slack, and keep your squad unified through

> "The way you 'do life'—from your workflow to time management—is undergoing a massive reorganization."

technology. If you've been resisting teamwork because you dislike managing people, the Saturn-Uranus squares might force you to step up to a new level of leadership; one that involves delegating with clarity and compassion.

That said, you'll need to be ultra-discerning about who you work with. All that glitters ain't gold, and even people who claim to be down for a cause may simply be self-interested. Do a thorough background investigation before signing on with anyone. You work too hard to have your good name sullied by someone else's misdeeds!

The Saturn-Uranus squares may shift what you actually do for a living, leading you toward cutting-edge fields, especially ones that "raise the vibration" of humanity. From shadow work therapy (or shamanism) to renewable energy (wind, solar), you could be part of a huge societal reinvention. With these two planets in modest fixed signs, you run the risk of undercharging for your services—or, in some cases, swinging to the opposite extreme and making them inaccessibly expensive. Pay attention to what the market can bear.

57

Honestly, Aries, this shift may not even require you to increase your earnings. As boundary-hound Saturn pulls the emergency brake on Uranus in Taurus' impulsively indulgent influence, you could learn some big lessons about the problems of excess. We're not saying you'll turn into a minimalist, but you could definitely learn to live well with less in 2021.

Chiron in Aries: The key to unlocking the Saturn-Uranus squares.

April 17, 2018–April 14, 2027

The key to finding the balance between boundary-hound Saturn and disruptor Uranus lies with the comet Chiron, which bobs between the two planets in the asteroid belt. Chiron is known as "the wounded healer" in astrology. Until 2027, it's weaving through your sign, an event that only happens every five decades. Chiron's symbol is represented as a key-shaped glyph, showing how this comet unlocks the healing gifts that you've developed by overcoming pain and personal struggle.

Aries born between March 26 and April 2 will feel Chiron's influence most intensely in 2021, since it will travel between 5° and 12° Aries this year. But all Rams are on this nine-year journey of transformation together. It's likely you've already begun to drill down to your core wounds since April 2018, exploring family of origin trauma and childhood pain. Through this, you're learning how you block your full self-expression.

Do you turn cold instead of expressing your anger…or misuse your warrior energy to intimidate people? With Saturn in your collaborative eleventh house, your surly edge or devil-may-care "free spirit" may be a cover-up for pain around belonging (or not belonging). As you reflect on group interactions, look at behaviors you developed in order to "fit in." Do these serve you any longer?

Perhaps your competitive urges are stopping you from being a true team player, which in turn is blocking you from greater leadership or increased abundance.

Against the backdrop of Uranus in Taurus, you may see where you traded independence for security or popularity—and where it's time to develop your own clear-cut values instead of "going along to get along."

For many Aries, this is the year where you'll be pushed forward as a healer. Pay attention! You may hear a loud clarion call to share your intuitive gifts with the world. Your mission, should you choose to accept it: to fearlessly forge ahead and pursue any calling that will revolutionize the world and make it a safer place for everyone. Unconventional techniques may be involved, which could range from AI to shamanism. Whatever the case, you are ready to step into your authentic powers—society's judgments be damned.

Jupiter in Aquarius & Pisces

January 1: Aquarius (since December 19, 2020)
May 13: Pisces (retrograde June 20)
July 28: Aquarius (retrograde until October 18)
December 28: Pisces (until December 20, 2022)

Jupiter in Aquarius

December 19, 2020–May 13, 2021
July 28–December 28, 2021

Popularity: Rising!

Expansive Jupiter dips in and out of Aquarius this year, sending a burst of jubilant energy to your eleventh house of community and collaboration. The red-spotted planet has been buzzing in this zone since December 19, 2020, and hangs out here until May 13. Then, on July 28, Jupiter rejoins Aquarius, fist-bumping Saturn in this "cool kids' club" (the eleventh house) until December 28.

Most Aries are in their element playing to a crowd, and you captivate best as a solo act. But this year, you'll flourish as part of ensemble cast, especially one that allows you to be your outspoken and original self. With the right collaborators, your star will shine brighter, making your witty impersonations even funnier or your philosophical rants more thought-provoking. So don't worry about others stealing your thunder. They'll only draw a bigger crowd and broaden your reach.

You've got the mic, so what do you want to do with it? Think long and hard about that, Ram. The eleventh house is about social justice, changing the world to fit the most progressive ideals of equity and human rights. With outspoken Jupiter here, you won't be shy about addressing these timely matters. In 2021, you could become deeply immersed in politics—maybe even starting an organization or running for office. (Never say never!)

Then again, you might make your statement from a more punk-rock domain, which is often the Aries way. Record a hip-hop album or make disruptive public art installations, like one Aries we know did during the Occupy Wall Street movement. From a grey van with tinted windows, he used a high-powered projector to beam messages about economic disparity onto high-rise office buildings around New York City.

Although Jupiter wasn't in Aquarius then, our friend exemplified the kind of action this transit can evoke—including his choice to move into a communal house with other artists, dumpster-dive for egregiously discarded food outside of Brooklyn's production plants, and take his first of many trips to Burning Man. In true Aries fashion, he charmed his campmates by playing Chief Nightlife Motivator—so much so that they quickly forgave him for showing up to the desert festival with exactly one duffel bag and zero gallons of water.

Regardless of your GPS coordinates, Jupiter's two circuits through Aquarius will expand your sense of community. This is a year to explore new social and extracurricular avenues that connect you with like-minded people. Since Jupiter rules global and cross-cultural ties, you could link up with a diverse, even international, crew around a common cause. Together, you might do some volunteer travel or go on tour with a socially-conscious cultural initiative (think: film festival, public art installation or music for charity). Hello, inspiring #SquadGoals!

Jupiter is in Aquarius until May 13 and again from July 28 to December 28, drawing key players and savvy collaborators who are keen to explore the cutting edge with you. An online platform, podcast or TV venture could emerge, so cast a wide net! Global Jupiter in your eleventh house of broadcasting helps you spread a message that resonates across continents.

Could you be the next YouTube or Instagram sensation? Since Jupiter rules publishing and teaching, you could earn your salary as an influencer or by teaching online courses. If you need to update your digital skills, become an avid student of webinars—or consider teaching a few yourself. Since eager Jupiter creates FOMO, be sure to pick your platform and craft your message consciously.

Jupiter reveals where we take risks, but you could be tempted to leap without looking. Watch what you post on social media or upload to the cloud, especially while Jupiter is retrograde (backward) from June 20 through October 18. A hasty drag or controversial comment could come back to haunt you. During this time, you might also pull back from a couple of group associations or friendships that are overtaking your free time or just not giving a fulfilling ROI.

UFO sightings, animal communication, micro-dosing—with Jupiter in your cutting-edge eleventh house you could really geek out over some left-of-center concepts. You might explore Kabbalah or other mystical principles that are linked to modern-day science and help you understand human nature. Heck, you might even dip into a philosophical debate about the existence of aliens or other sci-fi topics.

Aquarius (and the eleventh house) are associated with the metaphysical mind, and this Jupiter cycle could "open up" your third eye chakra. Throughout this awakened year, you may develop a fascination with activating higher states of consciousness. There are many ways to do so, Aries, like breathwork, meditation, and certain yoga practices designed to awaken kundalini life force energy. Check out Dr. Joe Dispenza's book *Becoming Supernatural* or his video series on the pineal gland. Aries willing to wander even further could find themselves at a plant medicine ceremony or studying the works of "psychonauts" like ethnobotanist Terrence McKenna and the researchers at MAPS (Multidisciplinary Association for Psychedelic Studies).

Overall, these could be lively and fun times, a real boon for your social life. Romance, on the other hand, may be a sidebar subject for much of 2021. The eleventh house rules platonic connections, making it hard to get swept up in a passionate bubble-for-two. Single Rams may enjoy dating casually—if at all—preferring low-key hangouts to high-pressure hookups. That said, you could meet some worthy prospects through mutual friends, group activities or even virtually. Even so, you'll be in no rush to make anything exclusive, as you're really savoring this liberated and bohemian Jupiter transit.

As for attached Aries, it might take a village to keep your bond going strong, and we mean that in a playful way. Socialize with mutual friends or create a new social group with people you both enjoy. Get involved in community activism and hobby groups together while also honoring each other's autonomy. Under this boundary-loosening Jupiter banner, you could experiment with some new bedroom techniques from tantra to toys. Some Rams might even flex the boundaries of traditional monogamy, dabbling in an open relationship or different polyamorous configurations. But if your primary relationship was shaky to begin with, proceed with caution. Overconfident Jupiter can make you minimize the downsides of your risks.

Even if you remain happily devoted to your longtime plus-one, your life can't and won't center around just one person this year. Give yourself some breathing room and go explore the wider world. Absence—and room to roam in whatever capacity works—will make your wild heart grow fonder.

Jupiter in Pisces

May 13–July 28
December 28, 2021–May 10, 2022
October 28, 2022–December 20, 2022

And...cut!

From May 13 to July 28, the action slows to a near-halt, as Jupiter plunges into Pisces and your twelfth house of rest, healing and endings. Fold up those butterfly wings and turn inward, Aries. Trust us, there's a reason for this celestial sabbatical: It's prepping you for a new 12-year life chapter that begins on May 10, 2022, when Jupiter moves into Aries for the first time since June 2010.

Before then, you need to recharge your batteries and take a fearless inventory of your life. As you direct your attention inward, you'll likely find yourself feeling more tired than usual, craving extra sleep and downtime. Honor your limits, as inconvenient as they may be to your grand plans. Like it or not, this is a transitional cycle that cannot be rushed. If something is heavy, put it down. It's time to ask yourself the honest, albeit painful, question: Should it stay or should it go? You don't have to make the final cut this year. Jupiter returns to Pisces

> **"While it might feel frustrating, Jupiter in the twelfth house is leading you through 'spiritual baggage claim.'"**

again from December 28, 2021, until May 10, 2022, opening another space of surrender.

Responsive Rams will benefit from mindfulness techniques, such as wei wu wei, a Taoist term that translates into "action that is not action." Rather than flying into fix-it mode, sit down—on an embroidered silk meditation cushion, naturally. Observe your emotions; name and claim each one. The decisions you make after this high-minded, Jupiterian reflection will be far more beneficial and could bring long-term gains, like resolving an ongoing family feud or unlocking a career path as a healer.

While it might feel frustrating, Jupiter in the twelfth house is leading you through "spiritual baggage claim." You want to travel lighter, letting go of burdensome situations and codependent relationships that are holding you back from your path. But in Pisces, Jupiter can inflate victim consciousness. Are people really expecting you to carry their weight? Or could this be a sneaky deflection?

Your demand for creative control may have taken the wind out of your collaborators' sails earlier in 2021. Sure, your game-changing vision was probably better than any of their "safe" ideas. But a refusal to bend left you saddled with all the work! In the twelfth house, Jupiter's boundary-loosening influence helps you release that tight grip. As you step back and create a space for contribution, the "slackers" might step up and lift your burden.

63

Is it actually time to go? Rushed endings can leave you stewing in rage and regret…even if a situation is a clear-cut "Hell, no!" Our advice to Rams on the run? Make the most graceful exit possible, for everyone's sake. In weepy, emo Pisces, Jupiter amplifies every emotion, from grief to guilt. Bring gratitude and compassion (including self-compassion) to this process, but don't let yourself off the hook too fast. If you need to make amends, Jupiter passes you an enchanted olive branch to extend…several times, if necessary. And if you need to hold others accountable, call them out as gently as you can. Revenge is a dish best left off the menu in 2021.

There can be losses during this time. Jupiter in the transitional twelfth house reminds us that while our souls may be eternal, our bodies are not. If you're grieving a lost loved one, you can expect to receive many signs of their presence. Your "soul squad" is eager to help you from the other side. You might even speak to a medium or develop your own clairvoyant abilities. Dreams can be vivid and even prophetic. Signs and serendipities will pop up regularly, like repeating number sequences that show up on food tabs, addresses and random clocks. Or three people recommend the same spiritual book to you within a week, then you spot it in a shop window days later. These guideposts are leading you somewhere…but don't stress about the interpretation. Take them as a confirmation that your ancestors, angels and spirit helpers are present and protecting you.

During this Jupiter period, many people meet (or should we say "reunite with") a soulmate. That being can even come in the form of a lover, a pet, a child (birthed or adopted). An accidental yet meant-to-be pregnancy could be in the stars, as your divine demeanor is magnetic to souls seeking to incarnate.

Just know that the twelfth house is also the realm of fantasy. You can get swept away by a wildly romantic figure during this Jupiter cycle whose manipulative traits are concealed during courtship. Take your time.

The twelfth house rules health, but more on the mind-body-spirit interconnected level. If you deal with any wellbeing issues, trust that the universe is issuing a wakeup call: Slow down, focus, remove negativity from your life. You might check out Louise Hay's book *You Can Heal Your Life* to see where any aches or pains could portend a deeper emotional issue. For example, if your lower back is hurting, you may need more support. Persistent bladder infections can be a sign that you're literally pissed off! This is a good time to try anything from therapy to soul retrievals to past-life regressions and hypnosis. During this karmic period, you may do some deep forgiveness work or meet kindred spirits whom you feel like you've known for many lifetimes. (Maybe you have…)

Career-wise, Jupiter in Pisces can be a richly creative time, especially for artists, musicians, writers and anyone doing "right-brain" work. But on the outside, it may feel like results have slowed to a crawl. That's an illusion, Aries, so keep producing work behind the scenes and tying up loose ends. Molecules are moving and things are shifting. Think of it as a baby gestating in the womb—a new life is forming, even if you can't see the process. In the meanwhile, you could produce a masterpiece—or at least, give your soul some joy and fulfillment. Trust that your efforts will pay off by the time the red-spotted giant sails into Aries on May 10, 2022.

Should you find yourself unemployed, don't rush to get a new full-time career unless you have to. You might do better with a flexible bridge job that pays the bills but doesn't consume all of your energy. Could you swing a gap year or a mini-sabbatical between May 13 and July 28? See what's possible. You could use the in-between time to take classes, travel and explore new options—including new cities to live in or career paths you might genuinely enjoy. A photographer friend of ours used this cycle a couple of years ago to couch-surf her way around the world, taking headshots in exchange for some stunning accommodations.

A note about "doing"—we live in a culture that's addicted to action, results, making things happen. It's a very "yang" and masculine energy. This is the exact antithesis of what Jupiter in the twelfth house dictates. Instead, this is a time to receive, allow, be supported—to adopt a more "yin" and feminine pace. Admittedly, this isn't natural for most Aries. You're the sign of the Ram, accustomed to diving headfirst into your goals. But forcing things will only cause frustration now. So instead of fighting the current and swimming upstream, try to let the tides carry you.

Jupiter's last tour of Pisces was from January 17, 2010, through January 22, 2011. A similar cycle may emerge between May 13 and July 28, and again, once Jupiter re-enters Pisces for five months on December 28. If you're feeling lost at sea, look back to that period on your timeline. Projects you shelved a decade ago may be ready for a retro revival. Or you could suddenly regain interest in a creative passion you haven't touched since 2010.

The trick is to give up the need to know what's next. With Jupiter in your soul-stirring twelfth house, the universe actually does have a better plan than one you've created out of fear and scarcity. Trusting this, however, will be a challenge, especially when your intuition clashes with your material-world goals. You could think of it this way: If you're driving through the night, your headlights only illuminate what's 25 feet in front of you. Yet, if you simply focus on that 25-foot range and keep driving, you'll reach your destination.

That's what Jupiter in the twelfth house is like. You can't see where you're going beyond a certain point, so you have to focus on the things you CAN control and change. It's very much like an astrological 12-step program, guided by a celestial Serenity Prayer. And much like in recovery, you'll thrive by taking things one day at a time and staying present in the moment. Soon enough, you'll discover that the magic happens in this slowed-down space.

Eclipses in 2021

May 26: Sagittarius Lunar Eclipse 5°29′ (7:13am ET)
June 10: Gemini Solar Eclipse 19°42 (6:52am ET)
November 19: Taurus Lunar Eclipse 27°17 (3:57pm)
December 4: Sagittarius Solar Eclipse 12°17 (2:42am)

Expressing opinions isn't exactly a problem for the blunt Aries—but could your message use some massaging? For the second year in a row, a series of eclipses activates the Gemini/Sagittarius axis, bringing an "extreme makeover" energy to the communication houses of your chart. Simple tweaks won't cut it now. You may be ready for a full-on rebranding. If you're breaking into a new field, carefully define your market position before you start posting wildly. You only get one chance to make a first impression—and your quick-to-judge sign knows how potent those can be!

If you've been trying to get your point across to a wider audience—or perhaps a more elite crowd—these game-changing lunations could refine your approach. Teaching, learning and writing are all highlighted. These eclipses might also bring thrilling opportunities to expand into new territory while also gaining popularity close to home.

> "The lunar eclipse could see you capturing media attention, considering a return to school or making an important long-distance connection."

Two of this year's eclipses are in Sagittarius, which rules your ninth house of travel, publishing, entrepreneurship and higher learning. This burst of energy may be a welcome power surge. The May 26 Sagittarius lunar (full moon) eclipse could see you capturing media attention, considering a return to school, or making an important long-distance connection. You may log airline miles near this date or launch an exciting startup venture that takes flight quickly.

Welcome to the expert industry? For more seasoned Rams, wisdom you've gained from personal experience is ready to be shared! You could start a podcast, record a TED talk or publish a book. This truth-telling full moon may also bring a searingly honest conversation that clears the air. Afterward, you'll know exactly where you stand, which sets you free to move forward in a distinct direction.

This summer, change happens closer to home. On June 10, a Gemini solar (new moon) eclipse will touch down in your third house of communication and community. You could get the green light on a media project, enroll in school or launch a pop-up shop that revives an area of town that was hit hard by the pandemic. Meetings, pitches, marketing campaigns and anything that puts your ideas on loudspeaker may bring unexpected gains. A social media post could go viral.

In short, make sure you're circulating through every viable outlet near June 10! Stay receptive to input. Feedback from a colleague or peer could finally help you crack the code on how to market yourself. With your mind thirsty for new knowledge and inspiration, you may find an author or speaker whose words hit you like a lightning bolt of truth, perhaps even driving you into deeper study of this person's concepts and philosophies. A sibling, neighbor or kindred-spirit type could play an important role in events sparked by this eclipse. You might clear the air around a lingering conflict or even put your superpowers together for a dynamic duo undertaking!

With June's eclipse influencing your social life, you may dial down participation with one group of friends as you discover a squad that's more in alignment with 2021 you. Or maybe you'll finally just sign on as a full-fledged member of this crew, rather than taking a one-foot-in approach. This eclipse will inspire you to think about the way you come across to others. If you normally fill every quiet moment with chatter, make an effort to listen more. If you hold back from sharing about yourself, challenge yourself to be more of an open book.

Bold money moves are in the stars this November 19, when the lunar (full moon) eclipse in Taurus initiates a fresh, two-year eclipse series across the Taurus/Scorpio axis. As the rulers of your solar second and eighth houses (the "financial districts" of the zodiac wheel), these signs catapult your earning powers into rare form. But how you make income and invest could go through big changes as these eclipses reveal unseen opportunities, as well as hidden roadblocks.

Taurus governs your second house of steady paychecks, so November's manifesting lunar eclipse could boost your org-chart status and, for business owners, rev up revenue. Recruiters might ping you with a job offer. Even if the circumstances aren't totally ideal, this may be too enticing to pass up. Fast action is required to capitalize on the brief, but karmic, window of possibility these eclipses open up. Have faith, Aries! Stuck energy is moving, which may be the most important win of all.

On December 4, the Sagittarius solar (new moon) eclipse pushes you into adventurous terrain. Solar eclipses launch super-powered fresh starts—ready or not! Prepare to take a bold risk, to leap without looking into something major.

68

This is a time when, as the saying goes, you'll throw your hat over the wall then figure out how to get it. Just say yes, Aries.

Venus Retrograde in Capricorn: Rethinking the long-term game.
December 19, 2021 –January 29, 2022

Love and money goals get serious this November 5, as Venus moves through Capricorn and your traditional tenth house until March 6, 2022. Largely, 2021 will be an experimental, even non-committal, year for Rams. But come November, you'll change your tune from "let's just see where life is taking us," to "let's design our Future (with a capital F)."

Don't expect the master plan to formulate itself overnight. From December 19, 2021, to January 29, 2022, Venus dips into retrograde, a backward journey she takes every 18 months. During this time, bind up loose ends from the past and deal with "attachment issues" that creep up every time you get close to bonding with your boo or a prospective business partner. For example, when they step closer, do you feel smothered and suddenly want to go MIA? Does anxiety flare up when you sense someone's dissatisfaction or feel neglected? It's all human nature, Aries, but learning how to respond to it proactively—rather than reactively lashing out destructively—helps you graduate to a new level of emotional intelligence.

Venus governs our values, from the people we hold dear to the pleasurable ways we spend our hard-earned cash. In career-centric Capricorn, the harmonizing planet helps balance your professional goals with your romantic ones. But here's the rub: As much as you want to "have it all," you tend to be single-focused, charging toward victory without looking right or left. This all-consuming tendency makes it hard to pivot. Someone interrupting you from work mode— even for a sweet little hug—can throw you off for hours!

Similarly, when you're in the throes of "new relationship energy," dealing with the duties of daily life is so not on your agenda. A recently engaged Aries friend

Instagrammed his whirlwind courtship through wineries, beaches and gorgeous hiking trails, inspiring deep envy among friends who were stuck in WFH mode during 2020's quarantine. He'd mastered the art of the four-hour workweek and had room to play, once again demonstrating the trailblazing power of being born a Ram.

Knowing this, you may simply choose to spend this four-month window focusing exclusively on your career or a relationship. For Aries juggling both, make sure you aren't biting off more than you can chew in these arenas. For example, you may need to dial back elaborate New Year's plans if you're launching a business—or delay said launch until 2022 so you can enjoy a sweet holiday homecoming with your love. Whatever it is you're creating, getting too detailed while Venus is in reverse is just a buzzkill. Discuss your dream scenario in broad strokes instead of trying to perfect a "five-point plan" on an Excel spreadsheet.

Venus in Capricorn can be a bright time for your career, so pick up the pace on your 2021 goals during Q4. Nurturing business relationships is top priority with convivial Venus at the helm. That said, you'll need to navigate professional relationships with kid gloves while Venus is in reverse. Reconnect with colleagues from your past during the retrograde. Send that basket of artisan treats or reach out with a "Happy Holidays!" text. From these interactions, you may discover that your current paths dovetail beautifully—and profitably.

Pro tip: Create a buffer in November by building stronger bonds with your colleagues or top clients, taking extra care to listen to their needs. You don't have to kowtow to demands but give them space to vocalize their opinions. Sure, you may totally disagree with their methodologies and think they're doing everything backwards. But diplomacy can lead to productive discussions instead of fiery debates. Aries business owners might have to dig deeper—both for client leads and creative inspiration—as the year winds down. Take on the challenge, because one fateful connection could change everything!

Retrogrades aside, Venus in Capricorn can be a powerful period for bringing some of your long-held romantic dreams to life. Clarify what you want and take action to get your life in alignment with what will bring you happiness. Maybe you've always dreamed of opening a metaphysical retreat center with a partner or relocating to a loft in the heart of a bustling metropolis. Whatever the vision, Aries, share it with potential plus-ones!

Warning: This may be bittersweet. For example, if you've never wanted kids and are dating someone who talks nonstop about freezing eggs and IVF treatments,

> **"Clarify what you want and take action to get your life in alignment with what will bring you happiness."**

well...differences may be irreconcilable. Real talk is essential during this Venus cycle. Venus is the diplomatic negotiator of the skies. Creative solutions may emerge as you generate the courage to vocalize your desires.

Picking a 2021 wedding date? Tying the knot is ill-advised any time Venus is in reverse, so we recommend crossing December 19, 2021, to January 29, 2022, off the calendar. If you do have a holiday season matrimony planned, here's an idea: Head to City Hall some time in November or early December and have your nuptial "officialized" while Venus is direct. You could also wait to sign your marriage license until after January 29. Not possible? Commit to renewing your vows on your one-year wedding anniversary. Since Venus only turns retrograde every 584 days, it's guaranteed that she'll be in direct motion during the next year, leaving you free and clear to bind your love without cosmic red tape.

In a relationship? Set up systems to stay on the same page as your sweetie. Create a shared calendar that syncs with your mobile devices. Earmark one or two nights a week that are sacred "just the two of us" time. You may also discover that your professional objectives don't mesh so well with your mate's. Try to work out compromises instead of breaking things off—and consider a few couple's therapy sessions to help you hash out a better plan.

Since retrogrades stir up the past, this holiday season could be especially nostalgic. Single Rams may reconnect to "the one that got away" or discover a surprising romantic dimension with someone who has been in the friend zone for years. If it was merely bad timing that messed things up, Venus' backspin can provide a do-over.

Just take things slowly, because you won't get a clear read until after January 29, 2022 (more like mid-February 2022). Glorifying the past can be a pitfall of Venus retrograde. If you reunite with an ex, don't gloss over the issues that broke you apart the last time around. Instead, dive into a shared exploration of how things fell apart—including the role you both played in the meltdown.

Moving through these blocks can make your bond rock solid. Yes, it will take some work. Such is the beauty of a long-term relationship, Aries. "Conflict-free" connections can be dull and stifling, but growing through the dissent brings a beautiful evolution for your relationship and for each of you as individuals. ✳

Taurus

HOROSCOPE

2021
HIGHLIGHTS

LOVE

Steady, enduring relationships are the preference for many Bulls, and with Jupiter and Saturn united in your tenacious tenth house for most of 2021, you're playing the long game. But don't rule out sexy exploration! (That can happen within the container of a committed bond, you know.) Not only is shock-jock Uranus spending the entire year in your sign, making you extra spontaneous, but when Jupiter electrifies your liberated eleventh house from May 13 to July 28, you could rebel against structures that feel confining. The trick? To feed both your traditional side and your naughty one. On November 5, Venus kicks off a four-month-long tour through Capricorn and your adventurous, free-spirited ninth house. Cross-cultural connections sizzle and long-distance arrangements thrive. Looser restrictions can also be fun for couples, but be warned! When your romantic ruling planet turns retrograde for six weeks on December 19, chemistry experiments could blow up if you race into anything impetuously—or without clear agreements.

MONEY

Three of the year's four eclipses charge up your money axis, revealing hidden opportunities to earn and learn. You work hard for your cash; now, make sure it returns the favor by investing in things that grow in value or bring a compounding interest. Career goals will consume many Tauruses to the point of obsession, thanks to Jupiter and Saturn in your ambitious tenth house. Focus and charge ahead because this could be one of the most successful years you've had in over a decade! Looking to reinvent yourself or embark on a new path? The Jupiter-Saturn combo helps you artfully transition. Don't throw out the baby with the bathwater or quit five minutes before the miraculous payday. Past experiences are building blocks to future gains, and you may get one last windfall from work you've done for years—especially near the Taurus lunar eclipse on November 19!

WELLNESS

In 2021, achieving optimal health is a marathon, not a sprint. That's good news for your methodical sign since you understand the game-changing power of a routine. Set a measurable goal, like training for a charity 10K or lowering your blood pressure. Then get a practice in place, even daily. With Jupiter and Saturn both in your tenth house of authorities, work with experts like coaches, trainers and nutritionists if you need support. When Jupiter's in your teamwork zone from May 13 to July 28, joining a support group (online or IRL) can keep you motivated! Thinking about trying anything risky, like rock climbing or cycling through urban traffic? Learn correct posture and invest in properly fitting gear. This is not the year for chancing an injury.

FRIENDS & FAMILY

Busy Bulls won't have time to toast the town in 2021, but don't let relationships falter with your VIP friends and relatives. Block out slots on your calendar for your inner circle, like Sunday dinners or Tuesday game night. Planning ahead will be essential, even if you're only meeting up monthly or for a seasonal vacation. With your prestigious tenth house activated by Jupiter and Saturn in Aquarius, there's a nonexistent line between socializing and networking. Plant yourself among people of notable status. Join clubs or get yourself nominated for an elite organization. Warning: When Jupiter chills in Pisces from May 13 to July 28, you may feel like deactivating your membership in any exclusive societies. This "one love" transit will connect you to some colorful characters, iconoclasts and activists!

75

Taurus POWER DATES

TAURUS NEW MOON
May 11 (2:59 PM ET)

TAURUS FULL MOON
November 19 (3:57 PM ET) Lunar Eclipse

SUN IN TAURUS
April 19 – May 20

The only constant in your life has been change, but 2021 brings some much-desired stability to the mix—at last.

Saturn in Aquarius: Time to build.
December 17, 2020–March 7, 2023

Sketch out the blueprints and call in the contractors! It's time to build your legacy, Bull, as planets call you forth to leave a meaningful mark on the world. On December 17, 2020, disciplined Saturn ascended to the top of your chart, setting up shop in Aquarius and your tenth house of success, ambition and leadership until March 7, 2023. This powerful manifestation cycle only comes around every 29.5 years, rewarding can't-stop-won't-stop dynamos with security, prosperity and prestige.

Saturn rules time and karma. Where have you put in your "ten thousand hours," as Malcolm Gladwell writes about in *Outliers?* This could be the year you cross the threshold from novice to pro. People may tap you for your expertise, looking up to you as their role model or guru. Or maybe you've always wanted to build a house, write a book or become an organic farmer. Whatever the dream, Saturn can help you crack the code on how to bring it to fruition. Don't deliberate, start researching and figuring out the "how."

If you've been working hard to achieve a goal—especially over this last seven-year Saturn "quarter"—you could rise incrementally through the ranks or gain prominence in your industry. But with integrity-hound Saturn blowing the whistle, there won't be any shortcuts. Refuel on midnight oil and prepare to pay your dues. Hustle and muscle are still required to give a mission one last push. The good news? Structured Saturn helps you streamline your efforts. Instead of scattering your energy in a million directions, put your horns down and charge toward that single point of focus.

Don't get it twisted, Toro: We're not suggesting you bear the weight of all this heavy lifting. The tenth house is the "executive suite" of the zodiac, and Saturn is grooming you as a leader between now and March 2023. Learn to delegate, project manage and plan before you jump in. After-hours work sessions might be unavoidable, but don't make it your new normal. A sleep-deprived Bull is a dangerously cranky creature. If you're tossing and turning with 3AM worries about sales figures, or pulling consistent all-nighters to finish client work, consider it a sign to enlist support. Use technology, too! With savvy Aquarius governing this chart zone, upgraded software and apps may be the answer to your time-management prayers.

Fortunately, this Saturn circuit helps you radar in on expert-level coaches, wise mentors, even older relatives who can provide guidance. Some of these way-showers may have appeared last year, when Saturn zipped through on a brief "preview" tour through Aquarius from March 21 to July 1. While the pandemic shifted the trajectory for people of every zodiac sign, the impact was definitely felt by Bulls. Sidelined goals forced you to dig deeper, learn and try new techniques. If you used the 2020 quarantine time to gain mastery of a craft, that vigilance could pay off soon.

Future plans still vague? Slow and steady Saturn helps you architect a long-term vision—one that's worthy of your efforts. Meticulous Bulls prefer to take things one step at a time, but in 2021, focus your planning and projections a little further into the distance. Where would you like to be in, say, seven years, when Saturn completes its next quarter?

The tenth house sits at the very top of the zodiac wheel, and it's the most public, prominent and status-oriented zone of your chart. With prestige-loving Saturn visiting, it's time to figure out what you want to be known for in the world. Steep as the learning curve may be, just start walking in your desired direction. Momentum will carry you along—especially in 2021, as adventurous Jupiter co-pilots the mission through Aquarius.

The tenth house is the realm of mastery and public image. Saturn will help you upgrade the way you present yourself to the world. Everything from social media profiles to presentation materials get a sophisticated overhaul. Your image matters now, which isn't exactly a news alert for your stylish, Venus-ruled sign. Of course, "power dressing" doesn't have to mean stuffy, boring or even "classic." Invest in polished pieces that are tailored to your physique, even if they cost a little more, then dress them up with statement accessories.

Taurus business owners may be ready to break ground on your next empire. If so, put down that shovel and call in the cranes. This is not a DIY job! It's also time to break the Taurus habit of avoiding discomfort. For example, you may be a charismatic salesperson, but once the deal is closed, you "forget" to finalize the paperwork. Or perhaps you keep stalling on building your website or posting on social media because you don't feel "ready." Stern Saturn snaps his fingers: It's time to face your resistance and fears. Once you do, you'll be rewarded handsomely—both with lasting inner security and an upgraded lifestyle.

Saturn in Aquarius will form a stressful square (90-degree angle) to your Taurus Sun sign, which could bring a few extra speed bumps and growing pains. At some point between now and March 7, 2023, you may have a professional identity crisis. This will either propel you onto a new path or bring you closer to what you really want to be known for in the world. With authoritarian Saturn in rebellious Aquarius, you may clash with management or walk out of a job because you disagree with their corporate ethos. Or, you may leave your current industry to pursue something completely new. There could be a company-wide restructuring or a changing of the guard which initiates your new trajectory.

> **"Saturn will help you upgrade the way you present yourself to the world. Everything gets a sophisticated overhaul."**

Health-wise, this square can amplify stress-related injuries. Are you putting too much strain on your joints? How you sit, stand or position yourself during your daily activities matters, Taurus! Invest in a better chair, mattress or supportive gear to keep yourself in ergonomic alignment. Since Saturn is associated with the bones and teeth, you may discover that you're grinding your teeth at night. Get that mouth guard, sure, but also look at where you can dial back anxiety-producing activities and relationships.

The tenth house rules men and fathers, so you may also experience a tough but necessary evolution in your relationship with your dad, brother, son or a key male-identified person in your life. Want to build a stronger bond? Start putting in a steady effort. Set up weekly phone calls, or meet up for Sunday dinners once a month. Be inquisitive instead of making small talk or doling out advice.

Relationship expert Alison Armstrong, who researches behavior and communication patterns among men, advises following her "30-Second Rule." In her findings, men are like deep wells. "When you ask them a question, they consider it seriously and 'go to the well' for the answer," she writes. "If you wait and give him a chance to draw up another bucket, you will get to hear what is beneath the surface. With each bucket, you will get to hear what is beneath the surface."

Whether you buy into Armstrong's philosophy or not, this exemplifies the type of patience that Saturn rewards. And who couldn't afford to sharpen their listening skills? It's certainly worth a try. See what happens if you don't fill that pregnant pause. A safe space could be created with an important guy in your life.

Saturn's last visit to Aquarius was from February 6, 1991, to May 21, 1993, and June 30, 1993, to January 28, 1994. If you were alive then and old enough to remember what was going on, you may see some recurring themes. And if you happened to have been born during those dates, you will experience a challenging but powerful life cycle called the Saturn return—a cosmic rite of passage that can bring maturity, tough lessons and even a life reinvention. While this can seem daunting, it's actually setting the foundation for the next 28 to 30 years of your life, ensuring that you move forward on a rock-solid base.

Saturn in Aquarius Square Uranus in Taurus
February 17, June 14 & December 24

You're a zodiac sign known to prize stability, but in 2021—and for the last three years—you've made a radical departure from that reputation. For this you can thank changemaker Uranus, which entered Taurus in May 2018, its first trip to your sign since 1942. Between now and April 2026, Uranus will completely overturn your notions of "normalcy." As it sweeps through your first house of self and identity, everything from your beliefs to your career path to your lifestyle is up for an overhaul. Even your appearance could dramatically transform.

Maybe bohemian Uranus inspired you to swap the buttoned-up and tailored Taurus look for casual chic. Think: flowing hair and diaphanous dresses more suited to a meditation circle in Tulum than a corporate luncheon. If you favor more of the toughened-up Taurus look (leather, tattoos and heavy boots), you might opt for a softer, more sophisticated style.

And while you may have first greeted the destabilizing energy of Uranus warily, over time, many Bulls have learned to embrace and even enjoy it. Spontaneity lends a certain air of aliveness. Aha, that's what you've been missing all these years! But your new go-with-the-flow vibe may be challenged in 2021 as Uranus drifts into three 90° squares—on February 17, June 14 and December 24—with structured Saturn.

These two planetary powerhouses only clash this way every 22 years. Until March 2023, Saturn will be anchored in Aquarius and your rule-adhering tenth house. As unconventional Uranus battles for freedom and stalwart Saturn campaigns for consistency, dueling desires ratchet up. On the one hand, you're a Taurus—and you need stability. You like to achieve, and you want to be acknowledged for your hard-won accomplishments. Saturn in Aquarius could serve up opportunities to lead, to establish a business or to create long-term success.

Normally, this would be music to your ears. Taking a steady, well-paying gig? A total no-brainer. But with Uranus sideswiping Saturn, you need to consider how much of your freedom you'll be asked to sacrifice in exchange. Is there a way to have it all—wild success and boundless liberty? The tenth house rules authority figures, men (or the male-identified) and fathers. With "teenager" Uranus in your outspoken first house, you could clash mightily with anyone who seems to be telling you what to do, believe or think. The slightest whiff of paternalistic or confining energy could send you over the edge.

The cure for the conflict of a stressful square is balance. Compromise. How can you satisfy your need for the unstructured freedom to "do you" (driven by Uranus) and the desire to build something of lasting value, to invest in long-term security? You don't want to be entirely adrift without purpose. But you also don't want to be locked into anything that stifles your growth. After all, security can be an access point to freedom. Once you cover the basics, you don't have to be saddled by mundane daily stresses, like how to pay the bills or where you'll live. Could you scale back some of your expenses or responsibilities to create more breathing room?

Jupiter in Aquarius & Pisces

January 1: Aquarius (since December 19, 2020)
May 13: Pisces (retrograde June 20)
July 28: Aquarius (retrograde until October 18)
December 28: Pisces (until December 20, 2022)

In 2021, Jupiter will shift back and forth between Aquarius and Pisces. Normally, Jupiter makes an unbroken trek through a single sign for 12 to 13 months, but in 2021, we'll see the planet of fortune and growth in two signs.

Jupiter in Aquarius

December 19, 2020–May 13, 2021
July 28–December 28, 2021

To the top!

Express elevator to the top of your game! Lucky and enthusiastic Jupiter is riding shotgun to Saturn through Aquarius, charging up your tenth house of career, leadership and long-term goals. The red-spotted planet holds court in this "financial district" for two prolonged phases: from December 17, 2020, to May 13, 2021, then again from July 28 to December 28, 2021.

While Saturn demands a plan, Jupiter gives you a high-roller's instinct. It's a heady combination for success, Bull, but it's also quite the paradox! Steady Saturn keeps you from blowing off course, while intrepid Jupiter invites you to wander down a side route and pursue your life path like an exhilarating adventure. Saturn is all about the destination while Jupiter revels in the journey. This is a year to enjoy both the "end" and the "means" with zero obligation to justify your choices to anyone.

Risk tolerance increases mightily for Bulls in 2021! With galactic gambler Jupiter spurring you on, there's room to go off script—and you could shock yourself with the ease at which you throw caution to the wind. What do you want to be when you "grow up," Taurus? What legacy would you like to leave behind? Lofty questions like these are worth pondering and pursuing.

Just make sure you're aiming high enough! Hosting lucky Jupiter at the top of your chart is like having an influential friend gift you an all-access pass to the VIP lounge. Doors will swing open, beckoning you into elite social circles. Don't waste a second wondering, "Do I belong here?" (You wouldn't be standing there if you didn't!) If you can accept these cosmic gifts, you'll expand your reach mightily. Stay alert when out in public. This serendipitous cycle brings "chance" encounters with helpful, well-heeled people. Jupiter only traverses this sector every ten to 12 years, so strike while the iron is hot!

The tenth house rules traditional corporate structures, big business, government and hierarchy. It's an interesting position for Jupiter, since this planet is all about freedom, entrepreneurship and taking chances. The trick is to combine these two contrasting energies to take calculated risks, or to become an "influencer" within a well-established industry. One metaphor might be a food blogger whose recipes capture the attention of literary agents—then boom, they become the darling of the epicurean world. Or the viral startup app hatched in someone's tiny apartment that gets a seven-figure buyout offer. (This happened to a Taurus we know.) There are ways you can gracefully rise to the top without selling out, and the Saturn-Jupiter combo is all about traversing both worlds.

Maybe you've just deferred a dream—for instance, you work in digital marketing, but you want to be trained as a doula. (If the fertility field is literally calling, check out Bull babes Latham Thomas of mamaglow.com and Alisa Vitti of floliving. com.) Or, you love your industry, but long for a position that gives you more power, flexibility and creativity. Search out recruiters and make your LinkedIn profile sparkle. Working with a coach, mentor or seasoned expert could pay off in spades now.

Ready for a career evolution? Expansive Jupiter can give you the courage to leave your current line of work and start something entirely new. Always dreamed of starting a wellness brand, remodeling old homes into boutique hotels, or working in the corporate offices of a company whose ethos you adore? Desires like these should not be dismissed, even if you have zero experience in the field. Jupiter rules education—both in the ivory tower and the boots-on-the-ground experiential kind. Embrace the learning curve and remember: You don't have to do it all by yourself! The tenth house is the "executive suite" of the zodiac wheel. Sharpen your leadership skills as the project manager instead of the DIY maven who wears 15 different hats. Plus, jovial Jupiter makes everything fun. We're betting that people will enjoy working under your capable command.

Speaking of education, your process-oriented sign has a special talent for teaching. With school systems turned upside-down from the pandemic, there's an opening in the market. Could you be the one to spearhead a timely reform? Maybe you'll lobby for policy change or create the template for a cooperative home-schooling system that parents in any neighborhood can plug into. Or you could unleash your passion for adult education with a series of training videos or mastermind groups. Don't rule out one-on-one consulting income either. Seasoned Bulls can earn a lucrative hourly rate as advisors.

Even if you don't leave your job or industry, you'll crave new challenges within your current role. Adopt the spirit of an "intrapreneur" now, someone who changes the system from within. Bold requests could be met with a faster "Yes!" than you expect. It might be time to spearhead a special projects division, or, since Jupiter rules global travel, go open your company's new office in Brazil or Berlin (or work remotely, if international borders aren't open).

Jupiter's last trip through Aquarius was from January 5, 2009, to January 17, 2010. Think back to that time. You may see similar themes repeating. Or, a cycle that began back then could now come to an end. It's time to set some new #Goals, Taurus—ones that match the person you've become.

On a personal level, Jupiter in Aquarius could bring a big evolution to your relationship with your father, male-identified relatives or men in general. We aren't big on genderizing astrology, but traditionally, the tenth house has been associated with the "divine masculine" energy that lives within all of us, regardless of gender identity. Bulls who have unresolved "daddy issues" (and really, who doesn't have one or two?) might find freedom through working with a counselor or doing self-development courses on the inner child. Jupiter helps you see your dad or a father figure as a human, rather than demonizing or idealizing him. Taurus fathers may go through a renaissance period with their own children, craving more time, visits and connection. If there's been a rift between you, Jupiter can help you close that chasm.

Endurance and strength training are highlighted with Jupiter in this disciplined part of your chart. You might enjoy the challenge of working with a trainer, tackling a triathlon or doing boot camp workouts by app. Exercising under the guidance of a seasoned expert could get you in amazing shape. Overall, this is a time to set goals, cut excess and streamline. Warning: Jupiter can be extreme and impulsive. Veer away from fad diets and save yourself an injury by warming up and learning how to properly use fitness gear. Remind yourself regularly that it's a marathon, not a sprint!

Jupiter in Pisces

May 13–July 28
December 28, 2021–May 10, 2022
October 28, 2022–December 20, 2022

Expanding your inner circle.

Feeling exhausted at the thought of all that hard work? Take heart, Taurus. A celestial sabbatical opens up from May 13 to July 28 when Jupiter darts forward into Pisces for a brief spell. With the jovial planet paddling through your eleventh house of teamwork, technology and activism, your social life gets a much-needed revival. Both virtual and real-time collaborations can take your ideas to new levels. Now, it's time to share the wealth and let your soul squad help you make even more significant strides!

If it is indeed about "who you know," then this Jupiter cycle will be a boon, as supportive people emerge to collaborate. Make time for parties, industry events and just to connect with longtime supportive friends. Since Jupiter rules travel, you could organize a fun reunion with your favorite kindred spirits. Meet for a mastermind weekend—or to relax in between coworking sessions at a gorgeous vacation rental.

Don't forget to have fun for fun's sake! Jupiter in the eleventh house invites you to let your hair down and be socially experimental. (Sexually, too, if that's your jam.) Inspiring new friendships will bring out your rarely seen quirky side. With the red-spotted planet in flowy, compassionate Pisces, you could find your extracurricular fulfillment through charitable volunteer work or in a healing circle or artist group.

With Jupiter here, no character is too wacky for you to entertain—at least for a conversation. Soften your social boundaries, but don't dissolve them completely! Your sharp instincts for people may become distorted by the rose-colored lens of Jupiter in Pisces. There's a risk of getting sucked into a radical or dystopian ideology now, especially if you're feeling (justifiably) disenchanted with the politics of our times. Gurus and charlatans can also hold sway. Litmus test it: Are you hoisting someone up onto a pedestal? That's a sign to pull back and get in tune with your own inner guidance.

85

Thankfully, that shouldn't be hard. The eleventh house rules the higher mind and all things metaphysical. While Jupiter dips into these waters, you could develop a powerful meditation practice or become a yoga devotee. You may even dabble in shamanic ceremonies, plant medicine or breathwork that activates your pineal gland. The point is to get in tune with your thoughts. During this liberated cycle, you need to question every assumption and ideal. That doesn't mean you can't align with a school of thought…just make sure said "school" prizes individuality over herd mentality.

Jupiter rules publishing, travel, study and entrepreneurship. This tech-savvy circuit is an ideal time to launch a podcast (and go viral!) or start a small business that brings in passive income through savvy Internet marketing. Enrich your skills with online courses and webinars by experts in your field. If your digital skills are lacking, you might polish them up with virtual training.

The eleventh house rules platonic love, so this Jupiter vibe is more about enjoying the company of many, rather than focusing on just one person. Coupled Bulls should make an effort to socialize together, hosting parties as a power duo or taking vacations with a shared friend group. Independence also makes the heart grow fonder. If you've been attached at the hip, carve time for separate interests and friendships. There's no rule that says you have to do everything together to keep a relationship strong. Couples' therapist and author Esther Perel makes a strong case for mystery and autonomy as the key to ongoing erotic attraction.

The unconventional eleventh house might even spark discussions of an open relationship or polyamory, although with philosophical Jupiter here, exploring can be as fun in theory as it is in practice. (Certainly a lot less complicated, but that's your call!)

Since the eleventh house rules technology, upgrade your toy drawer or experiment with new sexy scenes, and possibly a guest star or two in your bedroom. Single Bulls might have a Tinder tidal wave, successfully swiping into some interesting interactions. Although you may not be quick to settle down, you could meet some genuinely fascinating people—and you never know where that could lead.

Eclipses in 2021

May 26: Sagittarius Lunar Eclipse 5°29' (7:13am ET)
June 10: Gemini Solar Eclipse 19°42 (6:52am ET)
November 19: Taurus Lunar Eclipse 27°17 (3:57pm)
December 4: Sagittarius Solar Eclipse 12°17 (2:42am)

Gemini/Sagittarius Eclipses

Financially motivated.

From 2020-22, a series of economically stimulating eclipses lands on the Sagittarius/Gemini axis, bringing exciting momentum for your money moves. Three of 2021's four eclipses will occur here, sweeping through the houses of your chart governing work, money and long-term finances. This could shift the landscape of how you earn, spend, save and invest. Buckle up, Bull! Eclipses expedite change, which could come at a galloping pace that's not exactly familiar (or comfortable) for your sign.

On May 26, a Sagittarius lunar (full moon) eclipse will land in your eighth house of joint ventures, real estate and shared financial resources. Is it time to make a collaboration official? This lunar eclipse could bring a big payday—or perhaps an unplanned expense. A passive income opportunity may cross your path, or you could find ways to "make money while you sleep" through royalties, rental income, affiliate earnings and the like. You might decide to take a radically different approach, sitting down with a financial planner, buying or selling property or simply putting away funds for retirement.

Since the eighth house also rules your intimate emotional ties, the May 26 eclipse could bring huge changes to a relationship status: an engagement, a breakup, a pregnancy or plans to move in together. Couples may deal with joint funds together, perhaps merging your bank accounts and assets—or suddenly splitting them up. A relationship or financial source might be literally "eclipsed" out of your life, clearing the decks for something better, but in an abrupt way. A legal matter, especially one related to shared property, might be settled now.

Next up, the June 10 solar (new moon) eclipse will land in Gemini, blowing a gusty tailwind through your second house of work, money and earned income. This eclipse could expedite a job transition or reveal a moneymaking opportunity that's been hiding in plain sight. A change of guard at your office may throw you off your game temporarily but could also reveal an unforeseen growth opportunity worth applying for. You may suddenly and unexpectedly part ways with a client or leave a position. Or, you'll field an incredible offer that's too good to refuse.

That said, impulsivity isn't advised during the chaotic energy of an eclipse. Even if you're being rushed to sign on the dotted line, take the time you need to conduct due diligence and make sure this is the right move for you. Since the second house rules self-worth, this eclipse could deliver a much-needed confidence boost. You might also change your daily habits, prioritizing your spending, time management and routines to reflect what matters most to you.

Q4 could be a lucrative one if you play your cards right—budgeting, saving and investing wisely. But you can also rely on your natural charms during the holiday season. The December 4 Sagittarius solar (new moon) eclipse makes you a money magnet—and just generally magnetic, Taurus! This lunation heralds a bold new beginning for financial decisions and relationships. Even if you didn't hustle as cosmically directed all year, this final new moon gives way to a radically fresh start. Sizzling sexual chemistry could consummate, or you might meet a soulmate type you feel like you've known for lifetimes. (Hey, Taurus, maybe you have!) Plant yourself among the "right" people near December 4. Striking up a chatty conversation at the bar could evolve in some prosperous directions that unfold in early 2022.

Taurus/Scorpio Eclipses

Back in the saddle, baby!

Circle November 19 in neon pink ink! That's the day of the annual full moon in your sign, which is also a game-changing lunar eclipse in your trailblazing, self-directed first house! This is the first eclipse to hit the Taurus/Scorpio axis since 2012-14, igniting a game-changing series that spans until October 28, 2023.

Lunar eclipses are eye-openers. When they arrive in your sign, they force you to look at your own buried desires. There's a treasure trove waiting to be discovered within you, even if it feels "scary" or uncomfortable to do that inner work. This eclipse could herald a total identity shift, especially if you've gone as far as you want to with a certain job, relationship or way of life. True, you may shock the people who know you best when you announce that you're relocating south of the border or quitting your glamorous corporate job to open a Labradoodle rescue. But this eclipse series has a dual purpose. First, to get you intimately acquainted with your needs—and to remind you that you are a badass! Second, when the Scorpio eclipses begin next year, you'll "true up" your relationships, or upgrade to pairings that are in alignment with your authentic self.

Venus Retrograde in Capricorn: Calculated romantic risks.

December 19, 2021 –January 29, 2022

Destination: Experimentation! On November 5, ardent Venus boards a long flight through Capricorn, logging miles in your worldly, adventurous ninth house until March 6, 2022. With your radiant, romantic ruler in this intrepid position, love can be a fantastic voyage. Travel beyond the familiar instead of cleaving to traditions. Old-fashioned romance has its merits—and you're its loudest ambassador, Taurus. But that doesn't mean you can't expand your pleasure palate!

Cross-cultural connections, long-distance dating, looser "restrictions" within a relationship? All such things are fair game during these liberating four months… with a caveat: Venus will pivot retrograde from December 19, 2021, to January 29, 2022, a six-week signal jammer that could throw off your navigation system. Just as you reach cruising altitude, circumstances get intense, forcing you to make an emergency landing, so as to ground you in reality again.

Frustrating? For sure, Taurus. It takes something extra for you to be this exploratory in the first place, so when adventures yield strife, you can be super hard on yourself. Yet this four-month journey out of the comfort zone could be one of the most beneficial periods you've had in years! Maybe eight years, in fact, because Venus was last retrograde in Capricorn and your ninth house from

December 21, 2013, to January 31, 2014. Flip back to that period and see if any recurring themes are arising.

Canceling Cupid can be a tempting proposition when Venus shifts into reverse every 584 days. (The last Venus retrograde was from May 13 to June 25, 2020.) But wait! Rerouting romantic plans might be enough to tamp down turbulence during this six-week spell—as long as you don't slip into denial. Putting on the blinders would mean missing the gifts of this transit! What are those, you may ask? Retrograde Venus provides a powerful window for excavating your emotional landscape. Yes, you may have to deal with buried "attachment issues" and fears that spin you in the opposite direction of bonded, fulfilling love. But once you recognize them, you can begin to free yourself from their grips.

For example, if you and the LOYL keep getting ensnared in the same damn argument, dig deeper to unearth the root of the conflict. Goals for the future may be leading you on divergent paths. And so? By finally admitting this, you may unearth creative ways to support each other through these "separate but together" journeys.

Newly dating? Perhaps you became too ambitious about future planning when Venus first moved into Capricorn on November 5. It wouldn't be surprising with the love planet in the high-striving Sea Goat's realm and your "bigger, stronger, faster" ninth house. Re-evaluate: Maybe it is too soon to bring your new love interest home for the holidays, especially if your family hazes newcomers mercilessly and you're attracted to "sensitive" types. Plus, are you actually ready to move in together? Or would that shared financial obligation be a buzzkill for your sexy honeymoon phase? Question everything and slow things down if needed. Rewrite the script so it works for you (and your S.O., of course). Our advice? Avoid any major "stress tests" from December 19, 2021, to January 29, 2022, and instead, do things to strengthen communication with your potential soulmate.

Single Bulls who can't get off the treadmill with a toxic type could do some deeper repair work on the machinery of your hearts. Venus is spending four months in your ninth house of education and wisdom. There's the excuse you need to sign up for that healing retreat in Hawaii or to work with a renowned therapist or love coach. Not in the budget? Read books on attachment styles, watch TED talks on vulnerability. Schedule intuitive readings, find out your Enneagram type, get massages and acupuncture. Treat the retrograde like an

> ## "Venus provides a powerful window for excavating your emotional landscape."

extended vision quest. The goal? To become intimately acquainted with your patterns. That way, when they threaten to blow you off course in the future, you can catch, correct, and communicate powerfully with the one you adore.

Need help falling under Cupid's spell? Before December 19, revisit a location that makes you feel like your most beautiful and magical self. You can journey solo or with a plus-one, but the point of the exercise is to connect to your power and the sensual parts of yourself that haven't gotten enough attention for a while.

Planning a wedding? Astrologers never recommend marrying while Venus is retrograde. Alas, that timing will put a kibosh on New Year's nuptials in 2021. What to do if you've already planned a small destination wedding—or a giant, traditional affair—between December 19, 2021, and January 29, 2022? One option is to get hitched at City Hall earlier in December. If that kills the romance for you, make sure you renew your vows a year later (in late 2022 or early 2023). Because Venus only turns retrograde every 18 months, you'll be in the clear for your first anniversary.

Venus also rules our valuables—and what we place a high premium upon. In classy Capricorn, your appetite for luxury increases, but so does your practical, earthy nature. Want to treat yourself to something special for the season? Invest in sophisticated upgrades, using your keen sensibilities to find high-quality, heritage label goods at killer prices. (A Taurus Venn diagram if ever there was one!) From a tailored blazer to a sleek sports car, Venus can help you hunt down the perfect *objet*.

Mind the retrograde warning: Purchases made from December 19, 2021, to January 29, 2022, need to come with a solid warranty, or better yet, a lifetime guarantee!

Money matters are on the table for all Bulls now, and Venus in Capricorn helps with long-term planning. Financial goals have changed for many people after 2020's economy-skewing pandemic. By November 5, you may be looking at the future through a very different lens. What's important to you, Bull? And, if you're in a relationship, what is your partner's outlook on spending and saving? In all your closest connections, it's time to put long-range goals on the table and see how they align.

Though discussions may reveal that you want different things, this isn't the end of the line. Use Venus' four-month tour through Capricorn (both while retrograde and direct) to cleverly brainstorm ways you can support each other's dreams. That might mean reconfiguring finances temporarily so one of you can afford to go back to school or finally get a better car for daily commutes. Put it all on the table and discuss!

Gemini

HOROSCOPE

2021
HIGHLIGHTS

LOVE

Meant-to-be mates or star-crossed lovers? Whether they emerge for a reason, a season or a lifetime, relationships have a destined quality in 2021, thanks to the karmic South Node spending the whole year in Sagittarius and your partnership-oriented seventh house. Two tide-turning eclipses in Sagittarius, on May 26 and December 4, could bring rapid (and potentially exhilarating!) developments in your love life. The trick to seeing people's true colors is to remain as "in the now" as you possibly can—even if every part of you wants to project a fantasized future. That said, happily coupled Gems could embark on a grand adventure this year, like traveling the country by van for three months or starting a bespoke business from your kitchen table.

MONEY

Your career is on an exciting upswing this year as cosmic collaborators Jupiter and Saturn team up in Aquarius and your enterprising ninth house. Jupiter is the galactic gambler while Saturn likes to play it safe. Their paradoxical energy advances your efforts in a way that's both cutting edge and stable—how Gemini is that?! From May 13 to July 28, Jupiter rises into Pisces and your tenth house of achievement and status, which could usher in work with an established company or long-term client. Ready to pivot? Studious Saturn lends support for Geminis who want to enroll in school or create a curriculum to teach whatever you've mastered.

WELLNESS

Drop and give us twenty! Saturn, the planetary "personal trainer," hypes you up for a fitness challenge. Enlist support from a coach or community; track your progress by app. This is the year to push way past your perceived edges. With your nature-loving ninth house lit, outdoor exercise and sports are your jam in 2021. The Taurus lunar eclipse on November 19 could inspire a pre-holiday detox or renew a meditation practice. This is the first in an eclipse series on the Taurus/Scorpio axis, inspiring two years of holistic healing that impacts your mind, body and soul.

FRIENDS & FAMILY

Indie-spirited Gemini, don't forget your people! Jupiter's breezy tour through Aquarius will expand your social circle, turning strangers into BFFs in the blink of an eye. But "instant intimacy" doesn't replace time-tested trust. Make time for the friends who have had your back over the years. Visiting far-flung family, or even touring your ancestral homeland, could make a worthwhile vacation in 2021. Leave some blank spaces on that calendar! As the North Node in Gemini activates your autonomous first house, your "me time" will be more precious—and productive—than ever.

Gemini
POWER DATES

GEMINI NEW MOON
June 10 (Solar eclipse) (6:51 AM ET)

GEMINI FULL MOON
December 18 (11:35 PM ET)

SUN IN GEMINI
May 20 – June 20

Get ready for a year of structured expansion, Gemini—and a major reinvention of the image you present to the world!

Saturn in Aquarius:
The student becomes the master.
December 17, 2020–March 7, 2023

So many interests, so little time? As the zodiac's dabbling dilletante, you like keeping your (nail-art-bedazzled) hands in many pots. But in 2021, you could switch up your M.O, going from "jack of all trades" to "master of one." (Okay, fine, Gemini…master of two, but no more than three, okay?)

For this you can thank studious Saturn. On December 17, 2020, the cosmic coach rose into high-minded Aquarius, activating your ninth house of wisdom and global expansion until March 7, 2023. Saturn only visits each part of your chart every 29.5 years, and its three-year journeys definitely have an impact! Wherever the ringed planet parks will be an area of life that feels a lot like boot camp. You have to wake up early, push through the reps and "feel the burn" in order to get the rewards. But you'll also be motivated to take on the challenge!

Fortunately, Saturn's tour of the ninth house is one of its most rewarding circuits. Although Saturn is restrictive by nature, the ninth house rules expansion. Despite that paradox, you'll feel ready to embrace this planetary push—even if it requires you to go into beast mode.

As astrologers, we have witnessed Saturn's ascent into the ninth house (in either the natal chart or the solar one, as described here) to be a bountiful time for our clients. And it's a welcome relief after the past two Saturn cycles through your seventh house of relationships (December 2014 to December 2017) and your eighth house of intense, binding entanglements (December 2017 to December 2020). You've been paying your dues—personally, monetarily, karmically—and at long last, you'll start to gain real traction for all that hustle.

While you'll still break a sweat with Saturn touring Aquarius, it won't feel like an endless series of tests from the universe. In fact, you might realize that all those hard knocks of the past six years built some serious character and expertise. Step up, sensei! For the next two years, you could be tapped to teach something that you learned in the trenches. Create a curriculum or record live demos on YouTube. This could become a great source of income. Get to work on those lesson plans! Got a TED talk brewing or the words for a "how I mastered this" book? Disciplined Saturn will support your development efforts.

The ringed planet already embarked on a brief recon mission into Aquarius in 2020, from March 21 to July 1. Under normal circumstances, this may have sent you on an educational voyage to a far-flung destination. If not for the virus, you might have spent part of 2020 studying plant medicine alongside a Peruvian shaman, mastering French cooking techniques in Provence, or cycling through Southeast Asia to raise funds for a global charity.

Buuuuuut…sigh. Saturn's restrictive nature coupled with a pandemic put the kibosh on those sorts of plans. As such, many Twins found ways to travel in the philosophical sense, discovering new schools of thought. Maybe you connected to the nature-loving aspects of the ninth house, finding freedom in the great outdoors.

After reading Clarissa Pinkola Estes' *Women Who Run with the Wolves,* our Gemini astrologer "sis-Star," Miz Chartreuse, began a daily running practice through the woodsy trails near her suburban Chicago home. The joy-inducing treks were so profound that she began recording videos and leading her Instagram followers through inspiring daily meditations as she traversed the greenery.

The ninth house rules diversity and inclusivity—and with Aquarius, the sign of social justice, governing this sector of your chart, you may have been a vocal participant in 2020's activism. This was true for our Gemini friend, Aramis O. Hamer, a gifted artist who made a name for herself in Seattle as an interactive painter and muralist. Last June, while Saturn was in Aquarius, she was tapped to paint a letter in the Black Lives Matter street mural in the heart of Seattle's activist zone. The piece was featured on global news channels, in style magazines and on thousands of social media feeds.

"I couldn't imagine all this would happen as I painted this gold chain for the V," she wrote on her Instagram @aohamer, "I thought about the institutionalized chains that keep us bound by a system that was built on the dehumanization of Black and Brown people."

In 2021, Twins will feel another powerful pull to help spread a meaningful message. Whatever your métier—art, music, dance, or engineering the mechanics behind it all—your efforts will resonate with likeminded people across the globe.

No matter where you're located, Saturn's tour of Aquarius will activate your quest for knowledge, truth and your highest purpose. Since the ninth house rules higher education—and Saturn is all about credentials—you might "legitimize" one of your self-taught skills with formal training. Is a degree program calling your name? Enrolling in university classes, even part time, can position you for professional ascent in March 2023, when Saturn climbs into your tenth house of career.

The AstroTwins' 2021 Horoscope　　　98

Saturn in this sporty position can inspire you to take better care of your body. If you work a sedentary job, consider getting a standing desk, or making daily movement a priority. With the "personal trainer" planet parked here all year,

> ## "Twins who are feeling restricted by relationships could bolt on the very people who provide a sense of security."

pushing yourself (without overdoing it) can pay off with greater flexibility and more muscle tone. Saturn loves a program and a plan—and you, Gemini, get motivated by community. Participating in a fitness coach's 30-day challenge, for example, can provide a healthy, inspiring kickstart.

Saturn in Aquarius square Uranus in Taurus
February 17, June 14 & December 24

As the student becomes the master under Saturn's watch, don't make the mistake of thinking you can rise to the next level alone! While Saturn in Aquarius revs up your independent spirit, it can also make you a wee bit overconfident. Life is going smoothly at last, so it's natural to think things like, "Maybe I don't need therapy anymore" or "I can let my assistant go and schedule appointments myself." Twins who are feeling restricted by relationships could bolt on the very people who provide a sense of security, simply because you're bored.

Screeeeeeeech! While it's true that you may require a more advanced level of support in 2021, being a one-Gemini army could actually cause you to regress a few steps back on the gameboard. We realize that relationships are never quite the same once that early-onset dopamine rush fades—always a huge crash for your high-key sign. But don't underestimate the importance of stability and solid ground beneath your feet. In 2021, balancing variety and routine is essential to your sanity!

The reason for this? Three times this year—on February 17, June 14 and December 24—game-changer Uranus throws disciplined Saturn a curveball, forming a challenging 90-degree square. From May 2018 to April 2026, Uranus is side-spinning through Taurus and your twelfth house of healing, spirituality and wise guides. The twelfth house also rules endings. There is a sense of boundlessness with rebellious Uranus here, as if you're hovering between the Earth plane and the spirit plane, picking up otherworldly signs and signals. At times, this can make you feel like a superhero who has transcended the three-dimensional world, soaring across the energetic plane. But Geminis who lose touch with the material realm could wind up battling demons like addiction, delusion, isolation, melancholy and other self-destructive behaviors that can cause your mood and wellbeing to plummet.

As Saturn fires three warning shots to Uranus from your vitality-boosting ninth house, think of them as wakeup calls to tend to your physical and mental health. Our advice? Put some grounding practices in place as soon as the year begins! Physical exercise can do wonders to keep you in your body, as can eating and sleeping on a regular schedule. With Uranus in your ethereal twelfth house, this is an optimal time to get a meditation and/or yoga practice underway. The Gemini mind may never be quiet, but you can slow down your thoughts, learning to create space between stimulus and response.

On the plus side, the Saturn-Uranus squares can rev up both imagination and innovation. You'll be prone to romanticizing everything near these three cosmic events. Before you pull the trigger on any major life moves, consult your wise tribunal of advisers and elders. Getting a second, third and fourth respected opinion can help you massage the plan of action so you can enjoy the fairy tale without getting eaten by any big, bad wolves.

Visions may come to you while you're dreaming, rousing you from your sleep. Heads up: Neither Saturn nor Uranus will make you a "morning person" this year, but staying up all night on a creative tear should not be the "new normal" especially if you have to home school a kid or report for work at 9AM. Avoid sleep deprivation if you want to stay on an even keel.

Choose your gurus wisely! It might take a village to keep you on that healthy path this year, but you are worth the investment. Don't think of this as indulgent, Gemini. Caring for your wellbeing will positively impact everyone around you.

Jupiter in Aquarius & Pisces

January 1: Aquarius (since December 19, 2020)
May 13: Pisces (retrograde June 20)
July 28: Aquarius (retrograde until October 18)
December 28: Pisces (until December 20, 2022)

Jupiter will shift back and forth between Aquarius and Pisces in 2021. Normally, Jupiter makes an unbroken trek through a single sign for 12 to 13 months, but in 2021, we'll see the planet of fortune and growth in two signs.

Jupiter in Aquarius

December 19, 2020–May 13, 2021
July 28–December 28, 2021

For the first time in over a decade, bountiful Jupiter is visiting Aquarius and your ninth house of global expansion, publishing, entrepreneurship and higher learning. It's time to fly free and explore new horizons, to see how other parts of the world live. The only catch? Grounded, sober Saturn is riding shotgun, insisting that any journeys you take be purposeful. Thankfully, Jupiter gets you off the runway and into the air!

As long as you've cleared your flight path and have some idea of where you're headed, 2021 could invite you on a fantastic voyage, either literally or figuratively. Maybe you'll take a break from your duties and tour another continent for a month or sign up for a degree program that you can earn online. Whether you're actually boarding a plane or interfacing on webcam remains your call. But don't be surprised if opportunity knocks (or WhatsApps you) from a far-flung continent.

Feeling fenced in? While expansive Jupiter is in airy Aquarius and your global ninth house until May 13, then again from July 28 to December 28, you will not take kindly to anyone clipping your wings. Jupiter is the natural ruler of the zodiac's ninth house, tripling your willingness to throw caution to the wind. While there are no guarantees, you're likely to land on your stylishly soled feet with the planet of luck working overtime on your behalf.

Have you always visualized yourself as a business-owner or on staff at a game-changing organization? You could roll the dice on an independent venture or work for a humanitarian agency whose mission you believe in. Even if you work in a traditional corporate environment, you may interface with long-distance clients or serve as "brand evangelist" for the company. With your natural enthusiasm, you are the perfect ambassador to help spread their message.

Personal growth falls under the ninth house domain, and with eager student Jupiter at the helm, you might sign up for self-development workshops to explore your own human potential. Metaphysical studies, Buddhism and Eastern philosophy could also hold special appeal under the "New Age" influence of Jupiter in Aquarius. As cool and unruffled as Geminis come across, your sign can be plagued by a deep sense of anxiety—and an overanalyzing tendency that can give even the most neurotic Virgo a run for their money! Jupiter in Aquarius will teach you how to take a breath and lean into the Law of Attraction. Search for tools that can help you remain in an abundant mindset.

After all the loss and grief of 2020, you may find yourself adopting a "carpe diem" mindset, vowing to live each day as if it could be your last. But dial down the hedonism, Gem, especially while Jupiter is retrograde from June 20 to October 18. With the red-spotted raconteur in your "no limits" ninth house, you won't have a clear sense of "enough." This could materialize as unhealthy weight gain, addictions to sweets, booze, compulsive shopping or gambling. Responsible Twins are liable to veer in the opposite direction, taking on too much work or letting "scope creep" overrun what was once a manageable project. Instead of adding more irons to the fire, pause to finish what you've already started. And don't be afraid to downsize in the name of getting your Version 1.0 to market!

Romantically, you may prefer to fly free this year—or at least, to carve out time to follow your independent whims. One thing you won't tolerate: being confined by a needy mate. The codependent caretaker vibes that may have pushed you to your limits in 2020 (or before) have officially ended in 2021. Amen! The person who gives you space to roam without getting clingy or jealous wins your final rose this year. Maybe you'll drive off in an RV with a sexy co-adventurer who wants to see the world with you.

Jupiter's last visit to Aquarius was from January 5, 2009, to January 17, 2010. If you can, flip back to that time in your personal history books. You may see some familiar themes threading through your current life or history repeating itself.

Jupiter in Pisces
May 13–July 28
December 28, 2021–May 10, 2022
October 28, 2022–December 20, 2022

Mid-May, Jupiter lunges out of your wild and adventurous ninth house, tearing off a tie-dyed T-shirt and revealing a power suit underneath. The red-spotted planet will make a brief first impression in Pisces and your ambitious tenth house, supersizing your goals. Having a dreamy, creative zodiac sign like Pisces governing the flow of your career is a bit of a head trip. It may explain why so many Geminis struggle to pick a professional lane and often swim from one job (or path!) to the next. Even Twins who do have a steady nine-to-five can often be found moonlighting in some metaphysical field. To wit, one of our dearest Gemini pals is a Silicon Valley marketing director by day and a gifted psychic medium who works with private clients on weekends and evenings.

The last time Jupiter visited Pisces was from January 17, 2010, to January 22, 2011. What goals did you have on the agenda back then? Some of those may come full circle now. Grab the #BossGoals bull by the horns—or at least start gearing up for the climb! Jupiter will resume a longer tour through Pisces at the end of this year, on December 28, boosting well-prepared Twins up the ladder of success.

From May 13 to July 28, however, cast your gaze toward stable terrain. This might mean applying for a job with a steady paycheck or figuring out how the heck you can monetize one of the grand ideas that keeps popping up during your explorations (and meditations) while Jupiter was in Aquarius during the first part of 2021.

With free-spirited Jupiter in this power position, you may pick up consulting work for an established and traditional company. Expansive Jupiter might bring a promotion, an exciting offer, even an entirely new path! Since Jupiter only visits this part of your chart every 11 to 12 years, some Geminis might outgrow the industry they've been in for the last decade or so and move in a new direction.

The tenth house rules business, but with venturesome Jupiter in Pisces, even the steadiest of jobs will come with an indie-spirited twist. Maybe you'll be an "intrapreneur," spearheading a new division within your company or being tapped to oversee a coveted, envelope-pushing project. (Totally your speed!) Since Jupiter rules travel and global connections, you might interface regularly with a foreign office, relocate for an impressive new position or deal with clients in far-flung locations. A global reach is easy these days, so if you're a business owner, you might target promising new markets abroad.

This goal-oriented groove will also influence matters of the heart. Coupled Geminis can plan for the future, setting aside a nest egg for important things like retirement or home ownership, but also earmarking funds for, say, a kitchen renovation or an infrared sauna.

Unattached Geminis will get a lot choosier about your prospects, filtering out the flaky candidates and being upfront about your agenda. If you want kids or long to live somewhere else, don't be shy about voicing that desire if it helps you weed out incompatible people. (That said, you may not want to enter a first meeting wielding a huge checklist!) You might even attend singles' events or work with a traditional matchmaker if you're really serious about settling down.

Men, fathers and anyone male-identified fall under the domain of the tenth house, and with Jupiter here, you could heal any past trauma that's been plaguing the relationship between you and your dad. Or, you'll just evolve into a more adult relationship, moving past an outworn parent-child dynamic. If your biological father is not part of your life, you can still find an elevated position of forgiveness or closure with him.

Remember, forgiveness doesn't mean you condone someone's wrongful actions. It just means that you stop carrying around the pain from that. Set yourself— and the person in question—free. A helpful or supportive man, possibly a boss or a mentor, could open doors for you during this Jupiter cycle. Bring on the goodfellas!

North Node in Gemini: Major reinvention.
May 5, 2020–January 18, 2022

The dharma-directing lunar North Node spends all of 2021 in Gemini, activating your trailblazing, self-possessed first house. If you've been hiding your light under a bushel, you might as well surrender that M.O. This special "point" in the sky only traverses your sign once every two decades (for 18-19 months), demanding that you step into your higher calling.

This fateful cycle began on May 5, 2020. As such, you might already be in action around one of your visionary projects. If not, 2021 is the year to discover it! This path doesn't even have to be associated with your career. It could show up as a "meant to be" mission (perhaps one with a vacuum for leadership) or a passion project that consumes every minute of your downtime.

But here's the rub: Just because you're drawn in this direction doesn't mean you'll sail forth to effortless success. To maximize the gifts of the North Node, you have to wander into unfamiliar terrain. Mastering this energy, even when it's activating your zodiac sign, is like learning complex choreography…as one of Beyonce's backup dancers, not some playful TikTok amateur.

Lean in and say "yes" to the challenge! The fancy footwork you learn during this fateful phase may never become your natural gait. But it will get you treading down a fulfilling new path. We like to call North Node terrain "the Zone of Miracles," in fact. The universe will reward you with many blessings if you spring out of your safety zone. Take it in small bites, Gem! If projects have grown overly complex, wrestle them back to a manageable state. By the time the year is through, you could have a brilliant collection of works assembled and ready for a big reveal.

You're bound to discover plenty about yourself along the way, which might even provoke a short-term identity crisis. The person you thought you were becoming (or were meant to be) might not fit your direction anymore. While that can be unmooring, surrender to a higher guidance. Allow yourself to play with different roles—at work, in relationships and in your social life. Think of it as a costume party for your alter ego(s). You can always take them on and off until you find a "lewk" that fits.

Check your archives: The last time the North Node visited Gemini was between October 14, 2001, and April 14, 2003. If you're old enough to remember what was going on then, you might see some recurring themes crop up.

Eclipses in 2021

May 26: Sagittarius Lunar Eclipse 5°29′ (7:13am ET)
June 10: Gemini Solar Eclipse 19°42 (6:52am ET)
November 19: Taurus Lunar Eclipse 27°17 (3:57pm)
December 4: Sagittarius Solar Eclipse 12°17 (2:42am)

Gemini/Sagittarius Eclipses

Me vs. we.

The relationship rollercoaster brings more peaks and valleys, thanks to a series of eclipses that began on June 5, 2020. Three times this year—on May 26, June 10 and December 4—the momentous moonbeams will activate the Gemini/Sagittarius axis, forcing you to examine the balance between "me" and "we."

Eclipses are game-changers, and not always in a "rah-rah" kind of way…at first. If you're resisting the next level of transformation, these lunar life coaches will push you off the fence, bringing the kinetic energy needed to make real change. The challenge? Not scurrying back to your safety zone when things get uncomfortable…because they will. Every 8-9 years, these lunations take place in your sign as well as the sign opposite yours (Sagittarius), which makes these accelerated developments even more personal. Relationships will be mirrors as the traits you've rejected become reflected through your interactions with others.

Like it or not, Gemini, it's time to take an unflinching look at the role you play in relationship breakdowns. You're happy to embrace the "it takes two to tango"

106

mantra when everything's on the upswing. But when conflict throws a wrench in the plans, you tend to swing between extremes. You're either dragging the frenemy through a tangled mass of grapevines as you gossip about them to anyone within earshot or you're bearing the full brunt of the blame ("It was all my fault!") instead of holding your partner accountable.

Evil twin? Saint Gemini? We're happy to report that there's a world of options beyond those two. As 2021's eclipses push for deeper reflection, you can stop

> "Whether a bedmate, bandmate or business associate, you need to take command of the situation and deal."

ping-ponging between these extremes. But get ready to glimpse your shadow in the process (glug). That's exactly what eclipses reveal, both literally and metaphorically.

The first eclipse of 2021 is a lunar (full moon) eclipse in Sagittarius on May 26. Jaw-dropping intel could come to light involving one of your partners in life. Whether a bedmate, bandmate or business associate, you need to take command of the situation and deal with it already. This eclipse is the manifestation moon of the Sagittarius solar (new moon) eclipse that took place on December 14, 2020.

If you and your "other half" have been working in earnest to strengthen your partnership, May 26 would be a milestone moment worth celebrating! Someone (you, possibly) could be dropping to a knee with a velvet ring box in hand. Or maybe you'll get contracts drawn up to set a deal in stone. As long as everything's on the level, well, Gemini, why not? Just look for hidden clauses, which can be par for the course with eclipses.

On June 10, the only new moon in Gemini of 2021 also represents as a galvanizing solar eclipse. Talk about a supercharged springboard for your individual growth! You might want to earmark this visionary date as a one-day personal retreat.

As the silhouette of the moon blocks out the light of the Sun, you have a prime opportunity to turn inward (and away from distractions) to find out what is true for you! For your externally stimulated sign, it's necessary to step away from the lure of people-pleasing and performing in order to connect to your own center.

Warning: A host of emotions may arise, from sadness to resentment, but you don't want to rush into reactive mode. Instead, allow yourself to feel it all, then ask yourself, "If I was free and clear to live my life any way I chose, what would I do next?" You'll have six months of peak manifesting time (until the December 18 full moon in Gemini) to invest in your self-development. Sign up for courses, apprentice with a master, relocate for a fresh start. Just remember that this eclipse is all about sharpening your talents and getting them out into the world! PS: That might mean walking away from something (or someone) that is holding you back from fully blossoming.

On December 4, the final eclipse of 2021 arrives as a solar eclipse in Sagittarius and your seventh house of partnership. New openings for relationships could arrive out of the blue. You might be heading to City Hall to say "I do" or finalizing the paperwork for an exciting tag-team effort. Whatever you sign on for will take off at a gallop and could lead in unexpected directions. Unleash your spontaneous side and enjoy the ride!

Taurus/Scorpio Eclipses

On November 19, a new eclipse series begins with the lunar (full moon) eclipse in Taurus. For the two years to follow, these eclipses will strike the Taurus/Scorpio axis, activating your twelfth house of spiritual illumination and your sixth house of healthy routines. The mind-body-soul connection will be undeniable, so check your thoughts and begin shifting your mindset.

How often do you tell yourself "I can't!" or "That's not possible for someone like me." Those limiting beliefs might evaporate before your eyes near November 19 as you're called to support the people you love most. But don't do it at the expense of your sanity and self-care. Learning to "be there" and still have boundaries? It's not only possible, Gemini, it's high time!

Venus Retrograde in Capricorn: Seduction, round two?

December 19, 2021 –January 29, 2022

Santa baby! A sexy "winter warmer" could keep your libido out of hibernation this November 5 as sultry Venus sashays into Capricorn and struts down the catwalk of your erotic eighth house until March 6, 2022. Since this is the "red light district" of the zodiac wheel—and you'll be in a seriously seductive mood—mistletoe is not required!

> **"Venus' pivot could bring an old flame back into the picture who actually has soulmate potential."**

Typically, Venus hangs out in a zodiac sign for three to five weeks. But due to her every-18-months retrograde—this time from December 19, 2021, to January 29, 2022—she'll hover in Capricorn for four times longer than her usual spell. You know a lot about that, Gemini. Last year, the love planet lingered in your sign from April 3 to August 7. It was illuminating in many ways, especially when Venus turned retrograde in Gemini from May 13 to June 25, 2020. Suffice to say, that backspin was complicated for the zodiac's Twins! (Thankfully, Venus won't turn retrograde in your sign again until 2028.)

Go ahead and break out that crystal ball, Gemini. When Venus flips into reverse from December 19, 2021, to January 29, 2022, some of that seduction may turn into intrigue, and those cat-and-mouse games could send you scurrying down one-way streets. Forget about relying on your intuitive senses during this six-week signal-jammer.

Retrogrades stir up the past and Venus' pivot could bring an old flame back into the picture who actually has soulmate potential. If the connection is still strong, it may be worth exploring, but don't expect to get a clear read on the situation until after January 29, 2022. (Though a NYE liplock is not out of the question!) If you

109

hear from a toxic ex, don't waste time trying to be "just friends." If nothing else, conduct a ritual to clear their energy from your field.

Feel like getting closer to a special someone? If you want to create intimacy, you're going to have to pry open your chamber of secrets and get vulnerable. The good news is that Venus retrograde can help you plunge into deeper waters and develop trust.

If you raced into a relationship without getting real about practical considerations (like, say, incompatible spending habits or totally different views on raising a family), retrograde Venus will force you to take an unblinking look at how realistic a future together actually is. Or maybe you've been hiding something that's really important to you and you're afraid to say it for fear of pushing your person away. Baring your soul is the only way forward between December 19, 2021 and January 29, 2022. Eventually, anyone you "get in bed with" (literally or metaphorically) will find out who you really are—and who your alter ego is, too! But that's the magic of relationships, Gem: being loved for all of your complex and contradictory parts.

Conversely, you might sense that your love interest has a deep, dark secret to reveal. While you don't want to come across as suspicious, you need to investigate what this distancing is all about. The trick is to create a safe and judgment-free space for conversation. Venus retrograde can dredge up past relationship traumas, and fear can come up on both sides.

You don't have to freak out if you discover something sketchy from their past. But don't try to play therapist either! Between November 5, 2021, and March 6, 2022, strengthen the trust along with the lust. This might take hardcore negotiation, but thankfully, that's one of your savvy sign's strengths! With some healthy and honest dialogue, you could end up closer than ever. ✳

Cancer

HOROSCOPE

2021
HIGHLIGHTS

LOVE

Ready to set new depth records in the Love Olympics? Serious Saturn and adventurous Jupiter plunge into Aquarius this year, making waves in your eighth house of intimacy, seduction and shared resources. Surface encounters were never your sensitive sign's thing to begin with, so you'll navigate these seas with greater ease than most. Still, the transformational energy of the eighth house can bring some stormy endings, scintillating beginnings and a lot of ups and downs in between. Erotic exploration can get downright freaky during wild-child Jupiter's two laps through Aquarius until May 13 and again from July 28 to December 28. Business partnerships can also get off the ground, whether you're raising funds for a startup venture or funneling savings into a group investment. While there's no such thing as "too close" for most of the year, you could get a case of cold feet when Jupiter darts into Pisces for a brief spell, from May 13 to July 28. During that indie-spirited circuit, relationships with plenty of breathing room will be your jam. But you'll be back into full-on twosome mode on November 5, when seductive Venus camps out in Capricorn, your seventh house of relationships, for an extended four-month spell. Head's up: radiant Venus goes retrograde from December 19, 2021 to January 29, 2022. This can reignite an old flame or revive a nostalgic activity you once loved sharing with your partner.

112

MONEY

Enterprising Jupiter joins power-broker Saturn in your eighth house of big money for most of 2021. Nothing wrong with working a stable job but think beyond the nine-to-five grind. Lump sum earnings could flow in from an advance payment, bonus, commission or property sale. Royalties or passive income from digital downloads, like music, e-books or online courses, can also pad your pockets. Cancers with funds to spare should invest wisely, balancing the caution of Saturn with Jupiter's high-risk appetite. With both planets in communal, future-forward Aquarius, you might do well putting money in the tech sector, socially responsible companies, even space travel! Group investments could be lucrative. Do you need to pay off debt? Summon the courage to settle up with creditors and tax collectors. You might even negotiate a payment plan or reduced flat-fee payout, clearing your record and getting yourself back into black. The Gemini solar (new moon) eclipse on June 10 activates your sixth house of daily work. If you're searching for a steadier income stream, this lunar lift can bring a gig that covers your baseline bills.

WELLNESS

Transformational energy is afoot in 2021, as Jupiter and Saturn square metamorphic Uranus throughout the year. Evolving can be exciting and stressful at once for you, Cancer. While you're ready to embrace new developments, the fluctuating energy might take an emotional toll on your comfort- and familiarity-loving sign. As anxiety ramps up, turn to meditation, breathwork and music to find your chill. Mindfulness practices can also be game-changing, as you learn to observe your thoughts without reacting to them. With your eighth house activated, take extra care with sexual and reproductive health. Some Cancers may explore fertility treatments or new forms of contraception that work better with your hormones. Three eclipses, on May 26, June 10 and December 4, land on the Gemini/Sagittarius meridian, emphasizing healing on every level. Process trauma with a therapist while releasing stress from your body through dance, yoga or other flowy exercise. Jupiter's quick dash through Pisces from May 13 to July 28 could bring a major vitality boost. Drink more water!

FRIENDS & FAMILY

Tighten up the radius of your inner circle…yes, Cancer, just a smidge more. While you've always preferred a close-knit crew, 2021's intimate vibe makes one-on-ones your favorite way to bond. Here's the chance you've been waiting for to create memorable moments with a favorite relative or a new potential BFF. Coupled Crabs, if you've fallen into the habit of making your partner your everything, branch out. Developing a close friendship (or two) outside of the relationship is a wise tactic this year. Not only will the outside support take the pressure off your partner to meet your every need, but it can do wonders to revive the sexy dynamics between you. The November 19 lunar (full moon) eclipse in Taurus boosts your popularity both far and wide. With this new eclipse series activating your cooperative eleventh house until October 2023, the people you connect with near the end of this year, especially online, could usher you into new social circles, introducing you to cultural hotspots and extracurriculars that revive your *joie de vivre*.

Cancer
POWER DATES

CANCER NEW MOON
July 9 (9:16 PM ET)

CANCER FULL MOON
No full moons in Cancer in 2021.
(Hey, you had two in 2020, it's only fair!)

SUN IN CANCER
June 20 – July 22

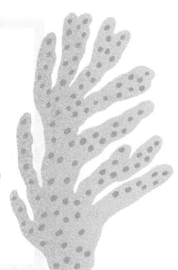

After a year that put compromise and partnerships in the spotlight, 2021 pushes you to go even deeper. Intimacy and investments are the key themes of your year.

Saturn in Aquarius: Money, power and soul-centered moves.

December 17, 2020–March 7, 2023

Money, power, respect—and a serious dose of sex magic! These heavy-hitting themes will permeate your 2021, as karmic Saturn rolls through Aquarius and your alchemical eighth house. The ringed guru settled down at this helm on December 17, 2020, and remains here until March 7, 2023, teaching you a masterclass in turning lead into gold. Enter the lab, Cancer: Figuring out the most palpable formula for security and seduction is all a matter of chemistry. How you share resources, and with whom, can make or break you while Saturn is in communal, future-focused Aquarius for two-plus years. Find your soul squad and your soul mate(s). Then merge energies, join forces. The eighth house has similar qualities to Scorpio, the eighth sign of the zodiac, where loyal bonds are everything.

The eighth house governs the life cycle from birth to death to reincarnation, and the esoteric realm of spirituality. With sober Saturn here, your mood may skew melancholy at times—not that you can't handle that! As an introspective water sign, you appreciate the dimension that comes from surfing the waves of the emotion ocean. Plus, Saturn only tours this evolutionary zone every 29.5 years (the last time was February 6, 1991, to January 28, 1994). To uncover the most valuable gems, you must mine your own soulful depths. This potent opportunity is worth embracing! The reward will be an inside-out transformation that sets you on the path to even greater security.

Where will you beam your diving light first? Your universe could look markedly different by the end of this year, if you're willing to submerge yourself in the process. Trigger alert: You may have to completely let go of something beloved and familiar that you've also outgrown. That ain't easy for a sensitive Crab! Your sign is famous for clutching onto relationships long past their expiration dates, filling your storage spaces with "sentimental objects" that rarely (if ever) see the light of day, and taking the concept of family duty to an almost sacrificial extreme. In 2021, boundary-hound Saturn blows a whistle on your addiction to comfort, shifting your priorities toward personal growth over all else.

Relax, Cancer. We're not suggesting you rip your entire life down to the studs overnight. But get honest about where you'd like to make some seismic shifts. With process-driven Saturn guiding your hand, you can disassemble these frameworks piece by piece instead of hitting them with a wrecking ball. (Think: deconstruction rather than destruction.)

Saturn made a brief visit to Aquarius last year, from March 21 to July 1, 2020, dovetailing with one of the most intense periods of modern history. While the planetary taskmaster was putting you through paces, the rest of the world was having an extreme makeover, too, grappling with a pandemic, quarantine, uprising and economic meltdown. Well, um…at least you weren't suffering alone? Saturn builds backbone. This preview cycle through Aquarius may have illuminated your own hidden strengths. Did you step up in unexpected ways during the pandemic's first pass? Free yourself from unfulfilling obligations? Learn the power of saying no? You'll continue building fortitude over the next two years.

Early on in 2021, take an honest inventory of your relationships, both business and personal. A once-flourishing partnership may be feeling like a serious drain on your soul. Whether you're leaking money or zapping your energy by caretaking, boundary-hound Saturn demands that you draw bright lines. Nurturing Cancers forget that most people lack your sensate attunement. While you're busy intuiting everyone's needs, you often fall into the trap of over-functioning. (You'll know this is the case if the people you've been "helping" seem to be getting lazy or complacent, while you keep working harder.) Did the once-dashing lover or dream client start treating you like their personal resource center? Enough's enough! A hardcore U-turn may be required to rebalance these exhausting—and utterly unsexy—dynamics.

Before you start handing out eviction notices to your inner circle, hit the brakes. Remember: We teach people how to treat us, Cancer. There are certainly a special handful out there who just "get it" and don't take advantage of your compulsive caretaking. But if you dig a little deeper, you may discover your own culpability in these lopsided relationships.

And no, it's not because you have a secret attraction to narcissists. Covert control issues could be the driving force. In a sneaky way, being the "giver" also allows you to maintain the upper hand in relationships. Sure, you may feel resentful, but you also remain emotionally debt-free. Since you aren't dependent on people, no one can pull the rug out from under you or threaten your security. Nor do you have to worry about how to reciprocate favors or wonder if there's a catch in these "generous" offers.

If this resonates for you, Cancer, please be kind to yourself. A fear-based reaction stems from the survival-driven part of your brain. Perhaps your parents lacked the tools to empathize with your feelings, much less recognize and validate them. Each time you were left alone to fend for yourself, your protective shell thickened. But as a result, receptivity was blocked. And if the people who cared for you as a child were unstable, you may outright distrust anyone who wants to tend to your needs. In 2021, Saturn gives you the courage to tackle these inconvenient truths head-on.

With Saturn in the eighth house of merging, you can begin to heal from any defensively autonomous behavior patterns. Start slowly, remembering that practice makes perfect. For example, your first pass may involve asking people for small acts of support, like a ride to a doctor's appointment or to feed your cat while you're away for a night. Don't qualify your requests with words like, "I don't mean to bother you," or add any bargaining chips like, "I can help you with X later." Just ask. Breathe through the uncomfortable feelings that arise as you await an answer. Whether people say yes or no, respond with gratitude. They considered your request and you can always try again! Once you get past this basic training phase, you can move on to bigger asks, bringing your tools into the boardroom…and the bedroom.

The eighth house is one of the zodiac's financial districts, governing the "big money" funds that come in lump sums: royalties, property sales, tax returns, inheritances. With the planet of adulting here, you'll be even more interested in long-range security. Now's the time to build (or start building) a strong investment portfolio, increase contributions to your retirement accounts, or otherwise set yourself up for a wealthier life as you define it. Joining forces with talented folk can lead to mutual gain. With team-spirited Aquarius ruling this part of your chart, group investments could pay off, possibly in Aquarian sectors such as technology, socially conscious startups or even space travel!

How's your credit score, Cancer? Debt can be cleared up while wizened Saturn spins through this zone. Taking the first look is the hardest part, but trust us, it's worth it. Saturn's tour of the eighth house only happens every 29.5 years and it's a prime window for creating fiscal freedom. No, you might not pay off your grad school loans, three years of back taxes or condo mortgage by March 7, 2023. But if you're drowning under the flood of monthly bills, call the lenders and negotiate. Some may even be willing to settle with you, like one friend of ours, who reduced $25,000 of unpaid medical expenses from his back surgery into a payoff of $6,000 while Saturn spun through his eighth house. A few honest phone calls and a bucketload of courage (plus friends standing by to make sure he dialed) was "all" it took to liberate him from the chronic, nagging stress of creditor letters piling up in his mailbox.

Whether or not you manage to pull off such a feat (which is more doable than most folks realize), the lessons don't stop when you're debt-free. Boundary-hound Saturn helps you set limits with things like swiping your Visa or purchasing anything with a high-interest payment plan. During this circumspect cycle, you can create lasting practices to get back in the black and stay there!

Our own history with Saturn in the eighth house began with an unexpected IRS bill (quarterly taxes…oh $#!%!) which led us to work with our vigilant Scorpio financial advisor. Through weekly sessions, we learned how to reconcile our monthly balance sheet and create a strategic plan, projecting cash flow for an entire year. A decade later, we still work with him as a high-level business advisor and have used these tools to grow our company by leaps and bounds. Saturn's integrity is certainly behind a good deal of that equation. But our Scorpio advisor is also a firm believer in the Law of Attraction—which is the rule of the land when this planet circulates the eighth house. A year into our work together, he gifted us both a copy of Napoleon Hill's *Think and Grow Rich*, which taps into many of these arcane principles (albeit in the archaic, patriarchal language of its era).

Need to fill the coffers? Look beyond the nine-to-five grind. Creative Cancers might earn a larger lump sum payment, like an advance on a book or record deal. Profits from a property sale could bring greater freedom. You might get a signing bonus…or a performance-based one if you burn enough midnight oil. But don't spend all your time working harder instead of smarter! Look for ways to earn passive income, such as through affiliate or direct sales. Perhaps you'll create a downloadable product like a digital course that you only have to record once, but can sell for years to come. Between now and 2023, you could see a serious uptick in your net worth by funneling funds into a diverse portfolio of investments, like real estate or index funds that yield compounding interest.

Merging assets and sharing resources could increase your affluence during this Saturn cycle, especially with social Aquarius ruling this chart sector. Get serious and strategic about networking with industry heavyweights. Hang out with friends who are savvy with their coin. Their prosperous prowess will rub off on you quickly, Cancer! Remember, however, that with Saturn it's a marathon, not a sprint. You're not just changing behaviors, Crab, you're transforming lifelong habits.

Now for the sexier part of the equation: Since the eighth house is the realm of permanent bonding, one or two key relationships could really be locked and loaded before 2021 is through. This is the zone where "two become one," and thanks to Saturn's gravitas, you could find that rare unicorn who is not only seductive AF but also comes built with a secure attachment style. While you generally play the long game in love, you take your time to commit. Sensible Saturn can bring the discernment needed to radar in on the right partner for life, someone who will stand by you through thick and thin.

Brace yourself nonetheless: Even the most breathlessly erotic encounter can set off your vulnerability alarm bells. As much as you long for nightly spooning (and then some), you start to feel suffocated quickly when people are always in your personal space. Once again, vocalizing boundaries becomes the year's prevailing theme. Sitting through the discomfort of these talks is better than burning bridges with someone you love, then living in endless regret. Honor your desire for alone time before your bubble is "invaded" and you won't set off any false expectations that leave you pissed off, freaked out and searching for the nearest exit.

The eighth house is all about trust and intimacy, and the slightest hint of betrayal can send you into a spiral. Did you meet your mate while they were otherwise engaged? Fears of being cheated on or abandoned could plague you this year. Past infidelities (perhaps your own) must be reckoned with, but this doesn't have to turn into some form of karmic justice. Many couples go through scandals such as cheating or lies and come out stronger once they both do the emotional heavy lifting. Breaches in trust don't have to spell "the end" if both people are committed to working through the pain. These can be the bridge to character-strengthening and trust-building that you never dreamed possible.

We're fans of modern-love expert Esther Perel's book *The State of Affairs*, in which she takes an unflinching look at why people stray. Her theory is that we're trying to reconnect with a lost part of ourselves through an infatuation. And for a caring soul like yourself, Cancer, it's easy to forget where you begin and your lover ends. If you've disconnected from your sensuality or sidelined your creative hobbies, reclaim your "me time." Relationships thrive as you tend to your personal needs.

Health-wise, Saturn in the eighth house tunes you in to deeper forms of healing. If you struggle with addictions or mental health issues, preventative measures should be implemented to avoid a relapse. Go back to 12-step meetings or set a regular appointment schedule with your therapist. With Saturn in Aquarius, it can be harder than usual for you to negotiate healthy boundaries with people, so you're going to need extra support for that resolve.

Get a blood panel done to check all your levels. You may be iron deficient or, like most people, low on Vitamin D and in need of a supplement. Holistic healing, like acupuncture or cranio-sacral therapy, may be especially effective for moving blocked energy. That migraine could be digestion-related and your fatigue an allergy to foods like wheat, eggs or gluten. Don't just wave things off and hope they'll go away. Suffering is not a badge of courage, Cancer.

Reproductive parts should be given special attention now, no matter your #FertilityGoals. For example, maybe you need to find new contraception that doesn't throw your hormones out of whack or give you constant UTIs. For female Cancers, strengthening your pelvic floor through exercises like squats, bridges and kegels can benefit in a host of ways from better bladder control to more enjoyable sex through ages and stages. Hoping for a pregnancy in 2021? Saturn in the eighth house can slow your fertility plans, but fortunately, accelerator Jupiter will be co-piloting through this zone for much of the year. (Read on for that!) An unplanned pregnancy or IVF treatments might be part of this year's forecast. Knowing this, you may want to shift some habits accordingly, being more vigilant about contraception or saving up for medical costs so you can be ready when the time is right.

The AstroTwins' 2021 Horoscope — 121 —

Saturn in Aquarius Square Uranus in Taurus

February 17, June 14 & December 24

Can you play well with others, Cancer? Your *esprit de corps* will be put to the test in 2021, thanks to a trio of complex mashups between controlling Saturn and collaborative Uranus. Power struggles and power mergers are in the cards for Crabs throughout the year, but settling on the right division of duties will take something extra.

Cool-headed Saturn and chaotic Uranus influence us in drastically different ways. So when they assemble into three challenging squares (90-degree angles) on February 17, June 14 and December 24, there could be a shakeup in the Cancer Crew! With Saturn digging in his heels from your domineering eighth house (Aquarius) and Uranus rocking the boat in your eleventh house of teamwork (Taurus), trying to get everyone on the same page will be as easy as herding feral cats. In more extreme cases, life could imitate an episode of Game of Thrones. Uncooperative, even mutinous, behaviors could disrupt a once-harmonious vibe—and you may feel like crying, "Dracarys!" and burning the whole thing to the ground.

But, uh, don't?! Rash behaviors like these are bound to bring regrets, something Saturn will clearly underscore. The trick to navigating these squares is to find a hybrid of the two energies. Can you balance Saturn's old-school, hierarchical model of command against Uranus' modern self-regulating forms of governance? Maybe this is a matter of updating titles. Who needs a CEO when you can have a Chief Unicorn Wrangler or Social Media Sensei?

In personal affairs, you may tussle with the green-eyed monster, who could be the devil on your shoulder during these moments. Jealousy may rise up when a high-key BFF leaves you to fend for yourself at a party or your love interest fails to soothe your social anxiety during a triple date (and worse, seems to be paying more rapt attention to someone else's plus-one!)

Little things like this can set a sensitive Cancer off on the average day, but with high-minded Uranus in the mix, you have a unique opportunity to transform some age-old possessiveness struggles. Google the term "compersion," which is the antithesis of jealousy, defined as a buoyant feeling of joy that arises when you witness another person's happiness. This word emerged from the polyamorous community, ascribed to that hard (but not impossible!) ability to glean positive feelings by watching your partner share love with someone other than you. Whether that sounds like the worst idea ever or like a skill you'd be keen to master, don't be surprised if the Saturn-Uranus squares set you off on some bolder sensual seas.

With your erotic eighth house getting pinged by this Saturn year, you may be willing to play with different structures within a relationship. Throw in a visit from experimental Uranus? That could bring Cancers to outer reaches of exploration. And yes, innovative ways of relating can happen within a monogamous arrangement, too. Electrifying Uranus squaring Saturn could wake up slumbering desire, no matter what your status. Mark your calendar and open your mind!

Jupiter in Aquarius & Pisces

January 1: Aquarius (since December 19, 2020)
May 13: Pisces (retrograde June 20)
July 28: Aquarius (retrograde until October 18)
December 28: Pisces (until December 20, 2022)

In 2021, Jupiter will shift back and forth between Aquarius and Pisces. Normally, Jupiter makes an unbroken trek through a single sign for 12 to 13 months, but in 2021, we'll see the planet of fortune and growth in two signs.

Jupiter in Aquarius
December 19, 2020–May 13, 2021
July 28–December 28, 2021

Diving into the Depths.
Where does the realm of "me" dissolve into "we"? Saturn is not the only planet posing that question this year. Expansive Jupiter takes two laps through Aquarius and your eighth house of merging, from December 19, 2020, to May 13, 2021, and again this year from July 28 to December 28. While the galactic gambler

is in this position, risk tolerance increases for joint financial ventures, sexual exploration and permanent bonds.

The eighth house is a private domain where little can be gleaned from a surface review. Mysterious glances are exchanged, hush-hush meetings are arranged. Supernatural phenomena may take place that are too bizarre to be explained, like receiving signs from departed relatives or serendipities such as repeating numbers appearing on addresses and clocks. This astrological house encompasses a vast spectrum of topics—birth and death, shared finances and resources, sex and reproduction, emotional intimacy, spirituality and the psyche. The common thread is that all of these things involve deep and sometimes unspoken energetic alliances with another person or entity. And with experimental Aquarius governing this house for Cancers, it's no surprise that your sign is exceptionally open-minded (not to mention sensitive) about all things esoteric. In 2021, you may have an experience that alters your perspective and makes you view everything in a new and transformed light.

Live-out-loud Jupiter isn't always the best-behaved houseguest in this secretive zone. While Saturn tempers the red-spotted planet's brash influence all year, Jupiter will not be censored. You may feel like you're constantly on the verge of spilling something deeply personal—or worried that someone will expose every skeleton in your closet. Well, Cancer...what if? While Jupiter serves time in Aquarius, shame and vulnerability researcher Brené Brown could become your spirit guide. Keep a reasonable privacy policy in place, but notice where your guarded vibe blocks intimacy. And stop hiding behind social lubricants. Weepy, gin-fueled confessions won't add up to much if you're closed-off and distant when you sober up again. Aim for "refreshingly authentic" as you unspool personal data, bit by bit. Trust doesn't happen overnight, but with Jupiter in Aquarius, you can lock down some loyal connections at an accelerated pace.

In love, wild-child Jupiter could turn your boudoir into a full-on erotic scene. Invest in all the props: fur-lined handcuffs, blindfolds, paddles, whatever tickles your...er, fancy. Since the eighth house rules power and control, a foray into the world of BDSM could be game-changing. But choose your safe word— and a partner who respects it—since Jupiter plays fast and loose. Even if you're titillated beyond all good sense, wait until baseline trust is established before

124

accepting an invitation to someone's "smush room," sex cave or personal play pen.

Saturn may be riding the brake, but while Jupiter is in Aquarius until May 13, then again from July 28 to December 28, your other foot will be on the accelerator. Romantic developments can get serious fast, and with this reproductive realm activated, pregnancies, cohabitations and engagements are all possible…in any order!

Your sex life can go through an outright revolution. Since Jupiter rules learning, everything from tantra to OM-ing (Orgasmic Meditation) could be part of your "continuing education." With the worldly planet positioned here, you could travel for a couple's retreat or a session with a sacred sexual healer who works under the jungle canopy of a remote island. (Here's hoping you don't have to Zoom in for a virtual demo this year.) You may also be wildly attracted to a clandestine affair, as this Jupiter cycle can tempt you to enter secretive terrain. Proceed with extreme caution.

Financially, you could team up with a powerful partner, signing on for a binding joint investment or undertaking. The eighth house governs "other people's money"—versus the income you earn—which includes loans, investments, inheritances, taxes, credit cards, royalties, commissions and property sales (to name a few). You might pay off a chunk of debt—but you could also amass some if you throw caution to the wind and plunk down for an interest-bearing purchase.

Since the eighth house rules passive income, perhaps you'll roll the dice on a venture that makes you money while you sleep, so to speak. Just note that starry-eyed Jupiter amps up your gambling instincts. Carefully vet any network marketing structures to make sure you're not signing on to a pyramid scheme. If you're going to invest in a startup, take time to look at the projections and plans. Do they read as realistic or overarching? While there's always a measure of pumped-up optimism involved in such things, listen to your gut. Do you hear a starting gun fire or alarm bells clanging?

Home ownership is a dream for many domestically-oriented Crabs and this could be your year to take that leap. Work with a reputable realtor to mitigate risk. Be sure to shop around, even if you fall in love with the first place you walk through. Legal matters fall under this year's cosmic domain, so protect your rights and intellectual property, even if that means investing in an attorney's expertise. Your dreams are worth it!

Last year, Jupiter traveled through Capricorn and your one-on-one partnership sign, along with karma cops Saturn and Pluto. Business and romantic relationships went through quite the stress test! Thanks to 2020's extreme circumstances, the novelty wore off quickly—if you even managed to have a honeymoon phase at all. Connections that weren't built for endurance fizzled out. You may have outgrown a longtime alliance and (hopefully) amicably parted ways. What and who is left standing? As the ink dries on the business contract, the wedding high fades, the baby is born…everything becomes more real. Do you have the inner and outer resources in place to navigate this new phase? Jupiter is here to help you on this journey.

The eighth house is where we enter the point of no return with someone, which can be scary for any sign, but maybe less so for yours. Cancers are deeply loyal, which is why it takes you longer than most to fully get on board. Once you actually give yourself over to a relationship, you don't question the "why." Building, nurturing, and championing each other's dreams is where you prefer to focus. When the honeymoon ends, you embrace the learning curve, looking for new ways of keeping that connection alive.

This year you could move from romantic love into mature love, where it's not about wanting to screw like bunnies every second, but about devoting yourself to something larger that the two of you can co-create. To be honest, our culture doesn't really teach us these skills, so be patient, Cancer. This can be an excellent year for therapy, healing and personal growth work—anything that helps you understand the inner realms of your psyche, emotions and unconscious motives. If you've barreled too quickly into togetherness, take a step back to evaluate. After all, if you're going to invest for the long haul, it's worth making sure your heart and soul are truly in this.

Jupiter was last in Aquarius from January 5, 2009, to January 17, 2010, so scroll back to that period to see if there are any recurring themes in your financial and emotional life. Relationships that began then could reach a page-turning moment, or Jupiter may herald the return of an important figure who you haven't talked to in over a decade.

Jupiter in Pisces
May 13–July 28
December 28, 2021–May 10, 2022
October 28, 2022–December 20, 2022

Sweet relief!

Jupiter's journey follows an unusual trajectory in 2021. Normally, the mighty gas giant cruises steadily through a single sign for 12 to 13 months. But from May 13 to July 28, the red-spotted planet pokes its head into Pisces, activating your wise, worldly and truth-seeking ninth house. Take a sabbatical! After the melancholy vibes of both Saturn and Jupiter in Aquarius and your depth-plumbing eighth house, you'll be eager to swim up to the surface and enjoy the sparkle of sunlight and fresh air.

While Jupiter's in Pisces, the glass could look more than half-full. This is one of the benefic planet's favorite places to hang out. Pisces is one of the two signs that Jupiter rules (along with Sagittarius), and it shares the buoyant qualities of the ninth house. If you felt like Debbie Downer earlier this year, suddenly, you're Can-Do Candace, cheering everyone on to victory. The difference is as palpable as night and day, so carpe diem! Whatever you've been ruminating on behind the scenes since January 1 could evolve into a tangible project between May and July.

As Jupiter departs from your micro-focused eighth house and swings into your expansive, optimistic and wide-angled ninth house, you may suddenly see the big picture where before you couldn't stop obsessing over every detail. One thing's for sure—the timeout from the intense transformational period of Jupiter in Aquarius be a welcome relief. The work you'll do in the first part of the year is important, but it sure isn't easy. You're clearing the decks for a positive new perspective on life, which continues again when Jupiter returns to Pisces from December 28, 2021, to May 10, 2022. And if you happen to get some missions in motion, all the better. Don't panic if interest cools after July 28. It's sure to pick up again right before 2021 wraps, so set things aside as needed—but don't put them too far out of reach.

You may begin a voyage of personal discovery while Jupiter hovers in Pisces. Bucket list dreams are clamoring for attention. Which will you tick off first—is there one that's "manageable" enough to squeeze in during this brief, two-and-a-half-month window? Momentum for a midyear adventure could be strong enough to get you aboard a plane or into an RV. Just make sure you're not forcing an expedited timeline. Rushing could compromise the quality of the experience.

While you might not achieve total dream liftoff until 2022, build a "runway" by doing whatever foundational prep work is required. For example, are you thinking about trekking across one of nature's mystical vortexes or climbing a daunting mountain peak? Invest in a backpack and hiking gear and get serious about your training. Increase the weight of your pack and the slope of your incline incrementally, simulating with equipment during cold months.

Whatever the goal, Jupiter in Pisces will push you through the challenging prep work, or at least give you a sneak preview of what 2022 can bring. This exploration could include travel, a return to school, a startup venture or some other roll of the dice. If you've ever longed to take a quarterly sabbatical or to dabble in a startup venture, now would be your time!

Cross-cultural romances and friendships may blossom under this horizon-broadening influence. Make a point of branching out mid-year, consciously choosing social activities that will put you in contact with a wide range of people. Learning about racial equity and inclusivity could transform your entire approach to socializing. With Jupiter's idealistic influence, you might even join (or start!) a community group devoted to truly diversifying organizations, from the leadership down through the ranks.

While Jupiter in Aquarius puts the focus on your intimate connections early this year, intense one-on-ones may feel stifling between May 13 and July 28. Careful, Cancer! You run the risk of pushing a stable partner away mid-year, especially if you cross paths with someone deliciously different than your usual type. But when

Jupiter swings back into Aquarius on July 28, the novelty could wear off, leaving you in quite the relationship pickle. (Especially if your rock-steady partner has already moved on to someone new.) Sidestep regret if you're bored by injecting your relationships with adventure. Take the helm with vacation planning, sign up for couple's workshops, and yes, make sure you're also devoting ample time to your own independent pursuits. The thrill you may be missing is the connection to your own passions—not the crashing highs and lows of a turbo-charged affair.

Thirsty for more authentic connections? Truth serum will be your drink of choice during this candid Jupiter cycle. Even the most bottled-up Cancers could pop their metaphoric corks. Spilling confessions to friends is one thing, but would your story make for an inspiring tell-all or documentary? With the planet of publishing doubling down in the media-savvy ninth house, there's no time like the present to shop a manuscript, screenplay or other treatment. Always wanted to start a blog or a stirring social media feed? Yours could be an influential voice in the chorus while Jupiter paddles through Pisces' poetic, compassionate seas.

Eclipses in 2021

May 26: Sagittarius Lunar Eclipse 5°29′ (7:13am ET)
June 10: Gemini Solar Eclipse 19°42 (6:52am ET)
November 19: Taurus Lunar Eclipse 27°17 (3:57pm)
December 4: Sagittarius Solar Eclipse 12°17 (2:42am)

Gemini/Sagittarius Eclipses

Learning when to let go.

It's cleanup time! In 2021, that will be both an inside and outside job. Three of this year's four eclipses will continue to activate the Sagittarius/Gemini meridian, the rulers of health, service and spirituality in your chart. Eclipses direct our attention to areas of life in need of tuning, especially if we've been neglecting them. You may have a renewed interest in preventative medicine and fitness, along with exploring the connection between mind and body through meditative practices.

The May 26 Sagittarius lunar (full moon) eclipse ignites your physical sixth house, bringing a burst of motivation to prioritize self-care. Scan your body, Cancer. Are you feeling ongoing tightness anywhere? Have you been putting up with pain that's going from mild to acute? Your body is your soul's address here on Earth, and under this lunation, you don't want to ignore any loud knocks for attention. Schedule appointments with doctors and holistic practitioners. The diagnosis could be nothing at all, or something you have to treat, Crab. Get the support you need to heal instead of waiting for the condition to potentially worsen—or literally worrying yourself sick with self-diagnoses that are way more severe than what's actually going on.

Lunar eclipses can bring endings, epiphanies and sudden transitions. You may need to swiftly integrate new habits, like a change of diet or, say, taking a break from rigorous exercise that's putting a strain on your joints. You could get a surge of conviction that you want to use your life to help and heal others. If you have a doctor who treats you more like an insurance form or patronizes you while you're on the examination table, this eclipse might find you swiftly changing providers.

Isolation, depression, anxiety: In the wake of 2020's world-changing events, sensitive Cancers may be dealing with a host of inner challenges. Since the sixth house rules pets, a furry critter could become your new plus-one for therapeutic companionship and snuggle time. With this eclipse in Sagittarius, the zodiac's Centaur, open your mind to equine therapy. Through this experimental process, humans and horses engage in interactive exercises designed to bring you into fuller connection to your own intuitive wisdom.

Work can also be affected by the page-turning lunar eclipse of May 26. The sixth house rules selfless service, and with daring Sagittarius ruling this part of your chart, you could boldly leap into a new industry. You might decide to pursue a path that allows you to give back through your endeavors, or you may be offered a job in a "green" industry, the service sector or the wellness world. Need to brush up on your skills…or gain a totally new set of them? Sagittarius is the sign of higher education. This eclipse could be your cue to dive into a full-on degree program or apply to be part of a short-term certification course.

One eclipse this year will land in Gemini and your twelfth house of spirituality, healing and closure. Ready to wave the white flag or let a painful situation go?

> ## "Give up the idea that you're burdening people by sharing your troubles. You could discover the perfect healing support."

The solar (new moon) eclipse on June 10 is the starting block of a six-month process. While you don't have to rip off the Band-Aid, gently release what no longer serves you. Give up the idea that you're "burdening" people by sharing your troubles. Since the twelfth house rules "earth angels" and mentors, you could discover the perfect healing support this June. If you struggle with an addiction or a mental/emotional health issue, recovery and resources could be on their way. This may also be a huge intuitive or even psychic awakening, a big moment of forgiveness or a healing breakthrough.

In your love life, the June 10 solar eclipse could bring a mind-blowing fantasy encounter. Ooh la la! Conversely, someone could reveal their shocking true colors, as a scandalous secret comes to light. You might get so swept away that you ditch a few boundaries you swore you'd never cross. Peer carefully through those rose-colored glasses, Crab! While softening your tough shell can allow for positive movement, you are likely to filter out pertinent red flags. This eclipse has the potential to bring either magic or mayhem to your love life, depending on the state of honesty and transparency you're operating from at the time.

The dust will settle after the December 4 solar (new moon) eclipse in Sagittarius, which heralds a new and improved chapter for your health—inside and out. But you're not out of the woods yet! Seasonal temptations provide the perfect test kitchen for your salubrious new habits. It's true that most things can be enjoyed in moderation, but not where addiction is involved. Steel your willpower, Cancer. One glass of wine or a sprinkle cookie might not undo all your progress, but if you know that such things are a slippery slope, plan ahead. For example, if you're not drinking alcohol, whip up mocktail recipes or bring a selection of bitters to pour in club soda. Having a glass in hand can reduce social anxiety and save you the awkward moment of explaining why you're passing on that brandied eggnog.

Hunkering down by the fireplace is perfectly acceptable this December, but the solar eclipse can pull you out of any sedentary slumps. Add home-fitness equipment to your holiday wishlist—and hey, since eclipses can bring happy surprises, why not let the world know you'd like a fancy Peloton bike along with the more affordable grippy yoga mat and exercise bands?

Happily, the Sagittarius/Gemini eclipses will wrap up with this eclipse, setting your body and mind on a more even keel. Your mission for the year is to balance head and heart, discovering the connection between your body and your mind. Every breath you take has the power to calm your senses and flood your system with healing pranic energy. Slow down and focus your attention on this simple, natural gift.

Taurus/Scorpio Eclipses
Changes on the Crab Crew.

A new eclipse series blows in on November 19, starting with the Taurus full moon. This lunar eclipse activates your eleventh house of teamwork and technology, the first in a grouping of eclipses that will generate sparks across the Taurus/Scorpio axis between now and October 2023. How well do you play with others? Can you pivot between collaborating with an ensemble cast and playing the lead role? Situations will arise over the next two years that force you to negotiate the "we" (Taurus) and the "me" (Scorpio).

Near November 19, there could be casting changes to the Crab Crew, as well as an urgent need to update your digital equipment and workflow processes. Inspect your tech! Are you still using that phone with the cracked screen, outdated versions of apps, or other analog processes that are slowing you down? This could be your cue to modernize, futurize or inform Santa of your wishes for that schmancy gadget! Conversely, has an addiction to social media left you feeling more disconnected than ever? This eclipse could be your cue to unplug, Cancer. Less screen time and more literal face time can do wonders to reduce anxiety. Of course, many of us don't have the luxury of living close to our people, especially in the wake of this decade's health-related restrictions. Be more conscious about your virtual activities, setting your status to Away and scheduling Zooms with colleagues and family instead of keeping your windows open 24/7.

Venus Retrograde in Capricorn: Back to the future.

December 19, 2021–January 29, 2022
Venus in Capricorn: November 5, 2021 - March 6, 2022
Venus Retrograde: December 19, 2021 - January 29, 2022

As if 2021 needed any more partnership-powered momentum, just wait until November 5. Vivacious Venus parks in Capricorn, activating your seventh house of relationships for an extended four-month tour. Until March 6, 2022, the planet of love, beauty and seduction will swirl through this zone, charging every conversation with magnetic allure. One minute you're reviewing sales reports, the next, you're unconsciously twirling your hair with your finger while picking up subtle innuendos in every exchange. And so much for that protective shell! While Venus sashays through this sector, your impenetrable cool is replaced by a desire to co-create with people who can push you past your own creative or romantic edge.

Bring on the power-couple fantasies! While Venus struts through status-conscious Capricorn, you could link up with someone who amplifies your allure with their own superpowers. Forget about tucking away into a private little couple bubble. Anyone you join forces with between November 5 and March 6 is likely to attract attention for you both—doubly so! Attached Cancers can combine strengths in ways that draw major media attention, like opening a holiday pop-up shop that raises money for a food bank or starting a scholarship for girls who are interested in breaking into the still-male-dominated S.T.E.A.M. fields.

But aye, there is a rub. The reason for Venus' protracted voyage through your partnership zone is due to the retrograde cycle, which happens every 584 days. Highlight December 19, 2021, to January 29, 2022—the dates of the backspin— in neon yellow. Relationships that were seemingly on cruise control could hit a speed bump. Pull over and pop the hood, Crab, or you could veer off on a dangerous collision course. While the tension may drive up your anxiety, think of it as periodic maintenance. Check to make sure that everything is level with the VIPs in your world. Maybe you need to refill the "gratitude tank" or the "communication tank" with an important figure. Do so before it's completely drained and there's nothing you can do to fix the damage.

How can you strike a compromise without making too many sacrifices? With the celestial sensualist backstroking through your twosome zone you'll learn why people insist that "relationships take work." Syncing schedules could be an angst-filled process for coupled Crabs, and during the retrograde from December 19, 2021, to January 29, 2022, things could get downright chaotic.

We wish we didn't have to deliver this news, Cancer, especially since Venus' reverse commute goes down right at the peak of festivities. But we also know that an ounce of prevention is worth a pound of cure. Security-minded water signs like to be prepared. If the introspective energy of 2021 caused you to drift from important relationships, increase your shopping budget. A generous gift could begin the process of making amends. But don't just open the door out of guilt. Follow-up and follow-through will be required. Are you ready to devote quality time for heart-to-hearts and to do whatever other repair work is necessary to mend fences?

Attached Cancers might be the first in line for a couple's therapy appointment in early 2022. Fortunately, Venus retrograde is a great time for getting to the root of longstanding feuds that have choked out love and affinity in your relationships. Plus, even while in reverse, Venus lends a measure of added diplomacy. Don't wait until you hit crisis mode and start flinging around divorce threats or pondering a breakup. Start dealing with the fractures long before the retrograde, like, as soon as the love planet moves into Capricorn on November 5.

Cancers who are hosting holiday gatherings would be wise to make a seating chart. Friction could erupt around you, even if you have zero to do with the situation. Place your blue-state brother at the opposite end of the table from your single-issue-voting sister who insists that being "fiscally conservative" drives her choices at the polls.

Expect some blasts from the past after December 19. As the cosmic lovebird flutters along her retrograde flight path, people who played a key role in your life could audition to be part of a sequel production. (Home for The Holidays: Part Deux?) When you find yourself ruminating on "the one that got away," indulge in a social media search. If your love interest's Instagram feed is suddenly filled

> ## "Unless you've both done significant inner work, unresolved issues are likely to flare up again."

with solo travel shots and adventure sports victory highlights—and you have to deep-scroll to find any partner poses—well, go on and slide into those DMs. The timing might finally be right for the two of you to give this romance thing a go.

But, at the risk of sounding redundant...be circumspect about any developments after December 19! The strong current that sweeps you away while Venus is retrograde could turn out to be a riptide that pulls you further out to sea than you were prepared to swim. Losing sight of your own "safe harbor" is a danger of relationships that begin while Venus is retrograde. That doesn't mean you can't survive the waves, or even learn to ride them masterfully. But if you head out to sea between December 19 and January 29, know that you've got some serious lessons ahead.

For example, if you're giving an ex a second chance, don't just let bygones be bygones. Unless you have both done significant inner work (and even then), unresolved issues are likely to rear up again. Do you have the tools to greet them differently this round? That could give your Act II a fighting chance. Of course, if it was merely bad timing that kept you apart, fate may finally be in your favor!

Or, say, you've been in a long-term relationship with your partner and you want to spice things up. Before you start casting for a "third" or discussing polyamory, make sure you're not avoiding the ongoing issues between you. Experimenting together can be fun, but you want to start it off from a healthy place. Otherwise, the effects can be like tossing a stick of dynamite in a room that's quietly been filling up with explosive gas.

The good news is, with Venus in wise, stabilizing Capricorn, you can lifehack your way through any relationship rifts, using time-tested methodologies. Yes, there will be work involved, but in tenacious, persistent Capricorn, Venus can make the process feel smooth, or dare we say, enjoyable! Go in with a willingness to do the work, from discovering how to manage your anxious or avoidant attachment style to taking a tantric breathwork class that extends orgasmic pleasure in bed. Fence-sitting Crabs will generate the courage to take a bigger step, like moving into a 2BR apartment with your partner of three years, building your shared dream home with the outdoor rain shower and wraparound decks, or planning that bucket list RV tour around the country together.

The time you invest—and the regularity with which you invest it—speaks volumes after November 5. Yes, it's an extra effort to plug in all those pop-up reminders and keep your eye on the clock. But having the support of an amazing partner will make all these efforts worth every second. ✳

Leo

HOROSCOPE

2021
HIGHLIGHTS

LOVE

Relationships are your *raison d'etre* in 2021, as expansive Jupiter tours the most twosome-focused parts of your chart—Aquarius and your committed seventh house, and Pisces, the ruler of your intimately bonded eighth house. Indeed, pairing up can bring the greatest adventures this year! But there's a price of admission to enjoy those rides. Weighty, somber Saturn drops anchor in Aquarius (your seventh house) all year, bringing its maturing influence to the mix. The dopamine-fueled highs of "new relationship energy" that cascades through romantic, creative and business partnerships can keep you excited about possibilities, thanks not only to Jupiter, but also to a pair of exhilarating eclipses on May 26 and December 4. Simultaneously, Saturn demands "adulting." How do your values mesh emotionally, spiritually and financially? Are you and your other half stable enough to weather the long-range challenges that come with collaborating? All this and more will be on the table, but if you can negotiate your way through the highs and lows, you might be on solid footing as a dynamic duo before the year is through!

MONEY

Roll call! Is Team Leo operating at the highest level of integrity and professionalism? Who you work with in 2021 is as important as what you're doing for pay. People can make or break your passion for a project, shaping your own success profile for better or for worse. Be vigilant about who is in your crew and where your name is associated. A high-paying gig might not be worth the price if a sketchy character or company tarnishes your sterling reputation. Is it time to shake things up? By-the-books Saturn in your partnership corner locks into three dynamic squares with changemaker Uranus in Taurus and your tenth house of success on February 17, June 14 and December 24. Near these dates, you'll see who can step it up and who needs to step to the left. Leadership opportunities abound, which may throw power dynamics into a temporary tailspin. Hey, Leo, you can't hold yourself back just to spare someone's fragile ego. Play fair, of course, but keep moving forward. Groom yourself for a royal role, which could be yours for the taking near the success-boosting Taurus lunar eclipse on November 19.

WELLNESS

Last year, healthy living was a huge priority for Lions, as Jupiter, Saturn and Pluto mixed and mingled in Capricorn and your salubrious sixth house. Hang on tight to all the new rituals and routines you created in 2020. In 2021, both Jupiter and Saturn have moved on to Aquarius and your partnership-powered seventh house. During this relationship-focused year, you'll have to take extra measures to ensure that self-care doesn't slip off your priority list. Noble Leos love to give, and there will be no shortage of people lining up to take advantage of your wisdom and generosity. By the time radiant Venus begins her extended tour through Capricorn and your wellness zone (November 5, 2021, to March 6, 2022), your energy tanks may be depleted. The final quarter of 2021 brings a major boost to your vitality, but don't wait until then to enact self-care measures. For best results, turn fitness into a social activity that you can enjoy with dates, mates and BFFs. The June 10 solar eclipse could lead you to a healing circle, like a meditation group, running club or online coaching crew that brings a built-in support network for your body-loving goals.

FRIENDS & FAMILY

With so much attention on one-on-one interactions, your social circle could shrink considerably in 2021, which is not the worst thing, Leo. The quality of your interactions will thrive, even if the quantity of your Instagram followers takes a dip. *C'est la vie!* While Jupiter plunges into Pisces from May 13 to July 28, you'll be more introspective than ever. Assemble a small crew of intimates with whom you can share secrets, work through emotional blocks and provide supportive advice for one another. Family gatherings may be replaced with individual visits—a true relief, since you won't have to navigate everyone else's complex dynamics! Be extra mindful about your holiday season guest lists. With sociable Venus retrograde for six weeks beginning December 19, opt out of stressful scenarios, even if that means booking hotels for annoying relatives or ringing in 2022 on a remote beach!

Leo
POWER DATES

LEO NEW MOON
August 8 (9:49 AM ET)

LEO FULL MOON
January 28 (2:16 PM ET)

SUN IN LEO
July 22 – August 22

Make it a double! Committed partnerships are the theme of this year's skies, so prepare to team up with people who complement you to a tee.

Saturn in Aquarius: Royal courtship turns serious.

December 17, 2020–March 7, 2023

Are you fiercer together, Leo, or is it time to stake out your own square footage in the proverbial Savannah? Saturn, the planet of adulting, boundaries and responsibility, spends its first full year in Aquarius, bringing a maturing influence to your seventh house of partnerships. From romantic relationships to close friendships to business alliances, all of your closest ties could undergo a few stress tests in 2021. As the rubber meets the road, you'll see who is strong enough to be part of your royal court.

With the cosmic "lord of the rings" reigning here until March 7, 2023, you could become half of a bona fide power pair. But that doesn't mean you have to spend every waking minute in the couple bubble. As the planet of restriction settles here for two years, the best relationships are ones that draw clear boundaries between "mine" and "ours." Half of you is eager to merge, the other half is staunch about maintaining autonomy. Separate checks, separate rooms, separate offices. Believe it or not, Leo, this might be the recipe for longevity in your VIP connections.

When Saturn visits this part of your chart every 29.5 years, you're forced you to inspect the integrity of your bonds. Are they built on a mutual give-and-take or is one of you, for example, shouldering all the financial burden while the other is tethered with domestic duties? Maybe you've been so busy following your S.O.'s north star that you lost your own direction or allowed life's stresses to throw you into a spiral of constant anger or depression. It's impossible to ignore an imbalance when Saturn spins through your seventh house.

Leos got a taste of these disorienting dynamics last year, when Saturn briefly visited Aquarius from March 21 to July 1, 2020. For most of the world, this socially suppressive cycle synced up to Phase I of pandemic regulations. Coupled Leos who were sheltering in place with a mate and/or family, bore the extra brunt of Saturn's demand for maturity. People in your lair may have regressed into childlike behaviors, growing distant or domineering as they grappled with a loss of control. Fear about the future probably didn't bring out the best in you either, Leo. (Hey, you're not alone!) If you got a glimpse of your inner King Joffrey, the *enfant terrible* from *Game of Thrones*, here's hoping you've figured out how to send that alter ego to the timeout chambers.

If you weathered these tests like a champ in 2020, certain bonds could be feeling rock-solid as you march into 2021. Perhaps connections even deepened, reaching a more mature stage that's less about giving each other contact highs and more about providing comfort and stability through life's ups and downs. We wish we could say that your unions are 100 percent bulletproof now, but Saturn might put your partnerships through more paces in 2021. Don't resist these drills! What doesn't kill you makes you (and your bond) stronger.

Aquarius is your opposite sign, and with accountable Saturn here, it's like getting a birds-eye view of how you "do relationships," too. At some point between December 17, 2020, and March 7, 2023, every Leo will feel tested around key relationships since the ringed taskmaster will be exactly opposite your Sun, the giver of life-force energy. In 2021, Leos born from July 23 to August 6 will feel Saturn's pressure the most. This opposition will try your patience; you just won't have the energy to deal with demanding divas (a blessing in disguise). Who deserves VIP access to the Leo Lounge—and who needs to be sent back to general admission until they've earned their loyalty points? Some shuffling of the decks may be necessary.

By the same token, pointing a blaming finger won't pass Saturn's muster—not even if said finger is dripping with ethically-sourced diamonds. These transits will hold up the proverbial mirror, insisting that you take responsibility for actions that you may have projected onto others in the past. Examine the role you step into because it's comfortable or familiar. For example, if you rush in like a superhero to fix everyone's problems, it's more likely that they'll start dumping their responsibilities on you instead of stepping up as team players. If you want equality, you must train people from the get-go—or let them know there's a new, non-enabling Lion in town. Then follow through with action! Saturn rules boundaries, and lovebug Leos could benefit from putting a few clear ones in place.

Single Leos might take a time-out from dating or a draining friendship to assess the ROI. You could also cut ties with a work partner who's not pulling their weight. Or, you may decide to make a budding relationship official, following traditional Saturn to the wedding chapel or into a formal business deal.

Does absence make the heart grow fonder? In the right proportion, yes, but too much distance can make you drift apart. With border-defining Saturn in your relationship house, you may be separated from a key person due to physical distance. Even for committed couples, unavoidable duties could keep you geographically apart. For example, one of you may have to homeschool the kids while another is quarantining with an aging relative who needs special care. Saturn trains you to navigate the obstacle course of these circumstances by leaning into time-tested solutions. Setting up a shared calendar might feel invasive, but in 2021, it's probably your best bet for managing conflicting schedules—and finding more shared whitespace for together-time activities.

If a long-term relationship is steadily losing steam, the clock could run out under timelord Saturn's watch. But this is the planet of karma we're talking about. Have the two of you fulfilled your purpose as a pair? Don't throw in the towel without giving it one last effort—unless you're 100 percent certain things are over. A consistent course of couple's therapy (six months minimum) could help repair the cracks in your relationship's foundation. If you break up or divorce, do your best to keep things mature and civil. For some Leos, there could be a temporary split or a desire for more personal space—a "room of one's own" a la Virginia Woolf. You don't have to be up close and personal 24/7 to have a solid relationship, Lion, so loosen your grip and build some emotional resilience.

With Saturn hustling through Aquarius, work relationships demand the same level of integrity. The bottom line is this: Start investing in business relationships that will go the distance. Chasing clients who string you along or collaborating with people who don't pull their weight? Not in 2021! Give that exhausting trend the heave-ho and start working with people who pass Saturn's discerning tests.

As you evict the lightweights from the Leo League, start teaming up with heavy hitters who can take your big ideas to the majors. Experienced Leos may work with agents and representatives who can sell your work for a higher price than you could command on your own. Creative Lions may sign with a professional who negotiates your contracts and helps you gain traction with the public. Maybe you'll be the one getting your license and repping undiscovered talent. You never know!

Prior to 2020, the last time Saturn braved Aquarian waters was from February 6, 1991, to January 28, 1994. If you're old enough to remember that period of time, take a look back. Recurring themes and lessons may arise that shape the next few years of your life, especially in regard to partnerships.

144

Saturn in Aquarius Square Uranus in Taurus
February 17, June 14 & December 24

Business partnerships will get a boost from serious Saturn in 2021, but juggling career aspirations and relationship goals will not be the easiest. Three times this year—on February 17, June 14 and December 24—erratic Uranus in Taurus and your success-driven tenth house clashes into a combative square (90-degree angle) with stabilizing Saturn. These two planets have completely opposite agendas. Old-guard Saturn adheres staunchly to traditions while wrench-thrower Uranus lives to break the rules. Disruptions, disruptions! There's no plowing ahead with the blinders on during the Saturn-Uranus squares. Keep your foot near the brake, because you may have to pull over and make some important adjustments to your workflow, relationship expectations and grand plans for 2021.

Check in: Have you considered the impact your professional decisions will have on the people closest to you, Leo? Or are you giving their input too much weight, holding yourself back from pursuing opportunities because you're worried it might rock the relationship boat? Is someone in your life draining your financial resources, or (glug) vice versa? If so, these squares will set off alarm bells, forcing you to renegotiate. You work too hard for your money—and so do they—to pour it into a bottomless pit of expenses.

Nailing that elusive work-life balance will take something extra for Leos in 2021. During the three Saturn-Uranus squares, recalibrating will be essential. Can you actually juggle and "have it all"? Figure that out, Leo. If you don't, you may see important relationships slip away or get called to the carpet for delivering work that's less than the sterling quality you've built your professional reputation around.

Here's an interesting (ironic, even) twist to these squares: While uptight Saturn is parked in rebellious Aquarius, wild child Uranus is in conservative Taurus from May 2018 to April 2026. This only serves to make their mashups even more confusing, or, to put a positive spin on it, "dynamic." But hey, sometimes, the only way to grow is to hurl yourself headlong into uncomfortable learning experiences. The three Saturn-Uranus squares set up opportunities to do just that. Shake up that stagnant energy, Leo, and try something different.

Important reminder! Uranus' tour through Taurus and your status-boosting tenth house is grooming you to be a leader for the future. The side-spinning planet governs teamwork, technology and unconventional approaches. Keep honing your chops by paying attention to both Saturn's time-tested structures and being open to novel approaches. Leos are the jungle royals of the zodiac. As such, you aren't always comfortable sharing the power. In 2021, the more you delegate to capable cohorts, the happier you'll be. But don't make the mistake of dropping the reins completely. Just shift to a managerial mindset. Raise the bar, keep the larger mission present and hold everyone on Team Leo to impeccable standards.

Jupiter in Aquarius & Pisces

January 1: Aquarius (since December 19, 2020)
May 13: Pisces (retrograde June 20)
July 28: Aquarius (retrograde until October 18)
December 28: Pisces (until December 20, 2022)

In 2021, Jupiter will shift back and forth between Aquarius and Pisces. Normally, Jupiter makes an unbroken trek through a single sign for 12 to 13 months, but in 2021, we'll see the planet of fortune and growth in two signs.

Jupiter in Aquarius
December 19, 2020–May 13, 2021
July 28–December 28, 2021

Joining forces.
Long-distance love? Global partnerships? Although Saturn is weighing anchor in Aquarius all year, you don't have to sink to the bottom of the emotion ocean. Buoyant Jupiter will also traverse Aquarian waters for much of 2021, pulling you up to the surface when you need a breath of fresh air. Saturn contracts while Jupiter expands, creating the perfect system of checks and balances. Since their

Great Conjunction, an exact meetup in Aquarius on December 21, 2020, these planetary powerhouses have been working in tandem to balance your bonds.

Jupiter cycles through Aquarius for two extended laps this year: First, from December 19, 2020, until May 13, 2021, then again from July 28 to December 28. Both times, the indie-spirited star can help you develop a non-confining approach to commitment.

> **"With galactic gamble Jupiter opening your mind, you may embrace a whole new way of relating, merging and sharing with a significant other."**

Relationships are never 100 percent risk-free; in fact, playing it too safe is a surefire way to dull the passion for partners. (According to sex therapist Esther Perel, author of *The State of Affairs: Rethinking Infidelity*, this reliance on comfort might even increase the likelihood of cheating!) With Jupiter, the galactic gambler, opening your mind, you may embrace a whole new way of relating, merging and sharing with a significant other.

Dopamine plays a big part in the early anticipation of romance, and Jupiter in the seventh house could bring a hot-and-heavy attraction—or make you realize that you're missing those sparks. This neurotransmitter is the fuel for "new relationship energy," powering up feelings of limitless possibility and excitement about what could be. Alas, once the mystery ends, it's damn-near impossible to generate those early rushes and highs. But you can play with this, Leo, especially if you need to stoke fading embers! There's a reason that absence makes the heart grow fonder, but so does novelty. Growth agent Jupiter in experimental Aquarius can bring sparkle back to relationships—if you embrace its independent energy. Go forth and become a "new" person by expanding your own repertoire of hobbies, personal interests and individual pursuits. Your slumbering sweetie might wake up again as your new persona surprises the both of you.

When it comes to pairing up, get ready to meet some well-traveled and fascinating people who can open unexpected doors for you. Take advantage of this prolific window for creating advantageous alliances with folks around the globe. Cross-cultural connections have limitless potential while Jupiter traverses Aquarius throughout the year. Cast a wider net, whether you're sourcing materials for an upcoming project, or searching for a plus-one to share an important aspect of your life.

Looking for love? Diversify your dating portfolio. While broad-minded Jupiter scans the horizon of your seventh house, you could discover rich compatibility with people who come from vastly different upbringings. We're not saying you should blithely ignore non-negotiables, like extremely opposing religious beliefs, or differing financial values. But with candid Jupiter in the mix, discussions about race, culture and nationality could light the path to heartwarming hybrids that make life more interesting for all parties involved.

Jupiter's last visit to Aquarius was January 5, 2009, to January 17, 2010. Scroll back in your timeline for clues of what could resurface this year. In love, this cycle could bring a whole new way of relating, even a possible role reversal. Jupiter also helps you think outside the box when it comes to your dating habits. If you always pursue or push for a commitment (as high-intensity Leos are wont to do), you might take a more chill, receptive role with new love interests. Since Jupiter rules travel, a long-distance relationship could spark up. Coupled Leos might even consider an L.A.T. relationship (Living Apart Together), especially if you've fallen into habits that are more "old marrieds" than you like. One of you could get a job in another city or decide to go back to school, necessitating a second residence. With independent Jupiter here, you may prefer extending "visitation rights" over the habitual humdrum of seeing each other every day.

A longtime business partnership could end or go through some growing pains. Luckily, optimistic Jupiter's effect is usually positive, so try laying your cards on the table before you bolt. Discuss new roles, divide up responsibilities differently. It may be that your "work spouse" is craving change, too, but neither of you has had the courage to come clean about it. If you do part ways, Jupiter can help make this amicable—and swift! Be ready: It won't be long before a flood of new prospects arrives to fill that space. Since Jupiter rules global connections, you may make a fated one while traveling. You might relocate for work or continue digitally "commuting" from a remote office.

Just be careful not to make any sudden moves near January 17, when Jupiter in Aquarius tussles with spontaneous Uranus in Taurus and your tenth house of career. Every six to seven years, these two freestyling planets lock into a chaotic square (90-degree angle), driving up your rebellious urges. You may feel torn between relationship goals and a game-changing career opportunity, unsure how to pursue both without throwing your entire life into a tailspin. Do you have to cool off a passionate attraction because you're immersed in a dream project, or pass on a promotion because it will squeeze your personal time?

Everything is negotiable, Leo. Near January 17, stay calm and you can make the most levelheaded decision for your future. Remember that change of any sort always comes with an adjustment period. No matter what you choose, you won't be able to avoid at least a little bumpy terrain in the aftermath. And while relationships take precedence over most else in 2021, that doesn't mean you should sacrifice personal growth! Bringing your best self to the table is what makes partnerships thrive. When in doubt, ask yourself this: Will this decision make me resentful toward my partner? Life is too short to have regrets.

Jupiter in Pisces
May 13–July 28
December 28, 2021–May 10, 2022
October 28, 2022–December 20, 2022

Diving into the deep end of the pool.
Okay, so you're gaining some real skills with this "playing well with others" things, Leo. Nicely done! (We're joking, but TBH, sharing the controls can be tough for your take-charge sign!) You'll get a chance to test this cooperative mindset from May 13 to July 28, when Jupiter lunges forward into Pisces and your eighth house of intense bonding for a brief, two-and-a-half-month lap. While in Aquarius, Jupiter played fair and square, splitting everything down the middle. But when the red-spotted renegade splashes through the Fish's seas, a different form of division is applied. In this equation, one person may be contributing labor while the other puts up some cash, for example, with hopes of sharing bountiful long-term gains.

Similar to the seventh house (which is governed by Aquarius for you), your Pisces-ruled eighth house is fixated on relationships. While there's still plenty of sexy dopamine flowing here, this is the "lifer" part of the zodiac wheel, where we get inspired to commit mind, body and soul. Now, the rubber meets the road, and we can't lie: It could get intense!

The eighth house is a complex part of the chart that rules sex, death, taxes, investments, joint ventures, spirituality, reincarnation, research, psychology, soulmates, inheritances, real estate…and more. The common thread is that these things are binding and/or permanent. Mysteries that need to be investigated and explored also fall under the eighth house domain.

With eternally curious Jupiter here, you could delve into the most microscopic details, whether you're learning about the cryptocurrency, exploring tantra or training to be a meditation teacher. Under the deep-diving Jupiter in Pisces influence, you'll feel quieter or more introspective, if not outright consumed by a project!

Careful, Leo: To others, you could come across as moody or unavailable, hovering like a storm cloud around the house or office. There's a good chance you'll be processing some pretty deep emotions, which might make you unaware of the impact you're having in your space. Be mindful of the fact that relatives and roommates do not exist to be your 24/7 sounding boards. It's not that you can't lean on each other but regulate the flow! Rearranging shared space may be necessary to create more privacy. Set up a meditation cave befitting of your regal standards, then retreat to journal, ugly cry, Zoom with support group friends, whatever!

Struggling to be vulnerable and let someone in? Jupiter in your eighth house can amplify trust issues. Mid-year will be a good time for therapy, or even working with a spiritual healer to dismantle energetic blocks and cut cords binding you to unhealthy past relationships. With Jupiter in your karmic eighth house, a struggle-filled connection might even link back to a former lifetime. (Hey, you never know…)

Whatever you're dealing with, philosophical Jupiter can point you to resources, from books to TED talks to master teachers and (health regulations permitting) life-changing retreats. By doing the inner work, you'll regain access to your sunny side. Simultaneously, you'll increase self-compassion so you can process your way through the sad days instead of drowning in your sorrows.

We won't lie: Even this abbreviated visit from Jupiter won't be a casual, carnal cakewalk. An eighth house transit puts you squarely in touch with some of your

> ## "If someone sticks by you through a rough patch, you'll trust the power of their loyalty."

most complex and unexamined emotions. If the first five months of 2021 reveal the "for better" part of a partnership, Jupiter in Pisces may show you the "for worse." You could discover the kind of gritty resilience that a real commitment demands.

But these very trials are actually what make you better—as a person and as a couple. You never really know the fortitude of a bond until it's under stress, right? If someone sticks by you through a rough patch, you'll trust the power of their loyalty. And if you're called upon to be there for a lover in need, you'll discover strength you didn't even know you had.

Since Jupiter rules evolution, you could find yourself seeking a more meaningful bond with your current mate. If you've outgrown a longtime partnership, Jupiter in Pisces could push it past the breaking point, forcing you to surrender to the inevitable separation. The division of joint assets may become especially fraught with drama, driving up a lot of primal feelings. Try to stay focused on the big picture instead of getting petty, especially if you find yourself battling over money, custody, possessions or a home. With fortuitous Jupiter in your corner, you should do well in any legal battles, if not outright win them. Here's hoping you don't have to go there, Leo, but if you do, bring your "highest vibe" to the table and refuse to get dragged down into a dirty duel.

The eighth house rules "other people's money," such as loans, lines of credit, venture capital, inheritances. Between May 13 and July 28, Leos could come into a sizable bundle of cash. Maybe you'll take out a mortgage to purchase a home or a student loan to fund your PhD. There's always some form of interest involved with eighth house capital. Shop around (or try negotiating) for the best possible rate from banks—and read the fine print, especially while Jupiter is retrograde from June 20 to October 18. This is not the time to, say, gamble on a credit card that jumps up to 21 percent APR after the first zero-percent interest year—unless you're certain you can pay it back in under 12 months.

If lump sums come in mid-year from a legal settlement or money left to you by a departed relative, you may be feeling the bittersweet "emotional interest" of sadness mixed with gratitude. These are the life passages we often deal with when planets traverse the eighth house. Small consolation: During this psychically sensitive Jupiter cycle, you may connect to departed loved ones who send you "signs" or even visit you in your dreams!

Spiritually, you might develop psychic abilities, meditate or work with a medium this year. When you're not tracking the Dow Jones Index or perfecting the art of the G-spot orgasm, you might want to read (or reread) Scorpio Brian Weiss's seminal book on reincarnation and past lives, *Many Lives, Many Masters.*

Jupiter's tour of Pisces is extremely brief in 2021, but the galactic giant will pick up where he left off from December 28, 2021, to May 10, 2022. Get wind of visionary possibilities this year, but don't rush the timeline. This may be a better time to dive into behind-the-scenes prep work, like clearing up your credit or crowdfunding a down payment.

By 2022, we wouldn't be surprised to see you pulling the trigger on a long-held dream, like turning a plot of land to create a permaculture farm or moving to a modernized metropolis where you can enjoy a sex-positive lifestyle and have basically anything delivered to your front door. Or, like one of our Leo friends, touring the world to work with the best breakfast cooks before opening his own legendary morning meal spot!

Eclipses in 2021

May 26: Sagittarius Lunar Eclipse 5°29' (7:13am ET)
June 10: Gemini Solar Eclipse 19°42 (6:52am ET)
November 19: Taurus Lunar Eclipse 27°17 (3:57pm)
December 4: Sagittarius Solar Eclipse 12°17 (2:42am)

Gemini/Sagittarius Eclipses

Step into a starring role.

Turn up the heat or pass the torch? For the second consecutive year, a series of eclipses will activate the Gemini/Sagittarius axis, helping you strike a balance between your eleventh house of teamwork (Gemini) and your scene-stealing fifth house (Sagittarius). Your approach to friendship, dating and mating continues to evolve as three of 2021's four eclipses touch down in these signs. Spotlight-loving Leos could be vaulted into the public eye, perhaps inviting an ensemble cast to join you on your chosen stage or platform. Creatively, these eclipses blow open the doors to experimentation and play!

The year's first eclipse arrives with the Sagittarius full moon on May 26. This lunar eclipse could be a bountiful manifestation moment, since it's the follow-up to the total solar (new moon) eclipse in Sagittarius that activated your fifth house of fame, fertility and flamboyance on December 14, 2020. Whatever's been cooking in the Leo kitchen could come together in a spectacular finished product near May 26.

Get ready for your close-up! Media attention and other noteworthy acclaim could come your way. Not that you should wait. Strategic self-promotion can create a near-viral buzz. Whatever you're feeling passionate about near this lunar eclipse could be the inspiration for a YouTube series, livestream or a full-on marketing campaign. Creatively, this lunar eclipse could connect you to a deep well of inspiration, one that informs your efforts for the rest of 2021. In worldly Sagittarius, your work could be embraced across international borders. What Leo wouldn't want to spread your powerful message from Brazil to Bulgaria? Find your Eurovision alter ego and go play!

The May 26 Sagittarius lunar (full moon) eclipse could also bring a dramatic outpouring of emotions, baby news or a heart-opening moment for couples. Since the fifth house rules fertility, a pregnancy could be in the cards for many Leos—likely an unexpected one (oops!). Conversely, full moons can bring endings or transitions. A romance that's toxic or not going anywhere may abruptly end, clearing the space for a better match.

On June 10, the Gemini solar (new moon) eclipse spotlights your eleventh house of teamwork, technology, and humanitarian efforts. The big question: When is it time to be the star and when is it best to play a supporting role? While the May eclipse could put your name in lights, that's no excuse to behave like an obnoxious fame whore. Embracing the cooperative, communicative spirit of Gemini will be crucial in June. Ask yourself, "How is my newfound prestige serving something bigger than myself?" Use any influence you gain to help raise awareness for a social cause or to inspire others to shine. Lights, camera…action for all!

The final eclipse of the year is on December 4, a Sagittarius solar (new moon) eclipse that also completes the 18-month lunations that have been activating the Gemini/Sagittarius meridian. A new love affair, a surprise pregnancy or a sudden reawakening of your sensual desires could be on tap. You could get swept off your feet—either by someone new or through a rekindled connection with your mate. Some Leos may be promoted to a position of greater leadership as a result of work you've done since these eclipses began on June 5, 2020. Nice!

Taurus/Scorpio Eclipses

Who's on top?

On November 19, a new group of eclipses rolls in, with a Taurus lunar (full moon) eclipse. Until October 28, 2023, these moonbeams deliver a master class in balancing professional aspirations (Taurus) against the needs of your domestic life (Scorpio).

In our experience, the inaugural eclipse in a series can be the most potent, since it's the first one to illuminate a "shadowed" area of life, one where you haven't necessarily wanted to dig below the surface. Since this year's Saturn-Uranus squares have already directed your compass toward career goals, November 19 may herald a huge moment for success! If you're ready for a big reveal—and by "ready" we mean not just mentally prepared but also with all your presentation materials up to sophisticated Taurean snuff—this full moon could be a great day for a debut!

> ## "The big question: When is it time to be the star and when is it best to play a supporting role?"

There could be a change of guard at work, one that leaves a vacuum in leadership that you're tempted to step into. Or, you could get a surge of motivation to start your own biz. Some Leos may get a once-in-a-lifetime opportunity that requires you to leap!

Should you take that position overseas even if it means relocating your entire family? Say yes to the promotion that will require some extensive 14-hour days as you get acclimated? Think hard, if not long, Leo, because the window for capitalizing on an eclipse's offering is brief!

Venus Retrograde in Capricorn: Healthy loving.

December 19, 2021–January 29, 2022
Venus in Capricorn: November 5, 2021 - March 6, 2022
Venus Retrograde: December 19, 2021 - January 29, 2022

With so much planetary focus on partnerships in 2021, it would be easy to let self-care slide. But starting November 5, you'll have a welcome opportunity to lavish your body with love! Beauty queen Venus luxuriates in Capricorn and your sixth house of wellness until March 6, 2022, giving you a four-month window to prioritize Numero Uno. Yes, you should strap on your own oxygen mask before assisting other passengers, Leo. From there, how about booking an oxygenating facial, a full body scrub (plus seaweed-mud wrap), and a regular course of holistic, immune-boosting massage and acupuncture treatments?

Venus in Capricorn offers the chance you've been waiting for (whether you realized it or not) to get your body tuned up again. Sure, there's a measure of inconvenient timing, given that this cycle dovetails with the holidays. We're not telling you to deprive yourself of every seasonal indulgence. Leos could be the healthiest hedonists in town, whipping up warming mocktails, low-sugar desserts and plant-based dishes that get rave reviews around the table.

Rather than suffering through a boot camp workout (or trying to gin up the motivation to start one right after NYE), Venus in Capricorn can lead you to pleasurable forms of exercise, like dancing, cross-country skiing or riding the Peloton bike. Anything that allows you to socially engage (IRL or virtually) will also keep you motivated. How about joining a wellness coach for a 21-day reboot, where you can share tips, recipes and progress with people who cheer you on?

If you're in a relationship, use this four-month Venus circuit to get healthy together. Prepare nourishing meals, do buddy workouts, plan activity dates that involve outdoor exercise. Soon you'll be glowing from all those endorphins— and fired up for some Boudoir Olympics! Bottom line? Taking care of your own health could be a pleasurable experience with enchanting Venus here.

Since the sixth house also rules your day-to-day work, charming Venus could help you score some big professional wins in Q4. Tap into this enchanting, creative planet to level up your presentations and warm up the (Zoom) room for every single pitch. In driven Capricorn, Venus may cause you to transfer all your romantic energy from the bedroom to the boardroom (or whatever "studio" you do your work in).

If no one is counting on you for TLC, this might be the perfect moment to plunge headlong into your process. You could make huge strides as an artist or professional! Just be careful not to tap out. For hardworking Leos, dialing down professional stress could be the key to rebooting both your mojo and your imaginative powers.

156

But aye, there is a rub: The reason you're hosting Venus for this extended spell is due to the planet's periodic retrograde cycle, which crops up every 18 months. The next reverse commute is scheduled from December 19, 2021, to January 29, 2022, which could throw some wrenches into all those self-loving routines you started in November. Right before Christmas, your vegan holiday menu

"Maintaining consistency will require extra support, and perhaps some distance from triggering people."

may be vetoed by your sugar-obsessed sister-in-law, or you might succumb to social anxiety and start drinking those beverages you swore off in November. Maintaining any sort of consistency will require extra support—and perhaps some conscious distance from triggering people who don't respect your life-affirming quests!

You could be nitpicky and irritable with family or a love interest, suddenly seeing everything that's "wrong" about them. Body image alert! You might become hypercritical of your reflection during this time, fixating on perceived flaws and obsessing over your appearance. Beware making any cosmetic changes, especially permanent ones. Venus retrograde would not be the time to experiment with dramatic "new year, new you" haircut, injections or surgical enhancements. (The last thing a Leo needs to hear is, "Whoa—what happened to your face?")

Stay away from wellness fads, too, especially ones that encourage slashing an entire food group from your diet. That said, you could have an allergic reaction to something you eat (like nightshades), or you might break out in a rash from chemicals in a beauty product. Declutter your toiletry and makeup bag, tossing and replacing anything too old or harsh.

While romance planet Venus snoozes in Capricorn from December 19, 2021, to January 29, 2022, don't take anything at face value. Nope, not even with

157

the people you've loved for years. Folks who are known for churning up your anxiety should be handled with kid gloves, if not avoided altogether, during this time. We realize some of them may have given birth to you (or occupy a close branch on the family tree) but hey, Leo, if there was ever a year to not go home for the holidays, this would be it. And, while it might not be the most "political" maneuver, Leos who are hosting can leave disruptors off of your guest list.

Bottom line? Plan to ring in 2022 in a way that feels grounding and nurturing to you. If that means joining a meditation circle in Hawaii or renting a country house with your chosen family of BFFs, do it! With diplomatic Venus lending an assist, you'll be artful at smoothing over ruffled feathers with family…which we recommend doing long before the December 19 retrograde begins. Advance notice always helps keep upsets at bay. Keep your reasoning sweet and succinct. Queen Elizabeth's advice may work like a charm here: "Never complain, never explain." ✳

Virgo

HOROSCOPE

2021 HIGHLIGHTS

LOVE

Simmering passion gets turned up to a boil several times in 2021—especially if you've devoted ample time to self-care. From May 13 to July 28, boundless, bawdy Jupiter sails through Pisces, activating your seventh house of partnerships for the first time since 2011! During this cycle, which resumes again on December 28, you could liberate yourself from a restrictive relationship or rewrite the rules of romance. Long distance? Living Apart Together (LAT)? You may surprise yourself by being extremely open-minded. Both of the love planets, Venus and Mars, will visit Virgo in 2021. Glow-up goddess Venus swings through your sign from July 21 to August 16, joined by her dance partner Mars from July 29 to September 14. Hello, romantic and erotic renaissance! Venus takes an extended tour through Capricorn and your lovestruck fifth house from November 5, 2021, to March 6, 2022. This four-month cycle could bring anything from pregnancies to proposals to a passionate *affair de coeur.* But easy does it after December 19, when Venus ends the year in a signal-jamming retrograde.

MONEY

Werk, Virgo! With disciplined Saturn in Aquarius activating your industrious sixth house all year (and until March 7, 2023), you'll be a busy bee. Duties may feel a tad "lather, rinse, repeat," but you'll welcome the stability. Fortunately, venturesome Jupiter weaves in and out of Aquarius—from January 1 to May 13 and again from July 28 to December 28—which could set you on a steady growth trajectory. Figure out the right routine and you'll relish the work you do. In 2021, process and technique are as important as the results. On June 10, the solar (new moon) eclipse in Gemini touches the top of your chart, bringing promising possibilities for your career. If you want to make a name for yourself, you'll have to leap quickly!

WELLNESS

With Saturn, the personal trainer planet, doing reps in your salubrious sixth house all year, you're fired up for a fitness challenge. Since the ringed taskmaster likes to create lasting results, think of this mission as a marathon, not a sprint. Pay special attention to bones, skin and teeth, which are the Saturn-ruled body parts. Adventurous Jupiter will also weave through your sixth house (until May 13 and again from July 28 to December 28), which, along with boosting your energy levels, can expand your appetite. There's a tendency to put on a few pounds when the abundant planet visits this zone, so if you care, you may need to be stricter with yourself about what you ingest—and when!

FRIENDS & FAMILY

Your inner circle is always at the top of your priority list, but with Jupiter and Saturn regulating the flow from your disciplined sixth house, you could have a breakthrough around setting boundaries. You're the sign of selfless service, yes, but don't confuse that with being a martyr. With both planets in idealistic Aquarius, you could connect to a high-minded crew, especially if they are as devoted to healthy practices as you are. Depending on safety restrictions, you might join a meditation circle or a hiking club. Two Sagittarius eclipses on May 26 and December 4 activate your domestic fourth house, which could bring fast-moving developments involving your residence or family.

Virgo
POWER DATES

VIRGO NEW MOON
September 6 (8:51 PM ET)

VIRGO FULL MOON
February 27 (3:17 AM ET)

SUN IN VIRGO
August 22 – September 22

After a colorful 2020, you're ready for a bit more routine. This year finds you in a very Virgo groove, as you focus on bringing order and wellness back to your cosmic court.

Saturn in Aquarius: Structured living.
December 17, 2020–March 7, 2023

Exhale, Virgo. After a curveball-throwing 2020, this new year brings a lot more predictability. Since December 17, 2020, structured, methodical Saturn is parked in Aquarius, settling down in your sixth house of work, wellness and healthy routines until March 7, 2023. For the next two-plus years, incorporate new systems into your repertoire—and really make them stick. Wax on, wax off!

While this low-key groove might not be everybody's cup of antioxidant-rich matcha, it's music to a Virgo's ears. Devoting a year to self-development? Anchoring in healthy routines? You're so all about that.

You already got a taste of Saturn in Aquarius last year, when the ringed taskmaster briefly paddled into the Water Bearer's realm from March 21 to July 1. (Before that, Saturn's last visit to Aquarius was from February 1991 to January 1994!) For some Virgos, 2020's brief window served as a wakeup call to deal with your health. Chronic pain or a lingering issue needed to be treated seriously instead of simply managed. And thanks to Saturn's notoriously challenging onset, getting a doctor's appointment during a pandemic did not make this an easy trial!

Other Virgos may have gotten really excited about a fitness modality, like restorative yoga or boxing, only to have it taper off after July. If so, you could pick up where you left off—and take it much, much further in 2021. Suit up in your best athleisure. This year, Saturn wakes you up for sunrise yoga and pushes you to do one more set of mountain climbers because…results.

With the planetary personal trainer in your corner until March 7, 2023, improving your life will be a marathon, not a sprint. Instead of changing basic behaviors, shift your mindset and develop sustainable habits. Skip the 30-day challenges and instead, cultivate a practice, like daily morning breathwork, meatless Mondays, and balancing finances every Sunday morning. You might even write a mantra for your life—and get it inked on your arm, like so many sleeve-tatted Virgos we know. Whatever the case, Saturn in Aquarius can help you get your whole life tuned up!

But that's not to say you won't try a "fad" or two. Having an experimental, metaphysical sign like Aquarius ruling your sixth house explains a lot about Virgo behavior. Take, for example, your encyclopedic knowledge of holistic remedies from adaptogens to zinc. Or how you become the loudest ambassador for your favorite healing techniques…and if you're passionate enough, enrolling in teacher training, then selling supplemental products through an affiliate network. Nothing wrong with that! As far as your selfless sign is concerned, anything that improves your quality of life is meant to be shared.

When planets orbit through the sixth house—as both Saturn and Jupiter will in 2021—you can get back into your vibrant element, with some experimental Aquarian twists! Leave room for variety and spontaneity within your routines and you'll never get bored. One Virgo friend choreographs a new workout for herself each month, mixing up hip-hop, aerial silks and a few spicy pole-dancing moves. Virgo health maven Kris Carr, who authored *Crazy Sexy Cancer Survivor*, has a robust library of plant-based recipes on her website.

While your research-obsessed sign has been known to Google for health advice, make sure you're getting your guidance from the pros! Saturn rules mastery and expertise. If you're serious about exercise, consider investing in a (Zoom or IRL) session with a trainer who can correct posture and show you how to avoid injuries. When it comes to medical care, consult a board-certified doctor (MD or ND) for check-ups and procedures. As an earth sign, you may prefer natural remedies. Work with practitioners who integrate traditional medicine with techniques like acupuncture, Chinese herbs and CBD remedies. Prevention is the best "cure" of all.

Saturn rules the bones, teeth and skeletal system, and these may be sensitive areas in 2021. Pay special attention to your posture and make sure you have a decent mattress to sleep on. Regular visits to the chiropractor, along with therapeutic massage, may be necessary. Dental issues could flare up if you haven't been brushing regularly, especially around your gumline. And, yeah, Virgo: Don't forget to floss!

Gut check: The sixth house is associated with the abdominal area, which is also a sensitive region for Virgos. The enteric nervous system, often called the "second brain," is located in the gut, and is connected to the actual brain by a vast network of neurons. Astrologically, this may explain why Virgos can be dubbed "neurotic" or may struggle with amplified anxious feelings.

In 2021, get serious about creating serenity in your life. Among its many effects, tension can wreak havoc on your belly because when the brain triggers a stress response, the gut gets involved. With heavy Saturn in this energy center, it's more important than ever to keep your digestive system and G.I. tract flowing—and yes, calming down can support this. Undiagnosed food allergies (and sensitivities) may flare up, causing a host of symptoms, including fatigue. It would be worth it to have a panel of tests done to see how your body responds to things like wheat, gluten, dairy and other hard-to-process "inflammatories."

Even if you're not having issues, there are many benefits to strengthening gut health. Balancing intestinal flora (AKA "the good bacteria" that exists in your gut) directly improves your immune system. You might try taking a probiotic supplement, eating fermented foods like kimchi and tempeh, or doing a short-term cleanse.

Simple mindfulness practices can be game-changing for you in 2021. Virgos who are processing trauma or living with PTSD may benefit greatly from body-centered, somatic therapy. Karmic Saturn here supports deeper healing from issues that have been passed through family lineage. Generations of ancestral conditioning affect us on a cellular level. Who knows? By courageously addressing such trauma, for example, you could turn the tide in a healing direction for your entire family—present and future.

The sixth house governs your daily work—not so much your lofty career goals, but the administrative, plug-and-play duties that keep food on the table. In 2021, you may be more process-oriented than results-oriented. Efficient Saturn helps you upgrade systems in the name of "working smarter, not harder."

Be honest: What duties do you find draining? Instead of life-hacking to relieve the misery, consider long-range solutions like outsourcing or delegating. Not possible? Reorder your workflow and you may bring back pleasure to your productivity. For example, stop multitasking with ten browser tabs open in Chrome. Group similar tasks together so you're only switching on one part of your brain at a time. Pay attention to your natural ebb and flow. For example, if you're more creative in the morning, reserve 9AM to noon for focused tasks, such as writing and brainstorming. If you tend to be less disciplined in the afternoon, return calls and emails then, or do any online research then. Make it work for you!

With Saturn hustling through your sixth house of service, you may be drawn to roles that fall in the "essential worker" category. During this humble transit, you could be happy to step back and help others get their accolades. (Hey, "Best Supporting" is an Oscar-worthy role, too.) Social impact careers are a natural fit for your selfless sign. If you're feeling drawn to that sector, Saturn's tour of humanitarian Aquarius is an optimal time to pivot in that direction.

If you're just breaking into an industry, diligent Saturn in your service-oriented sixth house will reward you for a humble attitude. Even if you were the biggest fish in the pond you just leapt out of, you might be a mere minnow in a vast new ocean. Check any ego at the door, stat. Ask how you can help. Spend extra time brushing up on a company mission or learning new skills. Make yourself invaluable to the influencers. Some people believe you're never too old for an internship, so even a few weeks of working for "free" (in exchange for the pure gold of contacts, connections and an insider view) could be the best investment you make.

In tech-savvy Aquarius, some part of your job might also get very technical. The precise sixth house is all about the details. Is it time to learn graphic design, drafting, accounting or another specialized area? Give your skillset whatever brush-up it needs. Enroll in the training, even if you already have plenty of hands-on experience. Sharpening your axe with an experienced teacher is a great way to boost your confidence. The prestige of a degree or official certification never hurts while status-driven Saturn visits your work house.

That said, the formal piece of paper may not be necessary. With superconnector Aquarius ruling this part of your chart, someone you hooked up with in the past could do you a solid. By elite Saturn's standards, it's as much about who you know as what you know. Joining industry groups, coaching programs and masterminds can be a great way to beef up your contact database this year.

Surrounding yourself with people who are up on the latest innovations can be a brilliant business strategy. Be kind and patient when grooming a green person, though. Under CEO Saturn's tutelage, you'll want to treat the "little people" on Team Virgo like gold. Lead democratically, not as a dictator, and be open to their suggestions. Given the speed at which technology changes, a savvy sidekick might know some helpful shortcuts or have a few brilliant ideas that are right in sync with the current zeitgeist. You could be rewarded with a loyal and skillful wingperson who sticks around for the long haul.

Saturn loves to set up systems, so you could write an operations manual for your company or department, design training programs or delegate tasks to new hires then show them the ropes. Dabble with some project management apps like Slack, Evernote or Basecamp, too. Perhaps you'll hire a virtual assistant or an intern to manage your workload—or staff up on the homefront with a babysitter, house cleaner or dog walker.

Saturn in Aquarius Square Uranus in Taurus
February 17, June 14 & December 24

In case you were worried about becoming too much of a stereotypical Virgo, here's some news you may find heartening. (Well, relatively speaking.) Three times this year, spontaneous Uranus cannonballs into the equation, shaking up Saturn's stuffy influence. On February 17, June 14 and December 24, flip your perspective to a wide-angled lens as innovative Uranus forms a challenging square (90-degree angle) to old-guard Saturn. If you found yourself hyper-fixating on details or becoming way too myopic and controlling, these shakeups may be just what you need to refresh your perspective.

Just don't expect these moments to be a cakewalk! Saturn is plunked down in your meticulous sixth house, which is comfortable and familiar. Wrench-thrower Uranus, on the other hand, is in Taurus, expanding your horizons from your ninth house of travel, expansion and adventure. You'll be risk-averse one second, with the gambler's instinct the next. In a perfect scenario, you'll have everything you need to make a calculated move. But it might take until the third square on Christmas Eve before you gain the confidence you need to make any disruptive decisions—the life-changing kinds that you know are necessary for growth, but also scare the living daylights out of you because…change!

167

If you want to expedite this process, it can be helpful to sign up for sessions with a master teacher or learn all you can about the new league you'd be leaping into. No one can plummet down a search engine rabbit hole quite like a Virgo. Before the year is halfway through, we bet you'll be informed enough to, say, publish a walking guide of the cultural hotpots in the city you're considering for relocation. Or dispensing wellness advice on a social media feed, culled from all the experts you've now become obsessed with. Don't get too far ahead of yourself though! You may be called to the carpet for playing "insta-guru" if you don't cite your sources and put in the "I am not a professional" disclaimer.

The ninth house rules publishing, and the sixth house can be a beneficial zone for writing and research. Got an idea for a book, documentary or eye-opening media property? The Saturn-Uranus squares could spring you into action. These vitality-boosting mashups might inspire you to take on a marathon project—or literally train for a marathon (or 5K). Challenging goals will keep you in action this year, even if reaching them is a long shot. Uranus in the ninth house just wants you to try, Virgo, because it's through the process that you always discover the most epic growth.

Jupiter in Aquarius & Pisces

January 1: Aquarius (since December 19, 2020)
May 13: Pisces (retrograde June 20)
July 28: Aquarius (retrograde until October 18)
December 28: Pisces (until December 20, 2022)

Everything in its place…and everyone, too! You're on a mission to streamline and systematize as expansive Jupiter teams up with Saturn in Aquarius, weaving in and out of your sixth house of health and organization this year. This cycle began December 19, 2020, and lasts until May 13, 2021, resuming for a second round from July 28 until December 28, 2021. Talk about a galactic glow-up! With vital Jupiter in Aquarius, you may feel more energized and robust than you have in years.

A relationship revival may be in the cards from May 13 to July 28, as abundant Jupiter leaps into Pisces, beaming good fortune into your seventh house of partnerships. Pairing up will feel like a great adventure during these two and a half months, a cycle that resumes when Jupiter returns to Pisces on December 28, its home for a good part of 2022. Virgos who are just getting back into the dating world can taste all the offerings from Cupid's sampler platter, just as spring fever sets in.

Jupiter's back-and-forth dance between Aquarius and Pisces is actually rare. Most years, Jupiter hangs out in a single sign for a solid 12-13 months. But 2021 will be different. With the red-spotted giant generating excitement for work, wellness and relationships, this could be a jubilant year where you get to experience the feeling of "having it all."

Jupiter in Aquarius
December 19, 2020–May 13, 2021
July 28–December 28, 2021

Wellness adventures resume.

Less is more? That old paradox will make perfect sense when supersizing Jupiter sails into Aquarius and your downsizing sixth house. Until May 13—and again after July 28—your curatorial powers will be in rare form. Should it stay or should it go? Merciless discernment will be required in 2021.

Even if you're ready to go on a Marie Kondo rampage, determining the joy-sparkers is not as easy as it sounds. While Jupiter was in your "see it, want it" fifth house last year, your stash of material possessions may have swelled. Hey, retail therapy is a real thing…especially during a pandemic. Also, Virgos may be neat freaks, but contrary to popular misconceptions about your sign, you can be quite the collector and not exactly the minimalist. When you're into something, you dive deep, culling the finest, rarest, and most in-demand versions in the category. But while Jupiter is in Aquarius in 2021, you'll want to travel (and live) light, with a focus on necessity. Maybe you'll settle for a single pair of limited-edition sneakers rather than scooping up every release to hit Instagram?

The sixth house is the domain of wellness. While teamed up with Saturn in Aquarius, Jupiter could push you to get into great physical shape, both inside and out. You may be inspired to learn about health and nutrition, perhaps

169

enlisting a wellness coach or even becoming one. Flower essences, supplements, plant-based powders? All the shelf space you just cleared might start to resemble a health food store's vitamin aisle!

Bear in mind, Virgo, that Jupiter is the mythological god of the feast. When this expansive planet visits your sixth house, there's a tendency to put on a little "padding," no matter how mindfully you chew each bite or steadily you circuit train. Your appetite for everything may increase under Jupiter's influence, so even those raw vegan chocolates, when eaten without restraint, might, er, fudge the definition of "healthy decadence." To fill up, start each meal with a salad and fill at least half your plate with veggies—dark leafy greens and cruciferous ones if possible.

As an earth sign, outdoor exercise is your jam. Sedentary Virgos should peel off the couch and get outdoors for fresh air runs and bike rides. Exploratory Jupiter supports trying new techniques that keep you radiant. This would be the year to try smoking cessation hypnotherapy or intermittent fasting.

Since Jupiter is the planetary truth-teller, you may get some eye-opening news about health habits that need to be changed. Fortunately, Jupiter is one of the two "benefic" planets (the other is Venus), meaning its influence is overarchingly helpful and positive. Even if you're in perfect health, or feel like you are, it's best to get everything checked out and nip potential problems in the bud. If you're dealing with an ongoing issue, Jupiter brings the gift of early detection, guiding you to the best treatment options for a speedy recovery. Don't dismiss any nagging aches or pains. It's better to be safe than sorry. Look for a doctor specializing in functional medicine, which blends traditional and holistic remedies such as Ayurveda and acupuncture.

The sixth house rules the service industry and also all things "green," so if you're switching fields, you might look into a solid path such as nursing, accounting or human resources. You could also move into the eco-friendly or wellness fields, perhaps even launching your own small business thanks to entrepreneurial Jupiter. Higher education also falls under Jupiter's domain, so explore college/certificate programs and online courses to build your skills.

While Jupiter spins through Aquarius for much of 2021, the bulk of your luck will come from diligent, detailed duties—the kind your sign specializes in. But stay on top of the paperwork! The admin stuff could swell from a small stack into an overwhelming mountain if you don't stay on top of it. No matter where your aspirations are pointing, your success hinges on a carefully crafted plan and well-timed execution, along with attention to detail. Skip the shortcuts and follow the standard operating procedures. Reading the instructions can be eye-opening, sparing you potentially expensive mistakes. For many other signs, this would be a struggle, but it suits your methodical Virgo nature just fine.

If you're in between gigs or launching a new venture, you might consider taking a "bridge job" to pay the bills while you attend classes for certifications, grow a side hustle or dabble in different areas to find your passion. The flexible hours and secure pay will take the pressure off and keep the lights on. While Jupiter is retrograde (backward) from June 20 to October 18, it's an especially good time to research, refine, test and "try before you buy" before launching into a major life change.

If a recent hire on Team Virgo just isn't working out, you may have to let them go now, too. You could also connect with an old employer for part-time work. Or maybe that fresh-out-of-college person you mentored back in the day has risen through the ranks to an executive role at another company. Your good karma could be repaid with a job or a referral, so reconnect!

Jupiter in Pisces
May 13–July 28
December 28, 2021–May 10, 2022
October 28, 2022–December 20, 2022

It takes two.
Is freedom the secret to lasting love? That idealistic view isn't exactly an easy one for your security-minded sign to embrace. But surprise, surprise: A liberated approach to amour could suddenly hold sway when, from May 13 to July 28, untethered Jupiter soars into Pisces and your seventh house of relationships.

This is Jupiter's first dip in the Fish's emotion ocean since January 2011. Adjusting to the dreamy but unpredictable current may find you splashing around wildly, like a toddler in their first swim class. That said, you're no stranger to being swept away. With fantasy-fueled Pisces governing the action in your solar seventh house, your boundaries are a lot, er, softer, in the game of love. Caution you apply in other areas of life can evaporate when Cupid swings by!

There's no stemming the tide of romantic exploration while Jupiter's in Pisces, but don't lose sight of the shoreline this spring and summer. A charismatic lover could pull you into a powerful undertow, especially when Jupiter turns retrograde on June 20. Coupled Virgos may be scanning the horizon for potential adventures you can co-create—perhaps because you're feeling stultified by all the duties you heaped onto your shared plate earlier this year.

The million-dollar question is this: Have you built your partnerships on a firm foundation or a shaky one? This brief, indie-spirited Jupiter cycle will put your ties through the ultimate test. If you rushed into coupledom for security's sake, boredom could overwhelm you, and send you running for the door. Conversely, fiery sexual chemistry may dissolve into ash if you keep locking horns over daily responsibilities, like who's paying the car note or putting in the Instacart order.

If you settled into a static role, like "eternally supportive spouse" or "loyal business partner," Jupiter in Pisces could crash through the white picket fence and cast you into a totally different scene. What feels comfortable before May 13 could suddenly stifle your self-expression once Jupiter swings into "no limits" Pisces mid-year. Out of nowhere, you may rail against convention, wanting to run away from any relationship that feels restrictive. (Or perhaps dramatize your everyday affairs into something worthy of a reality-TV confessional!)

The trick to navigating these complex seas? Try viewing all relationships through Jupiter's high-minded, philosophical lens. Set aside knee-jerk judgment and avoid the Pisces pitfall of self-pity or a victim mindset. The desire to be romantically or sexually liberated is not shameful, Virgo! But blaming other people for feeling "trapped" or unhappy is not going to bring a solution. Maybe you didn't paint yourself into that tight little corner all by yourself. But if you're being perfectly honest, you laid down a few of those brushstrokes, even if you were being passive when you should have vocalized a boundary.

With growth-agent Jupiter in your seventh house, "unconditional love" is an essential concept to embrace. Allowing yourself (and your partner) to evolve could mean letting go, at least in part, of the way things have "always" been. Here's the rub: After May 13, the very rules you laid down might suddenly feel suffocating. Eating crow is never your favorite culinary experience, but with truth-telling Jupiter here, it could be on 2021's metaphorical menu.

We're not saying you'll break up with the LOYL or buy out the business partner from your 2019 startup. But if trouble's brewing, do whatever you can to fortify your bond. Traveling between May and July (or at the end of the year when Jupiter returns to Pisces on December 28) could be a healing salve with the nomadic planet in the mix. But honest-to-a-fault Jupiter won't let you gloss over the real talk. If viable solutions don't easily emerge, get extra support: couples' therapy, mediation, conflict-negotiation workshops. Better to sit through an hour of vulnerable conversation with a pro than get embroiled in a shouting match outside your RV when you missed the exit to your campsite and you both stayed up half the night driving on a two-lane country highway with a rampant deer population.

Abundant, adventurous Jupiter in Pisces could also bring new love to the fore. Someone you've known in another capacity could start showing a different kind of attention, and you'll be more willing to drop your guard. Is the writing on the wall in a relationship—or a prospective one? If so, it will be as obvious as neon pink graffiti while Jupiter is in your seventh house! It might take until December 28, when the red-spotted giant returns to Pisces for a longer cycle, before you're ready to take the full-on plunge. But pay attention to those pings and pangs. Are your butterflies excitement, dread…or a little bit of both? Break out your journal and observe, observe, observe.

Jupiter rules global expansion and cross-cultural connections. Single Virgos could meet someone from a wildly different background than yours, perhaps quite a departure from your usual "type." With Jupiter at the helm, opposites can and do attract! Although your tactile sign loves to cuddle up to a warm body, you might even contemplate a long-distance relationship. If you're feeling the love, you may surprise yourself and willingly withstand the WhatsApp chats across miles and time zones.

173

Couples might renew their vows or even start a business together, since Jupiter rules entrepreneurship. You could also find yourself trading roles—for example, the high earner in your relationship quits a full-time job and the other one steps up to cover costs, or the silent supporter moves into the spotlight. A long-distance move may also revive your bond as you forge life in a new terrain together.

Jupiter takes 12 years to make a complete cycle through your chart, so for some Virgos, a longtime relationship could run its course and you may amicably part ways. Or, you might move into the next big evolution of your partnership—for example, children leave the nest and you downsize your home, or you decide to get engaged after a few years of dating each other.

Jupiter in Pisces will also ease your workload at the office. After hustling and breaking ground early in the year, someone whose skills complement yours to a tee could become an official business or project partner. Since Jupiter rules long-distance travel, you might even team up with someone in another part of the country—even the world! Time to work with developers in India, Poland or Argentina, or to hire a career coach who works with you via Zoom?

Are you an artist, musician or creative type? Jupiter in your seventh house of contracts could bring a helpful agent, lawyer or broker to bring your talent into the public eye. Team up with people whose connections and experience can open doors, instead of taking a DIY approach. Let someone else toot your horn instead of trying to hard-sell yourself. Just because you can do it yourself doesn't mean you should.

And it goes both ways! As the zodiac's happiest, humblest helper, Jupiter in Pisces may lead you to work as an agent or rep. Where you struggle to stand up for yourself, you can be a fierce advocate for others. From talent management to PR, working for a commission could inspire you, especially if it means getting more up-front funding for your clients. You'll sleep well at night knowing that you, say, helped a budding artist get paid what they deserve for their hand-crafted textiles or a young scriptwriter not get jacked by the Hollywood machine. Enjoy your slice of the pie!

174

Eclipses in 2021

May 26: Sagittarius Lunar Eclipse 5°29' (7:13am ET)
June 10: Gemini Solar Eclipse 19°42 (6:52am ET)
November 19: Taurus Lunar Eclipse 27°17 (3:57pm)
December 4: Sagittarius Solar Eclipse 12°17 (2:42am)

Gemini/Sagittarius Eclipses

Work-life balance, reinvented.

Work hard, relax hard? For the second consecutive year, a series of eclipses will rumble across the Gemini/Sagittarius axis. These game-changing moonbeams could bring radical shifts to your lifestyle, family structure, career and goals. Gemini governs your tenth house of ambition and work while Sagittarius rules your fourth house of home and roots. Eclipses sweep in to shake up whatever needs to evolve. While it can be temporarily disorienting or chaotic, ultimately the purpose of an eclipse is to help us—or push us!—to evolve. There's no more dragging your feet or procrastinating. It's time to leap into action.

Two of 2021's four eclipses fall in Sagittarius, highlighting your domestic fourth house. The May 26 lunar (full moon) eclipse could activate a major change or a conflict with someone in your family. Even if you weren't planning to relocate, you might also pull up the stakes and move into a new home or realize that you're so done with a certain way of life. If you're a parent, a child may enter a different phase or stage of life, which could leave you with a sudden new set of responsibilities or even a bout of empty-nest syndrome.

Full moons can bring turning points, endings and epiphanies. When they coincide with lunar eclipses, one door may suddenly close or you might be shot out of the cannon into unfamiliar terrain. Like giant magnifiers they may also suddenly expose an area of your life where you've been confused or in denial. Brace yourself for a possible blowup or family feud that finally brings a stewing issue into the open. You'll have no choice but to lay all your cards on the table—at least if you want to bring back the love.

It may take until the December 4 Sagittarius solar (new moon) eclipse before you can really start fresh. In our experience, solar eclipses can be a little gentler, since new moons herald beginnings, rather than endings. Still, it may feel like you're groping around in the dark temporarily, which can be disorienting for a directional sign like yours. You'll definitely need to embrace the new and unfamiliar at the end of 2021, possibly moving, getting pregnancy news or meeting a powerful and influential woman.

June 10 features the first Gemini solar eclipse in this series, as the potent new moon charges up your tenth house of career, public prestige and leadership. Get ready: New developments are coming to your work, path and goals. Perhaps you'll just have an exciting awakening about your life purpose. Or, you could be offered an unexpected opportunity that boosts your industry cred. A mentor, influencer or powerful man may open major doors for you.

Your relationship with your parents and/or children could undergo big changes now. The fourth house rules mothers, women and feminine (yin) energy; the tenth house governs men, fathers and the masculine (yang) principle. Your own gender identity may evolve in ways that differentiate you from prior generations. Maybe you'll recalibrate the role you've been "expected" to play by the society or the culture you grew up in. If you've always been the martyr, you may begin asserting more boundaries. Or if you're always dishing out tough love, you'll become a bit softer and more compassionate.

Taurus Lunar Eclipse

Wanderlust erupts!

If 2021 has been a bit too predictable for your liking, just wait until the lunar (full moon) eclipse on November 19. This one falls in Taurus and your nomadic, expansive ninth house. Out of nowhere, your adventurous spirit comes rushing back. So, where to next? These moonbeams may lead you to a decadent destination, one that also satisfies your earth sign's desire to revel in the beauty of nature. (Food and wine country, anyone?)

As one of the zodiac's four mutable signs, you get restless when sitting still for too long. Virgo, you'll be happy to hear that this eclipse is the first in a two-year series kicking things up across the Taurus/Scorpio axis. While Taurus rules your worldly and expansive ninth house, Scorpio governs your third house of short trips and area adventures. Whether you're boarding a plane or planning a road trip, keep those WhatsApp notifications on. Just in time for the holidays, you could score an invitation to visit friends on another coast or continent!

The ninth house rules higher education. Some Virgos might be lured back to the ivory tower, applying for a winter semester course load or a virtual training. If you've always wanted to work with a spiritual teacher, this fortuitous eclipse could bring the opening you've been waiting for—perhaps including a soulful sojourn. Have guru, will travel!

Venus Retrograde in Capricorn: Romantic redux?

December 19, 2021 –January 29, 2022

Thought you'd slip off like a lone wolf for some holiday season hibernation? Not so fast! There will be too many interested parties hovering around the Virgo den for you to pull off any such disappearing acts. From November 5 to March 6, 2022, glamorous, romantic Venus sashays through Capricorn, strutting down the catwalk of your fifth house of fame and romance.

During this extended cycle, people will either want to date you or imitate you. As uncomfortable as you may be with that much attention, relish it! Venus normally hovers in a sign for a few weeks, but due to a retrograde from December 19, 2021, until January 29, 2022, the love planet will percolate in this passionate placement for four whole months. That's a lot of pull, Virgo, and you're here for it!

Venus turns retrograde every 584 days. If you trace these backspins over the years, they create a unique, five-pointed star pattern on the zodiac wheel. Every eight years, Venus reverse-commutes through the same zodiac sign—and Capricorn is part of that quintet. Whether in forward or retrograde motion, Venus's tour through Capricorn rustles things up in your love life, sparking excitement and drama. But if you haven't cleaned up the past, look out! Like cosmic review periods, retrogrades force you to parse through old situations so you can stop dragging baggage into every new relationship.

Check your calendar: Where were Cupid's arrows pointing from December 21, 2013, to January 31, 2014? This was the last time Venus retreated through Capricorn, and similar themes could arise in your love life as 2021 winds down.

Do you need to forgive someone, or perhaps extend an apology for your own indiscretions? We all make mistakes in the game of love; in fact, Cupid's playground is notoriously messy territory. Venus retrograde is prime time for making amends, dropping grudges or doing the therapeutic work that's needed to process old hurts.

Virgos on the hunt for new love will have bountiful luck while Venus makes a four-month visit to Capricorn. But during the retrograde, your mistletoe moments could be…misleading. From December 19, 2021, until January 29, 2022, question every urge to play Dial-An-Ex. (Yes, even if the sex was amazing, and you haven't found anyone who could set every cell of your body on fire since.) If it was just bad timing that kept you apart, reuniting with a bygone love interest might make for a legendary holiday season. But retrogrades aren't necessarily that literal. It may be that you need to look for someone who has your ex's best qualities—without the toxic traits. If you find a paramour who fits that bill, explore with an open mind and heart! This spicy new prospect might work in a completely different sector or hail from a cultural background you've never dated before. All the same, the similarity to your ex's values and mannerisms will be striking enough to pique your curiosity…and potentially draw you in to something real.

Attached Virgos may lock horns over unfinished drama that you knew, deep down, would resurface one day. With the peacekeeping planet in retrograde, tempers will flare fast. Your levelheaded nature could fly out the window at the slightest provocation. Take cooldown breaks instead of shouting something you'll regret. Better you should spend a night or two sleeping on the sofa than demolish the LOYL with a wrecking ball of harsh feedback in the heat of the moment.

Been with your partner so long you barely have any hygiene boundaries anymore? Look out, Virgo. An outside attraction could lure you in, especially if it comes with the sparkle of "new relationship energy" that's seriously MIA in your comfortable LTR. Even if nothing physical is happening, be honest with yourself: Are you sharing more sexual fantasies with your so-called friend than you are with your partner? Maybe it seems easier to open up to them because the stakes aren't so high, but ask yourself honestly if you're treading into emotional affair terrain. This newfound intimacy can be exhilarating at first, but you can only bare souls (if not other things) without forming an emotional attachment for so long. Expectations will creep in, making this too complicated to skillfully navigate.

If you're intent on making things work with your partner, take the Venus retrograde challenge and plunge in deeper. Have the gut-wrenching conversations and figure out where you took a turn in the "too close for chemistry" direction. Did you get so caught up playing "fixer" and life coach that you stopped being vulnerable? Have you borne the brunt of financial duties without a fair exchange? While you can never replace the dopamine-fueled buzz of the courtship phase, you might discover an equally titillating (and far more intimate) way to generate attraction with your tried-and-true honey. Simply sharing a new adventure has been proven to release dopamine and oxytocin, both important chemicals for sexual bonding. Pro tip: Leave the tacky reindeer sweaters in mothballs this holiday season and ring in 2022 with a road trip through the Southwest, or a week in a surfing village!

Then again, Virgo, you might be ready to explore a new relationship configuration. If you're staunchly monogamous, "opening things up" won't be your jam. But, if you're "monogamish," as sexpert Dan Savage dubbed it, Venus' four-month circuit through Capricorn could find you engrossed in books like *More Than Two* or having "what if" conversations with your longtime love. Heads up: These talks alone might just turn the heat back on with your sweetie. If you're going to dabble in this experimental terrain, start as slowly as you can—and if possible, long before the December 19 retrograde.

The fifth house rules fertility, so if babies are part of your plan, you could be celebrating a pink line on that pregnancy test (or adoption news) before spring officially hits. Already a parent? Plan to relive your childhood this winter with a calendar full of adventures, like tobogganing down a snowy hill or sipping artisanal hot cocoa by a roaring fire. Having trouble conceiving? While Venus is retrograde from December 19 to January 29, 2022, dive into a deeper investigation. Get recommendations for fertility specialists, possibly ones who incorporate natural approaches, such as dietary changes, into their treatment plans.

If you're still nursing a wound, use this six-week backspin to process the pain and fully heal. You could be back on the dating scene (and crushing it!) before March 6, 2022.

Check your creative compass, too: Venus' tour of your fifth house stokes your artistic fire, lighting you up with inspiration in the final quarter of this year. Don't fill your calendar with so many romantic pursuits that there's no blank space for the muse. The final act of that one-Virgo show you've been working on forever could finally unspool on the page. Life doesn't just imitate art while Venus is in reverse. Creativity is your catharsis! If you're sticking close to home for the holidays, your time off could be consumed by writing a book or unleashing a politically charged, mixed-media installation piece that can be displayed as public art. Whatever your métier, you'll feel unleashed!

Style could be the chosen statement-making medium between November and March, and contrary to the myths about Virgos, your look is anything but basic. From brightly colored, designer-vintage pantsuits to razor-cut bobs, Venus in the fifth house provides a serious glow-up. Splurge on self-care. When you treat yourself like a million bucks, your confidence soars. But hold off on more dramatic style shifts, like hair chops and tattoos. Put those on a Pinterest board until beauty queen Venus is back to her senses on January 29, 2022. ✷

Libra

HOROSCOPE

2021
HIGHLIGHTS

LOVE

Ready to create some lasting love in your life? Cupid is back in your corner in 2021, slinging golden-tipped arrows while simultaneously putting you through relationship boot camp. On the upside, expansive Jupiter soars through Aquarius, activating your fifth house of love, fertility and creativity until May 13, then again from July 28 to December 28. Amour could arrive from a long-distance locale or via a scintillating cross-cultural connection. Coupled Libras could take off on your dream trip or relocate to a juicier destination. Pregnancies may be on the agenda, or you could spend more quality time with the kids you already have. But there is a catch: Boundless Jupiter will share a flight path with restrictive Saturn, who is also in Aquarius all year (and until March 7, 2023). Even if you want to be swept off your feet, you'll feel like you're wearing heavy-soled combat boots instead of lightweight glass slippers. But hey, Libra, you're kind of a "warrior for love" in 2021. If it's worth having in your life, it's worth fighting for…or at least, putting in the necessary hard work that goes along with relationships.

MONEY

Cue the (Libra) Gwen Stefani, because those "if I was a rich girl" fantasies will be dancing through your head. Abundant Jupiter in your glamorous fifth house will whet your appetite for luxury, so you might as well make a budget. With Saturn riding shotgun, you'll have more discipline, so instead of scooping up every trendy treasure that beckons you with a shoppable Instagram link, think in terms of "building a wardrobe" or buying "investment pieces." At work, you could be called into a leadership role, or have an opportunity to make bank from your

The AstroTwins' 2021 Horoscope   182

creative talents. Get organized while Jupiter is in Pisces and your systematic sixth house from May 13 to July 28, a period that may require more "lather, rinse, repeat" work. Investments pay off near the lunar eclipse on November 19, the first in a two-year series that will rev up your money mojo!

WELLNESS

Overarchingly, 2021 will be an indulgent year, with a focus on pleasure— the kind that verges on hedonism, at times. But discipline returns with a vengeance from May 13 to July 28, as Jupiter lunges into Pisces and your wellness-obsessed sixth house for a brief voyage. Green is the new black— from the non-GMO food you put on your plate to the environmentally-friendly beauty products you add to your cart. Spring training may have a "no pain, no gain" element to it as you restrict certain habits in order to form newer, healthier ways of life. Book doctors' appointments and explore options for health care (and health insurance) during this time. An ounce of prevention is worth a pound of cure!

FRIENDS & FAMILY

A little space, please? After three close-knit years of bonding with your innermost circle, you're ready to break free and explore your autonomous side. It's not that you'll ditch your family in 2021, but you may limit the time spent together to quality over quantity. Groupthink is the last thing you want to get sucked into in 2021, but in order to formulate your opinion (and uncover your independent values), you may have to stray from the flock a bit. Two eclipses in your zone of peers, on May 26 and December 4, attract soulful friends and deepen your connection to relatives close in age, like siblings or cousins. Make up for lost time after November 5, when your ruler, sentimental Venus, dips into Capricorn and your family-friendly fourth house for four months. Holidays will be extra nostalgic due to Venus retrograde from December 19, 2021, to January 29, 2022—as long as you steer clear of difficult relatives!

POWER DATES

LIBRA NEW MOON
October 6 (7:05 PM ET)

LIBRA FULL MOON
March 28 (2:48 PM ET)

SUN IN LIBRA
September 22 – October 23

Back in the limelight! After a domestic and homebound 2020 that put you in touch with your emotions, you're ready for a year of fun, celebration and expression. Here it comes!

Saturn in Aquarius: From cocoon to catwalk.
December 17, 2020–March 7, 2023

The pressure is lifting, Libra! For the past three years, you've been shouldering a weight-bearing load as somber Saturn in Capricorn locked into a tough square (90-degree angle) with your Sun sign. But on December 17, 2020, the cosmic Lord of the Rings eased off the throttle, shifting into fellow air sign Aquarius

The AstroTwins' 2021 Horoscope   184

and activating your flamboyant and romantic fifth house until March 7, 2023. Talk about a heavenly holiday gift. Although Saturn never gives anyone a total pass, this will be a much lighter cycle, with more opportunities to enjoy life's pleasures—and far fewer existential crises and intense unpacking of childhood wounds. Frankly, you could use a break from all that inner work!

The beauty of Saturn's previous three-year tour through Capricorn (from December 19, 2017, to December 17, 2020) was that it anchored you in a true sense of home. Breezy Libras are easily unrooted, floating like a butterfly…then freaking out and stinging like a bee when they need emotional stability and have nowhere safe to land. Over the past few years, we watched many Libra friends heal this pattern through embracing their domesticity, settling into a stable living arrangement, even buying real estate.

Now that you understand that there's no place like home, you can stop clicking your ruby slippers. Next up: Getting them resoled with a six-inch heel! When Saturn moves from Capricorn into Aquarius, it's like you're emerging from the cocoon onto the catwalk. As Aquarius rules your fashion-forward fifth house, systematic Saturn is here to help you build a tastefully chic wardrobe—like Libra Fashion Week darling Kim Kardashian on a more conservative day.

Membership has its privileges while Saturn spins through communal Aquarius. Saturn can be restrictive, so think "exclusive and elite" and aim for quality over quantity when it comes to your human interactions. Are tryouts involved to be part of the team? Do you need to be nominated or voted into a certain club or masterclass? This is exactly the kind of affiliation to add to your C.V. now, as Saturn helps you build cachet.

Saturn briefly visited Aquarius last year, from March 21 to July 1, 2020, which doubled down on the social restrictions many felt during the first wave of the pandemic. Unfortunately, what was meant to be your cosmic coming-out party devolved into a celestial stay-at-home order. We could argue that Libras got more ripped off than most zodiac signs, but the truth is, Saturn's transits never get off to a rollicking start. Hopefully you made the most of your time indoors, sharpening your creative gifts, mastering the art of video chat seduction, even making headway on a project like writing a novel or perfecting your TikTok choreography.

For Libras who work in the arts, this Saturn cycle might produce some of your best work ever. You could rise slowly but steadily into recognition. This isn't the kind of Internet-famous, six seconds of Snapchat stardom. Rather, it's hard-won acknowledgment for your talents. So on that note, be mindful of what you put out into the public forum. If you've already had your metaphorical hit album, you could easily follow with a "sophomore slump" if you rush to drop a half-baked product. Take the time to hone your craft, Libra. Only attach your name to work that reflects your stellar taste. For example, if you're an actor who needs to take side gigs (a commercial, an indie film) between roles, make sure they're still respectable, even if you never put them on your reel.

Power couple fantasies come to life with Saturn here, and thanks to this persistent planet, one could bring the guarantee of staying power. Picture Libras Michael Douglas and Catherine Zeta-Jones whose marriage has lasted over 20 years, withstanding both a notable age difference, his throat cancer and her mental health struggles. Saturn knows that you have to take the bad along with the good. It's all part of adulting, a key lesson that the planet of time and maturity is here to teach.

Already in a relationship? While restrained Saturn slogs through Aquarius, it could take a little something extra to feel even a fraction as Balenciaga-glam as signmate Cardi B. Most Libras need no excuse to pamper themselves unapologetically, but in 2021, doing so is more of a necessity than a luxury. The catch? Basic blowouts and cosmetic treatments only provide a temporary hit, so think beyond the express manicure mindset. To access your galactic glow-up, tear a page from Libra GOOP maven Gwyneth Paltrow's playbook and indulge in healing treatments. Align your chakras with meditative breathwork, get your lifeforce energy flowing with Qi Gong and yoga, try facial acupuncture. Bringing your best self to the table is the recipe for living your best life with your partner.

Don't forget, Saturn is a planet with a plan! If you want those weekly date nights and sexytime to actually happen during this busy year, you might have to do something that seems antithetical to "spontaneity" and put them on a shared calendar. Relying on impulse is a recipe for disappointment. Carve out non-negotiable blocks for the quality time you crave. Couples who have done this successfully usually take turns surprising each other with date planning, trading off and having fun researching new venues and activities to explore. There's science behind this, too. Novelty releases dopamine, which increases the heat between you!

Aquarius governs your fifth house of romance, fertility and creativity, and under Saturn's tenure, these areas could turn into serious topics of conversation. What begins as a lighthearted love affair may steadily evolve into a real-deal relationship. Pregnancy could be an all-consuming topic for some Libras. Since Saturn can create slowdowns, conceiving might prove challenging. Libras may explore IVF treatments, or freezing your eggs if you want a kid, but not quite yet. Clear-headed Saturn can also bring a peaceful decision to not have kids (or more kids), and instead, to redirect your energy toward parenting a creative "child" instead. The larger message is to really make sure your life and relationship are strong enough to withstand some of the upheaval that can accompany the joy of a new family addition. Saturn loves a long-range plan!

Single Libras won't be in a rush to give up the curated life you've created for yourself. Hey, why rock the boat when you've already settled into peaceful harmony? You may be a romantic, but you labor few delusions about the "disruption" that an intimate relationship creates. This may be one of the reasons you're so hesitant to get involved. To function properly in the world, you need serenity! Many Libras have specific tastes, from a love of modernist furniture to a devoted raw-vegan diet. (And let's not get started on those complex, holistic beauty rituals.)

You probably won't take kindly to your mate's vintage velvet painting collection penetrating the spa-like atmosphere of your amethyst pillars and Green Tara meditation art…or their grab-and-go snacks tempting you away from your processed food detox. No, Libra, there's nothing like a relationship to reveal your edges. Maybe you aren't as willing to compromise as you'd have everyone believe. And that's okay! Let yourself go through this process and don't rush. It might take you until Saturn leaves Aquarius, on March 7, 2023, to arrive at the best decision for yourself. Weigh your options carefully, as only a Libra can.

Saturn in Aquarius square Uranus in Taurus
February 17, June 14 & December 24

Budget check! With status-boosting Saturn in your glamorous fifth house, your lifestyle costs could quickly creep skyward. It may be hard to discern a "want" from a "need" under this influence, especially if you're dazzled by a compelling sales pitch. But count your pennies—and plug your dollar bills into a money management app. Otherwise, you could be the victim of some unwelcome surprises to your financial picture.

The reason? Three times this year, Saturn gets t-boned by disruptive Uranus, which is parked in Taurus and your eighth house of investments, debt and binding relationships. On February 17, June 14 and December 24, the universe may test your resolve. Yes, there are some things that most people have to fund with a loan, like home, tuition, even cars. But wherever possible, avoid swiping that credit card or getting caught up in any expenses that involve high interest. If you do the calculations, you might discover that by the time you're done with those "low monthly payments," you could have refreshed your entire lingerie drawer for the price of a single set.

On the flip side, the Saturn-Uranus squares can push you to learn more about making your money work hard for you. Investing in things like index funds, which earn you compounding interest, might increase your long-term security. During these squares, you may be forced to weigh between a sparkly, short-term purchase that depreciates the minute you drive it off the lot versus an investment which will slowly but surely grow in value over time. With Uranus, the planet of technology and collaboration, governing your fiscally-savvy eighth house, you might even flow some funds toward a Silicon Valley start-up or team up with family to purchase a rental property in a developing neighborhood.

Romantically, the Saturn-Uranus squares can churn up confusion. Is this true love or just a steamy sexual connection? Lines could get blurry during this trio of squares, especially when the chemistry is so hot it's damn near exothermic. As Uranus in Taurus stokes your sensual nature, you may let your reptilian brain overtake your rational one. If you're free and clear to play, do so at your own discretion. Protect your privacy at all costs. Seriously, are there any cameras rolling? With Saturn in your fifth house, you need to check such things (Libra Kim Kardashian can testify). Of course, if you want to star in your own private cinema, well…lights, camera, action, baby.

Even happily coupled Libras may be tempted to play with fire near these dates, thanks to experimental Uranus seducing Saturn from your erotic eighth house. Okay, Libra, so maybe you've always wanted to have a threesome or explore some form of kink. You might screw up the nerve to talk about your fantasies under the influence of the Saturn-Uranus squares, but should you actually go there? We'd recommend waiting a good month after each of these cosmic mashups (February 17, June 14 and December 24) before you, say, set up an account on Adult Friend Finder or decide to surprise your partner with a Valentine's Day orgy. (Or, uh, something like that!) And if the allure is too strong to resist, well, don't say we didn't warn ya!

Jupiter in Aquarius & Pisces

January 1: Aquarius (since December 19, 2020)
May 13: Pisces (retrograde June 20)
July 28: Aquarius (retrograde until October 18)
December 28: Pisces (until December 20, 2022)

In 2021, Jupiter will shift back and forth between Aquarius and Pisces. Normally, Jupiter makes an unbroken trek through a single sign for 12 to 13 months, but in 2021, we'll see the planet of fortune and growth in two signs.

Jupiter in Aquarius

December 19, 2020–May 13, 2021
July 28–December 28, 2021

Creative evolution.

Ready for a personal Renaissance? Out of the cathartic ashes of 2020, great work could emerge from Libras in 2021. Jupiter makes two passes through Aquarius this year, awakening your fifth house of love, passion and creativity. Circle these dates and get ready for your debut: December 19, 2020, to May 13, 2021, and again, from July 28 to December 28, 2021. Jupiter enters a new sign every year, returning to each part of your chart every 12 years. The last time Jupiter was in Aquarius was from January 5, 2009, to January 17, 2010. You may see recurring themes pop up again now, especially around romance and artistic pursuits.

As unbound Jupiter joins structured Saturn in Aquarius on and off throughout the year, immerse yourself in the creative process. Whether you're building something tangible or making art for art's sake, push past your edges, exploring terrain where only true visionaries dare tread. While Saturn constrains, Jupiter expands, making you a "no limits soldier" when it comes to your passions. There's a real push-pull here. While Saturn disciplines, indulgent Jupiter in your festive fifth house can tip the scales more toward "play" than "work." A hit of hedonism will do you fine, but with excessive Jupiter at the helm, you won't be the one to set boundaries for yourself. While it's great to be in touch with your inner child, you could veer into bratty or selfish territory if you aren't careful.

This expressive cycle attracts fame and imbues you with a sense of authority. So, Libra, how ready are you for your closeup? With the spontaneous, red-spotted planet in this regal zone, there's no dodging the spotlight—or the call to a public leadership role. This year, you could become a style blogger's muse or sit on both sides of the camera as producer and protagonist. The trick is to be a class act— not exactly a tall order for your sophisticated sign. Turn some heads with your style ethos. Emerge as a prominent voice in whatever scene you feel compelled to join. Libras traverse every arena, like Democratic Socialist Congresswoman Alexandria Ocasio-Cortez to controversy-courting actress Bella Thorne, whose 2020 foray onto the OnlyFans website sparked outrage among sex workers when her earnings of $2 million in a single day caused a sitewide policy change which delayed payments to all members on the platform.

With expansive Jupiter pushing you out into the world, you're going to make some sort of statement in 2021. Just make sure the attention you're courting is the kind that you actually want. Jupiter here can make you a bit of a drama queen. There is such a thing as "bad press," and you don't need to wind up on the gossip blogs for acting like a rebellious teenager in a moment of frustration. Admirers will take notice, Libra, and since the fifth house rules that giddy, infatuated phase of love, single Libras may not want to rush to pare down their options. Enjoy the bounty of admirers that come your way now…and let yourself be courted, adored and spoiled.

Since Jupiter is the ruler of publishing, writers could see their names in print or pixels. Don't sleep on self-publishing with this independent planet at the helm. Musicians and performers could attract a global following, and, if restrictions lift, an actual tour—without having to sign on with a record label or sell your soul to a Hollywood producer!

Ambassador Jupiter can attract lovers from different cultures or spark interest with someone of a wildly different archetype than you normally pursue. Open up "borders" and you could be deliciously surprised by who, er, stamps your passion passport. Since the fifth house rules fertility, a pregnancy is possible for some Libras now. And if last year's suppressive vibes didn't do much for your love life, expect to get a dynamic do-over. No more playing it cool and coy! Your passion awakens and your desires are on fire. Or, you'll be "ripe" with original ideas, birthing a brainchild instead of an actual kid.

Long-term couples could get a burst of romantic renewal from this playful Jupiter cycle. Snap out of a sexy slump by reviving your honeymoon phase (yes, it is possible). Novelty is key, and adventurous Jupiter makes a great concierge for planning memorable, out-of-the-ordinary dates. Dress up for each other, turn on your flirty and seductive charms, and prioritize activities that generate joy. For Libras who are getting married in 2021, wedding planning could take a turn for the theatrical. Reprise the scene from your favorite movie or musical as you dance down the aisle or turn it into a theme for your guests—no matter how big or small of an affair you make it.

While tactile Libras need lots of touch, this could be the year where you explore a long-distance relationship or renting out a separate place from your long-term love as a means of regenerating magic. Autonomy can fuel passion, as long as there's enough togetherness to seal the bond. If last year taught us anything, it's that one can only employ the powers of video chat and texting to keep the vibe alive for so many days. (Although the term turned out to be longer than many expected!)

Is this connection strong enough for you to risk uprooting your life and relocating? Explore while Jupiter is in Aquarius (until May 13 and again from July 28 to December 28). Schedule a few longer visits, or talks about your options. You'll soon find out if the miles are worth crossing, or if they're masking problems you couldn't see from afar.

Jupiter in Pisces

May 13–July 28
December 28, 2021–May 10, 2022
October 28, 2022–December 20, 2022

Swap the stilettos for sensible shoes.

Party's on pause...screeeeech! A break in the action comes on May 13, when your hedonism gives way to healthy pursuits and a renewed dedication in your career. Bountiful Jupiter shifts gears, flowing into Pisces and your sixth house of wellness, efficiency and selfless service for two and a half months. (This cycle picks up again from December 28, 2021, to May 10, 2022.)

Here's hoping you swung from the chandeliers like Sia before May 13, because the closest you'll come to that midyear may be dangling from silks in an aerial yoga studio. But honestly, Libra, you'll appreciate the balance as you embrace your role as a "healthy hedonist." Fortunately, the learning curve won't be too steep. You may already be an ethical vegan (and unapologetically vain), understanding that eating well is the best beauty secret money can buy. Whatever the case, this is a time to expand your repertoire. If you currently consume a clean diet, incorporate preventative "medicine" like bee pollen to expel allergies or adaptogenic mushrooms to boost energy and performance. Since Jupiter is an international planet, you might add a worldly twist to your wellbeing, from Chinese herbs to Shamanic journeying.

In an oft-frustrating twist, people sometimes pack on pounds during this Jupiter cycle, even when they're exercising regularly. The truth? Boundless Jupiter isn't big on moderation. (Note: We believe beauty comes in all sizes, so no judgment. A little meat on your bones might do ya right!) Just bear in mind that even so-called health food can be deceptively unhealthy. Those cupcakes may be "vegan" or "gluten-free," but that doesn't mean they aren't packed with sugar and processed ingredients. You might try the technique of filling half your plate with veggies—cruciferous or dark leafy greens when possible. Since the sixth house is the systematic zone, use trackers for both food an exercise. Regulating your sleeping and eating cycles with set mealtimes and bedtimes can go a long way in stabilizing your appetite and biorhythms. If your doctor approves, you might see positive results, like weight management and energy boosts, from an eating plan like intermittent fasting or keto.

Jupiter is also the cosmic truth-teller, so if you've been neglecting your health, you may get some not-so-subtle wakeup calls. Book those overdue checkups, take advantage of your health insurance perks (or get some already), take inventory of habits that need to change. Since Jupiter rules travel, combine your vacations with healthy pursuits, even if you're relocating your WFH office to a cabin near stunning hiking trails.

With Jupiter in this orderly zone of your chart, you'll be in the mood to tidy up life across the board. Lighten your load—and your spirits—with a major decluttering and simplifying. Libra Marie Kondo is a household name at this point. Her KonMari method of downsizing begins with a gratitude ritual and ends with lovingly parting ways with anything that doesn't "spark joy." After you systematically parse through areas of your home, give your schedule the same treatment. Cut back on the multitasking and double-booking—a real pitfall for social butterfly Libras who can fall prey to FOMO. From May 13 to July 28, less is more! Organization, savvy systems and detailed agendas become your new obsession, as your dreams demand a solid backup plan.

As the sign of peace and justice, Libras crave work that makes a difference—and more than ever when Jupiter parks in Pisces from May 13 to July 28. The sixth house rules service and "giving back." With the red-spotted planet here, you could shift to a new sector, one that involves social justice, sustainability or anything green or ethical. Libras who are gainfully employed may find ways to weave such ethos into the work you're already doing. If it doesn't make sense for your day job, get your fix through volunteering. Pisces rules everything from the oceans to hospitals and jails. Jupiter here may guide you to support an environmental cause, raise funds for essential workers or support a cancer foundation. Maybe you'll become a vocal activist for prison reform laws or literacy programs for inmates.

Whatever work you do, Jupiter in Pisces will sharpen your intuitive powers, giving you a great "gut instinct." But in your systematic sixth house, you can't rely on feelings alone. This brief cycle teaches you the importance of doing things by the book. Ignoring rules and processes can bring huge and expensive mistakes while Jupiter is here. Slow down (as much as you can) and stop winging it! As the saying goes, if you fail to plan, you plan to fail. No shortcuts allowed during this Jupiter cycle, Libra. Your biggest growth comes through a strategic and well-timed approach. Do your homework, back up your claims with statistics and credible research.

And relax because you don't have to go it alone. (Music to your partnership-powered ears, we bet!) The sixth house rules employees and helpful people. You'll grow by leaps and bounds while Jupiter is in Pisces by delegating to talented people. From dog walkers to dry cleaners, babysitters to bookkeepers, Jupiter helps you upgrade Team Libra in a major way. Treat your service providers like gold, expressing regular gratitude for the ways they make your life run like a well-oiled machine. Guide them through your processes, even put together an orientation manual. Jupiter is the planetary educator, and if you're patient and tolerant through their learning curves, you could be rewarded with long-term loyalty.

If you're not already using toxin-free, non-GMO everything, this Jupiter cycle could turn you into a (Libra) Gwyneth Paltrow clone. Switch to environmentally-friendly cleaning products and natural fibers for your linens. Try chemical-free hair and beauty products for your daily grooming. With Jupiter here during planting season for many, you could discover a latent green thumb. Get those kale starts in ground—with a great set of leather gardening gloves to protect your nail art, of course—and fill your house with purifying plants. (Feel free to start with low-maintenance ones, like succulents and ZZ plants, before adopting a high-touch fiddleleaf fig). The sixth house also rules pets. Is it time to bring a kitten home from the shelter or spend quality time with the one(s) you've got?

Jupiter was last in Pisces from January 17, 2010, to January 22, 2011, so page back to that time in your life to see what might cycle around again. Perhaps you discovered yoga or a dance class you loved, conquered a chronic health issue or found soul-nourishing work. Apply any lessons learned during Jupiter's last go-round to make this cycle even better.

Eclipses in 2021

May 26: Sagittarius Lunar Eclipse 5°29' (7:13am ET)
June 10: Gemini Solar Eclipse 19°42 (6:52am ET)
November 19: Taurus Lunar Eclipse 27°17 (3:57pm)
December 4: Sagittarius Solar Eclipse 12°17 (2:42am)

Gemini/Sagittarius Eclipses

New conversations, fresh perspectives.

Pour the truth serum! For the second consecutive year, the cosmos serves up a series of mic-dropping eclipses across the Gemini/Sagittarius axis. You've got a message to spread, Libra, but do you have the right platform? Three of the year's four eclipses can help you sharpen your wording, snazz up your branding and crack the code on digital marketing.

Two of the year's eclipses will fall in Sagittarius, spotlighting your third house of communication, kindred spirits and local initiatives. As the zodiac's diplomat and socialite, this will be a welcome boost. It all begins on May 26 when the Sagittarius lunar (full moon) eclipse delivers major news, a tide-turning conversation or an exciting new social connection—whether you were expecting it or not! Someone from your peer group, like a sibling, roommate or coworker, could play a key role in developments, perhaps nominating you to be part of an elite organization or inviting you onto the launch team of a profitable start-up. Local activism may call so loudly that you step into a crucial organizer's role that fills your life with purpose.

Since the third house is all about "twinning," solo ventures may suddenly evolve into partnerships. Look no further than your own zip code for opportunity and fascinating dynamic duos! You might even link up with someone you met last year, near the corresponding solar (new moon) eclipse of December 14, 2020. Scroll through your timeline. A casual holiday season connection you made six months ago might blossom into a mid-year mogul mashup near May 26.

Since lunar eclipses can sweep away what no longer serves us, May 26 could mark a bittersweet passage. A friendship may abruptly end, or you could have a painfully honest conversation about "growing apart" from someone who's been an everyday fixture in your life. If you've been waiting for important news, you'll have a much clearer idea of where you stand now. Get ready to practice new connecting strategies, such as active listening, non-violent communication and mirroring.

Pack your bags for adventure during the June 10 solar (new moon) eclipse in Gemini! This event spotlights your ninth house of travel, study and entrepreneurship. Global connections are calling, Libra, whether that means visiting far-flung destinations or communing with an international fanbase through virtual platforms. New friendships and global connections might also spark up around these interactive eclipses.

The high-minded Gemini eclipse can also spark a metaphysical moment. Will you dive into the texts of ancient philosophers or crack open A Course in Miracles? Writing, teaching and media projects could beckon, or you might even find yourself enrolling in courses, either to pursue a degree or for personal growth and development workshops. The "lifelong learner" energy of this eclipse series will be a boon to your already-curious mind. This eclipse could bring a sudden opportunity to publish your work, teach or deliver a motivational speech. If you've been playing small, you'll get a glimpse of your limitless potential, as well as a rush of inspiration to pursue it.

The final moonburst of 2021 arrives on December 4 with the Sagittarius solar (new moon) eclipse. In our experience, solar eclipses can be a little gentler and less abrupt than lunar ones, as they herald new beginnings rather than grand finales. You could begin a writing or media project or step into a powerful role in your neighborhood. (Mayor Libra, anyone?) A like-minded soul you've been secretly sniffing out all year could evolve into a pivotal collaborator as the year winds down. Spark up that synergy! Trial runs are fine under the variable energy of the third house. Test the waters by co-hosting a seasonal initiative, such as a live music fundraiser, tree-lighting for charity or something local, like a progressive holiday dinner (or cookie-baking party) with beloved neighbors.

If you've got a project or idea to pitch, there's still time to knock it out of the park before the year wraps. If you're a business owner, this is a great time to rebrand, debut a new logo or updated look or to team up with kindred spirits on a joint project. Since eclipses are known for bringing surprises, your missing puzzle piece might even be someone you considered "the competition." Just like that, they could switch from rival to ride-or-die partner, which is always preferable for your peace-loving sign. Cognitive dissonance aside, embrace the evolution. Eclipses just work like that!

Taurus/Scorpio Eclipses

Magnetic superpowers.

On November 19, a new eclipse series opens across the Taurus-Scorpio axis, charging up your sex appeal and earning power for two whole years. This one is a lunar (full moon) eclipse in Taurus, the ruler of your seductive, magnetic eighth house. Manifesting mojo will be high, but be careful what you wish for, Libra! What (and who) you attract isn't bound to go away quickly. Chemistry that's been simmering could heat to exothermic levels near November 19! That's great if it fits with your 2021 life plans, but eclipses can also disrupt the status quo. This impossible-to-ignore attraction might be with someone outside your current relationship—and resisting temptation will require extreme willpower.

For some Libras, surrendering to passion will be the right choice. Just make sure there's equal amounts of trust to accompany the lust. This erotically charged eclipse is not for the faint of heart because it demands loyalty and long-term allegiance. If those ingredients aren't available with the object of your affections, you could get swept into a derailing obsession. (So not worth it, Libra!) By the same token, this eclipse could illuminate a soulmate—possibly one who's been hiding in plain sight for months…or years!

Financial partnerships will get a strong gust from these eclipses, since Taurus/Scorpio is your money axis. Money may flow in from unexpected sources during this two-year circuit. Other revenue streams may dry up, forcing an overdue career pivot. Eclipses are sometimes "cruel to be kind," eliminating outmoded activities that we are clutching onto out of sheer habit.

Venus Retrograde in Capricorn: Home life, interrupted.

December 19, 2021–January 29, 2022

Hygge season (in the northern hemisphere) will be rich and rewarding in 2021. For this, you can thank your ruler, convivial Venus, who will be hibernating in Capricorn and the cozy cave of your fourth house for an extended spell, from November 5, 2021, to March 6, 2022. Forget about settling down for any long winter's naps! You may be happy hiding out behind closed doors, but you'll be a busy bee all the while, planning family gatherings, turning your stovetop into a test kitchen and your dining room table into the site of a home-based business.

Venus is the planet of love and romance, and this four-month cycle will bring out your dutiful nature. In Capricorn, Venus plays the long game, helping you build an inspiring future and solidify a sense of emotional security. Tap into the law of attraction. Like attracts like, Libra! To magnetize the sensual and sensitive partner of your dreams, you have to be tuned in to your own internal workings. By holding a high bar to your emotionally intelligent self, your existing relationships will also thrive.

Raising your vibration will be extra-extra important beginning on December 19, 2021, when Venus dips into retrograde until January 29, 2022. Every 584 days, the planet of beauty, love and radiance pivots into reverse, which can be a powerful review period for assessing the progress of all relationships. Speedbumps are generally unavoidable during Venus' six-week retrograde…and in some cases, the backspin can bring a full-force meltdown. Here's hoping it doesn't come to that, Libra! But even if everything is copacetic in your mind, check in with your nearest and dearest. Are your futures aligned or have you hit a fork in the road, making it hard to support each other's goals without sacrificing core needs? New arrangements must be made if one or both of you feels perpetually dissatisfied. Thankfully, while Venus is in Capricorn, cooler heads prevail, increasing the likelihood of a civilized conversation.

Nostalgia and sentimentality are favored during Venus retrograde. With your fourth house of family lit up like a Christmas tree by radiant Venus in Capricorn, holiday season 2021 could be legendary. Direct people's attention

> ## "With Venus going retrograde in your domestic zone, you may have to negotiate some new household rules."

to fond memories. Beyond the feelgood buzz, it's a great strategy for avoiding blowups during this oft-stressful season. If you're hosting a gathering, prepare in advance! Mix multigenerational playlists, organize games, compile a carousel of family photos to project onto the wall. In short, create whatever warm-fuzzy distractions you can to reduce the tension. Subtle and subliminal cues are also recommended, like piping in relaxing essential oils through an aromatherapy diffuser and dimming the lights to an ambient setting.

With Venus retrograde going down in your domestic zone, you may have to negotiate some new household rules. Is your space being shared fairly or is someone (er, you?) dominating the square footage? Do you have ample privacy for meditating and doing your creative work? If not, draw up a more suitable floor plan. Of course, this may be too much of a luxury as our homes became multifunctional in the post-pandemic world. Some Libras may opt to rent an outside studio (even a shared space) for dance practice or new moon circles.

If you want to bless your nest with dreamier décor, get started around November 5, when Venus in Capricorn sharpens your aesthetic vision and makes you a pro at "sourcing" everything from vintage replica wallpaper to the perfect, creamy-textured paint. But hold off on any massive renovations until Venus is back on track after January 29, 2022. Make mood boards for every style you're drawn to, from clean-lined Scandinavian minimalism to opulent "bordello chic." After all, you need to weigh all options before you choose a favorite (and spend a fortune). It's a Libra's prerogative!

Want to bury the hatchet with a ghosting friend or challenging relative? Diplomatic Venus can help. But when the peacekeeping planet is off her game from December 19, 2021 to January 29, 2022, don't rush to patch things over. Retrogrades helps us drill down below the surface. Unless you get to the root of the matter, you'll only find the unresolved issue rearing up ten times stronger. Start with a phone call and maybe a coffee date on neutral territory after that. Or, just give yourself a breather if you keep hitting the same wall with your inner circle. Time heals all wounds.

Of course, we teach people how to treat us, Libra. In your moments of venting, you may have ignited their protective natures, making them worry unnecessarily about your emotional wellbeing. Be more mindful of how you present your "woe is me!" moments. Sure, you might spring back like an elastic band, but you can't expect loved ones to volley back and forth with your moods on an endless loop.

Venus retrograde is an optimal time to reunite with the people who will never be knocked off your favorites list, like chosen family, close-in-age cousins, and beloved parents. Set up that spare bedroom and invite guests, or better yet, meet for a New Year's getaway somewhere that feels like a sentimental spot to you all. Sharing home-cooked meals is the best way to bond during this Venus cycle. Rent a house with a giant kitchen and whip up those legendary family dishes that remind you of the good old days. ✳

Scorepio

HOROSCOPE

2021 HIGHLIGHTS

LOVE

Relationships take a turn for the intimate, which is just the way your security-loving sign likes it. As Jupiter and Saturn anchor in your fourth house of nesting and emotional security, closeness is what you crave. (As long as you have some sort of privacy, too!) Cohabitating, starting (or blending) families, building your dream house—topics like these could be on the agenda for coupled Scorpios. Single? Traditional types will make you swoon, but make sure there's enough "spice" to accompany the "nice." Bawdy Jupiter bolts into Pisces mid-year, setting your head-turning, romantic fifth house on fire from May 13 to July 28. Circle these dates as "high season" for love—and get ready for a sexy surprise at the June 10 solar eclipse! On November 19, the lunar eclipse in Taurus could cement a relationship that's been growing closer all year. Sharpen your communication skills when Venus embarks on a four-month tour of Capricorn starting November 5. When the love planet turns retrograde for six weeks on December 19, your words can make or break a relationship!

MONEY

Kitchen-table side hustle, anyone? As serious Saturn and enterprising Jupiter join forces in Aquarius and your domestic zone, you could set up shop at Chateau Scorpio and make a killing! A family-based business may be the path to prosperity. Just make sure everyone's turf is clearly marked! Three eclipses— on May 26, June 10 and December 4—activate your money axis. The way you earn and save could shift near these dates, or you might be invited to be part of a promising investment. Scorpio business owners could raise funds for a venture, especially if it has a socially responsible mission or incorporates technology. Powerful women may show up as mentors, or you could get involved with a company whose mission supports families, children and female-identified people. Jupiter's fame-boosting tour of Pisces, from May 13 to July 28, could draw media attention to your work. Camera-ready Scorpios can burst onto the scene as influencers, YouTubers or other public figures during this mid-year cycle.

WELLNESS

Nourish thyself! Food and mood are intricately connected under 2021's emotionally charged starmap. From anxiety to lethargy, what you put on your plate will affect the way you show up in your daily life. Experiment with new eating plans or work with a nutritionist. Treatments like acupuncture can ease digestion issues (which may express as migraines), as can natural supplements like digestive enzymes. Tend to your emotional health with therapy, support groups and stress-relieving workouts. Gentle exercise can do wonders to tune your body this year, so swap some of those power vinyasa sessions for yin yoga—and don't underestimate the healing properties of an oxytocin-boosting walk with a beloved friend!

FRIENDS & FAMILY

Gather by the hearth! Family (including chosen family) is a primary focus of 2021. That means you have cosmic permission to draw a tight ring around your inner circle and concentrate on the relationships that mean the most to you. Then again, Scorpio, is it time to cut a few cords? Relationships that have grown codependent buckle under Saturn's strain—and with Saturn in your domestic house, the struggle for individuality may involve your mom or a female child. Embrace the space! Adulting is healthy for everyone (who's over 21, at least). Once you get through this, you'll re-establish the bond on more equal footing. Siblings, coworkers and friends close in age will warm your holiday season, as convivial Venus cruises through Capricorn for four months on November 5. A holiday season reunion trip could be epic when Venus spins retrograde for six weeks on December 19.

Scorpio
POWER DATES

SCORPIO NEW MOON
November 4 (5:14 PM ET)

SCORPIO FULL MOON
April 26 (11:31 PM ET)

SUN IN SCORPIO
October 23 – November 21

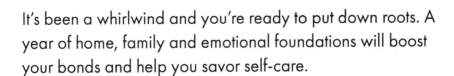

It's been a whirlwind and you're ready to put down roots. A year of home, family and emotional foundations will boost your bonds and help you savor self-care.

Saturn in Aquarius: Stop and drop anchor!
December 17, 2020–March 7, 2023

A security-building cycle is underway as stabilizing Saturn braves the waters of Aquarius, sailing through your fourth house of home, family and nurturing from December 17, 2020, until March 7, 2023. Nesting instincts are activated as the ringed taskmaster guides you toward savvier ways to live comfortably and economically.

How are things under your roof, Scorpio? As serious Saturn adds heft to your domestic plans, you may be ready to plant deeper roots, perhaps buying (or selling) property, renovating to create more privacy, or moving to a city with a more amenable cost of living. Creating a sacred oasis is a Scorpio talent, no matter how much square footage you have to work with. With your eye for beauty and attunement to mood and atmosphere, you literally feel "off" when color, light and energy are imbalanced in a space. To function in the outside world, you need a well-appointed home—the tidier, the better.

That said, shelter requirements may fluctuate over the next two years, as you evolve under karmic Saturn's adulting influence. You may come to the bittersweet conclusion that you've outgrown your digs, or conversely, feel inspired to live a more minimalist lifestyle under Saturn's austerity plan.

No need to rush any such process, though. As one of the zodiac's four "fixed" signs, embracing change isn't exactly in your DNA. Take a slow, methodical approach, but not so plodding that you fail to gain traction. Fortunately, risk-taker Jupiter will be co-piloting through Aquarius for much of 2021, which will help you hit the accelerator when cautious Saturn flashes you enough green lights to go! (More on that later in this chapter.)

Scorpios in relationships may opt to cohabitate. Is it time to take the grown-up plunge and start looking for your first love nest? Charged up as you may be with new relationship energy, Saturn warns us that only fools rush in. Major decisions should be rooted in both practicality and romance. Talk through every possible scenario, from how you'll divide up housing costs to the functionality of every room. That meditation cave you're envisioning might clash with your partner's desire for a home office—something to consider before you settle on a floor plan. For other Scorpios, restrictive Saturn may shift your lifestyle, limiting the time you spend together. Maybe one of you has to relocate temporarily for work or go help an ailing relative on a rotating schedule. There will be details to work out, so be patient!

Saturn briefly visited Aquarius last year—from March 21 to July 1, 2020— just days after sheltering in place was mandated in major cities around the globe. Quarantine was particularly heavy for many Scorpios, as this disruptive cycle forced you to reexamine your entire lifestyle. While privacy is essential to your inner serenity, you love sharing energy with good friends, usually over craft cocktails or artisanal coffee. Without your RDA of people-watching and

"What do you want your inner circle to look like in 2021...and beyond?"

shameless flirting, your mood may have tanked. The silver lining? Saturn's first lonely pass through Aquarius renewed your appreciation for the power of human connection. The next two years are sure to open your heart even wider.

Let's get real: Most people aren't your cup of oolong, Scorpio. With your psychic sensitivity, you can be picky about whom you let into your field. But those who pass the litmus test are rewarded with legendary love and loyalty. Which begs the question: What do you want your inner circle to look like in 2021...and beyond? Your vision could inform everything from your extracurricular plans to your home zip code in the next phase of life.

Saturn plays the long game, so think ahead. For example, if you're a culture vulture who intends have children within the next few years, you may sacrifice downtown proximity in exchange for more square footage or a place with a yard. You could opt to stay put in tight living quarters while you save up for moving costs or consider some other practical reasons (e.g., you can walk to work or stay in a particular school district). Since Saturn rules structure, you might benefit from building storage systems or working with a professional organizer. We're not saying new shelves will change your life...but we're not saying they won't, either!

This isn't going to be the easiest Saturn phase in the world, Scorpio. While in Aquarius, Saturn forms a challenging 90-degree angle (called a "square") to your Sun. Squares force us to stop procrastinating and go face the music. If your foundation has been shaky for a while, the coming two-plus years help you strengthen it. Learning to nurture yourself is part of the plan. Regimented Saturn wants you to schedule self-care, not just talk about it theoretically. Eat meals at regular intervals, go to sleep at the same time every night (yes, we said night, O' Nocturnal One), and incorporate fitness into your daily routine.

The fourth house rules women and female-identified folks. In 2021, you could align with a powerful group of ladies or become involved in an organization that forwards women's rights. A relationship with a female colleague or mentor could evolve into a serious business partnership, or perhaps you'll benefit from the wisdom of an older woman. On the flip side, you may find yourself stepping into this role, grooming a younger upstart or playing mentor-slash-momager to a colleague. An aging parent or relative may require more support from you this year which, in turn, could lead to you taking on a more grown-up role in your family structure.

Got mother issues? Maturity-planet Saturn in your maternal fourth house might spark a possible rift with your mom or child(ren). If you've been too close for comfort, weighty Saturn hands you the psychic scissors and commands you to cut the cord. Space and autonomy can strengthen your bond—even if there's grief involved with letting go. Cautious Saturn may delay your efforts to start or expand a family, or seriously change your lifestyle to accommodate children. Scorpio parents might struggle with a child going through a tough cycle (oh, those tricky preteen years) or feel the pangs of empty nest syndrome. During this stoic Saturn cycle, you may not have the usual warmth and closeness with your kin. It's a time when you need to "do the right thing, not the easy thing." Exert loving but firm boundaries, Scorpio.

And hey, that's a sound strategy for dealing with everyone in your life now. Saturn in your sensitive fourth house teaches you to lead with the right balance of head and heart. You may weather some tough lessons about people who prey on your (secretly) soft side or charm you into codependent enabling. This year, especially while Saturn is retrograde from May 23 to October 10, you may have to revamp (or even terminate) relationships that are draining and one-sided. Let others take responsibility for their grown-up choices, and you do the same.

That said, you don't have to be a one-Scorpio show. Saturn can help you build a solid, nurturing support system—whether it's a friend circle, a professional mastermind group or your own family. In 2021, you'll perfect the balance between shared goals and self-reliance.

Saturn in Aquarius square Uranus in Taurus
February 17, June 14 & December 24

Your inner circle is going to be mighty influential this year, but how much power do they have over your decisions? Allowing them to hold sway could lead to all kinds of frustration in 2021. Three times this year—on February 17, June 14 and December 24—boat-rocking Uranus in Taurus and your seventh house of relationships crashes into an eye-opening square with Saturn in Aquarius. These rare mashups can set off alarm bells. Ironically, the reason for said alarms is likely because you're playing it too safe, not that you're stepping into imminent danger.

Scorpios are family-oriented, fixed-sign creatures. People may be surprised at your preference for all things "kid-tested, mother-approved"—especially since this can run counter to your bawdy side. Oftentimes, you're the glue that holds everyone together in your crew. And yeah, that can involve a bit of clever coercion as you get wayward relatives to fall in line with your vision. But your ability to see the big picture is one of your strengths, and those who know you tend to trust in your decision-making powers.

So, Scorpio, what happens when the tables are turned, and you want to break away from the pack? You could be faced with that very conundrum during the three Saturn-Uranus squares. With Uranus in your opposite sign, you may suddenly feel a polar pull in a new direction. Possibly, this will involve forging a partnership with someone who doesn't necessarily fit in with your fam. Or hey, maybe they do, but you want to slip away into a couple bubble for a while and not be bothered by any "outsiders." Whether for business or pleasure, you may be annoyed by anyone who tries to wedge themselves into your dynamic duo.

Another way these squares could play out? Coupled Scorpios may find themselves longing to do more family-oriented activities. If parenting is on the agenda, you could get rather insistent about getting the babymaking, IVF, adoption paperwork, etc. underway. But is it really the right time? The chaotic energy of Saturn-Uranus squares could set you and your closest companions on edge, or even throw your relationships out of whack. Conversely, if your partner's relatives have been a thorn in your side, you may need to lay down some limits. Can you tell your mother-in-law to stand down without sending her away for good? Even if you handle this with kid gloves, bonds may fray. Don't do anything rash near February 17, June 14 or December 24.

If kids and family aren't the topic *du jour*, renegotiating boundaries could be. Do you share a home with anyone? Disruptive Uranus could reveal incompatibilities around the way you divvy up the space. Privacy-hound Scorpios: Maybe there is a way you could happily cohabitate without having to sacrifice your precious cave time. Let innovative Uranus open the doors to exploration.

Jupiter in Aquarius & Pisces

January 1: Aquarius (since December 19, 2020)
May 13: Pisces (retrograde June 20)
July 28: Aquarius (retrograde until October 18)
December 28: Pisces (until December 20, 2022)

In 2021, Jupiter will shift back and forth between Aquarius and Pisces. Normally, Jupiter makes an unbroken trek through a single sign for 12 to 13 months, but in 2021, we'll see the planet of fortune and growth in two signs.

Jupiter in Aquarius

December 19, 2020–May 13, 2021
July 28–December 28, 2021

Party at Chez Scorpio!

Regardless of Saturn's tour of your domestic fourth house, all will not be quiet on the Scorpio home front this year! Exuberant, adventurous Jupiter makes two passes through Aquarius in 2021, countering Saturn's somber effect. From December 19, 2020, until May 13, 2021, then again from July 28 to December 28, the red-spotted rabble-rouser makes waves in your fourth house of family, home and emotional security. How flexible can you be, Scorpio? Saturn restricts while Jupiter expands. With this planetary paradox activating such a deeply personal zone of your chart, you may welcome seismic shifts one moment, then hit the brakes the next.

The fourth house sits at the very bottom of the horoscope wheel, representing our deepest foundations and roots. Jupiter's presence puts the cosmic spotlight on your closest ties and the ways you support yourself. Your living situation could also go through some big and exciting shifts. Jupiter visits this part of your chart every 10 to 12 years. It was last in Aquarius from January 5, 2009, to January 17, 2010, so themes from that time period could repeat now.

This heart-opening Jupiter transit puts you squarely in touch with your deepest feelings—not that your passionate sign needs any help with that. But you keep some important parts of yourself safeguarded far within, fearing that others will hurt or reject you if they see your "broken bits." Live-out-loud Jupiter won't let you hide your humanity. This is a good thing, Scorpio! When you suppress your authentic nature, you can come across as intense, stormy or aggressively defensive. Other times, you lapse into "overfunctioning," playing caretaker to the world at your own expense.

Broad-spectrum Jupiter helps you reveal a wider range of emotions—and in turn, some inspiring and generous people could enter your orbit. New levels of honesty and transparency can strengthen your relationships. Let a few tears flow, cry on some shoulders, voice your feelings. On the flip side, if you're always the one being coddled, work on developing more emotional resilience. Sure, you can be "precious" every now and again. But too much of that high-maintenance energy can prevent you from forming an adult relationship based on equality and mutual respect.

Be patient with your process. No matter how hard you try to contain your feelings, they can be big and all-consuming during this sensitive cycle. But you don't want to drown in your own emotion ocean. Keep the "life ring" of inner circle friends active on group chat. You might even set up a weekly call to check in and support one another. Jupiter makes everything bigger, including your already-powerful sentiments. Counterintuitive as it may seem, challenge yourself to be more vulnerable!

Friendships that have hovered in a semi-casual zone for years could deepen, evolving into the "chosen family" category. Some risk is required! Instead of waiting for people to prove that they're trustworthy, spark up intimate dialogues.

You'll quickly see who passes the Scorpio sniff test. Can they host conversations about complex topics or do talks devolve into dragging and gossiping? Are they responsive to your invitations or are you working too hard for attention? Loyalty points must be earned, of course, but you've gotta start somewhere!

Jupiter governs travel and long-distance exploration, so having this globetrotting planet in your domestic zone can be a bit of a paradox. You may decide to take home on the road for part of 2021, perhaps spending a month traveling around in an RV or apartment-swapping with friends as you explore a seasonal residence in their cities. With growth-oriented Jupiter in charge, this year's starmap will help you feel at home or comfortable wherever you go. The key is to build a greater sense of security without becoming insular or a shut-in.

And if you don't emerge from your cozy cave that often, you can still bring the wider world to you. Join a mastermind group with participants from every continent—or a teacher who livestreams from a far-flung locale. Learn a foreign language that's spoken in one of your dream countries. Fluency in Italian will come in handy when you can finally rent that villa on the Amalfi Coast or scout out the best empanadas in Buenos Aires. This year, you might get a new roommate who hails from a different country, or a relative (perhaps a parent) could move in with you. Globetrotting Jupiter welcomes some interesting and colorful people into your quarters.

Women could play a key role in opening doors and inspiring you. Surround yourself with powerful females who "made it" without selling their souls. You might also go into business with a family member this year, or find work involving women's issues, children, hospitality, art or interior design. Your relationship with women, children and mothers (or maternal figures) could also undergo a major growth cycle. Some Scorpios will get pregnant or expand their families this year; others may move, even pulling up the stakes for a long-distance relocation.

The parent-child dynamic is one of the most pivotal bonds for water signs, but if yours is strained, Jupiter will help you evolve. Perhaps you're still trying to be the "hero child" and win your folks' approval, or just hiding parts of your life for fear they won't understand. Rethink that strategy, Scorpio. A series of honest conversations can free you up to relate to each other as adults instead of getting swept into constant power struggles and bids for validation. A visit to your hometown or to a nostalgic place from your personal history could help you put your past into a balanced perspective—or just warm your heart by reminding you where you came from.

Kitchen table start-up, anyone? Under enterprising Jupiter's influence, your household might become the bustling hub of cottage industry. Maybe you'll start a home-based business or figure out a way to make #WFH your permanent way of life. Who cares if you stay in PJs until 2PM when your productivity is sky-high? If you do your best work in a yoga pants with your Labradoodle by your side, this could be the year to launch that online store or turn Chateau Scorpio into a satellite office.

Nostalgic connections may surge while Jupiter is in Aquarius. Looking for love? You might reconnect with a childhood sweetheart or "the one that got away." (Funny how fetching you both look without the awkward braces or ill-fitting training bra…) Follow any intuitive flashes to get back in touch. If nothing else, you could finally get the closure you need to move on. But who knows, Scorpio? With so much history between you, there may be a lot to excavate. Plus, fortune favors the bold when Jupiter's in town. 'Fess up to your feelings, if you're still holding a torch. Reignited…and it feels so good!

Jupiter in Pisces

May 13–July 28
December 28, 2021–May 10, 2022
October 28, 2022–December 20, 2022

Come out of your shell again.

Cozy as 2021 may be, don't put every bandage dress and formal blazer into deep storage! Home might start to feel somewhat claustrophobic on May 13, as expansive Jupiter swings into fellow water sign Pisces, setting your fifth house of glamour, passion and self-expression ablaze until July 28. This brief and festive circuit will repeat again at the end of the year, from December 28, 2021, until May 11, 2022!

The spotlight beckons while Jupiter is in your flamboyant fifth house, perhaps bringing fame or recognition for your talents. An epic romance might even be in the cards or perhaps a pregnancy (the fifth house rules fertility). The clouds part and your stormy moods lift—at last! Say hello to a glittering cycle filled with high-key interactions, bursts of creative inspiration, and maybe an epic love story or two. The red-spotted planet hasn't visited this part of your chart since January 17, 2010, to January 22, 2011, so look back to that time for possible recurring themes.

A cross-cultural love connection may spark up while globetrotting Jupiter traverses Pisces' free-flowing seas. Coupled Scorpios can stoke the embers with a spiritual sojourn. If conditions allow, visit one the vortexes of the world, like Sedona, Arizona or Maui's Haleakalā Volcano. It's time to grow, follow your bliss and ask yourself: Does this make my heart feel expansive? If the answer isn't yes, put that activity on hold. With Jupiter here for only two and a half months, you can't afford to squander one of the most joy-inducing periods of the year.

Creative Scorpios will feel the strong guiding presence of the muse, so let your inner artiste or performer emerge onto a wider stage. In soulful Pisces, Jupiter ushers in divine downloads, especially when you can get your brain in a meditative state. Pisces rules the dream realm, so keep a capture tool on the nightstand. Who knows? You might just compose a symphony while you sleep!

Your career could take a turn for the public between May 13 and July 28, or again at the very end of the year. With the daring planet camping in your theatrical and self-expressive fifth house, artists, performers and creative types could gain major recognition. Get ready to be signed or discovered! An international fan base could be the first to spot your gifts, as global Jupiter carries your impact worldwide. Set it off virtually in Seoul, Copenhagen or San Francisco, Scorpio!

You might even decide to take a sabbatical mid-year so you can sharpen your gifts. Maybe you'll invest some hard-earned funds from your day job to shoot a music video or work with a private painting instructor. Even if you aren't in a creative field, Jupiter in Pisces could encourage you to explore hidden talents (we recommend picking up *The Artist's Way* by Julia Cameron), or developing yourself as an arts appreciator.

Eclipses in 2021

May 26: Sagittarius Lunar Eclipse 5°29' (7:13am ET)
June 10: Gemini Solar Eclipse 19°42 (6:52am ET)
November 19: Taurus Lunar Eclipse 27°17 (3:57pm)
December 4: Sagittarius Solar Eclipse 12°17 (2:42am)

Gemini/Sagittarius Eclipses

Hello, money magnet!

Three of 2021's four eclipses fall along your wealth axis, ramping up your earning power and revealing untapped revenue streams. These Gemini/Sagittarius eclipses transform the ways you spend, save, earn and invest. But don't cling to outmoded processes! Maybe it's time to downsize or reorganize. You've been raising your financial IQ ever since this eclipse series lifted off on June 5, 2020. Stay alert! These moon-sponsored masterclasses are in session until December 4, 2021.

First up: On May 26, the lunar (full moon) eclipse in Sagittarius could bring a well-deserved windfall or an epic career breakthrough. This full moon is the manifestation of events that ignited six months prior, during the December 14, 2020, total solar (new moon) eclipse in Sagittarius. If you've hustled through the first half of 2021, prepare for a lush harvest at the end of May.

The twist? This bounty could come from an unexpected source. Maybe you'll field multiple offers, but with a high-pressure deadline that intensifies the urgency to choose or lose. Adventure and novelty hold sway, but as you "secure the bag," think about the long term. Before you say yes to any tempting gigs, are the hours reasonable? (And by reasonable, we know nocturnal Scorpios don't mind burning a quart of midnight oil here and there.) Does the company offer benefits or a work environment that suits your lifestyle? Does this qualify as a growth experience, or can you build industry cred? If these "vital stats" check out, you could leap toward a game-changing opportunity mid-year!

The June 10 Gemini solar (new moon) eclipse is the only one this year to touch down in your eighth house of shared resources, joint ventures and long-term financial planning. You may suddenly buy or sell property, make an investment or combine your assets—possibly through a business alliance or romantic merger. The eighth house is the "big money" sector, ruling funds that come in a lump sum rather than at an hourly rate. (Think: passive income.) You may be inspired to create a product that pays in royalties, affiliate commission or that can be downloaded multiple times for a fee, like an online course. Applying for a grant or hoping to raise a round of funding? Get rolling on the paperwork and pitching near June 10!

Track your expenses, too, so there are no unpleasant surprises mid-June. Have you calculated the taxes from any increased earnings? You may have to deal with an interest charge or I.O.U. that comes due. This may be your cue to refinance a loan, such as your mortgage or college tuition. Explore debt consolidation plans, which can reduce monthly expenses. But make sure to calculate everything, Scorpio. Banks are happy to tack on upfront fees (from "transfers" or "service charges") which could increase the total amount of your loan. Do you add to cart compulsively, racking up credit card charges? This eclipse could spur you to dig deeper, perhaps working with a therapist, money coach or joining a group like Debtors Anonymous.

There's a larger message here: It's time to make your money work harder for you! Learn about investing, speak to a financial planner, up your retirement or 401(k) allocation. You may buy or sell real estate or begin saving up for a future home purchase. Need to raise a round of funding? People could line up to put dollars behind your dreams. Get that business plan going!

A steamy relationship moment may be in the cards near June 10. With the solar eclipse activating your erotic eighth house (AKA the Scorpio house), you could meet someone who ignites your passions on every level. A relationship that was percolating in the friend zone could reveal deeper potential, which you'll be uncharacteristically keen to explore. Lusty chemistry aside, are you dealing with a trustworthy soul? Under the obfuscating shadow of the eclipse, it's hard to tell. Pace yourself, Scorpio…as best you can.

Then, it's back to business on December 4! The final eclipse of 2021—a Sagittarius solar (new moon) eclipse—plants the seeds for a fresh career path or money management style. Work duties may shift, and quite suddenly, under these metamorphic moonbeams. Network your way across the holiday party circuit.

A casual conversation near the eggnog station could evolve into synergistic talks about how to combine forces (for profit!) in 2022.

The best news? The December 4 solar eclipse is the final one to hit your money houses until 2029. While these lunar shakeups are ultimately helpful, they provoke their fair share of anxiety. Keep forging ahead with career goals through the holiday season. Be proactive. Near December 4, the runway to success will clear for takeoff. Off you go!

Taurus/Scorpio Eclipses

Balancing between "me" and "we."

Highlight November 19 in neon yellow: A new eclipse series begins across the Taurus/Scorpio axis, energizing your seventh house committed partnerships and your first house of fearless self-expression. Until October 28, 2022, these game-changing moonbeams usher in exhilarating developments for your relationships and your personal passions.

Is it time to make it official…or call the whole thing off? A partnership could hit a milestone moment on November 19, as the Taurus lunar (full moon) eclipse expedites developments with your love interest or a business partner. You and the LOYL could sign a lease together, get engaged or decide to move ahead with babymaking plans. Single Scorpios might meet a soulmate or have a major sexual awakening, as a combustible attraction blazes up out of the blue. This won't be a no-strings hookup though. With a karmic eclipse guiding the process, it could feel more like a past-life reunion. Let the dust settle before you decide that this is "meant to be." Even if you have a strong soul connection, everything has to add up in the material world, too.

Ready to bolt from a toxic relationship? November 19 could evoke a swift and sudden split. For some Scorpios, this eclipse may also bring a breakup or dissolution of a work partnership, as lunar eclipses push us off the fence into a firm decision. If you're the one left stunned by a departure, trust that the universe has something much better coming your way. Eclipses blow in and clear out anything that no longer serves us. Time will reveal the hidden gift.

217

Venus Retrograde in Capricorn: Romantic real talk.

December 19, 2021 –January 29, 2022

Cat and mouse game, anyone? Sultry Scorpios love to tempt and tease. But starting November 5, you'll be down to experiment with new seduction techniques. Love planet Venus swings into Capricorn and activates your articulate, variety-loving third house for an extended stay, taking up residence until March 6, 2022.

This cycle offers a chance to sharpen your "direct communication" axe. Instead of dropping hints, see what happens if you straight-up ask for what you want. No, this might not send as many frissons of tension rippling through the air. But if you're really being honest, how is that pursuer-distancer dance working out for you? Mystery can backfire—or blow relationships off-course—if you take too long to reveal your intentions.

Fasten your seatbelt, garter belt, whatever! Venus in the third house blesses you with a silver tongue, which gets the sexy action going a lot faster than you'd expect. As if you didn't already have enough ammo to launch a charm offensive this holiday season! Instead of dropping hints, you'll be flirty and forward. (Mistletoe game: skyrocketing!) Got an idea to pitch? A product to sell? Few can say no to you when Venus vectors through your third house—especially when you lean into Capricorn's authority and confidence.

But in your everyday interactions, how effectively do you spell out your needs? Do you listen attentively or cut people off mid-sentence? Do you divulge with the vulnerability of a post-TED-talk Brené Brown (who shares your sign)? Or, like the Scorpio researcher herself has admitted, do you struggle to give up true control?

Wherever you fall on the communication continuum, Venus will hold up the mirror. People's responses and reactions are the most honest reflection of what's going on inside of you. Want to improve your relationships? Change is an inside job during this four-month Venus cycle. Minor shifts—like taking a moment to validate someone's POV before countering with your perspective—can transform a potential diatribe into a productive dialogue. In some cases, being more expressive can thaw the frozen tundra of an icy connection. Stop giving 'em the cold shoulder, Scorpio, and start asking questions!

Fingers crossed, Venus' tour of Capricorn will set the stage for a holiday season filled with family love and renewed understanding. But…this Venus peace treaty comes with a rider attached. From December 19, 2021, to January 29, 2022, Venus slips into her biennial retrograde. This feather-ruffling cycle happens every 584 days, and when it does, pleasantries may fly out of the window. Formality has its place, especially when gathering in groups. But with Venus in snooze mode, you might not be able to stop yourself from picking a fight with your sister or pushing a friend's buttons with political commentary after your first flute of NYE champagne.

Should tension escalate between December 19 to January 29, 2022, don't storm off. TBH, you could use more real talk with your people, especially peers who fall under the third house's domain: siblings, coworkers and the neighbors you see every day. Selfish behaviors may have crept into your dynamics, or perhaps you've been secretly competing with one another.

Familiarity can breed contempt, Scorpio…we don't have to tell your prickly sign that. But if you want important bonds to stay intact, redraw boundaries while Venus is in reverse. Make sure that everyone has ample space, privacy and autonomy. Let yourself miss people, even develop a little FOMO by sitting out an activity here and there. You'll be much better company when you actually want to see the people you're with!

Looking for love? The friend zone could serve a bounty of unexpected options between November 5, 2021, and March 6, 2022. Warning: Feelings will run hot and cold while Venus is retrograde. What felt like a twin flame rekindling could get SO much more complicated than you bargained for at the year's end. Not sure anything will come of this? Stash your lusty feelings in the vault and see if they're still burning after January 29, 2022.

If you're baehunting during the retrograde, double check those ring fingers and ask obvious questions, like, "Are you in a relationship?" You could attract people who are charismatic but not 100 percent available—mirroring your own secret fears about being "trapped." Stay off that slippery slope. It's all fun and games until the sensitive Scorpio inevitably gets hurt, then stings!

If the sex magic cools off with your S.O. between December 19, 2021, and January 29, 2022, don't panic. The third house governs platonic love, offering a four-month window where you can strengthen the friendship aspect of your bond. Open up a safe space to talk about topics that might feel scary to broach. That's what you'd do for one of your BFFs, right? Even if the "say anything" discussions reveal different points of view, it will be a relief to have the truth out on the table…or the therapist's couch or in the breakout room of a couple's workshop. Scorpios play the long game in love, and you'll be more inspired to do so while Venus traverses traditional Capricorn. Why not learn some skills for mating and relating that can keep you in tune through your sunset years?

In all types of relationships, Venus retrograde tasks you with improving your communication style. People have probably told you (on multiple occasions) that you can be kind of intimidating, Scorpio. Soften the intensity of that penetrating gaze and wait before you start reading people, or guessing their zodiac signs, or investigating their intentions like a CIA agent. This cooperative Venus retrograde can bring a gentle wake-up call to take it from "me" to "we." For every two queries you make, offer up something personal about your own life. We're not telling you to trot out every scandal—but with people who are meant to be in your life for the long haul, we're certain you'll be swapping those stories, too. Sooner or later.

Every eight years, Venus pivots back through the same section of the zodiac wheel (minus two degrees). Scroll back through your timeline to December 21, 2013, to January 31, 2014, which was the last time the planet of love and harmony backtracked through Capricorn and your third house. Similar themes may arise now, even if players and circumstances have changed. You got through it then and you'll emerge stronger this time. Stay present and don't stop communicating! ✷

Sagittarius

HOROSCOPE

2021
HIGHLIGHTS

LOVE

Relationships don't have to be so serious, do they? In 2021, the answer is no...and yes. With the lunar North Node (destiny point) in Gemini, a meant-to-be bond could develop, perhaps in the afterglow (or aftermath) of 2020's events. But with sober Saturn and your ruler, adventurous Jupiter, mixing and mingling in your friendly, flirty third house, you'll be torn. Part of you wants to lock things down, but not at the expense of your autonomy. Lovers may accuse you of keeping them at arm's length, and it's kind of true. Thanks to the karmic South Node in Sagittarius all year, your lens is flipped inward. First step? Give yourself space to be authentic about what makes you feel happy and fulfilled. No, it might not be what society or your lover(s) say is the "right" answer. But thanks to a rare pair of eclipses in your sign on May 26 and December 4, you're ready to dig deep in the name of personal discovery. Once you're clear, Saturn and Jupiter will support you in communicating your vision and creating love by your own design. The June 10 solar eclipse in Gemini activates your relationship zone, which could shake up the status quo and spark a brand-new chapter in amour. When Venus turns retrograde at the year's end from December 19 until January 29, 2022, money matters could become a sore spot. Buffer yourself from the breakdown in advance! Spend this year learning to budget with your partner. Single? Start setting clear boundaries with dates and would-be-mates about who pays for what.

222

MONEY

Last year's Capricorn cluster (Jupiter, Saturn, Pluto, eclipses and the South Node) put major emphasis on your second house of income. Money was on your mind, and not just because of the economic and pandemic turbulence. This year, only Pluto will linger in the Sea Goat's sphere. If you've been pondering a job change, you could finally make the leap! Some Archers are ready to put better boundaries around your work so it doesn't spill into your "free time" 24/7. Innovative Uranus is well into its journey through Taurus and your sixth house of work and wellness. Many hands—along with digital solutions and apps— can lighten your workload. With Jupiter and Saturn in your zone of cooperation, partnering up with a sibling or friend could open up your schedule while paving the way to prosperity. These power planets are also activating your teaching and communication skills. Write that advice book, start your podcast or share your skills through a webinar series. When Venus turns retrograde from December 19, 2021, to January 29, 2022, make sure you have a cushion for unexpected expenses.

WELLNESS

Healing is both an inside and outside job for Archers in 2020. As the karmic South Node treks through your sign, circumstances that are out of alignment with your core needs will be impossible to push through and endure. But this intense transit may force you to deal with shadowy emotions such as shame, grief or your own people-pleasing tendencies as you learn how to take better care of yourself. A mindfulness practice can help you slow down and tune in. Your body will demand attention, too.

The AstroTwins' 2021 Horoscope   223

With disruptor Uranus in Taurus and your sixth house of healthy routines, you can't spend all day hunched in front of a screen. Stop for self-care breaks, dial down stress by setting boundaries and creating privacy. Infuse exercise and nutritious meals into your daily schedule. If you don't, you could get a wakeup call from the November 19 lunar eclipse, the first in a healing two-year series on the Taurus/Scorpio axis. Time is a precious commodity. Be choosy! Keep your schedule clear for well-paying opportunities that have sane deadlines. Remember: Before you say no, always try negotiating a counteroffer!

FRIENDS & FAMILY

Does it feel like everyone wants a piece of your time? You'll be quite the popular one this year, thanks to your ruler Jupiter's tour through Aquarius and your garrulous third house. Exuberant Archers were born with a raging case of FOMO, but saying "Yes!" to too many things could seriously drain you in 2021. Boundary-hound Saturn will crash into three tense squares with Uranus, illuminating the importance of discernment. We know you want to have it all, Archer, but that desire could mean losing out on something (or someone) truly meaningful because you've overcommitted. Is it time to cohabitate or change your living situation? Jupiter's brief visit to Pisces from May 13 to July 28 is an ideal window for dealing with domestic matters. Family pressures could become overwhelming, but you don't have to run away to liberate yourself. Let this candid energy help you speak your truth and enlist your family's support. Ready to pull up the stakes or do some renovations to your home? While Jupiter is in Pisces midyear, you could get this mission in motion, but it might take until 2022 before you make any major moves.

Sagittarius

POWER DATES

SAGITTARIUS NEW MOON
December 4 (2:42 AM ET) Solar Eclipse

SAGITTARIUS FULL MOON
May 26 (7:13 AM ET) Lunar Eclipse

SUN IN SAGITTARIUS
November 21 - December 21

If last year felt like all work and very little play, that will change. To your relief, variety is the spice of 2021 —with lots of people, projects and great conversations that keep life interesting.

Saturn in Aquarius: Say what?!
December 17, 2020–March 7, 2023

Stand firm and speak your truth! Heavy-hitter Saturn, the planet of maturity and structure, is broadcasting from Aquarius and your communicative, cooperative third house all year long. Your words carry more weight than ever during this cosmic cycle, which lasts until March 7, 2023. If you plan to open your mouth or press "publish" on a post, step into your power first. Saturn, the cosmic disciplinarian, challenges you to be impeccable with your messaging. Know your hashtags and stay abreast of the cultural conversations. Whether you're building a platform or already standing on one, weighty Saturn gives you influence.

You first got a taste of this power in 2020. From March 21 until July 1—literally one of the most game-changing periods in recent history—Saturn ran a preview lap through Aquarius, its first visit to this realm since 1994. Whether you were supporting an activist cause, raising funds for someone affected by the virus or simply figuring out how to even post at all, you had to think through every word. That mindfulness will come in handy again.

The trick with Saturn? Get to the point and keep it brief. When there's business to take care of, skip the clever wordplay and philosophical meandering (aka "Sagspeak"). Brevity is the soul of wit when timelord Saturn is in this position. And honestly…what a relief! Mastering this "less is more" approach to communication is a discipline that could open up tons of room in your schedule, Archer.

What will you do with all those extra minutes? And, moreover, asks Saturn…with whom will you spend them? Free-spirited Archers like to roll with a motley crew of characters. You'll become insta-BFFs with anyone—from the steel-drumming street performer to the I.P. attorney who specializes in digital acquisitions. As long as they can hold down a captivating conversation, you're in!

But in 2021, bringing all these friends together for a "come as you are" moment could get tricky. You may feel judged by the company you keep, or worse, get stuck in the middle of tense ideological debates. Yes, 2021 may present prime opportunities to play Cultural Activities Ambassador or superconnector. But there's a time and place for everything. When you're doing business, make sure everyone in your crew can be vouched for and verified. You'll never complete the mission if you're bogged down brokering peace deals.

How you say things matters, too—right down to your inflection. If you've adopted the millennial-era habit of ending every sentence with a question mark, consider that this "upspeaking" may signal a lack of confidence and authority. Ouch! You could go as far as working with a vocal or dictation coach, but really, you could start by recognizing that your thoughts are valuable. No more apologizing for your candid opinions, Sagittarius. That said, check your facts and get your data from credible sources. You could get #Cancelled for shooting from the hip or spreading fake news.

Refining your message could pay off in other ways. You may rise into recognition as a writer, blogger, podcaster or media-maker in 2021. If you've mastered your medium, you might generate revenue as a teacher or motivational speaker. Saturn likes things polished and refined, so don't rely on your ad-libbing gifts. Work from a script or outline. Make sure you really have something to say—and stay focused, please. Again, brevity is the soul of wit.

If you're a business owner, refresh your branding so everything (fonts, logos, colors) is consistent. While Saturn is retrograde (backward) from May 23 to October 11, it's a great time to revamp your marketing materials, presentation style and social media profiles. That curated image will take you far! Writers, artists and inventors should protect intellectual property with trademarks, copyrights and even patent applications. Saturn likes to do everything by the book. If, for example, you "fell into" a job as a life coach but never got certified, diligent Saturn could prompt you to get some formal training under your belt. Trust us, Sagittarius: You'll feel free to charge more when you do things with integrity. There's no cutting corners under Saturn's reign. Luckily, Saturn in Aquarius forms a relatively easy sextile (60-degree angle) to your Sun, so you'll welcome an intellectual challenge or stretch.

The third house rules siblings, neighbors, colleagues and kindred spirits. With wizened Saturn here, you might have growing pains with one or more of these people. Or, you may formalize a collaboration with someone whose skills complement yours. Take those dynamic duo developments slow and steady. Test your synergy by doing a joint project and seeing how that goes before diving into an official partnership. You could also rise into a leadership role in your community, becoming an advocate for a cause you care about. As your fellow Archer Mos Def once said, "That idea of peace and love toward humanity shouldn't be nationalistic or denominational. It should be a chief concern for all mankind."

Love could also arise from the friend zone this year, and it's not bound to be a casual affair. With serious Saturn here, you could fall hard for someone you never saw "that way" before. If you've been in a relationship for a long time, you may need to consciously seek new ways to bond. Pro tip: Start by stimulating your intellect and let your body follow.

No matter your status, with Saturn in unconventional Aquarius, you don't have to plug relationships into a traditional script. Since the third house can bring things in pairs, some Sagittarians may be torn between two lovers, or three! Or maybe your affections are split between a person and your personal passions, and you want to devote equal time to both. All that Saturn really requires is integrity and stability. If you're willing to be honest—and to put in the work that's required to listen and communicate effectively—you really could architect a love life that suits you to the core.

Saturn in Aquarius square Uranus in Taurus
February 17, June 14 & December 24

Word is bond…or is it, Sagittarius? Under 2021's friendlier skies, it may feel perfectly reasonable to rush into collaborations based on a "good feeling" or "mutual understanding." But…screeeeeeech! You might be the zodiac's gambler, but those are the kinds of risks that ruin friendships, and frankly, can screw you over big time in 2021.

Three times this year, wrench-throwing Uranus in your hypervigilant sixth house crashes into a challenging square (90-degree angle) with Saturn in your communicative third. Impatient, eager and optimistic you may be, but you'll need to put those qualities on ice near February 17, June 14 and December 24. Paperwork, contracts, budgets and schedules? Dealing with this stuff can feel downright torturous to many a Sag. And sure, you can outsource these tasks to a degree, but you won't want to keep your head in the sand in 2021. Know the finer points of any contract you sign, the interest rate of any loan you take out, and the expectations of any project partner you take on.

We understand that this can slow down your ambitious timelines. But when wild-child Uranus throws watchdog Saturn off his game, taking precautionary measures winds up being a time-saver. There are too many loopholes to consider and details to finesse this year. Speeding through these could result in costly mistakes. Dot every "i" and cross every "t" the first time around.

Even then, the squares could cause your outdated systems to break down. Upgrade, update and bring things to code! With techie Uranus in Taurus and your sixth house, invest in quality solutions from reliable brands—even if it costs you more upfront. With Saturn in digitally savvy Aquarius, new software, apps and virtual support staff can keep your life running smoothly.

New service providers may also be incoming near February 17, June 14 or December 24. While this can bring a bittersweet parting with people who are legit loyalists and friends, you can't be a martyr about such things. Get the right support or your own life could suffer. Helpful people who you once relied on might suddenly move on to pursue new aspirations. While you may feel blindsided by their departures, they've also helped you see which shoes need to be filled. With a little dedicated searching, you might find someone who's an even better fit for the 2021 you.

Jupiter in Aquarius & Pisces

January 1: Aquarius (since December 19, 2020)
May 13: Pisces (retrograde June 20)
July 28: Aquarius (retrograde until October 18)
December 28: Pisces (until December 20, 2022)

In 2021, Jupiter will shift back and forth between Aquarius and Pisces. Normally, Jupiter makes an unbroken trek through a single sign for 12 to 13 months, but in 2021, we'll see the planet of fortune and growth in two signs.

Jupiter in Aquarius

December 19, 2020–May 13, 2021
July 28–December 28, 2021

Expanding your reach.

Although heavy-hitter Saturn is restricting your candor, forget about drifting away on any silent retreats in 2021. For much of this year, your ruling planet, outspoken Jupiter, will join Saturn in Aquarius and your expressive, outgoing third house. Translation? You can still be the loud, proud Sagittarius you were born to be. You just need to articulate your thoughts in a more polished manner.

Most of the time, Jupiter spends 12-13 months in a single zodiac sign, but 2021 is different. This is one of those rare years when your red-spotted ruler will ping-pong between two signs: your Aquarius-ruled third house of communication and local activity and your Pisces-ruled domestic fourth house. Both areas of life will blossom in unprecedented ways. Jupiter is the galactic gambler, increasing your risk appetite and demanding major growth.

While Jupiter is in Aquarius from December 19, 2020, until May 13, 2021—then again from July 28 to December 28, 2021—you'll have more opportunity to connect to an audience and seek out kindred spirits. Raise your voice and share your unique ideas with the world, both in real-time forums and through social media or digital channels. Jupiter in Aquarius helps you bring people together and dive into inspiring collaborations. Seek variety: The energy of the third house is all about trying new hobbies and short-term projects. And while spinning through geeky, humanitarian Aquarius, you could find your soul family everywhere from a Twitch broadcast to an organized protest on City Hall.

Jupiter is the planet of higher learning, travel, publishing and entrepreneurship. While in Aquarius, your thirst for knowledge could lead you to eye-opening new books, podcasts and classes. Maybe you'll even create your own! Sagittarians are gifted and engaging storytellers, so find creative ways to package your message. Variety adds spice. You could juggle a few part-time gigs while growing a passion project, or even create multiple income streams.

Major personal growth and evolution are Jupiter's hallmarks. You may find that some of your friendships feel flat, or that you've drifted in different directions. It happens. The good news? Jupiter in Aquarius could bring some intriguing new people into your sphere. Revamp your social circle! And hey, no need to ditch all your old friends, Sag. Just take the initiative to evolve your bonds. Instead of venting over "wine o' clock" outings that leave you both drained, go for a walk, form a mastermind group, or consciously introduce new and positive topics.

While your brilliant ideas could have a long-distance reach, there's treasure to be mined in your own backyard. The third house rules all things local, so start close to home, using your ingenuity to drum up ways to connect with people while being mindful of health guidelines. See something that can be improved in your zip code? Join (or start) a food co-op, run for office, support a progressive political candidate in your district.

The travel restrictions of 2020 were not easy for your peripatetic sign. Sagittarians live to travel! But the silver lining of "sheltering in place" was that many of you learned to "travel in place." Did you bond with neighbors? Discover hidden gems, like a woodsy walking trail or a lot that had space for an outdoor market? Entrepreneurial Jupiter could spark new ways to generate revenue close to home, perhaps even collaborating with one of the area businesses that could use a post-COVID economic boost.

Jupiter's globetrotting influence might lead you to seek out a new zip code or a "second city." If you've always dreamed of being bicoastal or spending part of your year in wildly different scenery, make it happen. Do a home or apartment swap, find a short-term rental (or rent your place out while you travel). If you're feeling stifled in your current living situation, Jupiter invites you to explore other options. Start hanging in a different part of town to see how you like the vibe. Plan short trips to new cities and pretend you live there, trying them on for size.

Jupiter in Pisces

May 13–July 28
December 28, 2021–May 10, 2022
October 28, 2022–December 20, 2022

Redefining "home."

You'll get a short breather from the social whirlwind between May 13 and July 18. As Jupiter darts forward into Pisces, attention flows toward your fourth house of home and family. Remember those people you quarantined with back in 2020? While you may all have been relieved to get a little space from each other early this year, when Jupiter springs back into Pisces mid-May, you may feel pangs of longing for their company. With your good-natured spirit, you can revive the closeness in no time.

Hosting adventurous Jupiter in your fourth house of nesting can feel like a bit of a paradox. Your free-spirited sign doesn't relish staying in any one place for too long. If you planted deep roots, you may suddenly feel the urge to pull them up after May 13. But Jupiter's energy can be rash! Before you give up your rent-stabilized apartment lease or put your Midcentury house on the market, how about testing the waters with a "home away from home" experiment? Nomadic Jupiter in Pisces might finally incentivize you to give #VanLife a whirl, all while having a subletter cover your mortgage. Or maybe you'll relocate to a boho-chic beach town while Jupiter swims through Pisces' esoteric waters. Hello, island life!

Are you ready to cash out? Property sales can be quite lucrative while Jupiter lends his Midas touch to your fourth house—and they may happen fast! Just make sure to get the listing up before the red-spotted risk-taker turns retrograde on June 20. This could also be a prime two and a half months to get a sweet deal on land...or an Airstream trailer. Living life by personal impulse is the Sagittarius way, and if you only get a taste of it this year, note that Jupiter will return to Pisces again from December 28, 2021, until May 10, 2022, and for a third time between October 28 and December 20, 2022. You'll have two more chances to redefine home as you know it.

Already happy with your housing sitch? Enterprising Jupiter in Pisces could turn your kitchen table into the workspace for a promising side hustle. Family, even neighbors, may get involved in this revenue-generating venture. A roommate, relative or close friend, could help offset your cost of living by contributing to the rent. You might go into business with family or move closer to your clan for emotional support as you pour your energy into a time-consuming venture. If you're a parent, you could take time off for child-rearing (if you live/work somewhere with decent benefits) or flex your schedule to allow more time with your little one(s).

Your relationship with your mother, a child or a key female could go through an important growth cycle between now and December 20, 2022. If you've been locked into an outmoded or codependent pattern, Jupiter helps you evolve into a healthier dynamic.

In your love life, a touchy-feely and nurturing cycle is ahead. Perhaps you and your partner will renovate a home or prepare it for a new family addition.

Getting more in tune with a maternal figure—or your own nurturing side—can benefit your love life. Just be careful not to "mother" your significant other too much (hello, turn-off), or to turn coziness into coddling. A little baby talk, a

> ## "Keep the emo vibes under control and focus on coming from a more heart-centered and compassionate place."

cutesy nickname here and there? Fine, within reason. Turning your partner into your mommy-slash-therapist? Notsomuch. Keep the emo vibes under control and, instead, focus on coming from a more heart-centered and compassionate place with dates and mates alike. Give people the space to be human, messy and real…including yourself.

Overall, Jupiter in Pisces gets you more in tune with your sensitive side. Note: This is not your cue to throw diva-style temper tantrums or to excuse bad behavior by saying you were moody or upset. Take responsibility for your part of the relationship, Archer. With positive-energy planet Jupiter here, use your supersized feelings to connect authentically with people and even to forgive those who have hurt you in the past.

Lunar South Node in Sagittarius: Karma calling.

May 5, 2020–January 18, 2022

There's no escaping your calling in 2021—and for the second year in a row, this mission will rock the very core of your soul. On May 5, 2020, the lunar nodes began their 18-month pilgrimage across the Gemini/Sagittarius axis, their first return since October 2001 to April 2003.

Every 18.5 years, the South Node comes to your sign, which is a phase you're in the midst of now. (Nine to ten years later you'll host the North Node, FYI.) Like an astrological adjustment, you're being "trued up" to your authentic nature. So, Archer, who the heck do you think you are, anyway? Are you living life by your design, like inspiring Sagittarius signmates Janelle Monae, Miley Cyrus and Jane Fonda? Or have you put your real desires on hold, out of fear, shame or guilt?

The South Node's karmic correction may leave you feeling lost and unmoored in moments but have faith! There's a reason these tests are pushing you past the edge of reason. You literally need to "break" (or crack a little) in order to have an honest look inside of yourself. Even if you think you've dismantled your ego structure, there may be more "unlearning" to do.

You don't have to treat this like radical shock therapy either. The Nodes remain in Gemini and Sagittarius until January 18, 2022. Until then, keep bravely looking into the shadows—with as many coaches, healers, therapists, shamans and guides as you desire. Examine your assumptions and your knee-jerk tendencies at every turn. Coasting is not an option!

If you've outgrown certain situations, you don't have to cut anyone off. In fact, you probably shouldn't. The transformation of the Sagittarius South Node is an inside job. Plus, you never know: As you shift, the people around you might be inspired to make their own long-overdue changes as well. That said, you do need ample alone time. Figuring out what makes you happy, regardless of whether or not others approve, is a process. Set up a sanctuary, chill space, meditation room, whatever, so you can slip off for solo reflection. The sooner you start thinking about these quiet spells as "personal growth and development sessions," the faster you'll evolve toward your true north.

The hardest part for many Sagittarians will be setting aside your urge to merge and people-please! With the destiny-driven North Node in your opposite sign of Gemini, your seventh house of partnerships is being activated by this 18-month cycle. When the inner work feels too hard, you might want to go for your favorite fixes—firing up a steamy romance or giving friends advice on their problems. But don't! This is just an avoidance technique. Be careful about creating distracting drama in existing relationships, too, for the very same reason.

Bottom line: Forget about living for the applause and approval ratings. Validation-seeking is the way to stray in 2021. Dig deep and structure your life according to your own principles, even if you're still discovering what those ideals actually are!

> "Forget about living for the applause and approval ratings. Dig deep and structure your life by your own principles."

Eclipses in 2021

May 26: Sagittarius Lunar Eclipse 5°29' (7:13am ET)
June 10: Gemini Solar Eclipse 19°42 (6:52am ET)
November 19: Taurus Lunar Eclipse 27°17 (3:57pm)
December 4: Sagittarius Solar Eclipse 12°17 (2:42am)

In 2021, there will be four eclipses, superpowered events that always arrive with new and full moons. Should you hit the gas or slam on the brakes? Eclipses can speed up results, but they can also destabilize our lives. Even if you aren't looking directly into the sun, it might feel like you need special glasses to understand what's happening during these lunations. Eclipses reveal shadows: Literally, the shadow of the Earth on the full moon or the shadow of the moon across the Sun—or figuratively, our own hidden emotions or opportunities that have been sitting, unrealized, right under our noses.

Two of these eclipses will occur in your sign: A total lunar eclipse with the Sagittarius full moon on May 26, then a total solar eclipse with the new moon in Sagittarius on December 4. Woosh! This pair of lunations pushes your personal needs into the spotlight. If you've been playing Best Supporting at the expense of your own destiny, look out world! You could literally snap from the pressure of trying to take care of everyone around you. But that doesn't have to be the case if you start setting boundaries ASAP.

The May 26 lunar eclipse could bring an exciting bounty! This is the culminating full moon of last year's new moon in Sagittarius—the December 14, 2020, solar eclipse. Who knows? You may be ready to embrace a totally new identity or lifestyle. If you've been hustling tirelessly toward a personal goal, you could cash in or decide to debut the results near May 26. Just make sure you have all your ducks in a row and your intellectual property protected. Eclipses are known for bringing surprises, and not always pleasant ones. You can't predict what will be revealed, but you can make sure that your own presentation is as bulletproof as possible.

On June 10, the first solar (new moon) eclipse of the 2021's pair lands in Gemini and activates your seventh house of partnerships. A wave of "new relationship energy" could sweep through as you're drawn to a tantalizing new potential plus-one. Already attached? Buried issues may surface, but face them head-on. You might not wrestle the relationship demons overnight, but this could be the start of a six-month process that sets the stage for the honest dialogue a Sagittarius needs in order to stay committed. An unpredictable business partnership or creative collaboration could also emerge.

Ready to make some money moves? A brand-new eclipse series ignites on November 19 as a lunar (full moon) eclipse in Taurus lunges into your sixth house of work and wellness. If you've been burning the candle at both ends, you could soon be snuffing out that stressful routine. An exhausting client or job may be "eclipsed" out of your life, paving the way for a more fulfilling (and better paying) opportunity.

Archers who have been hustling toward a goal could hit an important milestone. Keep your eyes peeled for hidden opportunities and, when it comes to collaborators, diamonds in the rough. You may finally get the resolve you need to slay an unhealthy habit, like a raging sugar addiction. Getting your blood levels checked near this date could reveal deficiencies that can be cleared up with natural supplements, refilling your energy stores in a matter of weeks (if not days).

P.S. This is the first in a two-year eclipse series shaking up the Taurus/Scorpio axis until October 28, 2023. The connection between mind, body and soul will be underscored by these moonbeams, which could push your life in a more "woo" or holistic direction. Where can you simplify and where can you add more specialized touches? Let the inquiry begin!

> **"Saturn will help you upgrade the way you present yourself to the world. Everything gets a sophisticated overhaul."**

On December 4, the final solar (new moon) eclipse of 2021 falls in Sagittarius. As it reverberates through your trailblazing first house, you'll get an early burst of "fresh start" momentum. No need to wait until 2022 to launch a new initiative. With this cosmic tailwind at your back, the final month of the year could be downright transformational!

Venus Retrograde in Capricorn: Slow down and savor.

December 19, 2021–January 29, 2022

Holiday season could find you ruminating on "the one that got away," or perhaps revisiting a nostalgic chapter with your longtime love. For this you can thank Venus, the legendary love planet, which turns retrograde on December 19, reverse-commuting through Capricorn and your sensual-but-sensible second house. This is also your money zone, and Venus governs the valuables that we treasure. You may be rethinking every line item on your expense report, asking, "Is this really a necessity?"

Venus turns retrograde every 584 days, when she shifts from being an evening star—visible at dusk—to a morning star, appearing in the sky just before dawn. Metaphorically, Venus' backspins are a time for putting old romantic issues down for a long winter's nap. As you do, you clear space for an unscripted chapter to emerge.

Fascinating fact: Every eight years, Venus' backspin will hit the same point on the zodiac wheel (minus two degrees). Venus' prior U-turn in Capricorn dovetailed with the December 21, 2013, solstice and lingered until January 31, 2014. Scroll back on your timeline. What was going on in your love life then? Were you seeing anyone special? Locking horns with your partner about a particular issue? How were you earning your paycheck? Romantic and financial themes could repeat themselves at the end of this year.

Venus was retrograde from May 13 to June 25, 2020—a cycle that hit Sagittarians especially hard. Because it took place in Gemini and your seventh house of relationships, it packed a double-strength punch. You may still be picking up some of the pieces from whatever broke down back then…or reminding yourself that it's not cool to bring up that argument again.

With Venus backing up through your grounded second house, this retrograde cycle will be a lot easier on your heart. But don't expect to dodge all surprising events. These planetary pivots can be as nostalgic as they are nerve-wracking, especially if old chapters reopen and paramours from your past reappear. Reuniting with a soulful sweetheart can be a touching affair if wonky timing was the only thing keeping you apart. Running into your ex and their new spouse at a NYE party? You could probably do without that. But this holiday season, you'll need to chill and be still instead of reacting to every disruption in the field.

Venus first cruises into Capricorn on November 5, extending a "buffer zone" prior to the December 19 retrograde. When the backspin ends on January 29, 2022, the love planet will hang out in the sign of the Sea Goat until March 6, 2022, giving you an integration period to make sense of any changes that arise. That means Venus will trek through Capricorn for four months, which is also quadruple the length of its usual lap through a single sign.

What should a Sagittarius do? For starters, light some candles and put your softest sheets on the bed. Set up a speaker in your boudoir for soothing audio, from meditation tracks to sultry slow jams. Just note that you might be doing this for your own sleep sanctification rather than to entertain a special guest star. Capricorn rules your tactile but traditional second house. You may feel surprisingly old-fashioned for the entire time Venus lingers here (November 5,

2021, to March 6, 2022). Good things come to those who wait, and in this case, that might include letting would-be lovers with unproven track records show you exactly how much effort they are willing to put in.

> ## "Get all those 'where is this relationship going' conversations hashed out prior to the retrograde."

Already seeing someone? Before Venus' U-turn, flood your "emotional bank account" with as much feel-good energy as possible. Get all those "Where is this relationship going?" conversations hashed out prior to the retrograde, while you're in a more levelheaded space. Book ample quality time, cuddle up for movies and go on winter season adventures. That way, everyone's love tanks will be filled before December 19.

The second house rules our security, and abandonment issues may flare during this Venus retro. Instinctually, you'll feel like clinging to your partner. Insecurities could snowball quickly, which is not a good look. Worse yet, being smothering and needy will only push them away. Should those "Don't leave me!" fears ignite, book yourself a therapy session or talk to a relative who is experienced with long-term relationships. Then, call your friends and get some hangouts on the books.

Filling your life with soul-nurturing activities will be a whole lot more effective than making teary demands for reassurance. Stubbornness and (self-) righteousness could also interrupt your peaceful coexistence between December 19 and January 29, 2022. You'll have to try harder than usual to be a better listener, even if you have smoke pouring out of your ears during the talk.

This is also a crucial moment to review your finances. As much as you'd love to spoil everyone with luxe stocking stuffers, you might have to streamline your gift-giving splurges—as well as your own holiday indulgence budget. Dial back the retail therapy binges, and devise tricks to get the books back to black. It's fine

The AstroTwins' 2021 Horoscope 239

to be fanciful, sensual and decadent, but this year, you might have to "holiday" on a budget.

Self-care can go a long way to keep you grounded! If you want to loosen up your belt in any category, let it be for things like massages and organic produce. Eat clean, get eight hours of restful sleep nightly, drink two glasses of water for every mug of coffee you down. Move your body daily and make sure you break a serious sweat at least three times a week. If other people want to act the fool, well, that's their business. Buffer yourself against their antics by giving your body lots and lots of love. ✳

The AstroTwins' 2021 Horoscope   240

Capricorn

HOROSCOPE

2021 HIGHLIGHTS

LOVE

Curate a playlist of sexy slow jams. They're the perfect soundtrack for 2021's chilled out vibes. With Jupiter and Saturn mingling in Aquarius and your sensual second house for most of the year, you're not rushing toward any climactic finales. Take your time and enjoy the buildup of sweet affection. (And if you're feeling it, lean into the experimental Aquarian energy!) Make regular deposits in the "emotional bank account." Prepare healthy breakfasts for two, send supportive texts before your partner's big meeting. Show that you can be trusted by keeping your word and being on time for plans. These considerate actions might seem small, but they'll be important capital when Saturn in Aquarius gets embroiled in three squares with chaotic Uranus in Taurus and your fifth house of romance on February 17, June 14 and December 24. Jupiter's brief tour through Pisces activates your flirty third house from May 13 to July 28. Intense feelings could cool, or you may require a little more space before making a big commitment near the year's end. You'll be back to love magnet status by November 5, when Venus embarks on a four-month tour through Capricorn. You may have a big announcement near the Taurus lunar (full moon) eclipse on November 19, like a proposal or pregnancy. A past "situationship" could heat up again when Venus pivots retrograde for six weeks, starting December 19.

MONEY

After three years of hustling and paying your dues, 2021 could bring well-deserved compensation. While this probably won't arrive as a huge lump sum deposited in your bank account, a Jupiter-Saturn mashup in your second house of financial stability promises a reliable flow of income. Expenses may increase under Jupiter's watch, and sensible Saturn could inspire you to tuck away more retirement funds. Budgeting and careful planning will be important to maintain in 2021. Some Capricorns may have to tighten your belts or work a lower-paying "bridge job" as you continue breaking into a new industry. If you're on the hunt for more gainful employment, circulate near June 10, when the Gemini solar (new moon) eclipse opens unexpected doors to opportunity. Throughout the year, Jupiter and Saturn in Aquarius and your money zone will clash with spontaneous Uranus in your luxe-loving fifth house. Your competitive or status-driven side could flare, but curb those inclinations. Keeping up with the Joneses will send you down a slippery slope during these planetary squares. Instead, quantify "enough" and make that your magic number for 2021. Simple pleasures satisfy!

WELLNESS

Hardworking Capricorns have no problem sprinting into action, but when was the last time you considered your resting state? In 2021, give your body a chance to recover and repair itself. Lift weights, endure long runs, hit the rock-climbing wall, but also start incorporating stretching and gentle yoga into your routines. Sanctify your sleep, turning your bedroom into a peaceful oasis. Repetitive exercise, even if you're only at a "6 out of 10" level, can create lasting good habits under the watch of your ruler Saturn. Train yourself to eat and sleep at regular times. Your system will appreciate that rhythm! Three eclipses, on May 26, June 10 and December 4, rev up your axis of healing, marking good times for a dietary detox and a series of holistic treatments. Working through trauma or anxiety? Body-based somatic therapy can remove those blocks. Whenever possible, lean into your earth sign signature. Get out in nature, work in a garden, take your fitness routines to the park. Venus in Capricorn gives you a glow-up after November 5. Embrace a cleaner, greener beauty routine!

FRIENDS & FAMILY

Aquarius and your traditional second house, you'll feel happiest in the cozy company of the people who know you best. Take the reins, gathering your inner circle for Zoom check-ins and IRL vacations. When Jupiter zips through your friendship zone from May 13 to July 28, your social calendar will fill up quickly as you mingle with both new and old friends. The local scene could become a buzzing place for Capricorns to make your mark. Get involved, whether you're hosting gatherings at area venues or becoming a vocal activist in your community. Head's up: Pleasure planet Venus is retrograde in Capricorn from December 19, 2021, to January 29, 2022, a time where you may feel more introverted. Step back from holiday hosting duties and let someone else organize the menu, decorations and other details that you'd normally insist upon handling. Being a guest can be fun, too!

Capricorn
POWER DATES

CAPRICORN NEW MOON
January 13 (12:00 AM ET)

CAPRICORN FULL MOON
June 24 (2:39 PM ET)

SUN IN CAPRICORN
January 1 – 19; December 21 – 31

Last year's extreme pileup of planets in Capricorn left you both exhilirated and exhausted. Now, how can you take the fresh-start energy and build it into something tangible?

Saturn in Aquarius: Build your dream.

December 17, 2020–March 7, 2023

Boot camp is over, Capricorn, and you can finally exhale. After three grueling years, drill sergeant Saturn (your galactic guardian) has officially moved on from Capricorn, freeing your first house of self-expression and initiative from its restrictive grasp. Who have you become since December 19, 2017? Saturn's strength-training influence created a serious identity shift for many Capricorns over the past three years. Do you even recognize yourself?

Hustle paved the way for career breakthroughs since late 2017. But as you put in that sweat equity, you became aware of old structures and habits that were ready to be dismantled. One of our Capricorn mogul pals decided to downsize the portfolio of businesses she'd been operating since the 1980s. Fortunately, she sold off two venues pre-COVID for a decent profit. But sadly, when the virus shut down foot traffic near her downtown district, she had to shutter a beloved location that had only been open for a year. Another Capricorn moved his coaching practice to Costa Rica with plans to open a retreat center. For now, he is settling into the flow of virtual sessions and hoping to revisit the brick and mortar dream when travel restrictions ease up.

Gains were matched with losses since late 2017, which is not the ROI formula your achievement-oriented sign prefers. But learning to ride those waves was the point of Saturn's exercise. After all, Capricorn, you are a human being…not a human doing. Even if you scored epic victories over the past three years—like one Capricorn friend who is rising through the leaderboard as a top insurance agent in the Pacific Northwest—you also learned that happiness is at least as much an inside job as one to be measured by external validation.

Saturn only visits your sign every 29.5 years. That means you're free of this intensity for nearly three decades—woot! But you're probably still picking up some pieces as 2021 dawns. Last year was particularly challenging since transformational Pluto and expansive Jupiter were riding shotgun through Capricorn. Pandemics, economic insanity, elections, massive life changes! The ceaseless tests required you to tap reserves of strength you didn't even know you had. If you bottomed out here and there, it's understandable. Please, keep dosing yourself with massive love and forgiveness!

Wherever you're standing as this new year begins, the ground beneath your feet should feel a bit more…solid. Deep sighs of relief? Let them out! Just don't loosen your belt too many notches. Saturn tours Aquarius from December 19, 2020, until March 7, 2023, playing Chief Budgetary Officer in your second house of financial security. New lesson for 2021: How to not burn as much as you earn. Or, if you're already mastering the art of saving and investing, how to compound your profits. It's time to make that hard-earned cash work just as rigorously for you.

Saturn briefly visited Aquarius last year, from March 21 to July 1, 2020. Did you scale down...or up? While minimalism is a bit too severe for your status-loving sign, you may feel compelled to live well with less this year. Once again, the ringed guru is camped out in Aquarius until March 7, 2023, adding heft to your second house of values, financial foundations and sensuality. Ease up and stop "going HAM" on every project you take on. During this cycle, stop clinging to the competitive edge and create sustainable security instead.

Are you a chronic over-spender? With communal Aquarius ruling this zone, tap into the sharing economy instead of reaching into your own pocket every time. Maybe you can keep on enjoying all those lavish (and practical) goods without breaking the bank! As the zodiac's provider sign, you like to be prepared. But do you really need to own everything outright? (Your storage unit says "no!") Pool funds for lesser-used items from yard-care tools to commuter vehicles. As long as your pod is made up of trustworthy, integrous people, this model could work out swimmingly. And hey, you can always split the cost of an insurance policy to cover any potential repairs.

Slow and steady growth is a hallmark of Saturn in the second house, which might frustrate you at times. Tenacious, persistent Capricorns don't mind taking things step by step, but you can get anxious when the numbers on the scoreboard aren't trending in your preferred direction. Results could take longer to roll in this year, testing your patience. Don't give up! When there's a pause in the action, focus on fortifying your foundation. What can you do to strengthen your base? Do you need better tools? Are you collaborating with people who have enough expertise? Monitor your daily routines: What tasks are slowing you down? Outsource, delegate or tap into technology to speed up your processes.

While you're comfortable with titles like boss and CEO, Saturn's tour of the second house might pull you into a more modest position, especially if your career compass is now pointing you toward a nascent industry. In liberated Aquarius, this Saturn cycle may take you from hired gun to an independent contractor or consultant role. You might even embrace the opportunity to work as part of a team or a think tank, a departure from your take-charge M.O. And if work doesn't provide this opportunity, join a mastermind, incubator or group coaching circle. Tap the hive mind for stabilizing solutions, which will come as a relief after these three frenetic years.

Want to lighten your workload? Start by streamlining and simplifying. That way, you can focus on tasks that are directly in your wheelhouse. Then, consider ways to redistribute duties. Would it make sense to bring in a business partner, hire an employee, outsource to a contractor, get an intern?

If you're working your way up the ladder, humble thyself. Yes, you busted your butt to break into this field during Saturn's residence in Capricorn. Now that basic training is over, you must hone your practice. The next two years may be a "chop wood, carry water" tour of duty as you gain mastery from repeating tasks over and over until they become second nature.

Without all that performance pressure bearing down, you may feel (and look!) younger than you have in years. Saturn rules aging, and while it toured Capricorn, you've learned to appreciate any grey hairs and wisdom lines that appeared. But the stress of this period might have dimmed your radiance, especially if you lost sleep worrying about all the changes swirling around.

With Saturn in Aquarius, you'll get a different kind of galactic glow-up, one that comes from luxuriating in beauty rituals that you "didn't have time for" last year. Strike the idea of rush hour from your mind. Wake up a little earlier in the morning to bathe and primp. Start winding down sooner for bed. Sleep sanctification is a big theme of this Saturn cycle. How can you make your nighttime hours more restful? Upgrade to a more supportive mattress or pillows. Wind down by listening to binaural beats, which deliver tones in each ear at a slightly different frequency—in this case in the theta (dreams) and delta (deep sleep) range.

In personal affairs, Saturn's tour of this sensual sector bodes well for lovemaking techniques. Learn the art of partner massage, or lean into the Aquarian high-minded experimentation and take a tantric workshop to connect breath and body sensations. Developing rituals can keep Capricorns connected to your favorite people. Savor quality time together, preparing special meals and watching movies.

Processing trauma, anxiety and grief? After 2020, most people are. In addition to any aftershocks of the past year, you may be ready to tackle longstanding blocks

> "With Saturn in Aquarius, you'll get a different kind of galactic glow-up by luxuriating in beauty rituals you didn't have time for last year."

that show up as physical sensations. With Saturn in your tactile second house, somatic therapy could be especially effective for releasing pent-up pain. This body-centered healing modality combines psychotherapy and physical therapy to free you from blocks. Tension may be especially noticeable in your neck and shoulder area. Here's the excuse you've been waiting for to make massage a monthly (or weekly!) indulgence.

Saturn in Aquarius square Uranus in Taurus
February 17, June 14 & December 24

Slow and steady wins the race this year, but don't get too comfortable in your routines. Novelty and excitement add color to your world, setting off a rush of sexy, motivating dopamine in your brain. But when your "fun tanks" get depleted, you slip into a melancholy mood, seeing the glass as half-empty instead of overflowing with promise and opportunity. That's no way for a Capricorn to live!

Three times this year—on February 17, June 14 and December 24—staunch Saturn in Aquarius and your humdrum second house gets electro-shocked by spontaneous Uranus in Taurus and your playful, romantic fifth. As the two planets assemble into dynamic 90-degree squares, you will quickly see where you're plummeting into a rut.

There's only one thing to do, obviously, which is to redirect yourself up and out of those holes! But how? Rebellious Uranus can call forth your wild side, even taking you in a destructive direction if you aren't careful. And in your drama-loving, romance-obsessed fifth house, the side-spinning planet pushes your envelopes to places you didn't know you would (or could) go!

Fortunately, sensible Saturn is tapping the brakes, which can send you on a detour route right before you hit the Scandal Superhighway. From lovers to friends, choose people who lift you up without throwing you off course. This is a year where you must be mindful of the company you keep. Those thrill-seeking "trustafarians" you seem to attract? They have Mommy and Daddy to bail them out of the messes they make. But who knows if they'll have your back (or post your bail *cough*) if the chips are down?

You may have to temper some of your lust. How else will you screen out the hot-AF-but-so-wrong-for-you types? Yet, this trio of squares can help you nail the elusive balance between excitement and stability. For single Capricorns, that could arrive in the form of a game-changing lover who is as excited about adventure travel as they are about co-creating a gorgeous home. Coupled Capricorns might start saving up to tick some must-do items off your shared bucket lists.

Speaking of savings, difficult conversations about money could finally surface during the Saturn-Uranus squares. If you're sharing funds with anyone, how aligned are your financial goals? One of you may like splurging on top-shelf tequila while the other wants to tuck the discretionary income into a Roth IRA. Whatever the case, don't leave anything up to chance. Get clear about your goals before initiating dialogue, so you can come to these conversations with tangible discussion points. But with Uranus in the mix, stay open to experimental ideas and innovative ways to earn and invest.

The AstroTwins' 2021 Horoscope   250

Jupiter in Aquarius & Pisces

January 1: Aquarius (since December 19, 2020)
May 13: Pisces (retrograde June 20)
July 28: Aquarius (retrograde until October 18)
December 28: Pisces (until December 20, 2022)

In 2021, Jupiter will shift back and forth between Aquarius and Pisces. Normally, Jupiter makes an unbroken trek through a single sign for 12 to 13 months, but in 2021, we'll see the planet of fortune and growth in two signs.

Jupiter in Aquarius

December 19, 2020–May 13, 2021
July 28–December 28, 2021

Cashflow and confidence on the rise.

Cha-ching! Here's another reason why your self-worth and your net worth are set to rise in 2021. Risk-taker Jupiter co-pilots with Saturn through Aquarius for two prolonged laps, bringing massive growth to your second house of money, work and self-esteem. Their first circuit began on December 19, 2020, and lasts until May 13, 2021; then the red-spotted planet rounds out the year in Aquarius again from July 28 to December 28. Roll up your silk charmeuse sleeves, Capricorn, and get ready to reach epic levels of productivity and profit! Your personal life can also get on solid footing during this stabilizing cycle.

Jupiter in Aquarius is an industrious but expansive time, when taking calculated risks can yield epic results. In fact, 2021 could bring notable financial growth wherever you invest the time, resources and attention. Making money is only part of the equation (and the part most Capricorns do well). But how are your budgeting and money management skills? While Jupiter tours Aquarius, you could start putting funds into retirement and saving accounts, or increasing the amount you set aside for your nest egg each month that you can later use to invest, buy property or grow.

New to your field? Jupiter in the second house rewards a humble attitude. In order to get ahead, you may have to pay dues and put in some sweat equity. But no matter what your level, that hardworking attitude is essential. Do the rigorous but rewarding work to solidify the foundation of the Capricorn empire, brick by brick—or pixel by pixel. In tech-savvy Aquarius, the more digital skills you get under your belt, the better. Learn the finer points of social media marketing, podcast editing or using apps like Canva to level up your visual presentations.

Sidebar: You may have to bring in some temporary security measures while you're building toward your ultimate dream. Certain skills can't be rushed, Capricorn. Maybe you'll take on a part-time bridge job or hire yourself out as a consultant. That way, you can keep the lights on while you volunteer-apprentice alongside a master or develop your art without the pressure to produce income from it.

With globetrotting Jupiter in Aquarius, you could relocate for work, receive a major promotion or get word of a raise. Last year was all about making a name for yourself and trying new things. Now you'll make choices in the name of security—ones that may not look as fierce on social media, but that build an enduring sense of comfort and ease. The trick is to make sensible choices that give you a high ROI. If that means moving to a new city, switching jobs or revamping your lifestyle, enthusiastic Jupiter will buoy your courage.

In affairs of the heart, Jupiter's flights through your second house can be both experimental and grounding. Many people end this transit engaged or in a stable partnership, but since quirky Aquarius rules this part of your chart, you might find yourself attracted to someone who totally breaks from type. Comfortable and consistent are important qualities, but that doesn't have to amount to boring. The lowkey person you dismissed last year may seem like a total catch in 2021 when you realize how well you "parallel play" alongside one another. For example, your partner quietly cooks a gourmet meal while you're designing your website, or you read in bed while trading off DJ duties with your playlists.

Since the second house rules self-worth, Jupiter could bring some divine lessons about accepting yourself as whole and perfect, just the way you are. Status-conscious Capricorns like to signal an achieved and successful vibe to the world. While that's never going to change entirely, you may realize the divine comedy of playing that game. What's the point of trying to prove yourself to people who are worried about proving themselves to you? What if you could all relax and just be yourself? Practice makes perfect…or should we say, perfectly imperfect. Jupiter in Aquarius helps you embrace a more easygoing vibe. That laid-back and content energy could attract a completely different type of person.

For coupled Capricorns, these two Jupiter cycles are an ideal time to start building something lasting as a duo. You might buy a house (or remodel part of the one

> "With globetrotting Jupiter in Aquarius, you could relocate for work, receive a major promotion or get word of a raise."

you already own), open a joint account or even start a cottage industry together, thanks to entrepreneurial Jupiter's influence. With travel-loving Jupiter in this decadent part of your chart, a high-end vacation for two could give you epic lifelong memories—yes, even if you have to follow more restrictions in order to enjoy this luxury.

Overall, Jupiter in Aquarius can help you streamline your lifestyle so you feel wealthier—not just financially, but with a joyful, well-rounded life. Not sure how to achieve that lofty goal? Start by taking inventory of your daily routines: eating and sleeping patterns, fitness habits, extracurricular commitments, work style. Are these serving your highest good or are you just autopiloting through the motions? Take classes, read books, work with a coach—explore ways of healing and strengthening these vulnerable parts of yourself.

Many people end this Jupiter cycle with happy, solid relationships and friendships. That's the result of owning all the parts of yourself, including the ones that might not earn you any bragging rights. Growth can be a messy process at times, but challenge yourself to let go of the control. It's the key to your happiness in 2021.

Don't squander these horizon-broadening moments, even if they require you to tighten your belt a bit. Growth-agent Jupiter only cycles through this "financial district" of your chart every ten to 12 years. The last time was January 5, 2009, until January 17, 2010. You may see recurring themes if you reflect on that period. To get the most out of this cycle, you will have to gamble a bit more than your sign is comfortable doing. With swift Jupiter at the wheel, don't miss out on a grand adventure by waffling or playing small! We're not saying to leap without looking. But if you get the job offer of a lifetime, or your soulmate lives on the other side of the country, don't cling to the past out of habit. At a certain point, you can't avoid risk or demand guarantees. You just have to go for it! And with pragmatic Saturn traveling alongside Jupiter, you won't lose sight of the safety net. Nothing ventured, nothing gained.

Jupiter in Pisces
May 13–July 28
December 28, 2021–May 10, 2022
October 28, 2022–December 20, 2022

Assessing the local talent.
As you're fortifying your base and master-mixing your formulas, how will you share your ideas with the world? On May 13, outspoken Jupiter springs into Pisces and your third house of messaging, local happenings and kindred spirits for a short spell, staying until July 28. During this brief cycle, which picks up again from December 28, 2021, to May 10, 2022, you'll get a chance to test-drive some of your plans and collect valuable feedback.

Get ready to connect with kindred spirits through multiple channels—broadcasting, teaching, community action, social media. You could share your avant-garde ideas through a podcast or your own YouTube series. Since Jupiter rules publishing and the third house governs writing, this might be the year that your novel, screenplay or self-help book finds an eager audience. If you've developed mastery in an area, there's no better time to launch a workshop or a DIY starter kit helping others learn your craft.

If you've been in nonstop "Go!" mode since 2021 began, Jupiter's move into Pisces pulls away from your workspace and shifts your focus to interactive tasks. Solo projects could evolve into exciting partnership opportunities as you embrace

254

the spirit of cooperation! Someone you formerly dubbed a competitor could be your missing puzzle piece after May 13. Just make sure you spell out roles and ownership rights explicitly.

Your social calendar may be packed, along with a bustling lineup of pitch meetings, brainstorming sessions, conferences and coffee dates. As you've been

> ## "Hello, Mayor Capricorn? Getting more involved with your neighborhood will be richly rewarding."

redefining your values and creating a new lifestyle, your agenda should reflect these new priorities, both on and off the company clock. Try to get the most important meetups scheduled before Jupiter turns retrograde from June 20 until October 18. During that annual four-month reverse commute, backstage developments take priority over public productions.

Hello, Mayor Capricorn? The third house rules neighborhoods and getting more involved in yours will be richly rewarding. With charitable, compassionate Pisces ruling this zone of your chart, you could leave a powerful mark on an organization that helps underserved members of your community. Fundraising might be your specialty, or maybe you'll pass along your wisdom volunteering as a mentor.

Not totally in love with where you live? While Jupiter is in Pisces mid-year, start exploring new districts or even frequenting a "second city" that becomes your part-time or satellite home. A friend may be up for a summer apartment swap, giving you a chance to test out permanent residence in a new zip code before you rent the U-Haul and put in notice at work. Spoiler alert: Jupiter's next cycle (starting May 2022) will be in your fourth house of home and roots. So if you're not sure where you want to reside on a permanent basis, or you're thinking of investing in a vacation home, mid-2021 is the perfect time for some adventure-filled research.

The AstroTwins' 2021 Horoscope   255

Eclipses in 2021

May 26: Sagittarius Lunar Eclipse 5°29' (7:13am ET)
June 10: Gemini Solar Eclipse 19°42 (6:52am ET)
November 19: Taurus Lunar Eclipse 27°17 (3:57pm)
December 4: Sagittarius Solar Eclipse 12°17 (2:42am)

Gemini/Sagittarius Eclipses

Prioritizing self-care.

Time for an inside-out makeover? Since June 5, 2020, a healing eclipse cycle has been vibrating across the Sagittarius/Gemini axis, touching your sixth house of wellness (Gemini) and your twelfth house of closure, release and healing (Sagittarius). In 2021, three more eclipses will fall on this zodiac "ley line," revealing the need for clearer boundaries in the name of self-nurturing. Eclipses sweep away what no longer serves us, making room for a new and better fit. It's time to let go of outmoded habits and make room for better ones, especially around your emotional, physical and mental health.

On May 26, the Sagittarius lunar (full moon) eclipse activates your healing twelfth house, which could abruptly end a situation that's been draining your joie de vivre. While losses are never easy to process, this one is likely to be accompanied by a spiritual epiphany or transformation. Tenacity is a Capricorn trait and you don't let go without a fight. Sometimes it takes a situation being "eclipsed out" of your life to help you understand the power of letting go. If you've battled an addiction or codependence, this eclipse could rocket you from rock bottom into recovery. You may finally surrender to powerlessness over your demons and get the support you need to make life manageable again.

Just be careful not to get stuck in a victim mindset, a pitfall of a twelfth house eclipse. There's strength in acknowledging that you're a survivor who's gone through a harrowing injustice. But you don't want to get mired in eternal pain. While it may seem logical to pinpoint one person as the source of all your angst, the real growth comes when you can (self-lovingly) find the power to change the situation. Work with a therapist or qualified healer to pinpoint the roots of this struggle, such as childhood incidents or limiting beliefs you picked up from your family of origin.

The May 26 eclipse supports you with healing these patterns—and replacing them with healthy new behaviors and thoughts. Forgiveness work may be part of this process. We're not suggesting that you justify a person's wrongful deeds. It just means that you free yourself from carrying around this pain by accepting that this trial of spirit took place, and that you can go on and create a happy future. On the flip side, if you've been overly punishing, you may finally release an ancient grudge and rekindle a relationship. Has this person attempted to make amends, learned their lesson and grown since the transgression? Maybe it's time to bury the hatchet, Capricorn.

The June 10 Gemini solar (new moon) eclipse will power up your sixth house of health, organization and fitness with motivating vibes. Welcome any improvements in this area, but hold tight, because big changes might be ahead. You may need to revamp your habits completely, possibly with doctor's orders attached. (Who knew you had high blood pressure or that you could be a candidate for a knee replacement if you keep going with those long-distance runs?) Since the sixth house rules pets, and you may meet (and adopt!) your furry soulmate near this date. Bonus: Bonding with animals can lower your blood pressure, so consider it a contribution to your wellbeing.

The sixth house rules support staff and service providers. Good help could be surprisingly easy to find near June 10! If it's time to call for backup, spell out your requirements. What experience level are you looking for? What values are essential for members of Team Capricorn to hold? At the same time, be open to surprises! This eclipse could usher in a candidate who's even better than you expected, like a virtual assistant who also has experience reading contracts or managing social media.

Ranks could reshuffle on the Sea Goat Squad surrounding this Gemini new moon eclipse, and that includes hiring and firing. You might let a once-reliable contractor go, or this person could suddenly "eclipse" themselves out of your life. Staffing changes at your nine-to-five could upset the apple cart, forcing everyone to scramble as you pick up the slack or adjust to new duties. If you're a shameless control freak, stop micromanaging and start delegating. This systematic solar eclipse can revolutionize the way you work. Welcome new lifehacks and productivity tools. Try project management applications like Asana or Slack.

You might be offered a job in the service industry, or a gig at a company focused on wellness or the environment.

The December 4 Sagittarius solar (new moon) eclipse is the final lunation in the Gemini/Sagittarius series. As the year winds down, you could celebrate big results for any healing work you began near June 2020. For many Capricorns, this process has been both an inside and outside job. The December 4 solar eclipse will catapult you into a new level of spiritual and emotional resilience right before 2021 is through. Pop-up alert: You're stronger than you realize! You could also have a spiritual awakening or receive a psychic "download" near December 4. Pay attention to your intuition and the strong messages you receive in the form of serendipities and signs like repeating numbers on clocks or multiple people mentioning the same resource.

Taurus/Scorpio Eclipses

Romance and friendships ignite.

On November 19, a new two-year eclipse series ignites with the Taurus lunar (full moon) eclipse. Until October 28, 2023, these lunations send frissons across the Taurus/Scorpio axis, which rules your fifth house of romance and fame (Taurus) and your eleventh house of teamwork, tech and activism (Scorpio). Forget about hiding out under that blanket coat, Capricorn—and even if you do, the spotlight will still find you. November 19 is a prime moment for posting new photos, celebrating the launch of a project or starting a buzz for one of your passion projects.

Speaking of passion, chemistry that's been bubbling since mid-May of 2021 could go from lukewarm to exothermic! An attractive romantic prospect could blow in like a surprise nor'easter, shaking up the current status of your love life. Single and free? This will add warmth and excitement to your holiday season. But if you're otherwise engaged, this soul connection could send you into a bit of a tailspin. Should you acknowledge the feelings or wait for them to pass? Pure romanticism may cloud your judgment—or compromise your ethical stance on "commitment." But if you truly feel like this is a once in a lifetime connection, you may have no choice but to pursue. Happily coupled Capricorns could have a big announcement to make near this eclipse, such as an engagement, pregnancy or other big step you'll be taking together. Whichever way you leap, make sure you're having fun, because this Taurus full moon is as playful as it is practical!

Venus Retrograde in Capricorn: What do you really want?

December 19, 2021–January 29, 2022
Venus in Capricorn: November 5, 2021 to March 6, 2022
Venus Retrograde: December 19, 2021 - January 29, 2022

Hello, your royal hotness! A long winter's nap will be the furthest thing from your mind come November 5. Pleasure planet Venus embarks on a four-month tour through Capricorn, blessing you with amped-up magnetism and allure. You

> "Don't waste time on types who can't be bothered to make an Open Table reservation, much less a coffee date."

may want to hibernate while the celestial seductress lingers here until March 6, 2022—but that doesn't mean you'll be alone (or even sleeping much at all) in your sexy cave. Unless, of course, you want it that way...

During this sultry cycle, the Law of Attraction is on your side! Focus on what you want to create in your existing relationships. Then, pitch the vision in the most intoxicating way possible, painting a picture of the future in vivid brushstrokes. Looking for a partner? Be your discerning Capricorn self while you're vetting candidates. There's a time to be "open to whatever the universe provides," but this four-month cycle probably isn't it. Know thyself and trust in that.

For example, if you like a human with a plan, don't waste time on the laid-back, flowy types who can't be bothered to make an Open Table reservation, much less commit to a coffee date. Or, if you're turned off by anyone too controlling, maybe you should pass on a friend's offer to fix you up with her really successful surgeon friend.

Keep a back channel open with the muse! Whenever the cosmic creatrix visits your sign, you aren't just divinely inspired, you're motivated to make actual art, music, poetry. Whatever your métier, release the pressure to crank out a masterpiece. Instead, think along the lines of "studies," setting aside your perfectionism (as best you can) and allowing yourself to play with the materials until you get comfortable. You never know, though! One of your random sketches or strums could be the foundation for a large-scale painting or studio-recorded single.

Plot twist alert! From December 19, 2021, to January 29, 2022, Venus will spin retrograde, a cycle that happens every 584 days. (The last Venus backspin was from May 13 to June 25, 2020.) Every eight years, Venus pings one of five points in the zodiac wheel during her reverse commutes, and uh, "lucky" you, Capricorn, you're on her short list. Scroll back in your albums and timelines: What was going down from December 21, 2013 to January 31, 2014, which was the last time the planet of love and beauty backed it up through your sign? Themes in love, pleasure and creativity could come full circle, including a few lessons that you thought you'd mastered but apparently need to sharpen.

Maybe you'll get a second chance to make things right with someone who was in your life eight years ago. If that old flame isn't rekindled, you could meet someone who stokes the same embers in your heart (and loins). Coupled Caps may have to rehash an issue that you thought was buried. But don't exhume those skeletons just to keep things "interesting." If you're feeling restless, stop projecting onto your partner and go develop one of your gifts instead.

Whatever direction she's paddling in, Venus is the planet of love, but during this six-week intermission, the lens flips inward. Take inventory: Do you keep winding up in the same arguments with your partner? Dating the same frustrating type in a different body, like the lovebomber who showers you with reverence then tells you, "I'm not ready for a relationship" at the first "threat" of attachment? Enough's enough. While Venus is in reverse, turn the tide on these trends.

Attached Caps might schedule a couple's therapy appointment for the first week of January. (Birthday gift that keeps on giving?) Single Sea Goats, how about treating yourself to sessions with a dating coach—or declaring January a month for self-love, where the only person you "date" is yourself!

Capricorns like to keep everything calm, cool and collected, but that's a double-edged sword. If you've been telling people what they want to hear instead of speaking your truth, relationships could grow flat or distant after November 5. Even if you adore someone, it's possible to O.D. on togetherness. Near December 19, you could wind up feeling like an involuntary inmate in the couple bubble. Set yourself free with an honest conversation about autonomy. Avoid cliches like, "I need space" which could make your love interest feel like they're to blame. It's up to you to set boundaries. This includes saying no to that poker night you're not feeling instead of trying to be a supportive partner and ante up when you'd rather be streaming a Netflix series from the cozy comfort of your bed.

On the flip side, the temporary uncertainty that arises during the retrograde can drive up fears. If you find yourself turning from confident to clingy, don't be surprised. But do enlist some supportive sounding boards who can talk you out of sending a barrage of indignant texts to your partner…especially in the middle of a workday!

While we aren't suggesting you ring in the New Year as a party of one, a little alone time can go a long way this winter. Engage in activities that you love doing, whether or not you have a partner. Join a book club, go snowboarding or cross-country skiing, learn a cooking technique like sous vide. Oscar Wilde summed it up best, "To love oneself is the beginning of a lifelong romance." This extended Venus in Capricorn cycle is all about cherishing yourself, with or without a partner or any sort of outside validation.

Has a connection drifted to the shallow end of the pool? Plunge in deeper! That's one of the beautiful offerings of Venus retrograde. If you've kept conversation on the surface (which can be a Capricorn defense mechanism), use the relaxed pace of the holiday season to deepen intimacy. Long talks will be heartwarming, but you have to be willing to open up and get vulnerable.

If that terrifies you, think of it like this: Start by showing your scars, not your scabs. Partially-healed wounds are easier to talk about than the fresh ones that are still stinging from a recent affront. From the listener's response, you'll know whether to trust them with the details of a painful personal situation—or not!

Warning: Venus retrograde can draw you towards sketchy encounters and people with pasts so concealed, you'd need to hire an FBI bureau to uncover them. But they'll look good on the surface, sweeping you in as their co-stars in a short-lived fairy tale romance. Luxury vehicles and couture labels might actually be red flags while Venus spins backward through status-conscious Capricorn near the year's end. At the very least, some deep Googling can put your mind at ease.

If you're otherwise engaged, beware the lure of an emotional affair after December 19, which, for you, can feel as erotically charged as "the act" itself. You'll know you're blurring lines if you can't stop thinking of excuses to send helpful tips to a "friend," or if you're counting down the minutes until you are together in the office/class/band practice, etc. Boundaries are a must!

While you'll be in festive spirits for most of this Venus cycle, during the retrograde (December 19 to January 29), people will fray your nerves. Plan ahead for the holidays by consciously not overbooking or taking on the lion's share of planning and hosting. With Venus off-course, it's too easy to fall prey to people-pleasing, which will only flood you with resentment as you count down to 2022. Warning: Relatives who always leave you feeling like "the responsible one" will be particularly aggravating. And if you have a bone to pick with them, it's gonna be hard to remain composed. For everyone's sake, don't volunteer your sleeper sofa to your drama-loving sister. Just help her find an affordable Airbnb.

Hold off on any "new year, new you" style updates while beauty queen Venus is in reverse. You may feel like chopping your hair into a platinum pixie or getting matching tattoos with your lover of two months, but radical changes have been known to go awry during these cosmic spells. Same goes for any major, non-refundable purchases. Get those gift receipts—and shop wisely for both holidays and whatever "treat yo'self" indulgences are on tap for your birthday. With value-driven Venus in reverse, your choices could be muddled, especially if you let your fluctuating emotions dictate spending. But here's a silver lining: Since retrogrades rev up the past, you might tap into a fresh income stream by reviving an old passion! ✷

Aquarius

HOROSCOPE

2021 HIGHLIGHTS

LOVE

Romance takes a back seat to solo pursuits in 2021, but that doesn't mean you can't get your fix! But you might have to opt for quality over quantity as serious Saturn and jovial Jupiter team up in Aquarius and your self-possessed, trailblazing first house. Personal growth and passion projects will be all-consuming at times. You're not purposely ignoring your heart! (Or regions further south.) But with so many dreams to pursue, you may find it difficult to focus on just one person. If you don't want relationships to wither on the vine, tap into Saturn's planning powers. Fostering healthy dialogue is especially crucial if you share a home or co-parent with a mate, since wrench-throwing Uranus (your ruler) is creating instability in your home sector all year. If you can only put one date night on the calendar per week (or month), make it a good one! Pull out all the stops and unleash your creativity. Circle June 10 as a power day for love. Under the Gemini solar (new moon) eclipse, you could unite with a soulmate, propose to the LOYL or leap toward another milestone like making babies or buying land together to turn into a retreat center. On November 5, Venus trails through your twelfth house of fantasy and healing, softening boundaries. But with the love planet spinning retrograde for six weeks starting December 19, you may be processing old blocks around relationships, too. Single? Freedom could be your aphrodisiac this year. Heck, even the most devoted Aquarians will require more alone time. Traveling, taking classes and exploring new interests will be a turn-on for couples. Bring on the shared adventures!

WELLNESS

"Let food be thy medicine," advised ancient Greek physician Hippocrates. In 2021, filling your plate with clean, healthy food could do wonders to keep you energized. Metaphysical Uranus (your ruler), is parked in Taurus and your fourth house of nourishment and security from 2018-26, which has forced many Water Bearers to be mindful about what you consume. Dial down the stimulants like caffeine and sugar and experiment with different eating plans. Dabbling with keto, intermittent fasting or the Mediterranean diet, for example, could reboot your energy levels. Use apps to track food and sleep, especially near the eclipses on May 26, November 19 and December 4. Even if you're in prime physical health, you may be dealing with anxiety or depression. Side-spinning Uranus in the fourth house can make it hard to feel secure or grounded. Get support from a therapist, start a meditation practice, learn breathwork techniques to keep your cool. The good news is, you have vitality-boosting Jupiter in your sign all year (except from May 13 to July 28). You could feel quite energetic under this athletic planet's care. While you may be in beast mode, go easy on your joints. Be vigilant about warming up and stretching to avoid injury. If you're a runner or weightlifter, swap in yoga or other low-impact workouts. Since Saturn rules the skin, bones and teeth, these body parts may require extra TLC. If you fall off the wagon, a cleanse or detox could get you back in the zone once Venus enters your twelfth house on November 5.

MONEY

Reinvention, mastery or a heaping helping of both? You're on the starting block of an unscripted chapter, Aquarius, which feels exciting and overwhelming at once! Enterprising Jupiter parks in your sign for most of the year, sparking a venturesome 12-year cycle! You could ditch the daily grind to helm your own business or work as an independent contractor. Prefer a steady paycheck? Take on an "intrapreneurial" role within an established company. Responsible Saturn—touring Aquarius until March 7, 2023—is grooming you for leadership, mastery and prestige! Ready to break into a new field? Jupiter gets

265

you off to a running start, but don't bank on overnight success. Saturn insists that you earn your chops with good old-fashioned hustle. Raise your rates or set up a salary review while lucky Jupiter takes a quick spin through Pisces, energizing your second house of income from May 13 to July 28. Need to brush up your tech skills or cast for a more capable cohort? Two eclipses, on May 26 and December 4, can point you toward the resources you need.

FRIENDS & FAMILY

Set your status to "away," Aquarius. With indie-spirited Jupiter and solitary Saturn stationed in your sign, 2021 could be quite the self-contained year. It's not that you mind having others around... as long as they don't interrupt your groove. You're enjoying your own company now, and there's nothing wrong with that! Surround yourself with people who understand the concept of "parallel play," where you hang out together, working on independent projects. Problems could arise when your autonomous ways clash with social and family obligations. You may bristle at people's "demands" for your attention, even if you were the one who put these house rules in place to begin with. Look out! Conflicts could boil over as your co-rulers, disruptive Uranus and boundary-hound Saturn, lock into three combative squares: February 17, June 14 and December 24. Changes on the homefront could shake up your living situation near the lunar eclipse on November 19. But hey, maybe it's time that your inner circle learned to fend for themselves—especially if they've been relying on you as their fixer. Just make sure your people know that you love them! You're going to need their support after November 5, when Venus spins into an emotionally tender cycle until March 6, 2022.

Aquarius
POWER DATES

AQUARIUS NEW MOON
April 11 (10:30 PM ET)

AQUARIUS FULL MOON
October 20 (10:56 AM ET)

SUN IN AQUARIUS
January 19 – February 18

Get ready for a bold new start! With both Jupiter and Saturn in your sign this year, big changes and new life structures are headed your way. Let the reinvention tour begin!

Saturn in Aquarius: Rebuild and refocus.
December 17, 2020–March 7, 2023

Where is the line between "we" and "me"? Can you contribute to the collective without sacrificing your renegade identity? As the zodiac's team-spirited individualist, you're a master at distilling everyone's needs, then designing the ideal compromise. But how satisfying is this for you…really?

The AstroTwins' 2021 Horoscope   267

In 2021, the stars send Ambassador Aquarius on a yearlong sabbatical. Bountiful Jupiter and boundary-hound Saturn are co-piloting through your zodiac sign, activating your first house of initiative, identity and independent activity. Translation? Instead of compulsively negotiating peace treaties, the question now becomes: What lights me up?

Drilling down to your desires is not as easy as it sounds. (Communicating them may be even harder!) Old scripts may be lodged in your psyche telling you that it's "selfish" or "narcissistic" to put yourself first. Expect to combat judgments from your inner circle, too, threatened by your pioneering efforts—particularly if you ask them to pick up some of the slack you've been carrying. Learning to assert yourself will be disruptive, uncomfortably so, at times. But consider the alternative: If you don't give your voice a stronger place in the chorus, you'll drown in resentment. Trust that relationships will rebalance in a liberating way as you evoke the spirit of "free to be you and me." (That's balm to the Aquarian soul!)

Hosting broad-minded Jupiter and control-freak Saturn in your sign can feel like having one foot on the gas and the other on the brake. But in truth, these planets can make beautiful music together. Jupiter is the galactic gambler, ready to roll the dice on every promising opportunity. Sound, stoic Saturn is the wise elder, who moves cautiously in the direction of success. As they check and balance each other, they attract luck while powering up your strategic mind. With this dynamic duo in your corner, calculated risks pay huge dividends in 2021.

Jupiter's visit is a shorter one, as the red-spotted planet only takes up residence in Aquarius from December 19, 2020, to December 28, 2021 (more on that in the next section). Saturn is anchored in your sign from December 17, 2020, until March 7, 2023. Heads up: Their most potent connection already happened on December 21, 2020, when Jupiter and Saturn aligned at 0°29" Aquarius. The "Great Conjunction," as this tete-a-tete is called, only happens once every 20 years. (The last one was on May 28, 2000.) But there hasn't been a Great Conjunction in Aquarius since January 6, 1405! (That's 616 years ago, if you don't feel like doing the math.) So yeah, this is a really major deal for you.

Feeling sparked? Great Conjunctions ignite, initiate and activate. On a global level, 2021's cooperative dance of Jupiter and Saturn pushes our collective systems and structures in an Aquarian direction. Hot topics for this year will include: social justice, shared resources, public health, technology, energy innovation, universal love, metaphysical awareness. Could it be that the rest of the human race is finally going to rise up to your elevated frequency? Certainly,

> **"Tag, you're it, Aquarius: the leader of the new school of thought. Guide others by living your truth, loud and proud."**

a greater percentage of the population will, Water Bearer. TBH, that may feel exhilarating and eerie at once. Originality is your calling card and it weirds you out when people "catch up" to your advanced outlook on life…not that they ever outpace you! Periodic ego checks will be necessary (along with a heaping dose of compassion) as you watch some "basic" types fumble through the enlightened concepts you've grasped since you were in middle school.

So…tag, you're it, Aquarius: the leader of the new school of thought! Teach and preach from a public podium, or guide others by living your truth, loud and proud. Just get ready for a lot more attention than your chill sign is used to. People may elevate you to guru status this year, studying (and yes, copying) the templates you set. That's a lot of power to wield, Aquarius.

Are you visibly uncomfortable right now? As one of the zodiac's free spirits, you resent when people become overly reliant on you. Don't freak out! Instead, shift from enabling to empowering. It's not your job to spoon-feed anyone solutions. Just encourage your superfans to figure it out for themselves. (You'll be amazed at the power of a "You've got this, babe!" in 2021.)

Define your limits right up front. Whether you're entering a romantic relationship or joining a dance troupe, be clear: What's your responsibility and what's theirs? How much compromise can you handle before you feel suffocated? Give yourself all the space and grace you need to reflect on this before you commit to any shared activities. People are just going to have to be patient with your process in 2021.

Let's dig into Saturn's influence before moving on to Jupiter. Before quirky, side-spinning Uranus was discovered by telescope in 1781, Saturn was considered the ancient ruler of Aquarius. Modern astrologers dub it your "co-ruler," and it remains one of your cosmic beacons. Whatever zodiac sign and house (solar and natal) Saturn is touring will influence your goals for approximately three years.

Saturn took a brief lap through Aquarius last year, from March 21 to July 1, 2020. (Read that again if you didn't just realize that this dovetailed with the first wave of pandemic lockdowns.) The restrictive taskmaster was hardly shy about announcing its entry into your sign. The term "social distancing" is basically a synonym for "Saturn in Aquarius." As the world grappled with new ways to commune without spreading a contagious, deadly virus, waves of loneliness and isolation forced us to use technology to stay connected. But Saturn brought its legendary buzzkill. TikTok overload, Zoom fatigue and public schools taught via Google Classroom. Suddenly, the mobile screens we couldn't stop staring at became the devices we wanted to hurl out the window in frustration! The united global uprising in support of Black Lives Matter, sparked by the brutal murders of George Floyd and Breonna Taylor, was at its strongest while Saturn toured your humanitarian sign.

A lot changed for everyone in 2020, but you, Aquarius, felt these seismic shifts more intensely than most. Saturn only visits your sign every 29.5 years. (Before 2020, Saturn's last pass through Aquarius was from February 6, 1991, through January 28, 1994.) We're not going to lie, Water Bearer, the next two-plus years could demand epic levels of resilience. With the planetary drill sergeant auditing your life, it's time to grow up! Get ready to confront every unworkable structure and immature behavior that you've staunchly defended.

Simultaneously, you'll see where duty-bound ideals may also be restricting your evolution. Principles you adopted from parents, teachers and modern-day role models will come under the microscope. Do these reflect your current values or are you trying to avoid conflict? Get ready for a master class in adulting, as Saturn reveals sophisticated strategies for self-expression.

It might help to think of the next two-plus years as astrological boot camp. To level up to the next phase of the game, you've gotta muscle through basic training. Daily drills will build strength, cement healthier habits and create neural pathways that allow for a legit mindset shift. Getting to Saturn's finish line is a triathlon, not a sprint. Unfortunately, delayed gratification is not the Aquarian way. That might add to your struggle with this planet's severity, alas. To motivate yourself, celebrate mini milestones and daily wins.

As one of the zodiac's lifelong learners, there's pleasure to be found in paying your dues. Embrace the process as much as the goal and you could crush this cosmic cycle. Saturn rules experts and elders. This may be the excuse you've been waiting for to train with a cutting-edge master in your dream industry. Climate change activist? Permaculture farmer? VR game designer? Somatic therapist? Pivoting in any direction is sanctioned by Saturn's occupation of your self-authorized first house. As long as you're willing to put in the work, Water Bearer, this could be the reinvention tour you didn't even know you needed.

Pristine levels of integrity and responsibility will be required for this journey. That's hardly a problem for most Aquarians, since you operate on high-vibe ideals. Saturn's demand for structure, on the other hand? That's another story. Expect to hit some walls, especially when navigating office politics or red tape. Clock-puncher Saturn can put the kibosh on your meandering workflow, forcing you to be accountable to other people's deadlines and schedules at a level you've never dealt with before.

Grrrr. We know you always get the job done, Aquarius. You'll even exceed expectations by independently deploying the most up-to-date methods and techniques. But good luck explaining that to your cohort in 2021. Deadlines will be deadlines under Saturn's reign. Respect due process, scheduling appointments instead of relying on "the universe" to create a serendipitous calendar overlap. Get in the practice of sending out formal meeting invites, ideally with a start and an end time to keep expectations clear. Spell out expectations and stick to them for best results.

As Saturn tours your first house of identity until March 7, 2023, give the Aquarius "brand" a review. Objectively critique all front-facing assets: websites, social media accounts, profile photos, merch. While we'd never suggest you give up your rebellious identity, seek a middle ground between "polished" and "punk rock." Saturn is the planet of maturity, inspiring a sleeker, more adult representation. It's fine to be the class clown, crystal collector or the Coachella VIP (or all of the above). Just make sure you show your full range and depth, Aquarius. People are ready to see your serious side, too.

To wit, Aquarius Paris Hilton took a stab at shedding her early-aughts image as a ditzy celebutante. Her documentary *This is Paris* debuted last September, shortly after Saturn's first pass through your sign. While the iridescent Fred Segal minidresses of her *A Simple Life* days were still in rotation, a throatier, well-spoken Hilton emerged. Self-reflective and bewildered by the "cartoon character" identity she created, Hilton shared candidly about the traumatic abuse she suffered at the hands of boarding school staff as well as physical violence she endured in romantic relationships. Now taking up the mantle of empowering survivors to break their silence, Hilton declared to the press that, "Activism and being an activist is the new influencer." Hear, hear!

Whether you care to walk a mile in Paris Hilton's Louboutins or march to the beat of a totally different drum, you may emerge as a powerful voice for a cause in 2021. Maybe it's time to get serious about building a personal platform, investing in equipment for livestreaming or podcasting. Already the reigning royal of (fill in the blank)? Water Bearers who have devoted their 10,000 hours (a la Malcolm Gladwell) to a craft may foray into the expert industry. Under Saturn's watch, you could make a bundle by developing and selling your own online curriculum. Not interested in DIY-ing your way to the top? You could become a brand ambassador or guest expert on someone else's channel. Design a sleek PDF one-sheet and send out a flurry of personalized pitches.

Before you begin blueprinting and building anything, however, survey your landscape. Saturn is the astrological architect. Old structures may be in need of a teardown or, at least, a renovation which will bring them up to code. Inspect vigilantly! Saturn wants you to create a historical landmark, not a pop-up shop. With that in mind, set realistic timelines so you don't have to rush development. This is not the year to cut corners or pass things off as "good enough." In fact, faking it 'til you make it could have detrimental effects. The good news is that you can boost your status and credibility in 2021. Just plan to put in long hours and sweat equity if you want to lay a solid foundation.

The first house is the "autonomous zone" of the zodiac, so be mindful of the guest stars you invite to be part of your crew. Benevolent Aquarians are always ready to hook up a friend, but your generosity could backfire if your posse is not qualified for the job. (Or worse, they might have "authority issues" that they start projecting onto you!) Bringing the amateurs up to speed could drain hours of your time; or, if you recommend them for a gig and they fail to deliver, it could reflect poorly on you. Save your superconnector skills for people whose sterling work ethic you can vouch for!

Feeling sleepy? Health-wise, Saturn's tour through your first house may temporarily zap your energy, especially if you've been slacking on self-care. Night-owl Aquarians may require more sleep over the coming two years. Tucking in early with a thick novel and a cup of lavender tea could sound downright exhilarating many evenings—a shocking departure from your "life of the party" status. Quiet time is definitely nice, but as this Saturn cycle wages on, make a concerted effort to boost your vitality. Clean up your diet, hydrate with water (instead of coffee or your favorite adult beverage) and have a blood panel done to check your levels. You may discover that you're low on Vitamin D or iron deficient. Routine-driven Saturn helps you build strength through daily practices. Start slowly if you must. A "Couch to 5K" program could be a game-changer if you need to turn potential energy into kinetic force.

Saturn rules aging and the first house governs appearances. Even the eternally youthful among you may want to put some clock-slowing practices in place. Relax daily with breathing techniques, meditation and time in nature. If you're considering cosmetic dermatology treatments, do careful research before you inject anything—and only book with recommended pros (even if you found a killer deal on Groupon). Note: Saturn will be retrograde from May 23 to October 10, which is not an optimal time for any such procedures.

Saturn rules the teeth, skin, bone structure and knees. In 2021, you'll need to get yourself a good dentist, aesthetician and chiropractor. Take off your makeup at night and swap in a moisturizer with sunscreen. Go easy on exercise that puts a major strain on your joints—and remember to floss!

Yes, this is a lot more thinking and strategizing than your spontaneous sign is used to, but here's the bright side of this transit: Planning is an Aquarius forte, as long as you're jazzed about whatever scheme you're cooking up. Opt in to activities that challenge and excite you, and delete the halfhearted engagements from your calendar. Saturn's streamlining influence will shrink your list of commitments and casual friends, but hey, that's more than okay! Time is the most precious commodity we have, Aquarius. Devote your hours to pursuits that give you a rewarding ROI.

Saturn in Aquarius square Uranus in Taurus
February 17, June 14 & December 24

Seismic shifts are ahead for Aquarians in 2021, but how will these changes impact your home and family life? Is your foundation stable enough to handle this much transformation? The Aquarius basecamp will go through a trio of stress tests this year as your cosmic co-rulers, Saturn and Uranus dance into dynamic 90° squares in the sky. These challenging formations—which take place on February 17, June 14 and December 24—could shake up life as you know it. Toto, we don't think you're in Kansas anymore.

Saturn is solidly anchored in Aquarius from December 17, 2020, through March 7, 2023, calling forth the mature, responsible part of your nature. Spontaneous Uranus, on the other hand, is stirring the pot in Taurus, the ruler of your fourth house of home, roots and security. Decisions you make in your own best interest may draw backlash from your inner circle. Worse, the more effort you put into gaining their support, the less likely they are to rally behind you.

The remedy? Serve up some good old-fashioned tough love. Stick to your guns, despite any unsolicited judgments from the masses. Close the opinion polls with "helpful" friends, too. Adulting by Saturn's standards is all about learning to trust your own inner guidance. If you make a mistake, you'll correct course and grow from the experience—but at least you'll know it was your decision! That's important this year.

Friends and family often count on Aquarians to be their unconditionally accepting rock. Oh, and also the entertainment director, the voice of reason, the IT specialist...shall we go on? But as Saturn directs your attention toward personal growth, patience will thin for people who treat you like their on-call life coach. You're so done being the fixer for perpetually distressed friends. Same for dramatic relatives who are their own worst enemies. Parents and children may be especially vocal in their pushback against a decision that you feel confident making. Time to wean yourself off that monthly stipend from the 'rents, in the name of regaining autonomy. Aquarius parents will need to lay down stricter guidelines with rebellious kids, underscoring that there are consequences to their actions.

Yes, Water Bearer, some serious blowups could erupt during the three Saturn-Uranus squares, forcing you to get real about your boundaries. Dynamics you've played out for years are suddenly up for grabs, throwing everyone into unknown territory. There could be major tension to weather as you settle into new roles. While there's probably no side-stepping the drama, do your best to detach and de-escalate. This will sort itself out, Aquarius, but you have to stand firm in your convictions.

Ready to reinvent your concept of home? Quirky Uranus provides an outlet for your adventurous side, but its destabilizing energy could pull up your roots. For example, maybe you enroll in a PhD program, then write your dissertation in an RV, visiting national monuments in between research sessions. Or you organize an apartment swap with three friends who live in different cities around the globe. Each quarter, you move to a new zip code, soaking up the culture of the area as a short-term resident.

Aquarians wishing to plant deeper roots could hit some walls, especially near the dates of these three turbulent transits. If you're purchasing property, have it thoroughly (and we mean thoroughly) inspected, for everything from ground water to black mold to property line conflicts that have never been legally resolved. Dream homes could turn into nightmares if you have to deal with loud construction, disrespectful neighbors or crime that you didn't notice when you checked out the place during daylight hours.

We're not saying you can't make a successful move in 2021. It's just that you might be happier with fewer domestic responsibilities. Then again, if being a homeowner (or land steward) is part of your Saturn in Aquarius vision for adulthood, let that factor into your house-hunting plans. By all means, consider the starter apartment, but if, say, you're looking to settle down in the next few years, you might be better off considering a single-family home with a yard and a decent school within walking distance. Or if you're of the age where you no longer want to hear your upstairs neighbor's 1AM kettlebell workout, the Saturn-Uranus squares could shuttle you off to a forever home that has "peaceful oasis" written all over it. Ahhhh.

Jupiter in Aquarius & Pisces

January 1: Aquarius (since December 19, 2020)
May 13: Pisces (retrograde June 20)
July 28: Aquarius (retrograde until October 18)
December 28: Pisces (until December 20, 2022)

In 2021, Jupiter will shift back and forth between Aquarius and Pisces. Normally, Jupiter makes an unbroken trek through a single sign for 12 to 13 months, but in 2021, we'll see the planet of fortune and growth in two signs.

Jupiter in Aquarius

December 19, 2020–May 13, 2021
July 28–December 28, 2021

Liftoff!

Fresh starts: incoming! Despite stodgy Saturn's occupation of your sign, you could still have one the most adventurous and energizing years in over a decade. Buoyant Jupiter sails through Aquarius for most of 2021—with the exception of a quick visit to Pisces from May 13 to July 28. This lends an upbeat, can-do perspective to all your personal projects. You're embarking on a fresh 12-year cycle now, so leave the last decade-plus in the rearview and keep your focus straight ahead!

Jupiter is the planet of good fortune, and when it's in your sign, you're inspired to gamble on a very worthy venture—yourself! A solo mission, a passion project, dreams deferred—whatever you've been putting off for "someday" could take front-burner status. And while Saturn might be tapping the brakes, Jupiter counters by putting the pedal to the metal. Until May 13 and again from July 28 to December 28, the red-spotted planet will fill your tanks with rocket fuel, ensuring that you move along at a faster clip whenever you're ready to hit the gas.

When Jupiter visits your sign, it's like you get a clean slate. While many Water Bearers could have a long list of ambitions, it's just as likely you have zero clue what you want to do next. That's perfectly fine, Aquarius! You may be starting with an utterly blank page, which is yours alone to write on.

Under such experimental skies, grant yourself cosmic clearance to explore all the options before picking a lane. Thrill-seeking Jupiter nudges you far out of your comfort zone. Without ignoring Saturn's cautionary guidance, you can still follow an inkling and see where it takes you. Maybe you'll discover a new passion; maybe you'll just be able to cross something off your bucket list. A vibrant and soul-expanding journey is in store either way.

The last time Jupiter toured Aquarius was from January 5, 2009, until January 17, 2010. Reflect back on that period: What interests were you engaged in then? Was there a particular crowd you couldn't get enough of? A passion you couldn't stop pursuing? You may find themes repeating now. Maybe you embarked on a new career path, relocated or totally changed your appearance from preppy jock to vintage glam. Perhaps it was a "coming out" year for you in some way. Every 12 to 13 months, expansive Jupiter changes signs, shifting the focus of your life. Now, it's made a complete revolution around the zodiac wheel and has returned to Aquarius. The past twelve years now mark a completed cycle. Set your sights on the future, taking all the wisdom and positive memories with you for the next voyage.

Not sure where to focus? Jupiter is the planet that governs travel, entrepreneurship, higher education and media-making. You may be inspired to explore one (or

The AstroTwins' 2021 Horoscope   277

more) of these areas in 2021. Launch your startup, film the documentary, take classes to sharpen your skills in an industry you'd like to break into. Philosophical Jupiter in your sign can lead you to life-changing personal growth classes or a metaphysical teacher who opens you up to a new dimension within yourself.

Jupiter is in your first house of appearances, so if you're an aesthetically inclined Aquarius, you could launch a cruelty-free makeup or holistic skincare line (or start religiously using one!). Where Saturn's severity can suppress your youthful fashion sense, Jupiter gives you permission to dress like a club kid, college student or athleisure-loving jock when you're off-duty. Without even trying, you could set a trend, one that has the potential to go viral under this world-expanding influence!

You could have a little planetary PTSD from the last Jupiter cycle, which took place from December 2, 2019, to December 19, 2020, in Capricorn and your twelfth house of closure, healing and surrender. But don't let it rattle you anymore. You're moving forward now, with the celestially supportive winds at your back. This is a highly independent cycle, an excellent growth opportunity. Aquarius is the sign of community, and you're rarely alone or without plans to get together with one of your zillion friends (yes, those Zoom hangouts count). Even if you savor your own company, community plays a strong factor in your decisions, and you may habitually opinion-poll your peeps before making any moves.

In 2021, the tide is turning toward a new, autonomous energy. Jupiter is in your independent first house, encouraging you to focus on yourself. If you're single, you might prefer to stay that way, savoring yourself as the main event—at least for a while! Attached Aquarians will require more free time (and "me" time). Put your love interest on notice: Quality time might come in shorter bursts! In fact, your inner circle will need to be a lot more self-reliant, because your independent projects will demand extra care and feeding. Take advantage of this lucky cycle and put your passions front and center!

Jupiter in Pisces

May 13–July 28
December 28, 2021–May 10, 2022
October 28, 2022–December 20, 2022

Abundance flows.

Make it rain, Water Bearer! From May 13 to July 28, lucky Jupiter takes a quick splash into Pisces, paddling through the seas of your second house of work and money. This brief cycle is a preview of what's to come. From December 28, 2021, until May 10, 2022, the red-spotted planet will return to the sign of the Fish to pick up whatever gets started in the middle of this year.

Hosting Jupiter in your sign sparked off 2021 with plenty of adventurous self-discovery. Exciting as it's been, your internal equilibrium may feel unbalanced from all the changes. After May 13, you may want to pick a lane, giving a novel idea a chance to become something tangible. Narrowing your focus won't feel limiting now—more like a welcome relief. Jupiter in your second house helps you build financial and emotional security. Roll up your sleeves and craft something that can stand the test of time. Although you only have a couple months for development this year, what you start now can be the base for an epic launch in 2022.

Abundant Jupiter in your money sector brings a boost to your bottom line. For some Aquarians, Jupiter's brief tour through Pisces could be a preview of the prosperity that's set to flood in at the end of 2021. Your net worth and your self-worth might rocket skyward midyear. It's also a powerful time to circulate among prospective employers or explore what else is out there.

Don't wait until opportunity knocks! Find out what qualifications are required, then polish your pitch. While your natural charm will open doors, a solid and consistent work ethic will win 'em over during this cycle. Freelancing Aquarians should set rates that are commensurate with your skills. If work has slowed, rethink your offerings. Create packages that fall in your ideal client's 2021 price range. If that means 30-minute sessions instead of 90-minute deep dives, for example, so be it. Once you get customers in the door, they're likely to return and upgrade services as they build loyalty with you.

Working a steady job, even if it's remote? Many corporations invest in their employees growth as a retention strategy. Refresh your resume, book a salary review, see if the company will fund your schooling if you agree to stay on for a set number of years. Toot your own horn and put your crowning achievements on display. You could boost your earnings and amass a sizeable nest egg. Jupiter rules publishing, entrepreneurship, travel and teaching, so you could even end up with a new job in one of these industries. Or maybe you'll relocate for a big opportunity. Time to open your company's satellite office on the opposite coast? Never say never!

Cash in hand is always a plus, Aquarius, but easy with the spending! Since Jupiter is the zodiac's gambler, you could get a little too generous with that newfound nugget. Treat yourself to some luxuries, including experiences you'll cherish for a lifetime. Enjoy your bounty but don't be wasteful. Respect your money and be sensible with how you allocate your funds. You can't take it with you—but please, don't spend it all in one place, either!

Eclipses in 2021

May 26: Sagittarius Lunar Eclipse 5°29' (7:13am ET)
June 10: Gemini Solar Eclipse 19°42 (6:52am ET)
November 19: Taurus Lunar Eclipse 27°17 (3:57pm)
December 4: Sagittarius Solar Eclipse 12°17 (2:42am)

Gemini/Sagittarius Eclipses

Defining "your people."

Should you dial up the passion or cool down the intensity? That's a line you'll keep on walking, as a series of change-making eclipses sweeps across the Gemini/Sagittarius axis for the second year in a row. Three of 2021's four eclipses land here, reshuffling the romantic ranks and changing the guard in your friend circle. Some fascinating new faces could join your lineup, shifting your perspective and opening doors to unforeseen possibilities.

On May 26, the lunar (full moon) eclipse in Sagittarius sends frissons through your eleventh house of teamwork and technology. Welcome to the collaboration nation! This eclipse could solidify your standing in a powerful posse. People you met near the corresponding solar eclipse, last December 14, could reappear, inviting you to participate in a game-changing venture. If you're leaning toward a "yes," don't deliberate! Eclipses open a brief, propitious window. Dive in and you'll figure out the details as you go. Feeling dissatisfied with the quality of your social interactions? Organize an intentional community of your own! By teaming up for a positive cause, you could shift the tide in your neighborhood, potentially drawing attention on a global scale. Looking for a way out of a draining obligation? This eclipse hastens your departure from a group that no longer reflects your values. No guilt! Make a swift exit and don't look back.

Got a digital venture to launch? May 26 could be a powerful release date! Since eclipses herald surprises, you might just go viral. Just make sure you've worked out all the bugs and thoroughly beta-tested any offerings. With Mercury turning retrograde for three weeks on May 29, there won't be a chance to scramble with last-minute fixes.

Romance takes center stage on June 10, when the Gemini solar (new moon) eclipse bursts into your fifth house of passion, fertility and creativity. You could meet someone and feel an instant, "past-life soulmates" click. You may also decide to finally end things with someone who's either strung you along or become more of a buddy than a bedmate. Happily coupled Aquarians might escalate temperatures by trying something "naughtily experimental" together. H-h-h-hot!

Caution: A fifth house eclipse can also provoke drama. Volcanic emotions could rush forth like molten lava, especially if you don't put clear agreements in place for your playful adventures. Your reactions will be especially strong near June 10, so try not to fly off the handle. An unexpected pregnancy may be in the cards near this fecund full moon. Not in the cradle-rocking demographic? You might give birth to a creative venture that arrives as a divine download during a conversation with friends.

Speaking of which, if you're an artist or performer (as many Aquarians are), the June 10 solar eclipse could thrust you into the limelight. Get ready for your marquee moment or to take a strut down the red carpet. Since this eclipse is ruled by Gemini, the sign of the Twins, you could break out as half of a dynamic duo. This bold eclipse may certainly launch you into new levels of prestige and recognition. You might also get a huge burst of inspiration that you need to immediately write, compose, paint, etc. The muse has arrived—and she's ready to get down to business!

Lastly, the December 4 solar (new moon) in Sagittarius eclipse could bring a breakthrough around a group project, especially one with a digital, activist or utopian bent. A world-bettering collaboration may take flight, or you might launch something online that makes a huge year-end splash. Aquarians who still have vacancies in your social circle could link up with an avant-garde new crew when this lunation brings fresh friendships and opportunities to expand your reach.

Extracurricular developments will simmer down after December 4, however, since this is the final eclipse in the Gemini/Sagittarius series that's been shaking things up since June 5, 2020. While it's been a colorful ride, you'll be grateful to downshift into a more settled social groove. With your squad solidified and everyone's romantic status (hopefully) clarified, celebrate the holidays in ideal Aquarian style, surrounded by the comforting presence of your favorite peeps. Pose for photos—in ironically tacky Christmas sweaters, maybe?

Taurus/Scorpio Eclipses

New plans for home and career.

On November 19, a new eclipse series ignites along the Taurus/Scorpio axis. Until October 28, 2023, you'll be juggling to balance Taurus-ruled domestic duties with the Scorpio-governed demands of your career. Chateau Aquarius could get the first hit of energy under the Taurus lunar (full moon) eclipse this November 19. Conflicts that have been brewing for nearly six months may boil over, forcing you to negotiate house rules with the other people living under your roof. Aquarians in the market for a move might radar in on the perfect listing, whether it's a primary residence, rental property or a piece of land that you'll cultivate for a visionary purpose. (Retreat center? Farm-to-table resto?) Buckle up! You could be living at a new address faster than expected. Love where you live? Plans could get underway for renovating, reconfiguring rooms or building an ADU that you can rent out as an Airbnb.

Venus Retrograde in Capricorn: Surrender and release.

December 19, 2021–January 29, 2022
Venus in Capricorn: November 5, 2021 - March 6, 2022
Venus Retrograde: December 19, 2021 - January 29, 2022

Desperately seeking…closure? Starting November 5, you'll get a prime opportunity to tie up loose ends, especially in matters of the heart. Venus, the planet of love and romance, embarks on a four-month journey through Capricorn and your twelfth house of surrender, spirituality and healing. Until March 6, 2022, you'll have a rare, extended opportunity to drill down to the root of an ongoing block. Have you never really dealt with a breakup, loss or a disappointing experience from your history? Does the same dynamic keep cropping up in every relationship—whether the love affair gets off to a bumpy start or you swear you've finally found your twin flame? It's time to turn inward, Aquarius.

We all have our blind spots, those issues that are so buried from our view that we project them onto other people, certain that they are to blame for our heartache. But what if it takes two to tango, Aquarius? What if the change begins with you? This kind of accountability can be a bitter pill to swallow, especially when the rawest feelings are involved. But Venus' tour through Capricorn gives you the courage to face down a demon that's dogged you for years. Drop the grudge and let the healing begin. Forgiveness might even be possible by March, but first, focus on yourself.

Fortunately, when Venus floats through your twelfth house, she'll swaddle you in support, making it easier to touch past pain and process it fully. Get ready for a deluge of feelings, from grief to rage to deep regret. Your heart may take a little

283

longer than your head to resolve this, so don't push yourself to "get over it" faster than is humanly possible.

This metamorphic spell may be most profound from December 19, 2021, and January 29, 2022, when Venus pivots into a six-week retrograde. During this time, you'll plunge into places that you've struggled to access for years. Do not fear these periodic backspins, Water Bearer. Venus turns retrograde every 18 months (the last one was from May 13 to June 25, 2020, in Gemini), opening up an important review period for all your close relationships.

And yes, that means Venus will be retrograde during the holidays. Take extra precautions to protect your heart from triggering situations. Guilt and denial have no place at your tables. Leave your anxiety-inducing aunt or boundary-challenged brother-in-law off the guest list if you know they'll suck the air out of the room. You might even choose to fete NYE in semi-solitude, lighting a bonfire for a spiritual ceremony in lieu of igniting noisy fireworks.

Fascinating fact: Every eight years, Venus turns retrograde in the same part of the zodiac wheel, minus two degrees. Flip back in your timeline to the period between December 21, 2013, and January 31, 2014. Themes from that time may recur—or, in some cases, people you haven't talked to since then could show up to make amends, get back in touch, or possibly reconcile a romantic relationship.

Retrogrades can act as do-overs, too. If you ended a connection prematurely, you may get a second chance with your ex between December 19, 2021, and January 29, 2022. Venus lingers in Capricorn until March 6, 2022, and it might take until then to figure out if the sequel is a great idea or an awful one. Check in with yourself always: Is the urge to "kiss and make up" coming from true desire, or a fear that you may never find someone who treats you the way you deserve? If the latter is the case, consider going on a dating hiatus so you can get centered in your own power again. Venus in your twelfth house can be a truly beneficial time to work with therapists, healers, and spiritual counselors.

Another way Venus in Capricorn could play out? You meet someone with legit soulmate potential. Pay attention to who shows up on your radar between

November 5 and March 6. Venus in your twelfth house can bring some charmed possibilities your way. Just keep the rose-colored glasses off your holiday wish list. As the planet of amour scripts a fairy tale with you as its swept-away star, you could lose your footing. And during the retrograde, there's a high risk that

"This deep-diving Venus cycle can bring some illuminating insights for you both."

you might totally detach from reality when it comes to love. Keep in close communication with a levelheaded BFF who can steer you back to reality before romanticism overtakes your good senses.

Alas, all the common-sense coaxing might not beckon you back…not when the dopamine rush of "new relationship energy" kicks in, or you suddenly get inspired about a lofty plan that will totally revolutionize your long-term relationship. The twelfth house rules illusions and denial. You're especially susceptible to falling into a rescue mission while Venus is retrograde from December 19 to January 29. As you wander through a deceptive hall of mirrors, it's impossible to not idealize the starving artist, broken bird or charismatic narcissist who wears childhood trauma like a seductive cloak.

Coupled Aquarians won't be able to sweep issues under the rug—and that's probably a good thing! This deep-diving Venus cycle can bring some illuminating insights for you both. Book a session with a therapist or sign up for a workshop that helps you heal issues and support one another through your self-discoveries. Has someone been a consistent crazymaker in your life? Whether you want to rip their head or their clothes off (or both), you may realize that it's time to say a final farewell or put up an un-crossable boundary.

If you're struggling to move on from a breakup, here's an idea: Create a mourning ritual for getting through the pain. Even relationships that end in shambles started out with some sort of promise. You wouldn't have wasted your time on them otherwise. Which parts of this person or experience will you always yearn for and really miss? Set up a temporary altar with photos or objects, allowing yourself to feel the pain of the loss fully as you sit before it. By January 29, 2022, you might even be ready to build a fire and do a ceremonial burning of a few of those mementos—or else pack them away in storage. If visual evidence of the past is too triggering, set aside a block of time each day to read healing books, journal, and give your emotions space to unleash.

Heavy as this sounds, take heart, Aquarius. Venus (along with Jupiter) is one of the two "benefics," meaning that even when in a challenging position, its effects are still gentle...and ultimately positive. The retrograde doesn't have to be a holiday buzzkill! Venus in the twelfth house is a stellar time for connecting to your spirituality, creativity and psychic gifts. As long as you protect yourself from energy vampires and surround yourself with people who can help foster your abilities, you'll be in good hands.

Have you always wanted to learn dream interpretation, dissect astrology charts or train to be a Reiki practitioner? With enchanting Venus in your corner, you could connect to a powerful mentor, guru or guide. And don't be surprised if a deck of oracle cards shows up in your stocking! ✳

Pisces

HOROSCOPE

2021 HIGHLIGHTS

LOVE

Love on the brain, Pisces? Your status as the hopeless romantic of the zodiac will be more obvious than ever this year, as serious Saturn and carefree Jupiter dance through Aquarius and your twelfth house of fantasy. You're ready to write the fairy tale and self-publish it—then livestream yourself getting swept away when exhibitionist Jupiter darts forward into Pisces for a brief visit from May 13 to July 28. Careful what you commit to though! Jupiter's fleeting tour of Pisces will revive your carefree, liberated nature. Relationships that are heavy and entangled could feel like an albatross around your neck, especially at the year's end, when Jupiter returns to Pisces for a longer stretch. But if you're excited to build a life together, create a home or make babies, the June 10 solar eclipse could accelerate developments. Commitments may be tested again near the November 19 and December 18 lunar eclipses. With a willingness to communicate and negotiate, you could wind up closer than ever. Being your S.O.'s best friend—and remembering that it takes a village to keep a relationship thriving—is the best strategy for staying together in the last quarter of the year. Assemble a supportive crew and lean on them instead of making your love interest play therapist, extra important when Venus turns retrograde for six weeks on December 19.

MONEY

Two eclipses in Sagittarius activate your professional tenth house, bringing your achievements into the spotlight. Payoffs for your hard work could be bountiful during the lunar (full moon) eclipse on May 26. Pisces seeking a new path might be ready to leap then, or during the solar (new moon) eclipse on December 4. Coaching may be required. With high-minded Jupiter in your spiritual twelfth house, studying with a sensei could sharpen your gifts. Some Pisces can finally commit to working in the "woo," generating revenue from your mystical gifts. Art, music and performance could also fill the coffers. Need a break to figure out your soul's calling? With both Saturn and Jupiter in your transitional twelfth house, a short-term sabbatical may provide the reflective timeout required.

WELLNESS

Healing is an inside job for you in 2021—and you're going to have to enter some deep chambers to access the riches. With diligent Saturn and exploratory Jupiter doing archaeological digs in your subconscious twelfth house, you could process buried feelings from guilt to shame to grief. Saturn helps you develop a practice, like daily meditation or journaling. Weekly sessions with a therapist might also be beneficial, especially if they're trained in modalities like hypnosis, EMDR or even shamanic journeying. When it comes to body care, 2021 is a year to investigate food-based cleanses and detox programs. Tackle addictions with professional support—and make sure you clue in your community so that they can support your efforts, not derail them! A healthy environment will guarantee success and smooth recovery.

FRIENDS & FAMILY

So many people, so little time! You may be feeling particularly tapped out after 2020's social lineup, and ready to retreat. You don't have to go M.I.A., Pisces, but one of your crucial lessons for 2021 is learning the art of the graceful "no." Setting limits is not the same as shutting people out. Cultivate connections with a spiritual or artistic community and spend time with people who understand your need to ebb and flow. By the same token, losing touch with important friends could happen during this drifty, dreamy year if you're not careful. You can't force yourself to be social if you're not feeling it, but you can be upfront about your need for space. On June 10, a family-focused solar eclipse may alter the configuration of people living under your roof. And your friend circle might undergo big changes during the lunar eclipse on November 19. If you're honest with yourself, some of these changes were probably a long time coming. While bittersweet, don't let nostalgia prevent you from opening up to new connections.

Pisces
POWER DATES

PISCES NEW MOON
March 13 (5:21 AM ET)

PISCES FULL MOON
September 20 (7:54 PM ET)

SUN IN PISCES
February 18 – March 20

Take a rest, Pisces...no wait, don't! This year, you'll be wrapping up one long chapter of your life while simultaneously starting an exciting new one.

Saturn in Aquarius: Retreating and defining boundaries.

December 17, 2020–March 7, 2023

Now they see you, now they don't? As the zodiac's "master of illusions," you could pull one of your famous disappearing acts this year. It's not that you're trying to hide away in your pearlescent oyster shell. It's just that diligent Saturn

291

dipped into Aquarius on December 17, 2020, and will be napping below sea level in your esoteric twelfth house until March 7, 2023.

This cycle, which only happens every 29.5 years, is like an extended artist's residence. Not only is your naturally vivid imagination activated, but you have a direct line to the divine. And with hardworking Saturn here, this is a powerful time for sharpening your creative gifts and your intuitive ones.

You already got a taste of Saturn in Aquarius last year. From March 21 to July 1, 2020, the ringed planet made its first visit to the Water Bearer's realm since 1994—which, in many places, dovetailed with the first phase of sheltering orders. More than one Pisces friend has whispered to us that, despite being freaked out by the pandemic, they secretly enjoyed that window of guilt-free solitude which quarantine provided.

So...what did you discover about yourself during that tide-turning quarantine? One Pisces friend, a talented painter, sold her first largescale piece and began working on series for a post-COVID gallery show. Another Fish deepened his skills as a medium and energy worker, staying up many nights learning how to identify spirits and clear entities from his living space—as well as the ones hovering in his girlfriend's 100-year-old house. True to Pisces form, our Fishy friend and fellow astrologer Stephanie Gailing wrapped the final edits on a dream interpretation book she'd been longing to write for years.

As the twelfth sign of the zodiac, the twelfth house is your native terrain. You're in your element when a planet orbits through this dreamscape—and in 2021 both Saturn and Jupiter spend time there. But here's the rub: Uptight Saturn is excruciatingly uncomfortable in the bohemian twelfth house. This planet loves boundaries, rules, status and structure. The twelfth house is boundless, spiritual, untethered and imaginative. Welcome to Paradox Central!

Learning to balance these polarizing forces could throw you into a precarious imbalance. But once you get your sea legs, look out, world: Mastering the mystical could become your 2021 quest! Saturn is the hardest working planet in the solar system. Wherever this cosmic mogul is orbiting, you'll willingly put in sweat equity. Over the next two years, you could enter a training program for something artistic or spiritual or even off-the-charts "woo," like getting certified as a meditation coach or an animal communicator.

While you're at it, how about monetizing some of your healing gifts so you can share them with the world in a way that also sustains you? No, it's not "un-

> ## "Drawing clear lines between work and rest time is another 2021 lesson."

spiritual" to charge for such things. Not if you look at money as a fair exchange for all the time, energy and love you devote to your craft.

Whatever you're called to learn and study, keep forging ahead. Don't squander the opportunity to explore the rich landscape of your imagination! At the same time, don't push yourself too hard. Drawing clear lines between work and rest time is another essential lesson for 2021. The twelfth house rules the dream state. With Saturn snoozing here, you will need more sleep than usual between now and March 7, 2023. (That's saying a lot for a sign that can give Sleeping Beauty a run for her high-thread-count satin sheet set!) Structured Saturn will also favor going to bed and rising at regular times. Get those circadian rhythms on a schedule!

This introspective Saturn cycle can feel heavy at times. Buried feelings could be dredged up, insisting that you feel, deal and heal. While you're no stranger to melancholy, pro-level support may be required to really process grief, shame or trauma that's been lodged in your subconscious since childhood. The effects may even show up as body pain, such as a persistent ache in your lower back or, since Saturn rules the bones, teeth and even your skin, with possible recurring breakouts that require a dermatologist's prescription.

While Saturn is in your twelfth house, you can do the deep inner work that banishes your demons for good. Even if you had an idyllic childhood, obstacles can still get in the way of you living your best life. The twelfth house rules the

293

subconscious, and in addition to "talk therapy," you might try other excavation techniques like sound healing, EMDR or hypnosis that can help you reach into those hard-to-access regions of mind and memory. If you're struggling with any sort of addiction, this Saturn cycle can be a powerful recovery period. Your devoted efforts—guided by well-vetted professionals and practitioners—can root out blocks you didn't realize were there. Spiritual healing modalities like hypnotherapy or a past-life regression might even help you access deeper regions of your subconscious.

Here's another way to use Saturn in the twelfth house to your advantage: This is a time for breaking unhealthy cycles of codependence and people-pleasing. There's no point in giving 'til it hurts anymore. That tactic will fall apart in 2021. Pisces who have been compromising core desires could slam up against a huge wall of resentment. Truth is, you can only live out other people's dreams for so long. With tangible, terrestrial Saturn in Aquarius, the next two years are meant for bringing your own visionary ideas to form. When the achievement-oriented planet shifts into Pisces on March 7, 2023, the effort you've been putting in now could bring you legitimate industry clout.

Since the twelfth house is the final wedge of the zodiac wheel, it's the realm of endings and closure, and with Saturn here, letting go of a beloved situation may feel inevitable. Endings are especially hard for your nostalgic, compassionate sign, but hanging on past the expiration date is a recipe for stagnation. Saturn's solution for Pisces in transition in 2021? Mourn, reflect, but do move on.

One Pisces we know sold the home she had bought 20 years earlier during Saturn's dip into Aquarius last year. Leaving behind the carefully chosen Italian marble countertops, the deck with the hot tub and the gorgeously landscaped yard (complete with a fountain system, fig tree and goddessy grapevines) was excruciating for this friend. But managing the property, which had also more than doubled in value, meant delaying retirement plans, so with heavy heart, she transferred title and deed and is now setting up a lovely residence in a smaller town which, incidentally, she paid for in full—with cash.

If something that once lifted your spirits is now leaving you drained, Saturn can help you map out an exit strategy that allows for graceful release. Mourn, grieve and ritualize the farewell process so that you can honor your tender feelings and the once-binding ties that you're loosening up for the sake of personal growth.

Saturn in Aquarius square Uranus in Taurus
February 17, June 14 & December 24

Who are the people in your neighborhood, like literally and metaphysically? Although you'll spend a great deal of 2021 drifting into the dream state, don't lose sight of your actual surroundings. Three times this year, you could come crashing back to reality as chaotic Uranus in your zone of peers and local activity sideswipes Saturn in your twelfth house of escape. On February 17, June 14 and December 24, they'll lock into challenging squares (90-degree angles) making it impossible for you to overlook the obvious…and non-obvious.

Changeable Uranus is on a longer journey through Taurus and your communal third house, from May 2018 to April 2026. During this time, your friendships and partnerships may have already taken on an ephemeral quality. "People come and go" might be a Pisces mantra on most days, but over the past few years, the turnover rate has been higher than ever. By the same token, those who can ride the waves of your mutable magic may have earned their permanent placement in the Pisces posse, ebbing and flowing when you were adrift, then providing a safe harbor when you needed to anchor down.

During the Saturn-Uranus squares, you may have to repay a debt of allegiance to people who have had your back over the past couple years. With Uranus in your zone of peers, this could be a close friend, sibling, neighbor, coworker, or someone who is a part of your day-to-day life. You're no stranger to sacrifice, and while it's important to keep some boundaries in place, you'll need to soften yours in order to lend the kind of support that's required. These are "in the trenches" moments, Pisces. While they don't come around often, you're wired and well-equipped to rush in for the rescue at times like these.

Check your strategy though! Empower, don't enable. People may be dealing with heavy matters, especially with sobering Saturn in your twelfth house. Addiction, grief, mental unwellness from trauma and anxiety: Along with holding space for their breakdown, help them find professional support to treat what ails them. These three squares will test your codependent tendencies. Empathize but don't play savior or collude with the unhealthy behaviors. That will only suck you both down into a bottomless pit of despair.

> ## "You could draw from your deep well of life experiences to help others."

Should some of your own unhealed wounds reopen during these dates, you may find yourself looking for people who can relate instead of folks who can help you process your way back to serenity. The last thing you need is a drinking buddy if you've been drowning your sorrows in a bottle, say. Get thee to a recovery program. Source referrals for therapists, healers and other practitioners from friends who have done their own work.

Uranus rules technology and the third house is the zone of communication. When Saturn squares the side-spinning planet, you could draw from your deep well of life experiences to help others. Broadcasting and writing may be especially potent channels for sharing your healing message with the world. You could set up a private consulting business, do card readings or distance Reiki.

Pisces who are trained as healers, whether with your hands (ruled the third house) or your psychic powers (governed by the twelfth), could see a boon in their business in 2021. Have you always wanted to learn a bodywork or energetic modality? Sign up for training or enroll in school.

Since the twelfth house governs the eternal realm, you may consider a certification program in an end-of-life (or afterlife!) field, perhaps as a death doula or animal communicator. There's no one more compassionate than you during life's passages, and with Uranus in your cooperative third house, you may feel compelled to sit side-by-side with your fellow humans during their most emotional hours.

Jupiter in Aquarius & Pisces

January 1: Aquarius (since December 19, 2020)
May 13: Pisces (retrograde June 20)
July 28: Aquarius (retrograde until October 18)
December 28: Pisces (until December 20, 2022)

If you're feeling adrift and introspective as the calendar turns, we wouldn't be surprised. For the first time since 2009, nomadic Jupiter is flowing through Aquarius and your watery twelfth house, joining Saturn there for most of the year. Low-key living—or a partial "gap year"—could be in the stars, especially if you're still figuring out what the next path looks like for you.

But don't expect to be incognito all year, because 2021 is extra special for Fish! From May 13 until July 28, Jupiter will dart forward into Pisces, reviving your risk-taking mojo and energizing you for big, bold changes! While this is a brief window, fear not: Jupiter will weave in and out of Pisces and your trailblazing first house again in 2022, motivating you to take a big leap.

In modern astrology, Neptune is the galactic guardian of Pisces. But before the hazy blue planet was discovered by telescope in 1846, traditional astrologers considered Jupiter your ruling planet. While Jupiter's now been demoted to "co-ruler" status, it's definitely your beacon. As the red-spotted planet weaves between the twelfth house of endings and the first house of beginnings, you may feel like you have one foot on the brake and the other on the gas. Just as you're about to advance, along comes a speed bump. But there will also be long stretches of superhighway between May 13 and July 28 where you can rev your engines. Expect to travel a good distance toward whatever's "new" and "next" for you!

The last time Jupiter visited Pisces was from January 17, 2010, to January 22, 2011. Look back on your personal timeline: What were you initiating then? Was there a dream you were chasing? Similar themes may arise mid-year, but this time around, you can pursue them with over a decade of maturity and experience under your skull-embellished, Alexander McQueen (a Pisces) belt.

Jupiter in Aquarius

December 19, 2020–May 13, 2021
July 28–December 28, 2021

Go where it flows.

So, what to expect during the transitional cycle of Jupiter in Aquarius? Well, Pisces, it's time to take a little break: More going with the flow, less pressure to perform. With expansive Jupiter in Aquarius and your dreamy and restful twelfth house, you may feel tired a lot of the time, as the vibe shifts from "fiesta" to "siesta." An erratic sleep schedule could leave you feeling even more out of sync with the world, but totally tuned in to spirit and the muse. Like it or not, you might be processing years' worth of feelings or dealing with a situation that consumes a lot of your emotional energy. The cure? Sleep on it!

Jupiter is one of the two "benefic" planets, meaning that it primarily brings good fortune and positive opportunities. However, Jupiter doesn't play small and, as the Great Expander, can drive you into excess or heedless risks. Be especially cautious with addictive substances or anything that you'd consider a slippery slope, like investing your life's savings into an unproven startup or quitting your amazing job to support a family business that is someone else's dream. Codependency could be especially amplified for much of 2021. Be vigilant about rooting that out in yourself and setting (or re-setting) limits when you start enabling someone else's helpless behavior or "victim mindset" at the expense of your own sanity.

The twelfth house rules the subconscious, and with Jupiter here, yours will be working overtime. Vivid dreams, bursts of creative inspiration during the late-night hours—the nocturnal muse is definitely "In." Keep a journal near your bed or even delve into hypnosis, mediumship and past-life regressions. Jupiter is the planet of growth, learning, entrepreneurship and travel. This Jupiter phase could inspire you to pick up a meditation or yoga practice, or to study with a masterful guru who can train you in a sacred technique. You may begin consciously seeking out coaches, consultants, shamans and other guides then signing up for every class, workshop and retreat they have to offer. There's good reason to invest in this kind of growth! Once Jupiter weaves back into Pisces on December 28 (or even during its May 13 to July 28 cycle), the Pisces student could become the master!

298

Someone close to you may need extra support—perhaps an elderly parent or a friend going through a rough time. You might need to take a time-out to repair your own health, especially if you're dealing with burnout or adrenal fatigue. Pace yourself, Pisces, and be gentle.

Many people meet a soulmate during this Jupiter cycle, or become unexpectedly pregnant. While you may grow especially close to one or two people, you could simultaneously check out on everyone else in your circle. You won't be terribly excited about logging in to social media or returning messages. As long as folks are on your mind and in your heart, they're "with" you, right? (Plus, you astrally travel to visit them basically every night, so why can't they appreciate that?)

Good luck explaining that to friends and family who want a piece of your time here on the 3D plane. If you want to keep relationships intact, schedule moments to swim up to the surface. Otherwise, key supporters could slip away, or move on to build a life with folks who are available right here, right now.

The twelfth house rules karma and you may need to make amends or do some long-overdue forgiveness work, especially while Jupiter is retrograde (backward) from June 20 to October 18. The red-spotted planet will buoy your courage and your candor. Take a chance and extend that olive branch. You're at the tail end of a long 12-year cycle, so you need to tie up loose ends, even if that means finally letting go of a connection that has run its course.

Most people resist the gift of Jupiter in the twelfth house, because it can feel like everything in your life is going awry. Some things fall apart or don't work out as planned. There can be losses and disappointments. Even your most diligent efforts and ace-in-the-hole tricks can fail you now. Some things might suddenly become difficult, and your inclination will be to push harder, only to find that you're spinning your wheels. And that can create a dilemma. We live in a culture that urges us to make things happen, to "just do it" and fight to the finish line. It's a masculine, yang and directional energy—and it will get you absolutely nowhere for the first four-and-a-half months of 2021, nor in the final five.

Keep this in mind, Fish: If things aren't working out, you're not cursed—you're blessed! It's the universe giving you a golden opportunity to make a radical change. Your luck during this Jupiter in Aquarius phase will come from adopting the Taoist practice of *wu wei*—"doing by not doing" or "action that is non-action." The universe is pushing you in its own divinely-ordered direction—one that doesn't necessarily line up with your agenda. Instead of fighting the current and swimming upstream, Jupiter's dictate is to surrender. That's something your sign knows how to do well!

Luckily, expressive Jupiter in the 12th puts the divine on speed dial. You can expect plenty of signs, messages and serendipitous moments. Your intuition is razor-sharp, so listen to it. When you quit fighting the tides, you'll be amazed at the flood of miracles that come your way. Marianne Williamson, an author whose work could be helpful this year, defines a miracle as "a shift in perception from fear to love." Those words hold the key to your happiness in 2021.

We know, you still probably don't believe us. Nobody ever does until this cycle ends—and trust us, we have been tracking it for over 20 years! Every year, another zodiac sign goes through this cosmic wormhole and 12-13 months later (or in 2021, midyear!), they emerge a butterfly when Jupiter soars into their sign.

So relax, Pisces, and don't squander this precious time. If you work as a healer, musician, dancer, actor, artist, therapist or energy worker, this could be an especially favorable time for doing the behind-the-scenes preparation. Set up an online presence so people can understand the depth and breadth of your work. Gather testimonials and social proof to help establish credibility in a crowded industry. Your status as an "emerging talent" or "indie darling" could make you a fan favorite—one who changes people's lives with a soul-stirring message.

Jupiter in Pisces
May 13–July 28
December 28, 2021–May 10, 2022
October 28, 2022–December 20, 2022

Pull back the curtains and open the doors.
Sweet redemption—at least the start of it! Exuberant Jupiter prances into your sign from May 13 to July 28, flipping the lights on and rebooting your energy levels. You're at the trailhead of a fresh 12-year life chapter—and also one of the

most exciting and adventurous years you've had in over a decade! You've earned it, Pisces, through devotion, hard work and tears. While 2021 may begin with uncertainty, emotional healing and flagging energy levels, by May 13, you'll feel like you've made it through the eye of the needle. You did some vital inner work, but you might also feel exhausted, drained and even a bit jaded.

Jupiter's tour of Aquarius was about sacrifice. Now, in a radical 180-degree turn, Jupiter in Pisces is all about you and your needs. Turn your attention to personal goals you've shuffled to the back burner. Believe it or not, all of the struggles leading up to this moment will soon make sense. You'll be rewarded for leaving toxic situations in the rearview as you move ahead into an enterprising new cycle. Jupiter's last visit to Pisces was from January 17, 2010, until January 22, 2011. Think back to that time. Did you start something new or make a major move? You may see themes from that era repeating. Either way, set your sights firmly on a challenging vision! You don't have to complete the mission this year. Just get the ball rolling!

With daring Jupiter in your sign, major moves won't seem so daunting. You could relocate, start a new relationship (or decide to fly solo), launch a new business or gain attention for one of your most cutting-edge creations. If you spent the first part of 2021 working largely behind the scenes, your hard work might pay off with recognition, even fame. Those seeds you were sowing now sprout up from the ground, revealing gorgeous blooms. As the Buddha said, "No mud, no lotus."

The only frustrating part? Jupiter's journey through Pisces only lasts until July 28 this year. Just as you gain momentum, you could get sleepy again, as the red-spotted planet drifts back into Aquarius and your healing twelfth house until December 28. Consider Jupiter's two-and-a-half-month visit to your sign like releasing a single while you're still completing your EP. You're gifted with a sweet, golden preview to explore new paths, experiment and seize life's most adventurous opportunities. Adopt a "carpe diem" philosophy, trying as many new avenues as you please and seeing what (if anything) sticks.

Don't worry too much about where it's all taking you, either. That will come at the year's end when Jupiter embarks on a longer circuit through Pisces

301

from December 28, 2021, until May 10, 2022, and again from October 28 to December 20, 2022. But do take note of what lights your fire this year. Next year, you'll have a chance to get those blazes going for real!

Eclipses in 2021

May 26: Sagittarius Lunar Eclipse 5°29' (7:13 am ET)
June 10: Gemini Solar Eclipse 19°42 (6:52 am ET)
November 19: Taurus Lunar Eclipse 27°17 (3:57 pm ET)
December 4: Sagittarius Solar Eclipse 12°17 (2:42 am ET)

Work-life balance: What's that? For the second year in a row, a series of eclipses is striking the Gemini/Sagittarius axis, teaching you how to live a productive life without sacrificing your free time. Both your personal and professional affairs could be due for transformation while these eclipses visit from May 26 to December 4, 2021.

As the zodiac's no-limits soldier, you throw yourself into everything you do with full passion and intention. But you often wind up feeling exhausted and emotionally battered from giving until you're drained. No mas, Pisces! In 2021, three of the year's four eclipses hit your fourth house of nurturing (Gemini) and your tenth house of ambition (Sagittarius). Whether you're underperforming or overdoing it, you'll get a wakeup call from these lunations to adjust your energy levels to more even settings.

The lunar eclipse on May 26 arrives with the full moon in Sagittarius, which could generate major movement for your career. Whatever you've been building since the corresponding solar (new moon) eclipse last December 14 could manifest into form. That's good reason to create consciously this year, Pisces. Focus on what you do want and be mindful of what you're building professionally, and with whom. Eclipses can exponentially increase the impact of your actions.

If you've been playing office martyr, look out! This culminating energy might herald a much-needed career change or a shakeup in the power structure at your job. In line for advancement? May 26 is your moment to leap, but not without some sort of safety net. The X-Factor of an eclipse is unavoidable, but you want to make sure your landing (wherever that may be!) is as soft as possible. With this worldly Sagittarius eclipse in your status-conscious tenth house, you might just find yourself in the C-Suite at an overseas location!

Home and family take center stage during the June 10 new moon, a solar eclipse in Gemini and your domestic fourth house. Nesting instincts could lead you in all sorts of new directions, especially since this one dovetails with peripatetic Jupiter's short tour through Pisces. Ready or not, you could be pulling up the stakes and moving across the country. Not that the shift has to be that dramatic. Renovation plans may get underway, or you could radically shift the usage of your space to accommodate 2021 you—which might involve anything from building a home recording studio to making space for your twin flame to cohabitate.

If you're ready to build a life with a partner or make some babies, the June 10 eclipse could accelerate the process. Pisces (like Rihanna) who have often dated the bad boys and girls could shock everyone and settle down with the nice, stable type, much like formerly fraught Fish Drew Barrymore, whose life now centers around parenting and supporting causes like anti-racist education for kids.

On November 19, a new eclipse series begins with the Taurus lunar (full moon) eclipse. Every six months until October 28, 2023, these momentous moonbeams will activate the Taurus/Scorpio axis. Taurus rules your third house of local activity, cooperation and communication. Scorpio is the delegate for your ninth house of worldly affairs and independence. This eclipse series will push you to balance your desire for companionship against your need for autonomy.

The first eclipse in a series is often the most intense shakeup, as it places emphasis on a new area of life and demands change! This November 19, your social circle could go through a huge shift. You may decide to "rebrand" yourself, revealing a totally new face to the world. Sure, you always knew that you could leap from physical therapist to world famous DJ without missing a beat. Or maybe you'll start dating people from a totally different gender—or decide to leave your posh downtown apartment to give homesteading a go.

Remember, most people aren't as nimble as you are, Pisces. You're not required to explain your choices to anyone! Just "do you" and before long, you're going to hear stories of how you inspired others to make a radical change in their own lives.

On December 4, the solar (new moon) eclipse could usher in fresh opportunities for your career. If you've been soul-searching to figure out where your true path—or the next one—lies, these moonbeams may bring major insights. Evoke your adventurous spirit! You might discover a burning passion to explore a new field, or even go back to school since Sagittarius rules higher education. With this lucky lunar lift spurring you on, you could wrangle a late registration into the January 2022 winter semester of a training or degree program. Nothing ventured, nothing gained!

Venus Retrograde in Capricorn: Experimental loving.

December 19, 2021 –January 29, 2022

Right-swiping royal? Belle of Bumble? Yes, we're talking to you. From November 5 to March 6, 2022, you could proudly claim such titles, when Venus spins through Capricorn and your tech-savvy eleventh house. If you've been complaining about your single status, "tap that app," Pisces. One lucky connection could be within easy reach. The eleventh house is the group sector of the chart. Joining a community, even a virtual one, may bring a high "clickthrough rate" with compatible matches. Just get out and mingle in whatever way you can. Friends could make a meant-to-be introduction, connecting you serendipitously to someone with soulmate potential.

If you're in a relationship, get ready to deck the halls in style and keep the New Year celebration going strong into 2022. Venus' tour of your outgoing eleventh house reinvigorates your social life as a couple. Your sex life gets plugged in, too! During this experimental time, it's anyone's guess what toys or temptations will make their way into your boudoir.

One caveat: You'll want to block out December 19, 2021, to January 29, 2022, as an "off season" period because Venus will be retrograde then. This six-week signal jammer happens every 584 days and could lead you astray from your best judgment. (Which, TBH has always been cloudy when your heartstrings are tugged.) Relying on pure intuition to guide romantic decisions is never a wise move while Venus is on its reverse commute. This is a time to sharpen intellect, common sense and take cold, hard facts into account.

That said, retrogrades revive the past. You might reconnect with someone you dated years ago—perhaps the last time Venus was retrograde in Capricorn from December 21, 2013, to January 31, 2014. If bad timing interfered with a sizzling connection earlier in the year, you may find your way back to each other for some mistletoe magic. Since the eleventh house is the friend zone, a platonic connection could get charged up with surprising romantic intensity. Proceed with caution during Venus' backspin, though, because you won't be able to overcome any regrettable line-crossing.

Don't be afraid to run background checks on those who make you swoon! A Google search could turn up more than you bargained for about your partner (or a potential partner). At best, you may discover some hidden achievements. Who knows? Maybe your Tinder date is a Tony-winning actor and has a screenplay in production with a major studio. At worst, you could realize you're dodging a bullet, even if it hurts like hell to cancel the fifth date with a sexy, soulful criminal whose transgressions you simply can't forgive.

Bottom line: It's better to be safe than sorry when the love planet turns into Rip Van Winkle every other year. You'll have to follow due process, which ain't easy for a free-flowing romantic like you! Slow down and, if you're still single, consider going out with multiple candidates instead of rushing into exclusivity.

Even if you've got a good one on the line, the hardest part of Venus retrograde in Capricorn will be managing your tendency to romanticize. Since the eleventh house rules the future, it's too easy to put the cart before the stallion. If you've only gone on a handful of dates, for example, stop tormenting yourself with questions like, "Have I met my twin flame?" And if you're gonna get freaky, choose a safe word and talk through boundaries and comfort zones thoroughly before you whip out the handcuffs or assume your Shibari knotting techniques will rope a lover in further.

If you've had an unrequited crush on someone who keeps popping in and out of your life, this would be the time to be more hardcore—with yourself. Limit the time you spend with the stringer-alonger. That way, you can open up space for someone who is actually ready to commit.

Coupled Pisces may have some real negotiating to do about your shared future, which could be a lively exploration. But get ready, because if you really probe, your partner might reveal some New Year's resolutions that don't easily dovetail with your own vision for 2022. You might even have strong emotions about it, feeling caught off guard, angry or upset. Try to remember that everything is a negotiation.

Maybe your partner wants to buy a small farm and develop the land while you've got your eye on a 19-foot RV that would be perfect for driving cross-country all year. Or suddenly one of you wants a baby, when last year, you were both sure that adopting a pair of Russian blue cats was more than enough caretaking. Life paths don't always line up perfectly, even when you love someone, and this Venus retrograde may reveal a fork in the road. Things like this don't have to be the end of the road, but perhaps the beginning of an adventurous new chapter. Get it all out into the open and see if you can actually play the long game together or not.

Who you do the holidays with matters as much as where you spend your seasonal celebrations. Idealistic plans to bring difficult family members together could go up in smoke—or seriously stress you out! Take the pressure off yourself to play peacemaker. The kumbaya vision is beautiful, but it's not gonna keep a narcissist from doing what they do. Know what you're getting yourself into before you send out those invites. A curated guest list is advisable, even if you "feel guilty" about leaving you-know-who off it.

On a lighter note, Venus' extended tour through Capricorn from November 5, 2021, to March 6, 2022, opens up an ideal window of time to reconnect to a beloved friend group…or get the dance troupe back together for a reunion tour. Venus is the pleasure planet, so why not upgrade? Think about doing something decadent, like renting an Airbnb in the heart of the forest with a giant room that you can use as a TikTok recording space. ✳

Plan it by the planets

Monthly Hotspots
CALENDAR

january

The New Year begins with Mars wrapping an extended six-month visit to pioneering Aries, a push to make bold resolutions. But we quickly move into practical mode when the red planet bursts into steady Taurus, the sign of the builder. Mid-month, expansive Jupiter and rebel Uranus get tangled in a cosmic conflict, forcing us to think outside the box. Late January brings the Day of Miracles, blessing us with good fortune when Jupiter and the revitalizing Sun unite. Back up your data and devices on the early side: Mercury ends the month with a retrograde pivot.

JANUARY 2021

SUN	MON	TUES	WED	THUR	FRI	SAT
					1 New Year's Day	2
3	4	5	6	7	8	9
10	11	12	13	14	15	16
17	18	19 Aquarius Season Starts	20	21	22	23
	MLK Day					
24	25	26	27	28	29	30
31						

Key:

HOTSPOT   LOVE HOTSPOT

Third Quarter   New Moon   First Quarter   Full Moon

MON
4

Mercury-Pluto meetup

Your words carry power, so wield them wisely. As expressive Mercury and secretive Pluto unite in strategic Capricorn, strong self-editing is advised. Even if you're tempted to blurt, hold back a few key details. Ask yourself: Has this person earned your trust? Saying less can create an air of mystery that works to your advantage. Use this focused transit to map a master plan. Connect important dots and watch the puzzle come together.

WED
6

Mars in Taurus through March 3

Motivator Mars charges into sensible Taurus, helping you pick up the pace without breaking the speed limit. A work or financial matter could heat up in the coming weeks. Don't rush to accept the first offer or plunk down your hard-earned cash without research. A bill may come due, and you could feel the pressure to pay it. Mars can ratchet up stress levels. While the red planet's in sensual Taurus, soothe anxiety by slowing down and savoring simple pleasures—art, music, nature—that don't cost a thing. If some extra funds do land in your wallet, treat yourself to a luxurious but practical splurge, like a new watch or a well-crafted set of speakers.

Lusty times beckon as smoldering Mars blazes into sensual Taurus, whetting your appetite for pleasure. You may be tempted to splurge on pricey gifts or, if conditions allow, an upscale date. The downside? Combative Mars in headstrong Taurus can lead to formidable fights where nobody backs down easily. But the sparks you set off with marathon makeup sex could be (almost) worth the trouble.

January 6

Third Quarter Moon in Libra

FRI

8

Mercury in Aquarius through March 15

Paging the hive mind! Clever Mercury leaves linear Capricorn and moves into innovative, collaborative Aquarius. Teaming up with avant-garde thinkers could take a project to new heights. Spruce up your online and social profiles now. A savvy digital presence will help you get your message across, especially when Mercury turns retrograde at the end of the month.

Mercury-Mars square

Everyone's entitled to their opinion, including you. But under today's stubborn sky, people will be talking (if not shouting) over each other. In the quest to be right, dialogue disappears. Avoid the arrogant posturing and one-upping mind games. Stay grounded in a spirit of humility and cooperation—two sorely-needed approaches that will be in short supply.

Venus in Capricorn through February 1

Instant gratification is never a bad thing. But with amorous Venus in conservative Capricorn for the rest of the month, long-term compatibility takes precedence over quick thrills. This is a lovely time for old-fashioned romance, from a more formal approach to courtship to easing slowly into physical intimacy. With Venus in this status-driven sign, potential partners will be viewed as a long-term investment. Will a relationship yield returns? If not, stick to a no-strings fling or friendship. Couples could team up on a business venture or tackle a shared goal.

SAT
9

Mercury-Saturn meetup

Pessimism alert! As mental Mercury and weighty Saturn unite, the glass looks half-empty. But adopting a doomsday mentality will only keep you stuck, wasting a potentially productive day. Step back and look honestly at what's not working here. How can you realistically improve this situation, one step at a time? Reach out to your network for resources. Someone in your circle could offer a great solution. Lean on the wisdom of their experience.

Venus-Mars trine

Bring on the lasting love! As affectionate Venus and passionate Mars harmonize in stable earth signs, you could have true romance with all the trimmings—sensuality and stability. Skip the "come here now go away" players and their mixed messages. A partner who makes you feel secure is suddenly the most attractive catch in town. Coupled? Mark a long-term relationship with a thoughtful gift to let your mate know how much you cherish them.

MON
11

Mercury-Jupiter meetup

A couple days ago, everything looked hopeless—and now, today's buoyant starmap brings a 180-degree turnaround! Hope renews as mindful Mercury hooks up with optimistic Jupiter, making your dreams seem possible again. Whew! Ride the wave of this magic moment, but beware: People are prone to exaggerating. If something sounds too good to be true, investigate before jumping aboard. Make sure you're not embellishing your own stories or promising more than you can deliver. Keep it real!

TUES 12

Mercury-Uranus square

Sure, rules were made to be broken, but what else might get shattered in the process? As mischievous Uranus battles mouthy Mercury, rabble-rousing could also destroy your integrity, trust and good name. Temper the urge to talk out of turn or post an incendiary social media rant. Is this truly a battle you want to fight? If you're presenting an idea, organize your points and research the facts. While it's great to be original, you don't want to be so "out there" that nobody understands your concept! Choose clarity over cleverness.

WED 13

Mars-Saturn square

Talk about a buzzkill! Excitable Mars has you motivated to go after your goals. But that high-flying starship could get grounded thanks to a jab from skeptical Saturn today. Be prepared to answer some probing questions or have a critic poke holes in your master plan. Avoid getting defensive! This could be a gift in disguise, inspiring you to tighten up your concept—or approach it from a fresh angle. Are your team members slacking? Listen to their complaints and try to reengage them. Cut loose anyone whose heart isn't in this—they'll only bring you down.

Venus-Uranus trine

Love is not meant to be static or stagnant, but rather, an evolving experience. As Venus forms a flowing trine to progress-driven Uranus, breathing new life into your relationship—or your approach to partnership—could ignite a romantic revolution. Tech-savvy Uranus may turn up a hot online match if you're single. For couples, doing something wildly off-script can put the passion back into your playbook.

January 13, 12:00 am ET

CAPRICORN NEW MOON

As the year's first new moon blossoms in goal-oriented Capricorn, your New Year's resolutions take root. What would you like to accomplish between now and the Capricorn full moon on June 24? Define your dream scenario, then tap a mentor, accountability buddy or coach to help you manifest it into reality. One action idea could lead to amazing results by summertime!

The AstroTwins' 2021 Horoscope   314

THUR
14

Uranus retrograde ends

Changemaker Uranus corrects course after a five-month retrograde that began August 15, 2020. The planet of genius, innovation and radical shifts will turn direct (forward) in security-seeking Taurus. Between now and April 2026, consider novel approaches to earning money and creating stability. Warning: When Uranus "stations" back to normal, people's behavior can be erratic and unpredictable. Give the energy a few days to settle before making any major decisions. While you may be headed for a big life change, it's not something to embark on impulsively.

Sun-Pluto meetup

Power surge! This once-a-year alignment of the revitalizing Sun and subterranean Pluto could reveal superpowers you didn't even realize you had. Intensity can run high and there may be a few large egos to navigate (gingerly) around. With these luminaries meeting in ambitious Capricorn, it's a great day to align with a VIP or decision-maker. Could they support your big project or advocate on your behalf? If you've been hiding your accomplishments, come out and let the world see what you're made of!

SUN
17

Jupiter-Uranus square

Genius idea—or pure chaos? As expansive Jupiter locks horns with radical Uranus, too much change could be activated at once, causing a crash. Yes, you've got to rip off the bandage sometimes. And today, that philosophy could be put into practice. Just be prepared to deal with whatever happens if you do.

WED
20

Mars-Uranus meetup

As speedy Mars and disruptive Uranus unite in Taurus, tunnel vision could send things flying off the rails at warp speed. But hey, maybe that's okay! You might hit on an ingenious idea, one that's both life-changing and lucrative. Just make sure you don't run anyone over in the process. Strong intellectual and sexual attraction can blaze up fast—when you least expect it!

January 19
Aquarius Season Begins

Futuristic Aquarius energy helps
us innovate, unite for social justice
and follow your
Utopian bliss.
As the zodiac's
mad scientist,
Aquarius helps
us think outside
the box and
connect with our
hopes and ideals.

January 20

First Quarter Moon in Aries

SAT

23

Mars-Jupiter square

Forcing an issue might win the battle, but it will ultimately lose you the war. Today, as headstrong Mars in Taurus squares idealistic Jupiter, people won't take "no" for an answer. What's going on here? If you've got a strong argument, plead your case. But remember, the heart can't be swayed by intellectual reasoning. A better approach: Try to understand what's going on emotionally on both sides. You may not get your way, but at least you won't burn a bridge by being a bulldozer.

Sun-Saturn meetup

Is self-doubt stealing your serenity? As the Sun makes its once-a-year conjunction with skeptical Saturn, your swagger could hit a snag. But don't let worry and insecurity overtake you. A too-cautious approach could cause you to miss an opportunity. Look both ways, then cross the street once it's clear! Have you been too heavy-handed or insensitive with someone? Make amends today. Then, get back out there—with plenty of grace and humility.

Aquarius Crystals

by MizChartreuse

Affirmations

I put on my crown of excellence daily.

I honor my gifts as a steward to the world.

I fortify myself first in order to be of service.

I enjoy the process of integrating polarities.

I am thankful for my forward-thinking perspective.

I collaborate with others to find solutions for the whole.

I recognize intersectionality and the many different ways to be human.

I am a pioneer of social responsibility.

I am worthy and whole because I exist.

I can productively dismantle to create anew.

I share my perspectives in a unifying manner.

I give thanks for my futuristic points of view.

I use my gifts as an innovator and trendsetter.

I raise the bar to a state of default excellence.

AQUAMARINE

Activates higher consciousness and a lighthearted spirit, protection from negative forces, may help regulate hormones

FLUORITE

Supports structure, unfolds creative potential, dissolves mental blocks, relief from joint pain

TUES
26

Sun-Uranus square

Brazen moves and inflammatory comments will come back to bite you as the ego-driven Sun and rebellious Uranus incite a fighting spirit. Flinging insults might give you a momentary rush (yup, you told them!). But later, you'll have to nurse a "shame hangover," knowing you traded your dignity to play the power-tripping provocateur. If someone pushes your buttons, do your best not to take their bait.

THUR
28

Sun-Jupiter meetup (Day of Miracles)

This annual conjunction of abundant Jupiter and the radiant Sun is often called the "luckiest day of the year" because the skies overflow with optimism and opportunity. Make the most of it! Focus on a miracle you want to manifest; then, ask the universe to make it a reality. But don't just sit around waiting for things to fall into your lap. Co-create with the cosmos and take a bold step on your own behalf.

Venus-Pluto meetup

What do you want for your romantic future? You may think you know, but today you'd be wise to take time to think deeply on the matter, as shadowy Pluto casts his smoldering gaze upon amorous Venus in tradition-loving Capricorn. You may be surprised by what you're actually thinking and feeling. Bottom line? Resist any knee-jerk reactions based upon passing fancies and get a fix on what you'd like to manifest for the long-term.

319

January 28, 2:16 pm ET

LEO FULL MOON

Rise and shine! The year's only Leo full moon brings out a spirit of courage and leadership. These magnanimous moonbeams will inspire generosity, something the world needs badly. Focus on setting a positive and confident example for others. And ask the full moon to help make your desires a reality! What do you want more than anything? Tune into your heart (the Leo-ruled part of the body) and let it point you in the direction of your dreams.

SAT
30

Mercury retrograde in Aquarius through February 20

Stop, analyze and review your grand plans! As clever Mercury takes a backspin through innovative Aquarius, you could have issues with technology, communication and travel. Group dynamics could get dicey now. Make sure to back up all electronic data and devices, which are susceptible to damage from Mercury's mayhem. Choose your words with extreme care, as this retrograde can muddle your message, especially on email and social media. Check in with your crew: Is everyone clear on their marching orders? Are there unspoken resentments to air? Pause to inspect and correct. A project could hit a snag or slowdown. Use this time to perfect your plans—then unveil them after the retrograde.

To find out how each Hotspot date will specifically impact your zodiac sign, read your Daily Horoscope at **Astrostyle.com**

https://www.astrostyle.com/horoscopes/daily

Aquarius Season *Journaling*

What do I love most about living in the digital age?

_____
_____
_____
_____

What does liberation look like to me?

_____
_____
_____
_____

If I could change one thing about the world, I would...

_____
_____
_____
_____

What kind of a team player am I?

_____
_____
_____
_____

What does "belonging" feel like for me?

_____
_____
_____
_____

HOME
Reset

Bring *OM* back home.

WITH FENG SHUI + ASTROLOGY

astrostyle.com/homereset

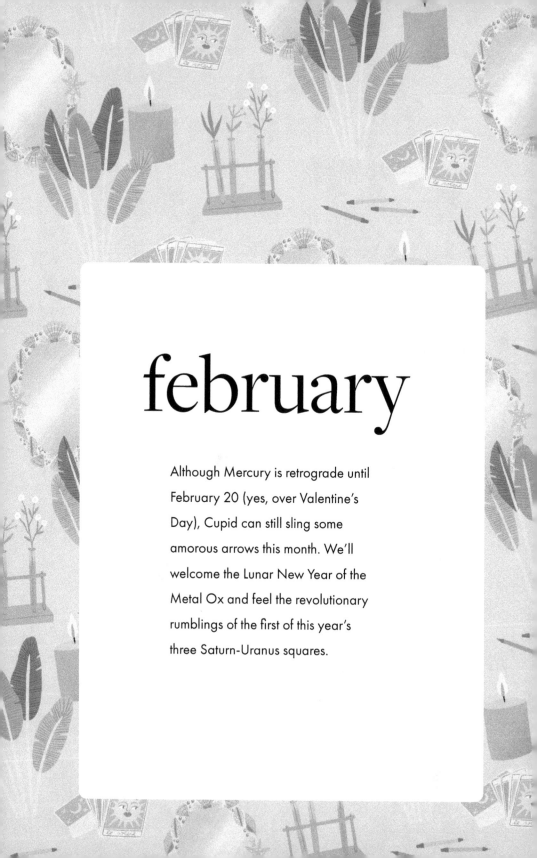

february

Although Mercury is retrograde until February 20 (yes, over Valentine's Day), Cupid can still sling some amorous arrows this month. We'll welcome the Lunar New Year of the Metal Ox and feel the revolutionary rumblings of the first of this year's three Saturn-Uranus squares.

FEBRUARY 2021

SUN	MON	TUES	WED	THUR	FRI	SAT
	1	2	3	4	5	6
7	8	9	10	11	12	13
14	15	16	17	18 ♓ Pisces Season Starts	19	20
21	22	23	24	25	26	27 ♍
28						

Key:

HOTSPOT　　LOVE HOTSPOT

Third Quarter　New Moon　First Quarter　Full Moon

MON 1

Sun-Mars square

Watch your temper today, especially if someone challenges you in a group setting. You can still stand up for your values without putting down someone else's. Emotions will heat up quickly, so be mindful not to push people's buttons.

Venus in Aquarius through February 25

Friendly fire? Love planet Venus will spend most of Valentine's month in Aquarius, the sign of casual connections and unconventional relationships. The atmosphere isn't exactly drenched in traditional romance (raincheck, Cupid?), but there's plenty of fun to be had. If group gatherings are permitted, you can celebrate the universal love of friendship and community. A mutual contact could play matchmaker, and online connections ignite with vixen Venus in this tech-savvy sign. For couples, this period can spark honest dialogue about the way you envision a happy union. Drift as far from the standard playbook as you want. No topic is taboo! From an open relationship to living separately to pursuing adoption, create an environment where you can discuss your secrets freely. Talking about them doesn't mean you'll actually pursue these things. The point is to banish fear or possessiveness, which will create breathing room for your individuality.

Februrary 4
Third Quarter Moon in Scorpio

SAT 6

Venus-Saturn meetup

As somber Saturn hooks up with love-maven Venus, relationships feel like serious business. You can no longer sweep a nagging issue under the rug—nor should you. This is a day for a "head over heart" approach. Have a no-nonsense conversation about boundaries or the future. Do you both still want the same things? Get real about it. Saturn rules experts, and if you can't get past a sticking point, a coach or couple's therapist could help. Single? Swipe past the players (even the hot ones!) and choose contenders with long-term potential instead.

Venus-Uranus square

Relationship goals, interrupted? On the same day that Venus and Saturn demand a serious look at your love life, rebellious Uranus barges in to stir the pot. The effect can be jarring, leaving you confused about what you really want. But consider it a reminder not to sideline your individuality just to be part of a couple. If it means losing yourself or feeling stifled, love might not be worth the price of admission. Can you stay true to yourself and still live "happily ever after"? Get authentic and you'll find out.

MON 8

Sun-Mercury meetup

You've got the gift of gab and the charisma to sway the masses as the bold Sun and expressive Mercury unite in tech-savvy Aquarius. Add some pizzazz to your profiles with a new headshot, tagline or a post that really gets your message out there. Just keep in mind that Mercury is retrograde, so make sure you're communicating clearly—and not overstepping any boundaries.

WED
10

Mercury-Mars square

Rivalry alert! A nemesis could push your buttons today, especially if they seem to be encroaching on your turf. If the green-eyed monster surfaces, remember: You don't have to succumb to his grips! Did a competitor receive buzz that could have gone to you? Instead of griping, send a congratulatory note or post a shout-out online. Signal-boosting them will only make you look (and feel) good! Remember, there's more than enough to go around.

~~~~~~~~~~~~~~~~~~

THUR
11

Venus-Jupiter meetup

Ah, that's better! The future looks bright and everything seems possible again as romantic Venus and expansive Jupiter unite in idealistic Aquarius. Venus and Jupiter are called the "great benefics" because of their positive, helpful influence. This once-a-year meetup opens your mind—and your heart—to a radically different kind of partnership. Bored? Do something different! You could be attracted to someone wildly different than your usual "type," perhaps from another culture or upbringing. Couples can break past plateaus by mixing up your routines and adopting a spirit of adventure. Ready for that next big step? Discuss it candidly today!

February 11, 2:05 pm ET

AQUARIUS NEW MOON
(Lunar New Year)

Don't hate, collaborate! The annual Aquarius new moon sparks unity, encouraging us to gather around common ideals or a community mission. Make sure to keep it inclusive! Welcome diverse opinions instead of creating an "us versus them" atmosphere. This evening also ushers in the Lunar New Year, as we bid adieu to the shrewd Rat and welcome the steady and hardworking Metal Ox.

The AstroTwins' 2021 Horoscope   329

SAT
13

Mercury-Venus meetup

With chatty Mercury pinging affectionate Venus, your mind and heart are in sync. Continue any dialogues sparked by the Venus-Jupiter meetup two days ago. Bring those big ideas out of the clouds and figure out how to make your romantic dreams a reality. Need to get something off your chest? Today's stars set the stage for a loving and compassionate conversation.

SUN
14

Mercury-Jupiter meetup

For the second time this year, idea maven Mercury conjuncts optimistic Jupiter, inspiring heartfelt dialogue and ideas that brim with possibility. But this time, Mercury is retrograde. Look back at grand plans that you discussed a month ago. Are they stuck in the "all talk, no action" phase? With Mercury in reverse, you can fill in the blanks or scale down to something easier to implement. Perhaps a phased approach would be smarter (and safer) than a big, splashy launch?

WED
17

Saturn-Uranus square #1 of 3

Should you fight for progress or stick to the tried-and-true? As structured Saturn in Aquarius makes its first of 2021's three destabilizing squares to disruptive Uranus in Taurus, the battle between order and chaos reaches a boil. Rebellious outbreaks will clash with iron-fisted bids for control as these next-door-neighbor planets wage war over their polarized agendas. Saturn and Uranus will square off again on June 14 and December 24, forcing change and toppling longtime institutions in the process.

February 19

First Quarter Moon in Gemini

FRI 19

Venus-Mars square

Uh-oh! The two love planets are at war today, making it hard to figure out whether you should stay or go. Venus in idealistic Aquarius wants freedom and space; lusty Mars in possessive Taurus is pressing hard for security. Can you build a commitment that feels safe but not suffocating? If you can't reach a compromise, take a time-out. Better to think it over than get lured into a blowout fight.

SAT 20

Mercury retrograde ends

Flip your focus back to the future! Mercury wakes up from a three-week retrograde in Aquarius, the sign of innovation, hopes and community. Since January 30, team efforts could have gone sideways due to internal politics and communication breakdowns. Shared technology may have gone haywire or perhaps private intel got into the wrong inboxes. Starting today, realign around squad goals, as you resume brainstorming. While it's important to be sensitive to everyone's needs, compromise is always part of the game. In the days ahead, you could reach a consensus around a shared mission.

February 18

Pisces Season Begins

The
dreamer
and healer of the
horoscope family, Pisces energy awakens
compassion, imagination and artistry, dissolving
the boundaries that divide us.

Pisces Crystals

by MizChartreuse

Affirmations

I balance work and play.

I look within to find my strength.

I overcome addictive behavior.

I give thanks for my beautiful soul.

I serve from a place of righteousness.

I distinguish between mind and emotions.

I decode the underlying causes of my choices.

I trust my natural intuition.

I am in tune with common sense.

I take constructive criticism in stride.

I am always grounded and protected.

I create boundaries to bring more freedom.

I raise my consciousness to the highest levels.

I believe others when they show me who they are.

AMETHYST

Enhances mental clarity, assists in detoxication and efforts to kick addiction; may ease pain, help you sleep and decode dreams

LABRADORITE

An "illusion-buster" that protects from us from over-serving others, enables big-picture thinking; powerful for meditation and insight

The AstroTwins' 2021 Horoscope   333

WED
24

Mars-Pluto trine

Competitive Mars and cutthroat Pluto can be fierce gladiators—and with both planets in staunch earth signs, their Game of Thrones intensity is dialed up even more. Luckily, they combine their superpowers today, giving us all formidable strength and stamina. No mission is too difficult if you stay the course! With sheer willpower and perseverance, obstacles will crumble in your wake. Your charisma can sway a decisionmaker, and your sharpened instincts could help you move ahead with your ambitions. Define your target and strike!

THUR
25

Venus in Pisces through Mar 21

Cupid makes a belated (and welcome!) arrival as Venus leaves airy, intellectual Aquarius and plunges into the fantasy-fueled waters of pleasurable Pisces. Over the next month, you can make up for lost time by indulging your erotic imagination. Surrender to sensuality and get lost in the depths of attraction. Just make sure to mark the trail so you can find your way back when reality comes calling. Connect with your amour du jour by sharing art, music and poetry, or by working on a heartfelt cause together.

To find out how each Hotspot date will specifically impact your zodiac sign, read your Daily Horoscope at **Astrostyle.com**

https://www.astrostyle.com/horoscopes/daily

The AstroTwins' 2021 Horoscope — 334 —

February 27, 3:17 am ET

VIRGO FULL MOON

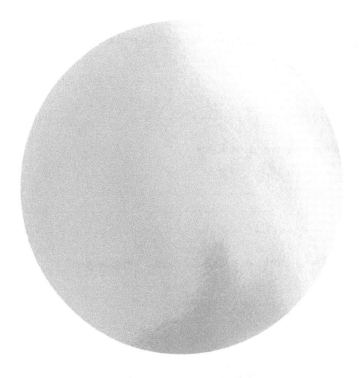

Order and simplicity are the mandates of the annual full moon in sensible earth sign Virgo. This lunar spotlight sharpens our analytical powers and reveals flaws in our thinking. Before you go primetime with your plans, do a thorough edit and run them past the toughest critics in your crew. Do you need more facts or research to back up your claims? Wellness check: The star sign of hearth, health and hygiene prompts us to purify. It's an excellent day for decluttering, deep cleaning and dietary overhauls.

335

Pisces Season *Journaling*

Where would I like to activate my imagination and creativity?

_____
_____
_____
_____

Which old hurts am I ready to heal?

_____
_____
_____
_____

Who in my life supports (or could) my deeper introspection?

_____
_____
_____
_____

If I could run away from one situation, what would it be?

_____
_____
_____
_____

What limiting beliefs are holding me back from my potential?

_____
_____
_____
_____

Visit the

ASTROTWINS **SHOP**

For books, charts, courses, gifts & more!

galaxy.astrostyle.com

march

If Valentine's month didn't deliver, March arrives to make up for it! With frisky Mars in Gemini, we'll all be searching for kindred spirits against the dreamy backdrop of Pisces season. Spring arrives at the March 20 vernal equinox, followed by a golden beam between go-getter Mars and structured Saturn that helps turn our passions into tangible form.

MARCH 2021

SUN	MON	TUES	WED	THUR	FRI	SAT
	1	2	3	4	5	6
7	8	9	10	11	12	13
14	15	16	17	18	19	20
21	22	23	24	25	26	27
28	29	30	31			

20 ♈ Aries Season Starts

Key:

 HOTSPOT   LOVE HOTSPOT

 Third Quarter   New Moon   First Quarter   Full Moon

WED
3

Mars in Gemini through April 23

Whatever you're selling, people will line up to buy it. As persuasive and passionate Mars blazes through talkative Gemini, employ the gift of gab to your advantage. A kindred spirit could pop out of the woodwork for business, pleasure or both! Caution: This transit can also bring out the fast-talking charlatans and devil's advocates who want to argue for argument's sake. Don't rush into any dynamic duos—they may not last. Monitor your screen time, too. With stressful Mars in this gadget-loving sign, a digital deluge of texts, alerts and electronic info could fray your nerves.

Mars in Gemini through April 23

Talk is cheap—and hot! Lusty Mars zooms into communicator Gemini, turning up the flirtatious banter and racy repartee. But in this breezy sign, attractions can be fast, fickle and fleeting. If your attention span is short, don't worry—just make sure you're not leading anyone on. Couples can argue more or treat each other with brusque impatience. Remember that respect is the foundation of any lasting relationship. If insults or contempt creep into your dynamic, stop and address the frustration behind your biting (and fighting) words. Or, save your edgy talk for the boudoir!

THUR
4

Mercury-Jupiter meetup

For the third time this year, idea maven Mercury and horizon-expanding Jupiter connect in Aquarius. Look back to January 11 and February 14—did you come up with an ingenious plot or a creative project at either date? At this final connection, you can add the finishing touches or perhaps start pitching the concept to a savvy, out-of-the-box thinker who can make it a reality. If you're negotiating a deal, put everything out on the table. Being open and honest will make it easier to satisfy everyone.

March 5

Third Quarter Moon in Sagittarius

WED

10

Sun-Neptune meetup

Lead with compassion! Under this heartfelt and imaginative cosmic conjunction, which happens once a year, showing your emotions will be viewed as a sign of strength, not weakness. For artists or healers, the confident Sun inspires you to hang your shingle or share your talents with the world.

SAT

13

Venus-Neptune meetup

A romantic and heartfelt sync-up of the two "mushball" planets gets those feelings flowing. Confess an attraction, express your gratitude in a sentimental post or make a sweet gesture. Feeling extra amorous? Surprise someone special with an over-the-top gift, just because.

March 13, 5:21 am ET

PISCES NEW MOON

Tune into the imagination station! The year's only Pisces new moon activates our dreams and divine connections, opening the floodgates of fantasy. Allow your softer, more receptive side to lead the way. Let intuition reign over logic. New avenues will open—and you'll see a pleasurable path to your goals. This lunar liftoff reminds you: Suffering is optional!

The AstroTwins' 2021 Horoscope   342

MON 15 — Mercury in Pisces through April 3

Communication planet Mercury swims into the dreamy Fish's realm, softening our speech and helping us relax into a more creative, compassionate mindset. What a relief! After Mercury's extra-long trek through intellectual Aquarius that started January 8, our weary brains could all use a break. Dial down the overthinking and get in touch with your emotions. Let intuition guide your decisions a bit more. Journaling, art and recording your dreams can lead to breakthrough insights.

SUN 21 — Mars-Saturn trine

Speedy Mars and cautious Saturn are like the cosmic gas pedal and the brake. When they combine their energy, it can be jarring. But today, as they harmonize in clever air signs, you could find the perfect pace for sharing your ideas without overwhelming people or sounding like a loose cannon. Be excited but a little restrained, confident but humble. If you strike that balance, you can come across as a charismatic and influential thought leader!

Venus in Aries through April 14

Bring on the confident swagger! As magnetic Venus zips into fiery and self-determined Aries, the next month could bring bold romantic adventures. Speak your desires without apology. Savor your independence. Play with new styles, even a head-turning makeover. The more you follow your bliss, the more turned-on you'll feel! Single stargazers could cycle through contenders quickly. Why waste time or settle? Thank you, next!

March 20
Aries Season Begins

The pioneer and trailblazer of the horoscope wheel, Aries energy helps us initiate, fight for our beliefs and fearlessly put ourselves out there.

March 21

First Quarter Moon in Gemini

TUES 23

Mercury-Mars square

Paranoid much? Today, you might twist your brain (and other people's) into knots by overanalyzing everything or freaking out before you have all the facts. Keep your knee-jerk reactions in check. Misinformation is flying about and can lead to unnecessary bickering and rivalries. Not sure if you should trust someone? Keep your secrets to yourself until you find out if this person is a true ally or a duplicitous gossip.

FRI 26

Sun-Venus meetup

As the confident Sun and affectionate Venus unite in lusty Aries, love could be a "hands-on" affair. It may sound cliché, but the more you love yourself—and walk through the world like you do—the more irresistibly attractive you'll be. Try it!

345

March 28, 2:48 pm ET

LIBRA FULL MOON

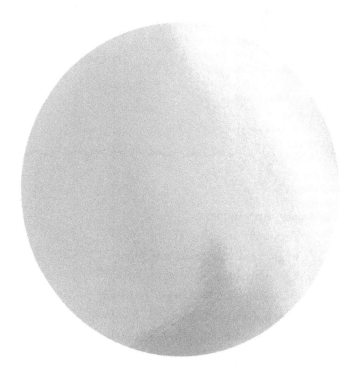

Bring on the balance and harmony! The annual full moon in Libra inspires compromise over competition, love over bitterness and sharing over self-interest. Under these patient skies, you can have a fruitful dialogue and resolve conflict. Be sure to listen as much as you talk—if not more! Feeling some friction? Get back on the same page with loved ones, business partners and friends under these magnanimous moonbeams.

Aries Crystals
by MizChartreuse

Affirmations

I prioritize my self-care.

I express my soul's vitality.

I trust my intuitive perceptions.

I release outdated emotional ties.

I channel my passion productively.

I embody discipline and self-control.

I am courageous in the face of danger.

I recognize toxic ancestral patterns.

I embrace my spiritual warrior nature.

I detoxify to experience true transmutation.

I cooperate with others and welcome assistance.

I release self-absorption and ego-centric mental blocks.

I acknowledge my mistakes to do better as I know better.

I validate myself by knowing my divine, inherent worthiness.

CARNELIAN

Good for protection
and supportive of new
beginnings; may alleviate
rheumatism and stimulate
absorption of vitamins,
nutrients and minerals

BLOODSTONE

Clears negative energy; may
boost the immune system,
stimulate the metabolic
process, detox the body and
reduce inflammations

MON 29 Mercury-Neptune meetup

Confusion and delusion might muddle your mind as foggy Neptune clouds the clear waters of Mercury. Instead of forcing yourself to (fruitlessly) focus, skip any tasks that require heavy mental lifting. Instead, surrender to the beauty of your imagination under these wildly creative skies (both planets are in dreamy Pisces). Have you been guarded and stiff with people? Let down your walls! Speak from the heart, even if you gush or get teary-eyed. Opening up to a trusted confidante can be incredibly soothing today.

To find out how each Hotspot date will specifically impact your zodiac sign, read your Daily Horoscope at **Astrostyle.com**

https://www.astrostyle.com/horoscopes/daily

Aries Season *Journaling*

Who are the people who inspire me to take initiative?

_____
_____
_____
_____

What am I most angry about right now?

_____
_____
_____
_____

What is the smartest way for me to fight back?

_____
_____
_____
_____

What and who is currently turning me on? (Meow, baby!)

_____
_____
_____
_____

What area of my life could use more excitement?

_____
_____
_____
_____

april

Aries and Taurus season make the first full month of spring adventurous and sensual. Later in the month, Pluto will turn retrograde, setting off a cycle of inner transformation and self-examination. When Mars enters Cancer on April 23, our social butterfly wings fold in a bit, and we get inspired to take on a home improvement project or to reconnect with family.

SUN	MON	TUES	WED	THUR	FRI	SAT
				1	2	3
4	5	6	7	8	9	10
11	12	13	14	15	16	17
18	19 ♉ Taurus Season Starts	20	21	22	23	24
25	26 ♏	27	28	29	30	

APRIL 2021

Key:

HOTSPOT   LOVE HOTSPOT

Third Quarter   New Moon   First Quarter   Full Moon

SAT

3

Mercury in Aries through April 19

With messenger Mercury in this assertive, me-first sign for the next three weeks, people will compete to have their voices heard. Make sure to listen as much as you talk, but remember: The squeaky wheel gets the premium-grade oil! Where do you shine? Pinpoint what makes your message stand out—a rare niche, a unique approach—and amplify that. Don't be afraid to break away from the crowd.

April 4

Third Quarter Moon in Capricorn

FRI
9

Mars-Neptune square

Don't believe everything (or anything) you hear today! With willful Mars battling hazy Neptune, people will make promises with no idea of how they'll follow through on them. A "user-friendly" person could butter you up to get what they want, then leave you hanging. On your end, make sure you can truly deliver before you commit to anything.

SUN
11

Venus-Pluto square

Control issues and power struggles can flare today as love planet Venus butts heads with calculating Pluto. Before you bare your soul, make sure the other person has earned your trust. Can they handle this delicate information? Honesty might not be the best policy under these volatile skies. Silence may be golden—for now.

353

April 11, 10:30 pm ET

ARIES NEW MOON

Make a fresh start! The new moon in trailblazing Aries inspires you to take a bold step forward on a pioneering project. How can you turn your passions into reality between now and the Aries full moon in October? Start talking about it, asking around and voicing your desires. You never know who might be listening.

The AstroTwins' 2021 Horoscope   354

WED

14

Venus in Taurus through May 8

Sweet sensuality! Affectionate Venus makes her annual homecoming in tactile Taurus, whetting our appetites for earthly delights. Indulge in a little luxury (it doesn't have to be expensive). Bask in beauty, from the gorgeous spring blossoms to a bespoke accessory. Pamper yourself and spoil the ones you love. "Too much of a good thing" feels like just the right dose now. Relationships can turn more serious under the stabilizing spell of Taurus.

~~~~~~~~~

FRI

16

Sun-Pluto square

Power struggle alert! This twice-a-year standoff between domineering Pluto and the ego-driven Sun can bring intense reactions to the surface. Although you have every right to be upset if you feel oppressed, a knee-jerk reaction could do more damage than good. If you choose to stand up to a bully, show your strength by remaining composed. But a warning: With both planets in haughty cardinal signs, it will be hard to resist taking the bait and losing control of your emotions. If things get heated, take a time-out and resolve this another day.

Mars-Jupiter trine

Enough "thinking about it"—it's time for action. As fortunate Jupiter and confident Mars support each other, it's your cue to take a leap of faith. We're not saying you should be reckless, but too much caution could lead to a missed opportunity. Embrace the unknown and stay open to possibilities beyond any you've ever manifested. One of your clever ideas may catch fire! Summon the courage to stretch beyond your comfort zone. You've got nothing to lose and everything to gain.

SAT 17 — Mercury-Pluto square

It's a tough day for pitching ideas, as people will be suspicious and resistant to anything new. Trying to get a key person on board? Charm won't persuade them one bit. Prepare to answer a lot of skeptical questions. The silver lining? Even if they say "no," you'll know exactly where you need to build a stronger case or do more research to make your plan absolutely bulletproof. If someone makes you an offer, do plenty of digging before you commit.

SUN 18 — Sun-Mercury meetup

Yesterday served up a tough crowd, but today's stars bring down their walls. Under a union of the bold Sun and articulate Mercury, you can speak in a compelling way that makes others take notice. Pro tip: Stick to key points and organize your information. A clear, compelling case—delivered with confidence—could win you a staunch new ally.

MON 19 — Mercury in Taurus through May 3

"If you fail to plan, you plan to fail," said the wise Ben Franklin. Make that your mantra as mental Mercury shifts into sensible Taurus, an ideal time to put concrete plans behind your lofty dreams. For the past couple weeks, you've had "April showers" aplenty when it comes to brainstorms. But can these concepts go the distance? Sort through the "crops" to pick a viable contender. Crunch the numbers, map out a few action steps and carve out set hours to methodically work on it. Investing a couple weeks will help you decide whether to dedicate more time to the project or move on.

April 20
First Quarter Moon in Leo

Taurus Crystals
by MizChartreuse

GREEN AVENTURINE

Promotes relaxation, regeneration and recovery; attracts monetary abundance

Affirmations

I am rooted in the earth.

I channel life force energy.

I explore my profound inner depths.

I embody love as an infinite resource.

I recognize my infinite, limitless nature.

I enjoy adventure and expanding my horizons.

I embrace my worthiness of abundance in all forms.

I trust my intuition.

I am one with all that is.

I am worthy of optimum health.

I understand my place in the universe.

I am open to all levels of consciousness.

I responsibly use my freedom of speech.

I embrace my role as a planetary guardian.

BLUE KYANITE

Removes physical and energetic blockages; may aid throat, brain and muscular system disorders

April 19

Taurus Season Begins

Taurus is the persistent provider of the zodiac, the sign that helps us seek security, enjoy earthly pleasures and get the job done.

THUR
22

Venus-Uranus meetup

Can you mix things up in your love life without completely capsizing a commitment? Today's mashup of Venus and unpredictable Uranus might throw you a curveball. For couples who've been stuck at a plateau, the change could be refreshing. But if you're feeling claustrophobic, this may spike your cabin fever, tempting you to bolt. Don't act impulsively. Maybe all you need is a little more breathing room…or to try some new bedroom moves?

FRI
23

Mars in Cancer through June 11

Home is where the heat is when excitable (and stressful!) Mars zooms into domestic Cancer for the next few weeks. Reduce the rising tension under your roof by decluttering, redecorating and making sure everyone has enough space to do their thing. The red planet's motivational influence may inspire a home-based business or a spring fitness challenge with roommates and relatives. (Who took the most steps a day or made the best-tasting smoothie? Winner!) Cabin fever can fan the flames of conflict, so make sure to get out of the house whenever possible. Channel your frustration into a healthy outlet, like sports or exercise.

SAT
24

Mercury-Uranus meetup

With these two clever cosmic players in savvy Taurus, a financial or work-related epiphany could be in the stars. If you've been frustrated with your interior design or struggling to figure out your spring "look," you might have a style breakthrough! Since both planets rule technology, setting up a Pinterest mood board can help you gather inspiration. Today may be a turning point for you in an important area of your life, as these two clever planets unite. Think (and seek!) outside the box for new opportunities.

SUN 25

Mercury-Saturn square

With mental Mercury crossing cautious Saturn, people's resistance to new ideas could be high. It's a smart idea to ask all the questions and do your own research. But if you're being overly skeptical out of fear, stop yourself. At a certain point, there are no guarantees. Taking a calculated risk might be the best you can do.

Mercury-Venus meetup

Let's talk about love! Chatty Mercury and affectionate Venus unite, making it so much easier to articulate your feelings. And as they connect in steady Taurus, you can be both sensible and sensual. Need to discuss a difficult topic, like money or family? Do it over a beautiful dinner. Clearing the air about a misunderstanding? A reassuring hug can offset any harsh words. Change the scenery and speak with an extra dose of compassion. This may be a great day to bring up that "next big step." Single? Scroll through the dating apps (or put the word out to friends that you're open to intros). Your efforts could turn up a couple of strong candidates.

Venus-Saturn square

On the other hand…on the very same day, Venus gets speed-checked by stern Saturn in future-focused Aquarius. Consider the ramifications of your heartfelt confessions. Are you leading someone on? Talk about your long-term visions of love, too. See where your values overlap and be frank about how they diverge. This doesn't have to be a dealbreaker. But you'll avoid heartache down the line by troubleshooting this now.

April 26, 11:31 pm ET

SCORPIO FULL MOON

Intensity ignites as the year's only Scorpio full moon fills the skies. With la luna shining her highbeams into this mysterious sector, a secret may be revealed. Can you let down your guard and be vulnerable with a certain someone? If they've earned your trust, take the intimacy of your connection— platonic, professional or otherwise—to the next level.

The AstroTwins' 2021 Horoscope 361

TUES 27 — Pluto retrograde in Capricorn through October 6

Shadowy Pluto slows its calculating roll, backing into retrograde motion for five months. This soul-searching annual backspin could lift the veil on something that's been hidden from you. It's a powerful time for inner transformation and forgiveness work, or to dive into research. Ready to solve a mystery?

FRI 30 — Sun-Uranus meetup

The only constant is change today. As the courageous Sun and radical changemaker Uranus make their once-a-year meetup, you'll be spurred to take action in a stagnant part of life. A plot twist could arrive out of the blue. Think fast! With both luminaries in stability-seeking Taurus, do your best to devise a sustainable solution.

To find out how each Hotspot date will specifically impact your zodiac sign, read your Daily Horoscope at **Astrostyle.com**

https://www.astrostyle.com/horoscopes/daily

Taurus Season *Journaling*

How can I bring the spirit of romance into daily rituals?

_____
_____
_____
_____

What do I spend the most money on?

_____
_____
_____
_____

What values do my closest friends and I share?

_____
_____
_____
_____

If I could keep only 5 items in my closet, what would they be?

_____
_____
_____
_____

How can I take better care of my health?

_____
_____
_____
_____

may

May flowers...or showers? It's a turning point month as lucky Jupiter leaves Aquarius and makes a short dip into watery and intuitive Pisces for the next couple months. Disciplined Saturn and communicative Mercury will turn retrograde, and the month caps off with a boldfaced Sagittarius lunar (full moon) eclipse.

SUN	MON	TUES	WED	THUR	FRI	SAT
						1
2	3	4	5	6	7	8
9	10	11	12	13	14	15
16	17	18	19	20 Gemini Season Starts	21	22
23	24	25	26 Lunar Eclipse	27	28	29
30	31					

MAY 2021

Key:

HOTSPOT · LOVE HOTSPOT

Third Quarter · New Moon · First Quarter · Full Moon

SUN
2

Mercury-Pluto trine

Your words are extra compelling today, so wield them with intention. As communicator Mercury syncs with magnetic Pluto, you could attract money and opportunity through your persuasive powers. The less you reveal, the better. A touch of mystery goes far!

MON
3

Mercury-Jupiter square

Oversharing alert! As mouthy Mercury and know-it-all Jupiter butt heads, you could easily say too much for your own good. And under these impulsive skies, it's a blurry line between fact and fiction. Negotiating? Ask lots of questions but don't be too quick to expose your intentions. Better to let others show their hand first.

Sun-Saturn square

Slow down! If you jumped the gun, you may need to retrace your steps today or ask for a do-over. Has your ego gotten a tad inflated? Humble thyself and bring it down a notch. The bold Sun gets body-checked by humble Saturn, a semiannual snag that demands we keep it real. Instead of rushing a project out the door, ask for a little extra time to do it right. No cutting corners allowed.

Mercury in Gemini through July 11

Communicator Mercury comes home to its native sign of Gemini. And the quicksilver planet will pay a protracted visit thanks to a retrograde that starts at the end of this month. In preparation, back up your electronic data and nail down important agreements. The sooner the better, since Mercury retrograde is notorious for messing with technology and transactions.

May 3
Third Quarter Moon in Aquarius

THUR
6

Venus-Pluto trine

Power and status are alluring today, but don't forget to check in with your values. An attraction could be amplified by someone's credentials. Make sure you're falling in love with the real person, not just their reputation. In a relationship? Dress up and play "power couple" tonight.

SAT
8

Venus in Gemini through June 2

Talk is cheap…and sexy, too! Romantic Venus heads into communicative Gemini, spicing up the next couple weeks with dynamic dialogues. Get your flirt on. Confess a crush. Dare to discuss a taboo topic or two—or question conventions that don't work for you. With Venus in this curious sign, the urge to experiment is strong. Just keep things honest and watch for mixed messages.

Venus-Jupiter square

Never enough? The grass looks greener in everyone else's relationship today, as Venus makes a cranky connection to insatiable Jupiter. If you've been settling for less than you deserve, this could be an important wakeup call. But if you're fixating on flaws, try making a gratitude list. Either write down the qualities you appreciate in your partner or, if you're single, the things in your life that you're thankful for right now. The shift in perspective will help you view this situation in a more balanced way.

The AstroTwins' 2021 Horoscope   367

May 11, 2:59 pm ET

TAURUS NEW MOON

Sweet stability! Start building one of your ideas into something tangible, as the material-minded Taurus new moon spawns a grounding six-month cycle. Want more emotional security, increased income or to see rewards for all your hard work? Set clear and simple intentions today. Your efforts could pay off by the time the Taurus full moon arrives on November 19.

368

WED
12

Mercury-Saturn trine

Be the adult in the room today. Wisdom and maturity will win the race as communicator Mercury pings serious Saturn. You don't have to be rigid, just realistic. It's a great day for strategizing, or to put a master plan behind your clever concepts. Listen to any pitches with a skeptical ear. Exciting as an offer sounds, will it pass the longevity test? Do your homework.

THUR
13

Jupiter in Pisces through July 28

Supersizer Jupiter cruises into imaginative Pisces, its first of three trips here between now and December 2022. Normally Jupiter remains in a sign for a solid year, but it will break up its tour between Aquarius, Pisces and Aries over the next couple years. Creativity and compassion will be amplified by Jupiter's presence here—and the world is certainly ready for this softer, more spiritual cycle.

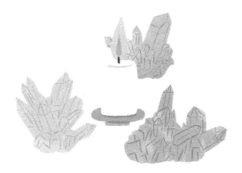

MON
17

Sun-Pluto trine

Don't hide your power today! As the bold Sun connects with crafty Pluto, a combo of confidence and shrewdness will take you far. Back up your bravado with a well-crafted plan for the win.

May 19

First Quarter Moon in Leo

WED

19

Venus-Saturn trine

Reality check? If you've put someone up on a pedestal, stern Saturn rips off the rose-colored glasses. It's never a bad idea to be honest about a love interest's shortcomings. Perhaps your life circumstances aren't neatly overlapping—for example, you live long-distance or your work hours don't sync up. Ask yourself: Can you live with these constraints? This doesn't have to be a dealbreaker. In fact, your willingness to address these factors could help you plan and problem-solve.

FRI

21

Sun-Jupiter square

Too good to be true? If an offer sounds that way, then it probably is. Today's fistfight between the bold Sun and cocky Jupiter has people talking a good game—with no real plan for how they'll actually carry it out. Make sure you're not overpromising either.

May 20

Gemini Season Begins

The most versatile and vibrant horoscope sign, Gemini energy helps us communicate, collaborate and fly our freak flags at full mast.

Gemini Crystals
by MizChartreuse

Affirmations

I express my truth.

I am the messenger.

I trust my inner compass.

I transform myself to evolve.

I am free to change my mind.

I embrace total self-acceptance.

BLUE LACE AGATE

Promotes mental clarity; aids in removing blockages from the nervous system and tension from shoulders and neck

APOPHYLLITE

Encourages peacefulness, openness; aids in healing grief and supports the lungs and respiratory system

SAT
22

Mercury-Neptune square

Thoughts are muddled as foggy Neptune obscures intellectual Mercury. And since both planets are in dualistic signs (Mercury's in Gemini and Neptune's in Pisces), people are likely to talk out of both sides of their mouths. Dodge those mixed messages and pause before you blurt.

SUN
23

Saturn retrograde in Aquarius through October 10

Pump the brakes! Cautious Saturn slips into reverse for its annual retrograde. This year, the planet of structure will back through futuristic Aquarius, putting visionary plans on hold. A team endeavor may need to be reorganized or scaled back. This could put a crimp on socializing and public affairs. Summer fun may be hampered by another round of restrictions, so prepare accordingly.

May 26, 7:13 am ET

SAGITTARIUS FULL MOON
(Lunar Eclipse)

Think bigger than big as the visionary Sagittarius full moon supersizes your dreams. Expand beyond the borders of what's comfortable and familiar. If you can't literally travel, seek fresh horizons through education, personal growth work and experiences that push you into inspiring new terrain. Nothing ventured, nothing gained!

THUR

27

Venus-Neptune square

Mixed signals and unclear messages can make for a challenging day in the love department. It doesn't help that foggy Neptune's interception also breeds indecisiveness. If people are moody or running hot-and-cold, let them be. Your own disenchantment with a romantic interest may confuse you. These fickle skies aren't great for decision-making. Accept these fluctuating feelings today without acting upon them.

SAT

29

Mercury retrograde in Gemini through June 22

A double dose of communication chaos could be in store as expressive Mercury, the planet of technology, travel and interactions, makes a three-week backspin through its home sign of Gemini. Hold off on buying electronics or anything with wheels (transportation will be impacted). If possible, wait to sign contracts and use this time to negotiate instead. Triple-check your words before you press "post" or "send." When in doubt, save to draft! Got an unfinished manuscript, podcast or workshop idea? Blow off the dust and revisit it. Stalled conversations may finally be resolved—get back into dialogue and really listen this time around.

Mercury-Venus meetup

Been holding your tongue? Today's cosmic entanglement may coax down your guard. Expressive Mercury, which is retrograde in chatty Gemini, connects with affectionate Venus. With the right dose of diplomacy and sensitivity, you can finally get this issue out into the open. It's a good day to tell someone how you feel—maybe even to say that "L" word for the first time?

MON
31

Mars-Neptune trine

Emotions can heat up quickly as exacerbating Mars in sensitive Cancer connects with empathic Neptune in delicate Pisces. An innocent comment could trigger an over-the-top reaction. Tread lightly! If you've been holding back your true feelings, they might come gushing out today—whether you finally clear the air about a longstanding hurt or express your appreciation to a special person.

To find out how each Hotspot date will specifically impact your zodiac sign, read your Daily Horoscope at **Astrostyle.com**

https://www.astrostyle.com/horoscopes/daily

Gemini Season *Journaling*

Who are my three favorite people to talk to and why?

_____
_____
_____
_____

In order to open up to people, I need to feel:

_____
_____
_____
_____

What ideas or activities get me excited and into motion?

_____
_____
_____
_____

What area of my life would benefit from being more organized?

_____
_____
_____
_____

My friends count on me to bring _____ to the party:

_____
_____
_____
_____

june

Eclipse season continues as a Gemini solar (new moon) eclipse arrives on June 10, followed shortly by feisty Mars moving into Leo (hello, summer lovin?) and the second of three seismic Saturn-Uranus squares. Jupiter and Neptune join the retrograde brigade, but in between, we can celebrate a peak moment when the summer solstice brings a burst of life-force energy on June 20.

JUNE 2021

SUN	MON	TUES	WED	THUR	FRI	SAT
		1	2	3	4	5
6	7	8	9	10 Solar Eclipse	11	12
13	14	15	16	17	18	19
20 Cancer Season Starts	21	22	23	24	25	26
27	28	29	30			

Key:

HOTSPOT   LOVE HOTSPOT

Third Quarter   New Moon   First Quarter   Full Moon

WED
2

Venus in Cancer through June 27

Naughty by...nurture? Affectionate Venus in touchy-feely Cancer has us all wanting to be coddled and cuddled. Enough talking about love—it's time to get out of your head and into your emotions. Let those deeper feelings emerge. Get sappy and sentimental. Ready to give each other a spare set of keys, meet the families or talk babies? Just be aware of how your fluctuating moods may impact a partner. If you're single, watch for neediness during this period, which can make you act too clingy, too quickly.

June 2

Third Quarter Moon in Pisces

FRI

3

Sun-Saturn trine

Clear communication and innovative ideas will win the race today. If you've been sitting on a cutting-edge concept, put together a proposal that bottom-lines your ideas. Once they're articulated in a structured plan (think: simple bullet points and non-cheesy graphics), it will be easy to make an impactful pitch on the spot. Make sure to back your ideas with data. Facts for the win!

Venus-Jupiter trine

Love wins! As the "benefic" planets (named for their helpful, positive influence) harmonize in sensitive water signs, hearts open. You'll be able to hear someone share their feelings candidly, even if it's about a hurt or upset. Honesty can be delivered with caring consideration—and received with a generous spirit rather than defensiveness. Happily coupled? Amp up the adventure by trying something totally new together. It's a beautiful day to let your favorite person know how much you love them. Feel free to express your feelings with a grand gesture!

SAT

5

Mercury-Neptune square

Mute those muddled messages today and don't speak until you're sure what you want to say. As communicator Mercury squares fog-machine Neptune, mixed signals abound. Sensitive info could slip through the confidentiality cracks. Keep secrets in the vault. While you might broach a difficult topic today, emotions could overtake logic fast. Take a time-out if things start to get irrational.

Mars-Pluto opposition

Thar' ...she blows? Two of the most volatile planets are at loggerheads today, turning a tense situation into a pressure cooker. It will be difficult not to react, especially if your sense of security feels threatened. Watch for anger and an impulse to seek revenge. You'll only end up hurting yourself. If you've been harboring resentment, clear the air—but don't burn a bridge in the process.

June 10, 6:52 am ET

GEMINI NEW MOON
(Solar Eclipse)

Ideas abound! This supercharged new moon in expressive Gemini sparks an outpouring of brainstorms and inspired conversations. Get all your thoughts into the open or captured on paper. With the sign of the Twins activated, kindred spirits could pop out of the woodwork. Explore synergies with a trial project. You'll know whether this dynamic duo has lasting potential by the December 18 Gemini full moon—and maybe sooner!

The AstroTwins' 2021 Horoscope   382

FRI
11

Mars in Leo through July 29

Restore your roar! Assertive Mars blazes into fierce and fiery Leo for the next few weeks, pumping up the amour and the glamour. Ready to see your name in lights? Express yourself boldly and wear your heart on your sleeve. Pursuing a passion could get you noticed. Nudge yourself into the spotlight, especially since the red planet only sashays down the Leo runway every two years.

Pump up the passion! Hot-blooded Mars roams into Leo, bringing out boldness in the bedroom and beyond. Unleash your wild side and don't be afraid to draw attention with a head-turning outfit or a showstopping performance. Pro tip: Tempers and diva antics can flare. If things start to shift from entertaining to argumentative, think twice about entering that cosmic coliseum. Work out your differences in the boudoir instead!

SUN
13

Sun-Neptune square

Self-doubt never served anyone any good. That said, have you overestimated yourself just a smidge? The confident Sun squabbles with delusional Neptune, skewing our perceptions. Not sure if your act is ready for prime time? Get a second opinion before you debut it. On the flip side, if insecurity is causing you to overthink and hide out, quit procrastinating! Tap someone who will be your personal cheerleader. They'll remind you how awesome you are as you take the courageous step of going public.

383

MON
14
Saturn-Uranus square

Where does your life need more stability…and where has it become so settled that it's turning stagnant? For the second of three times this year, rigid Saturn and rebellious Uranus get into a smackdown. Their conflicts could disrupt social circles, teamwork and financial solvency—all major issues this year. Consider how you can make major changes that don't completely topple your life. Curveball circumstances could force you to radically revamp your reality. Be prepared for that possibility. Look back to February 17, the first Saturn-Uranus square, for clues of what could resurface. The final faceoff, on December 24, will demand one more round of compromise and adjustment.

June 17
First Quarter Moon in Libra

SUN
20

Jupiter retrograde through October 18

Slow your roll! Expansive Jupiter eases off the gas pedal, starting its annual backspin. Until July 28, Jupiter will reverse through dreamy Pisces, snapping us out of illusion and delusion. Don't let this sobering reality check take all the wind out of your sails, though! From late July onward, Jupiter will back into visionary Aquarius, helping us refine our social circles and get teamwork back on track. While it's important to look ahead to the future (the domain of Aquarius), you also have to handle what's in front of you today. Carpe a little more diem and "be here now."

MON
21

Venus-Neptune trine

The summer solstice is drenched in romance, as affectionate Venus and enchantress Neptune entwine in heartfelt water signs. Keep the tissues handy—a conversation could move you to tears! But don't forget to keep healthy boundaries in place. Under this empathic starmap, it will be hard to distinguish someone else's emotions from your own.

TUES
21

Venus-Neptune trine

The summer solstice is drenched in romance, as affectionate Venus and enchantress Neptune entwine in heartfelt water signs. Keep the tissues handy—a conversation could move you to tears! But don't forget to keep healthy boundaries in place. Under this empathic starmap, it will be hard to distinguish someone else's emotions from your own.

June 20

Cancer Season Begins

The natural nurturer of the
horoscope wheel, Cancer
energy helps us connect
with our feelings, plant
deep roots and
feather our
family nests.

Cancer Crystals
by MizChartreuse

Affirmations

I trust my instincts.

I honor my sacred spaces.

I give thanks for mental flexibility.

I release confusion and baggage.

I cultivate heart-centered connections.

I use my inner vision as fertile ground to create.

MOONSTONE

Associated with intuition, feelings, the heart, and fertility

SELENITE

Encourages mind focus, calmness, and promotes fertility

TUE
22

Mercury retrograde ends

Bring on the mic drops, witty quips and savvy one-liners. Messenger Mercury snaps out of its three-week retrograde through its home sign of Gemini, where it was doubling its signal-jamming impact. Even the most basic communication came out sideways since May 29, causing rifts with all the Gemini-ruled people in your life: coworkers, neighbors, siblings, friends and peers. Ready the olive branch and put on your listening ears. It might take a few heart to hearts to bring back the love, but with Mercury back on track now, resolution is possible.

WED
23

Sun-Jupiter trine

Confidence will get you everywhere today, as the radiant Sun and optimistic Jupiter combine their superpowers in emotional water signs. If you can make people feel something, they'll eat out of the palm of your hand! Appeal to their emotions with a moving story or by authentically sharing your own experiences. While egos and personalities can get a little outsized today, it should all come out in the wash. Better to go big and miss the mark than to not even try at all!

Venus-Pluto opposition

Hold on tight! As delicate Venus goes head-to-head with powermonger Pluto, be sweet but self-protective. Other people's motives may not be entirely transparent. If you get a sketchy vibe or feel like someone's being manipulative, back away. Keeping the peace shouldn't happen at the expense of your dignity and self-respect. Do you feel like someone's gaslighting you? Politely excuse yourself from any conversations that push your buttons. Don't take the bait!

The AstroTwins' 2021 Horoscope   388

June 24, 2:39 pm ET

CAPRICORN FULL MOON

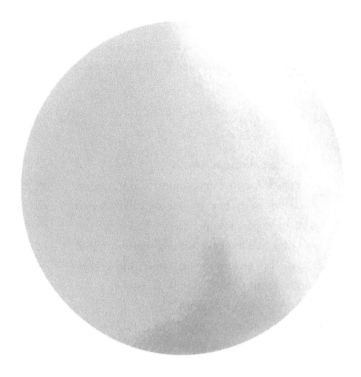

Galvanize your goals! The year's lone Capricorn full moon helps us think about the futures we want to create—and how we can turn ideas into tangible reality. Did you bring one of your 2021 goals to fruition? Celebrate the victory of reaching this milestone! If you've veered off-purpose, use this clarifying lunar light to identify any missteps and correct course.

FRI 25

Neptune retrograde in Pisces through December 1

Giving others the benefit of the doubt can be noble...but also naïve. As gullible Neptune powers down for its annual backspin, practice more healthy self-protection. Put safety first and don't feel guilty if you get a weird vibe from someone and need to back away. Allow yourself that moment to honor your intuition. It's possible you're imagining things and could hit it off on the second try. But maybe something truly is "off." Don't ignore your gut!

SUN 27

Venus in Leo through July 21

Put some allure in your purr! Love goddess Venus starts her annual catwalk through glamazon Leo, joining lusty Mars in the Lion's den. We'll all crave more attention and affection. Be generous with your praise and gracious about the accolades. If you're due for a romantic reboot, this could be a "renaissance period" for amour. Wear your heart on your decorative sleeve (or your backless bandage dress...or your slinky swimsuit).

To find out how each Hotspot date will specifically impact your zodiac sign, read your Daily Horoscope at **Astrostyle.com**

https://www.astrostyle.com/horoscopes/daily

Cancer Season *Journaling*

How likely am I to listen to (or ignore) my intuition?

_____
_____
_____
_____

How can I make my home feel like more of a sanctuary?

_____
_____
_____
_____

What self-care rituals can I add to my life to help me feel nurtured?

_____
_____
_____
_____

How comfortable do I feel expressing my desires?

_____
_____
_____
_____

A person I'd like to get closer to is _____ because _____:

_____
_____
_____
_____

july

The month begins with a speed check as hasty Mars and cautious Saturn face off. Are you ready to launch or do you need to slow down and enjoy the summer? Love gets a couple of reflective moments this month, when Venus makes uncomfortable contacts with a few other planets. Late July sees Jupiter ending its short visit to Pisces and returning to Aquarius until the end of 2021.

JULY 2021

SUN	MON	TUES	WED	THUR	FRI	SAT
				1	2	3
4	5	6	7	8	9	10
11	12	13	14	15	16	17
18	19	20	21	22 ♌ Leo Season Starts	23	24
25	26	27	28	29	30	31

Key:

 HOTSPOT

 LOVE HOTSPOT

 Third Quarter

 New Moon

 First Quarter

 Full Moon

THUR
1

Mars-Saturn opposition

Tap the brakes! As speedy Mars in passionate Leo opposes cautious Saturn in heady Aquarius, a fast-moving endeavor might benefit from a more measured pace. Have you put the right long-term plans and people in place? Think "big picture" rather than just about immediate gratification. On the other hand, if you've been hanging back and not sharing your grand scheme, today is your nudge to speak up. Gather some courage and a few talking points... then get out there!

July 1

Third Quarter Moon in Aries

SAT
3

Mars-Uranus square

As two temperamental planets butt heads in stubborn fixed signs, nobody wants to back down from being right. And the urge to win this battle could get heated, even ugly. Disruptive Uranus and hotheaded Mars can ignite strong reactions. Catch yourself before that knee-jerk response detonates. Losing your composure might leave you with a messy cleanup job.

TUES
6

Mercury-Neptune square

Logic or intuition? You could struggle to figure out which to heed today, as analytical Mercury arm-wrestles empathic Neptune. Don't rule out a hunch but make sure to back it with solid research.

Venus-Saturn opposition

Boundaries could get slippery today, as softie Venus clashes with tough-loving Saturn. You know you need to be consistent, but a strong attraction or a good heartstring tug is all it takes for you to go back on your word. Put in some reinforcements (like calling a friend) to stop yourself from caving so easily. If you reward bad behavior now, you'll only create a bigger problem later. On the fence about a certain relationship? This pessimistic starmap could make you overly judgmental. Don't sweep the downsides under the rug, but sleep on it before you call the whole thing off.

THUR
8

Venus-Uranus square

Suddenly single? You might feel like making a break for freedom today, as liberated Uranus T-bones romantic Venus. Your autonomy should not be the price of entry for partnership, so talk through a solution. If someone's smothering you, just take a day or two for yourself, rather than doing anything extreme. Radical moves are likely to be regrettable ones. If you've been biting your tongue a bit too much, vow to speak and act more authentically, starting…now!

July 9, 9:16 pm ET

CANCER NEW MOON

A heartfelt new chapter begins as the year's only Cancer new moon puts the focus on home, roots and emotional bonds. A nurturing person could play into events near this date. Has your own self-care fallen by the wayside? Recommit to relaxation and make sure you have enough support.

The AstroTwins' 2021 Horoscope   396

SUN

11

Mercury in Cancer through July 27

As communicator Mercury visits sentimental Cancer, make an extra effort to listen with compassion and speak gently over the next couple weeks. Scout clever ideas for home décor that will help streamline and cozify your space. Frame some family photos, install a closet organizing system or refresh with easy accents like hardy houseplants and new throw pillows.

MON

12

Mercury-Jupiter trine

Small ideas can have big potential, so don't dismiss a spark today, even if it seems silly at first. With supersizer Jupiter adding vision to Mercury's brainstorms, you never know where this could go! Caution: Both planets are in touchy-feely water signs today, so manage your moods. A gathering storm may turn into a tsunami if you let your emotions get out of hand.

TUES

13

Venus-Mars meetup in Leo

Rrowr! If you're not purring from the attention and affection of an admirer, get out on the prowl, stat. As the cosmic lovers unite in fierce Leo, adjust your crown and resume your heart-centered hunt. As for anyone treating you with less than regal reverence? Give them the royal flush!

THUR
15

Sun-Neptune trine

Ready to manifest a miracle? With the life-giving Sun boosting imaginative Neptune, your subconscious thoughts could take tangible form. Confidently ask for the support you need or push yourself to speak your desires aloud. Not only is the universe listening, a well-connected and helpful person could be, too.

Chiron retrograde in Aries through December 19

Where have you not been voicing your truth? Healing comet Chiron begins a five-month backspin, reminding us to advocate for ourselves. If you've been overly forceful with your opinions, reel it in a little and give others a chance to speak.

July 17

First Quarter Moon in Libra

SAT
17

Sun-Pluto opposition

Emotions can get intense at this once-a-year standoff between the ego-driven Sun and power-tripping Pluto. Be careful not to project your own frustrations onto others. Is it your issue or theirs? Assess before you accuse.

WED

21

Venus in Virgo through August 16

Earth gods and goddesses unite! Beautifying Venus moves into sensual and salubrious Virgo, restoring health to our love lives. Get physical—with self-care, a pleasurable exercise routine (solo or with your S.O.) and through lots of affection. Wanna know the sexiest thing you can do now, though? Slow down! Ramp up romance with massage. Prepare a beautiful meal with local ingredients or spend a day outdoors. Put phones away and connect through a long conversation. Listen generously, give advice only if asked and support, support, support.

THUR

22

Venus-Jupiter opposition

Never satisfied? The grass looks greener over every fence as indulgent Jupiter and thirsty Venus drum up dueling desires. With Venus in persnickety Virgo, someone's minor misstep could spiral into a dealbreaker, leading you to dismiss someone who might have actual promise. Do your best to stay grounded in realistic expectations. Couples could make mountains out of microdramas, and things might get ugly. Call a time-out before you blow. Not attached? Don't tie yourself down to anyone yet. Sample the bountiful buffet before you settle on a favorite dish.

July 22
Leo Season Begins

The drama queen and regal ruler of the horoscope clan, Leo energy helps us shine, express ourselves boldly and wear our hearts on our sleeves.

July 23, 10:36 pm ET

AQUARIUS FULL MOON №1

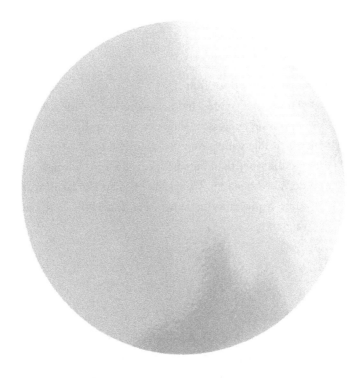

The first of two consecutive full moons in Aquarius shines the spotlight on our hopes for the future. Have you sidelined your ideals and gotten consumed by mundane tasks? Look up— and ahead! This is a day for inspiration. Take inventory of the people around you, as this full moon illuminates the zodiac sign that rules friendships, groups and community. Are your teammates aligned with your greater vision? You can still have your differences while working for a singular mission. Bring the crew back to cohesion or scout new collaborators.

SAT

24

Mercury-Neptune trine

Your intuitive powers may be borderline psychic today as clever Mercury and empathic Neptune unite in a flowing trine. Follow your instincts and investigate a hunch. Speak up if you get a strong gut feeling about anything!

SUN

25

Mercury-Pluto opposition

Drama, intrigue, hidden agendas? With calculating Pluto opposing expressive Mercury, it's best to keep your opinions to yourself. While your powers of observation are strong, there may be more to the story than initially meets the eye. Ask clarifying questions and do more research. Conversations can feel laced with subtext. If you sense a power struggle brewing, gracefully bow out before you get triggered.

TUES

27

Mercury in Leo through August 11

Restore your roar! Communicator Mercury spends the next couple weeks in Leo, making us all more creative and expressive. Got an idea to pitch? Use storytelling techniques and bold visuals to underscore your message. With affectionate Leo in the house, summer loving gets a boost. Take a chance and let someone know how you feel.

To find out how each Hotspot date will specifically impact your zodiac sign, read your Daily Horoscope at **Astrostyle.com**

https://www.astrostyle.com/horoscopes/daily

WED 28 Jupiter retrograde backs into Aquarius

Expansive Jupiter has been reversing through dreamy Pisces since May 13, making truth feel stranger than fiction. Today, Jupiter will back into Aquarius, the sign of teamwork and technology, for the duration of its retrograde. Between now and October 18, you may step back from a fast-moving friendship or cool your jets on a collaboration. Hold off on any outsized digital ventures and make sure all your plans are solid before taking any major risks.

THUR 29 Mars in Virgo through September 14

Turn dreams into reality! The action planet blazes into efficient and analytical Virgo, pumping you up to put plans, budgets and schedules behind your lofty ideas. Tidy up your cluttered spaces and ditch anything that doesn't "spark joy." With competitive Mars in this health-conscious sign, it's a great time to prioritize fitness. Make sure you warm up and stretch if you work out, as you'll be tempted to overdo it. Warning: When wordsmith Virgo collides with warrior Mars, people can get judgmental or critical. Simple conversations can combust into heated debates that get nasty. Follow the Golden Rule and "do unto others."

Bring healthy (and sexy) back to your love life! As racy Mars joins Venus in purist Virgo, there's no more stepping over stuff—the little things mean a lot. Being helpful and considerate is more of a turn-on than looking hot in your summer selfies. (That said, meticulous glamazon Virgo loves a good dressup date!) Get your hearts beating faster and your blood pumping by working out together. Be open to meeting someone through wellness pursuits or even sports (competitive Mars loves physical activity) if you're single. Watch out for a critical streak, as the red planet can dial up our flaw-finding tendencies while he's in this analytical sign. You don't have to settle but do remember that nobody's perfect!

July 31
Third Quarter Moon in Taurus

Leo Crystals
by MizChartreuse

Affirmations

I illuminate the darkness.
I honor the power of gratitude.
I am in tune with my highest self.
I magnetize success and prosperity.
I embrace and support my inner child.
I assist others to gain their heart's desire.

TIGER'S EYE

Removes creative blocks and confusion; can temper disorders and aid in digestion

CITRINE

Boosts new beginnings, is an anecdote to depression, encourages free expression

Leo Season *Journaling*

I feel energized when I:

_____
_____
_____
_____

I would like to feel more pride (and less shame) about:

_____
_____
_____
_____

I sometimes let pride or ego stand in the way of:

_____
_____
_____
_____

I have the easiest time taking the lead when:

_____
_____
_____
_____

I feel most able to be generous when I have:

_____
_____
_____
_____

august

Hello, innovation nation! This month features a rare second Aquarius full moon in a row. With passionate and creative Leo ruling the skies, roll out your most colorful ideas. But make sure you don't rock the boat so hard it tips over. Disruptor Uranus will turn retrograde mid-month, cautioning us to unveil our trailblazing ideas mindfully.

	SUN	MON	TUES	WED	THUR	FRI	SAT
	1	2	3	4	5	6	7
	🔥	🔥	💗🔥			🔥	
	8	9	10	11	12	13	14
	♌	💗	🔥	💗🔥			
	15	16	17	18	19	20	21
	♏	💗		🔥	🔥	🔥	
	22 ♍ Virgo Season Starts ♒🔥	23 💗	24 🔥	25	26 🔥	27	28
	29	30 🔥◑	31				

AUGUST 2021

Key:

HOTSPOT   LOVE HOTSPOT

Third Quarter   New Moon   First Quarter   Full Moon

SUN
1

Sun-Mercury meetup in Leo

Bold and clever ideas deserve to see the light of day. Pitch a creative concept today. Your courageous act might not get an instant greenlight, but it will certainly grab their attention. And who knows where that might lead?

Mercury-Saturn opposition

But wait…do you have a plan? Certain minds are closed tighter than Fort Knox as skeptical Saturn stares down talkative Mercury. If you're not ready to be grilled on how you'll execute your grand idea, let people know before you launch into a starry-eyed presentation. Or, hold off on sharing with the doubters and decision-makers, and spend the day putting a master map behind your brilliant, blue-sky vision. Keep it simple but don't skim over the technical parts. Make sure that people can clearly understand how you'll execute this, phase by phase.

MON
2

Sun-Saturn opposition

Reality check or total buzzkill? As the excitable Sun and cautious Saturn make their once-a-year standoff, it could feel like someone's poured a bucket of cold water on your dreams. Don't let it dampen your spirits. Extract the wisdom from any critical feedback or roadblock you encounter. This transit reminds us that less really can be more. Maybe you could stand to scale back, finish something you've started or put a more concrete schedule and budget behind your plans. Slow down—but don't stop!

TUES
3

Mercury-Uranus square

Paging Distraction Central! Buzzy Mercury in Leo already has you overbooked, juggling plans and fielding a million conversations at once. Today, as disruptive Uranus butts into the mix, that will multiply times ten. People may be contrarian just for their own kicks, so don't engage with devil's advocates if they turn out to be trolls. But do open up to unexpected ideas. If you've been rigidly sticking to one plan or POV, let yourself see this from a whole different angle. Welcome another approach, as long as it doesn't take you too far off course. Set a "hard stop" time for any brainstorming sessions to ensure you get your regular work done, too.

Venus-Uranus trine

An attraction could spark up suddenly today as romantic Venus pings the planet of surprises Uranus. For longtime duos, trying something out of your comfort zone could add a surge of excitement. Take a chance and suggest doing something a little daring together. With tech-savvy Uranus in the mix, widen your horizons and open your mind. Love could walk through the door when you least expect it!

FRI
6

Sun-Uranus square

Egos, tempers and tantrums, oh my! This volatile collision between the fiery Leo Sun and rebellious Uranus in stubborn Taurus could find people digging in their heels and taking shots at each other. If you find yourself walking on eggshells, diffuse the situation by exiting instead of provoking them further. Everyone is simply too committed to their own agenda to really hear anyone else. Avoid taking the bait if anyone pushes your buttons.

August 8, 9:49 am ET

LEO NEW MOON

A fresh start to your creative or romantic endeavors arrives with today's Leo lunar lift. Where have you not been voicing your feelings or sharing your ideas as openly as you could? Let these moonbeams loosen your tongue and make a vow to speak up. Do one thing to put your talents on display or draw attention to your gifts. Permission to graciously self-promote? Granted!

The AstroTwins' 2021 Horoscope   410

MON
9

Venus-Neptune opposition

Mixed signals much? It will be hard to tell if someone's interested in you or just being extra friendly. Don't assume anything under these obfuscating romantic skies. People could be extra sensitive today. Tread lightly to avoid pushing a thin-skinned person's buttons. Are you looking at someone through rose-colored glasses? Don't diminish the downside. Better to see people realistically, flaws and all.

TUES
10

Mercury-Jupiter opposition

Know-it-all alert! Today could feel like everyone is carrying on their own conversations and nobody's hearing anyone else. Don't add to the cacophony. Put on your headphones, turn on the white noise station or your favorite music for productivity and drown out the drama. Is someone trying to pitch you a big idea? If it sounds too good to be true, this starmap practically ensures that it is.

WED
11

Mercury in Virgo through August 30

Mental Mercury spends a couple weeks in his home sign of efficient, analytical Virgo. Bring order to any chaos by organizing, tracking and budgeting. With the communication planet in this healthy sign, you can successfully start (and sustain) new habits by writing things down and planning ahead. Keep it simple!

Venus-Pluto trine

Smoldering! As magnetic Venus and potent Pluto unite in earth signs, the definition of "sexy" could be a mashup of intense passion and a grounded, reliable connection. Can you possibly find that all in one person? If there was ever a day to, this is it! Couples could deepen their bond or revel in a mind-body-soul connection.

August 15

First Quarter Moon in Scorpio

MON

16

Venus in Libra through September 10

Home sweet home! Amorous Venus settles onto native soil, spending the next month in beautifying and affectionate Libra. Add romantic touches and decorative flourishes to everything. Give your closet a change-of-season update. Does it feel like everyone's flirting with you? That's how cosmic coquette Venus operates when she's in this lovely and gracious sign.

WED

18

Mercury-Mars meetup in Virgo

If you see something, say something! Have you observed a flaw in the plan? Speak up instead of just going along. Be diplomatic, as this transit can make you come across as rude or tactless. People could be overly critical or argumentative today. Don't get so hung up on the process that you lose sight of the bigger goal.

THUR
19

Sun-Jupiter opposition

Don't believe the hype—at least, not before you dig for the real storyline! Someone might talk a big game under this conflating cosmic confab. Enjoy the colorful stories but know the difference between the truth and a tall tale before you sign on. Be careful not to exaggerate or over-promise yourself.

Uranus retrograde in Taurus

As the unpredictable planet makes a five-month reversal through steady Taurus, your grip on finances, good habits and, well, reality, could get slippery. Plan with the best intentions but expect the unexpected between now and January 18, 2022. If money gets funny, pick up a side hustle or start an indie venture.

FRI
20

Mercury-Uranus trine

Eureka! The two most clever planets sync in sweet harmony today. As they merge their innovative superpowers in steady earth signs, put a thoughtful plan behind one of your big ideas. Then, get busy crafting it into tangible form!

SUN
22

Mars-Uranus trine

All fired up with…somewhere to go? As two of the most daring and impulsive planets align, you get the urge to take action on a unique idea. Ditch the status quo and approach an old problem from a fresh angle. Write with your non-dominant hand; take a new route to your usual destinations. Swing far out of your comfort zone in relationships and conversations. The novelty will give your brain a burst of mojo!

August 22, 8:01 am ET

AQUARIUS FULL MOON №2

Team up for the win! A rare second full moon in Aquarius (the first was on July 23) helps your collaborations take flight. An activist or community project could make a powerful impact. Seek out kindred spirits and people who think outside the box, then put your heads together for a common cause. Is a certain acquaintance worthy of being promoted to "true friend" or squad member status? These clarifying moonbeams will help you discern whether to open that door or keep them at arm's length.

MON
23
Venus-Saturn trine

As romantic Venus trines mature Saturn, love could take a turn for the serious. Single? Don't rule out a slightly older prospect or a stable person you might have written off as "boring." For couples, it's a great day to talk about the future and to make concrete plans for some fall activities you can enjoy as a duo.

TUES
24
Mercury-Neptune opposition

Your best attempts to make a decision could be in vain today, as communicator Mercury opposes foggy Neptune. Giving instructions? Check 'em twice or thrice. Your message will be easily obscured or misconstrued. Daydreaming again? Concentrating on anything for long will be a challenge, so take lots of mental breaks. If you need to remember all the details of a complex project, use a spreadsheet app or a good old-fashioned notebook and write it down!

August 22
Virgo Season Begins

The masterful helper of the horoscope wheel, Virgo energy teaches us to serve, do impeccable work and prioritize wellbeing—of ourselves, our loved ones and the planet.

Virgo Crystals
by MizChartreuse

Affirmations

I trust my inner guidance.

I am a messenger of truth.

I transform through the fire.

I serve others to heal myself.

I am impeccable with my word.

I embody the highest integrity.

PERIDOT

Known to calm nerves and tension, strengthen the digestive tract, and assist with childbirth contractions

MOSS AGATE

Good for mental stimulation and clarity, to boost self-esteem and reduce judgement

THUR
26   Mercury-Pluto trine

Make that big ask! Today's potent cosmic alliance gives you charisma and wit—along with irresistible powers of persuasion. Trust that you'll know exactly what to say in any situation. But if you need to write down a few talking points, tuck them in your pocket or jot them in your Notes app for backup.

MON
30   Mercury in Libra through November 5

Diplomacy is your path to progress as expressive Mercury starts an extra-long trip through measured and fair-minded Libra. Aim for mutuality and a balanced solution that takes all parties' needs into consideration. Even if it takes a little longer to make a decision, the long-term payoff is worth it. Hammer out any contracts before Mercury turns retrograde from September 27 to October 18, a tricky time to sign deals or officialize anything.

August 30
Third Quarter Moon in Gemini

To find out how each Hotspot date will specifically impact your zodiac sign, read your Daily Horoscope at **Astrostyle.com**

https://www.astrostyle.com/horoscopes/daily

Virgo Season *Journaling*

I would like to take better care of my body by:

_____
_____
_____
_____

What can I repurpose or upcycle? (DIY project time!)

_____
_____
_____
_____

How can I view a negative or challenging situation as a lesson?

_____
_____
_____
_____

What's the most fulfilling way for me to be of service to others?

_____
_____
_____
_____

Where could I ask for more support in my own life?

_____
_____
_____
_____

september

Time to play well with others! Partnerships
will carry us into fall as revved-up Mars
enters Libra, galvanizing our dynamic duos.
Libra season officially begins at the autumn
equinox. Another good reason to make deposits in the good karma bank? Communicator Mercury turns retrograde in this balanced
sign at the end of the month, when we'll need
an extra shot of goodwill and patience.

SUN	MON	TUES	WED	THUR	FRI	SAT
			1	2	3	4
5	6 ♍	7	8	9	10	11
12	13	14	15	16	17	18
19	20	21	22 ♎ Libra Season Starts	23	24	25
26	27	28	29	30		

SEPTEMBER 2021

Key:

HOTSPOT   LOVE HOTSPOT

Third Quarter   New Moon   First Quarter   Full Moon

THUR
2

Mars-Neptune opposition

Know thy limits! As relentless Mars opposes boundary-blurring Neptune, it will be hard to find the "stop" button or know how much is too much. But you'll be risking burnout if you push things too far. Take breaks in between your go-go-go activities today to replenish your tanks.

SAT
4

Mercury-Saturn trine

Take the time to think it through today. Whether you're making a big decision or finishing a project, wise Saturn rewards you for meticulous work. A well-connected or experienced person could help you get to the next level. Be prepared to return the favor by doing stellar work—and making anyone who recommends you look good.

SUN
5

Venus-Pluto square

Power struggles could pervade your love life today. Controlling, dominating or avoidant behavior will only heap fuel on the fire and deepen the divisive dynamic. Get to the root of what's really driving this tension. You may find yourself obsessing over you-know-who today. Hard as it is to stop your brain from fixating (and your fingers from Googling or texting), try to keep things above board.

The AstroTwins' 2021 Horoscope   422

MON 6

Mars-Pluto trine

Don't stop 'til you reach the top! As driven Mars and powerhouse Pluto commune, your competitive side comes out full force. Want something? Be proactive and strategic in your pursuit of it. Woo the decision-makers with heart and honesty and follow your instincts. Mars gives you the courage to make a big ask, while shrewd Pluto reveals different points of entry. Whether you get there through the front door, side door or the service elevator doesn't matter. The end justifies the means.

Venus-Jupiter trine

Take a chance on love! The "great benefics" Venus and Jupiter (named that for their helpful and positive influence) team up in breezy, communicative air signs. Let someone know that you admire them. Express appreciation and love. Be generous with your affection and you'll receive the same in return.

Sun-Uranus trine

Stuck at a plateau? Mix things up and keep trying different approaches. Under this innovative mashup, your bold and trailblazing attempts could bring a "Eureka!" moment.

September 6, 8:51 pm ET

VIRGO NEW MOON

How can you make a difference today? The year's only new moon in the sign of service, health and organization inspires you to get involved in meaningful projects. Look at ways you can give back through your efforts, even in small ways. Ready to get your fall fitness plans into motion? The fresh-start energy of this new moon inspires you to go clean and green.

FRI
10

Venus in Scorpio through October 7

When Venus shimmies into seductive Scorpio for a month, there's no telling what might transpire! No turn on is taboo if you're both into it. Get in touch with your eroticism through dance, sensual movement or good old-fashioned sexytime. Dive deep into emotional exploration to move past any blocks. A transformative four weeks await!

September 13
First Quarter Moon in Sagittarius

The AstroTwins' 2021 Horoscope   425

TUES
14

Mars in Libra through October 30

Self-doubt never served anyone any good. That said, have you overestimated yourself just a smidge? The confident Sun squabbles with delusional Neptune, skewing our perceptions. Not sure if your act is ready for prime time? Get a second opinion before you debut it. On the flip side, if insecurity is causing you to overthink and hide out, quit procrastinating! Tap someone who will be your personal cheerleader. They'll remind you how awesome you are as you take the courageous step of going public.

As driven Mars blazes into the sign of relationships, people will be eager to partner up. But don't lay on the pressure—or feel strongarmed into moving faster than you're comfortable going. Confidence, even a touch of cockiness, is a turn-on over the next few weeks.

Sun-Neptune opposition

Stuck in the muck? Blame nebulous Neptune, which can derail the best-laid plans. You may think you're focusing and moving forward, yet all too easily you'll get distracted or blown off course. Someone with an ulterior motive may not be showing their hand. Since you probably can't draw out the truth, work on something you can control.

THUR
16

Sun-Pluto trine

Your power is palpable today, so wield it responsibly! It won't take much to make an impact or even to come across as intimidating. Be conscious of how intense you're being. Want to increase your leverage? Hold back a little instead of being an open book. Mystery will work in your favor today.

FRI
17

Venus-Saturn square

If you've been charging full steam ahead in your love life, today's cautious cosmic clash could hit the brakes. Don't dismiss any reservations or nagging gut feelings. Instead, be grateful for this rare reality check from the stars. Considering a commitment? Make sure you're both on the same page for what you want long-term. The only way you'll know is by setting your emotions aside and talking it through. For couples, it's a good day for a serious talk about future plans or an unresolved issue.

MON
20

Mercury-Jupiter trine

With messenger Mercury and outspoken Jupiter teaming up in communicative air signs, word travels fast! It's a great day to pitch a visionary idea. But be careful that you don't inadvertently spread gossip or misinformation. Check the facts before you share.

September 20, 7:54 pm ET

PISCES FULL MOON

Let your imagination take the reins! The year's only Pisces full moon illuminates your subconscious and imbues life with a touch of magic. Who needs reality when enchantment beckons? Follow the coincidences and serendipities and see where they lead you. Music, art, poetry, dance—this lunar lift sparks creativity. The muse awaits! In compassionate Pisces, this full moon could inspire a healing conversation that builds a bridge to forgiveness.

WED 22 — Mercury-Pluto square

Duck! People are projecting their issues onto each other at every turn today, as expressive Mercury gets caught in combat with manipulative Pluto. Be careful not to play the blame game yourself. Under this moody square, you could spend the day ruminating over a recent problem. Catch yourself if you start obsessing. Tunnel vision won't get you where you want to go.

THUR 23 — Venus-Uranus opposition

Mood swing alert! Strong emotions might erupt like molten lava under today's explosive and unpredictable face-off. Try not to interact with someone who's behaving like a ticking time bomb. Feeling the urge for more freedom? You don't have to throw out the baby with the bathwater. It's totally possible to create more space in a relationship without calling the whole thing off.

September 22
Libra Season Begins

The balanced beautifier of
the horoscope family, Libra
energy inspires us to seek
peace, harmony and
cooperation—and to do it
with style and grace.

Libra Crystals
by MizChartreuse

Affirmations

I empathize with others.

I transmute my pain into wisdom.

I respect my boundaries and feelings.

I see relationships as divine assignments.

I give only from an overflowing cup.

I am worthy of unconditional love.

ROSE QUARTZ

Beneficial to all matters of the heart, helpful for fertility and relieving many body aches

AMETRINE

Good for promoting stability, brain function and body detoxification

SAT 25   Mars-Saturn trine

As speedy Mars and cautious Saturn merge their superpowers, you'll have the gift of timing on your side. There's a fine line between leaping at an opportunity and using the wisdom of discretion. Assess the pros and cons, then take a calculated risk.

MON 27   Mercury retrograde in Libra through October 18

Think twice before you speak, post or press "send." With communication planet Mercury backing through deliberate, fair-minded Libra, your judgment could be skewed for the next few weeks. Avoid jumping (or even walking) to conclusions before you have all the facts. Follow the Golden Rule: If you wouldn't want someone to say it to you, don't let it come out of your mouth.

~~~~~~~~~~~~~~~~~~~~~~~~

September 28
Third Quarter Moon in Cancer

WED

29

Sun-Saturn trine

Practice humility today, but make sure your accomplishments shine. You don't have to downplay your contributions. Just remember to acknowledge the "little people" who have worked hard to make these goals happen. By genuinely lifting them up, you make yourself look bigger!

Venus-Neptune trine

Romance reigns as these two enchanting planets unite in sensitive and sensual water signs. Compassion and creativity are also off the charts, making it a beautiful day to start a project as a duo or to listen generously to each other's POV. Under these healing skies, you can repair a rift. But use caution, as you may get a little too wrapped up in trying to solve someone's problems. This cosmic alignment makes everyone an emotional sponge.

THUR

30

Venus-Jupiter square

Feelings get magnified and exaggerated today, as inflating Jupiter butts heads with harmonious Venus. Being a know-it-all will definitely interrupt the harmony of a close relationship. How badly do you need to be right about this topic? With honest Jupiter off-kilter, telling the truth could set you a little too free! This might not be the best day to let it all hang out.

To find out how each Hotspot date will specifically impact your zodiac sign, read your Daily Horoscope at **Astrostyle.com**

https://www.astrostyle.com/horoscopes/daily

Libra Season *Journaling*

What is my vision of living a luxurious life?

_____
_____
_____
_____

What image do I (ideally) want to project to the world?

_____
_____
_____
_____

Where have I been too diplomatic, at the expense of authenticity?

_____
_____
_____
_____

People with these characteristics always catch my eye:

_____
_____
_____
_____

My most attractive qualities are:

_____
_____
_____
_____

GET YOUR DAILY, WEEKLY AND MONTHLY HOROSCOPE AT

Astrostyle.com

october

Back up those electronic files! Mercury is retrograde for the first half of the month, a dicey time for technology, travel and interactions. The cosmic trickster will treat us to his mischief, but luckily, we'll see three other planets—Jupiter, Saturn and Pluto—end their retrograde backspins this month, too. By Halloween, big projects should be sailing forward again.

SUN	MON	TUES	WED	THUR	FRI	SAT
					1	2
3	4	5	6 ♎	7	8	9
10	11	12	13	14	15	16
17	18	19	20 ♈	21	22	23 ♏ Scorpio Season Starts
24	25	26	27	28 ♌	29	30
31						

OCTOBER 2021

Key:

HOTSPOT LOVE HOTSPOT

Third Quarter | New Moon | First Quarter | Full Moon

FRI
1

Mercury-Pluto square

Think twice before you confide in someone or give away any state secrets. As mouthy Mercury squares off against sketchy Pluto, you never know if someone will keep this intel under wraps. Listen closely, ask questions and reveal as little as possible. Not sure of a certain someone's motives? Pay attention to what people aren't saying: Body language can reveal subtle but powerful clues.

~~~~~~~~~~~~~~~~~

SUN
3

Mercury-Jupiter trine

Lift the gag order! The secretive vibe of a couple days ago gives way to an outgoing and expressive energy. As talkative Mercury and outspoken Jupiter trine in social air signs, it's a great day for exchanging ideas or communing with your crew!

WED
6

Pluto retrograde ends

Back to your goals! Shadowy Pluto ends a five-month retrograde through Capricorn that began on April 27. If you've been unsure about whether to pursue a certain direction, this period of soul-searching may have helped. Now, you can get back to your mission with strategic focus.

October 6, 7:05 pm ET

LIBRA NEW MOON

Dynamic duos unite! The new moon in Libra, the sign of partnerships, sets the stage for teaming up with others. Bring harmony and balance back to your bonds. Seek new synergies. Ready to make a relationship official? Start discussing those next big steps.

THUR

7

Venus in Sagittarius through November 5

Broaden your search parameters in the game of love! With amorous Venus in worldly Sagittarius, you could be attracted to someone quite different from your usual type. Your backgrounds may be wildly divergent, but you could share common interests and philosophies about life. For couples, this is a great time to book pre-holiday travel, sign up for a fun course or venture outside your normal range of activities.

FRI

8

Sun-Mars meetup in Libra

Be a force of nature today! As the life-giving Sun and energizer Mars unite in diplomatic Libra, seize the opportunity to make a partnership official. Got an issue with a key collaborator or partner? Be direct but diplomatic.

SAT

9

Sun-Mercury-Mars meetup in Libra

Need a little time to think about it? The confident Sun unites with contemplative Mercury and action planet Mars. It's a good day to ask all your questions and research before making a big decision. But don't deliberate for too long or you could miss an opportunity.

SUN
10

Saturn retrograde ends

Reboot the revolution! Structured Saturn, which has been in powered-down retrograde since May 23, corrects course in Aquarius, the sign of teamwork, technology and social change. As the planet of "adulting" turns direct, it's time to put a plan behind your idealistic talk. If a group endeavor has been on shaky ground, you'll be able to get your crew aligned again.

October 12

First Quarter Moon in Capricorn

FRI
15

Sun-Jupiter trine

Adopt an experimental and open-minded attitude today. As the trailblazing Sun and adventurous Jupiter unite in air signs, thinking outside the box can lead to a breakthrough. Stuck in a mental rut? Go for a walk (or drive) off your beaten path. Read a website that's not in your usual feed. Novelty is the antidote!

SUN
17

Sun-Pluto square

Watch for power struggles today. If you're picking up cues that someone's being evasive or throwing subtle shade, you might be correct. But don't leap to conclusions! Make a point of observing before you jump into the fray. If you don't know how to react, it's better to keep your opinions to yourself than lash out. If you need to address an issue, step aside for a private chat.

MON
18

Mars-Jupiter trine

Quit talking and thinking: It's time for action! Go-getter Mars and risk-taker Jupiter unite in a harmonious trine, emboldening you to leap into the unknown. If your gut is telling you to take a chance, this is the day to follow it. But do look both ways before you swan-dive into something that you haven't researched. The combo of these two impulsive planets can tempt you to abandon common sense or get pulled into a pointless argument.

Jupiter retrograde ends

Forward! Auspicious Jupiter ends a retrograde slowdown that began on June 20. As the planet of expansion powers forward in visionary Aquarius, a cutting-edge collaboration could pick up speed. If a team has drifted from its original mission or purpose, you'll be able to come together again. Agreeing to disagree will be an easier policy to adopt now.

Mercury retrograde ends

Where is the love? Convivial Mercury wraps its three-week retrograde through peacekeeping Libra today, restoring harmony among feuding partners. Since September 27, communication has been strained, making it hard to see eye-to-eye with the people closest to you. An attractive opposite may suddenly have repelled you. Maybe you invited a toxic ex back into your world or made a destructive choice that impacted a relationship. While there may be damage to undo, start mending fences today. Break free from draining alliances and open up to collaborators who are a better match.

October 20, 10:56 am ET

ARIES FULL MOON

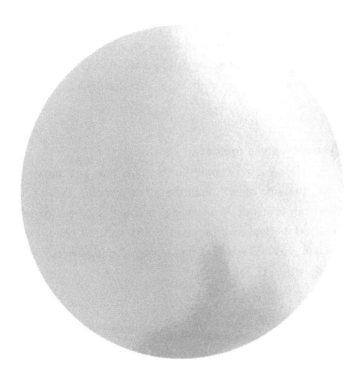

Ready to make a bold move? The full moon in passionate powerhouse Aries inspires us to take a daring leap toward a personal goal or to let your solo star shine. A project you've been working on for the past six months could come together. But don't wait to be noticed. Under these proactive, proud moonbeams, you've got permission to toot your own horn!

FRI

22

Mars-Pluto square

Deep-seated issues boil to the surface as aggravator Mars in Libra locks horns with power-tripping Pluto in Capricorn. A person who pushes your buttons could really get under your skin now. Do your best not to take the bait or worse, to fan the flames of conflict. Otherwise, things could get ugly! The direct approach is always best, but under these contentious skies, an upfront conversation might be best saved for another day. Stressed about a certain relationship? Take a time-out instead of demanding that they have "the talk" with you.

TUES

26

Venus-Neptune square

Hate to burst your bubble but...are you more in love with the idea of love than the actual person? Today's harsh square between romantic Venus and delusional Neptune snatches the rose-colored spectacles off your nose. Catch yourself before you get too lost in a fantasy and see this situation for what it really is.

October 28
Third Quarter Moon in Leo

October 23
Scorpio Season Begins

The most intense and focused of the horoscope signs, Scorpio energy helps us dive deep, merge our superpowers and form bonds that are built to last.

Scorpio Crystals

by MizChartreuse

Affirmations

I create my life.

I recognize the lessons in each moment.

I accept responsibility.

I spiral upward to wisdom.

I embrace all parts of me.

I rebirth anew and transformed.

I trust the process.

I recognize the suppressed aspects of myself.

I integrate my shadows.

I liberate myself from the underworld.

I embody true magic.

I productively magnify my power.

MALACHITE

Intense energy healer, works well with meditation; a stone of goddesses, assists female sex organs

BLACK OBSIDIAN

Powerful stone for deep insight, helps with blockages and can improve circulation

SAT
30

Mars in Scorpio through December 13

Intensity and intrigue build over the next few weeks, as potent Mars burrows into scintillating and secretive Scorpio. Watch for competitive or jealous flareups. Divisions of power can get more pronounced, but you also have a chance to ascend in a hierarchy. Make sure you don't come across as ruthless or only concerned with your own agenda. Bonds deepen and you'll gain a strong sense of who you can trust.

Sun-Saturn square

This twice-a-year conflict can make you feel pessimistic about the future, but it's also an important reality check. Don't get discouraged. Instead, go back to the drawing board or tighten up your plans. Consider this (brief) pause a blessing in disguise. You could spot an error or a flaw in your plans just in the nick of time.

Mars in Scorpio through December 13

Bring on the holiday season heat! As randy Mars slides into sexy Scorpio, a budding connection could burst into flames of full-on consummation. The red planet is all too happy to set your desire on fire. Warning: Jealousy and possessiveness could run rampant now. If someone's legitimately betrayed you, then use this courageous transit to walk away. But know that your raw emotions could also be provoking a bit of paranoia. Investigate before you accuse (and no, that doesn't mean snooping or invading privacy).

To find out how each Hotspot date will specifically impact your zodiac sign, read your Daily Horoscope at **Astrostyle.com**

https://www.astrostyle.com/horoscopes/daily

Scorpio Season *Journaling*

Where do I currently crave more privacy? Where do I feel isolated?

_____
_____
_____
_____

Describe the most seductive moment you've ever shared:

_____
_____
_____
_____

I would describe my attitude toward change as:

_____
_____
_____
_____

Powerful people make me feel:

_____
_____
_____
_____

How in touch with my own power am I?

_____
_____
_____
_____

The AstroTwins' 2021 Horoscope   448

november

Holiday shopping gets a cosmic twist! Not only does magnetic Venus (associated with both love and money) enter cash-savvy Capricorn for an extended visit, we have the debut Taurus lunar eclipse in a new series that will revolutionize our revenues over the next couple years. Hold tight for a Mars-Uranus opposition midmonth that could loosen tongues and heat up tempers. Looking for a quick pivot? Rapid changes could be afoot!

NOVEMBER 2021

SUN	MON	TUES	WED	THUR	FRI	SAT
	1	2	3	4 ♏	5 ♥	6
7	8	9	10	11 ☽	12	13
14	15	16	17	18	19 ♉ ♥ Lunar Eclipse	20
21 ↗ Sagittarius Season Starts	22	23	24	25	26	27 ♏
28	29 ♥	30				

Key:

HOTSPOT   LOVE HOTSPOT

Third Quarter   New Moon   First Quarter   Full Moon

MON
1

Mercury-Jupiter trine

Big ideas deserve the stage today, so banish those limiting beliefs and supersize your convictions! As clever Mercury and expansive Jupiter team up in lofty earth signs, words and notions carry magnitude—and can go farther than you think. Need to keep it real? Speak your truth, but "pre-edit" it so you don't inadvertently hurt or offend anyone. Take the high road and talk things through in a positive way rather than tearing others down! Be direct but kind.

TUES
2

Mercury-Pluto square

Keep it in the vault! With Mercury fighting secretive Pluto, don't give away any state secrets today. Do your research and check all facts before going public or buying into someone's pitch. People could represent themselves as bigger than they really are. Listen and ask questions, but hold your cards close to your vest.

THUR
4

Sun-Uranus opposition

Volatility alert! As the boldfaced Sun faces down radical changemaker Uranus, egos could get testy. Avoid thin-skinned people and rabble rousers who just want to push your buttons. This isn't the day to demand a firm answer or make a binding decision. Plans could change without notice. If you must pivot quickly, adopt a flexible attitude instead of digging in your heels. A completely unexpected approach could actually lead to a breakthrough.

November 4, 5:14 pm ET

SCORPIO NEW MOON

Dive into the depths! The year's only Scorpio new moon opens a new chapter for all of your investments: emotional, spiritual and financial. A bond that begins today could develop over the next six months. Can this connection go the distance? If it's got permanent potential, explore! Shared finances, passive income and property matters could be in the spotlight now, too.

FRI

5

Venus in Capricorn through March 6, 2022

Long-range goals are suddenly more important than instant gratification. Talk to your partner about taking a step toward greater commitment or, if you're single, make a list of the qualities you're looking for—and the deal breakers. A holiday season proposal could be in the stars. But take your time making things permanent, as the love planet will turn retrograde (backward) for six weeks on December 19. Venus normally stays in one sign for about a month, but it will linger in steady Capricorn for four whole months due to the backspin. Slow and steady wins the romantic race!

Mercury in Scorpio through November 24

Keep it under wraps? Messenger Mercury slides into secretive Scorpio, urging you to strengthen those filters. The next couple weeks are ideal for researching, editing and crafting your magnum opus behind the scenes. Hold off on the big pitches and press releases. Instead, perfect your presentation and make a grand debut at the end of this month!

The AstroTwins' 2021 Horoscope   454

WED 10

Mercury-Mars meetup in Scorpio

Retract your claws! Fights could get ugly and people could play dirty today. Don't fan the flames by tossing out cruel barbs. Discussions and negotiations could get intense, so make sure you know exactly what you are and aren't willing to settle for before you open talks.

Mercury-Saturn square

Rigid much? Watch for a tendency to be stubborn or argumentative today. When you find yourself resisting something "on principle," take a look at what that might really be about. Are you afraid of losing control or being exposed as not having all the answers? Keep the imposter syndrome in check but do make sure you've done all your homework.

Mars-Saturn square

One foot on the gas, the other on the brake? As speedy Mars and cautious Saturn get into a traffic jam, there could be unforeseen roadblocks. Just when you thought an ambitious project was about to achieve liftoff, it might hit a major snag. But is it as "terminal" as you fear? Today's constraining clash could make you see only the downsides. Step away for a day or two then reexamine. You might be pleased to find that things aren't nearly as bleak as you thought. In fact, this brief pause could help you catch something you wouldn't otherwise see.

November 11

First Quarter Moon in Aquarius

FRI
12

Sun-Neptune trine

Dream it, manifest it! Your powers of creative visualization are mighty under this golden trine. Make a practice of imagining the outcome you want with all your senses and doing affirmations to support it.

SAT
13

Mercury-Uranus opposition

Don't expect your mouth to be able to keep pace with your thoughts today! This cosmic collision sends your mind into overdrive. But hold your tongue before rebellious Uranus seizes the mic. In this case, the first thought probably isn't the best thought!

MON 15 — Sun-Jupiter square

Open minds, closed doors? Experimentation could be the key to solving a sticky conundrum today. But getting a certain decision-maker to buy in could be tough, particularly if their ego or status is at stake. Don't follow the herd: Share your bold ideas, even if others don't understand them (yet). Fortune favors the forward thinkers, especially those brave enough to voice their visions. Let others look at you sideways. In a few weeks, you'll be celebrated as the Nostradamus of your crew for your brilliant foresight!

WED 17 — Mars-Uranus opposition

Pure genius? Under today's combustible mashup, you could have a major epiphany that leads to a breakthrough. But play it cool. People will have hair-trigger tempers and could explode for no apparent reason. Dodge the dramatic divas and skeptical resistors. Spend your time around folks who are open to trying things a new way! Don't let your own quick-to-heat emotions get the best of you.

THUR 18 — Mercury-Neptune trine

Ask and you'll receive! Not everything requires laborious effort. Today, as mental Mercury tunes in to mystical Neptune's frequency, use the Law of Attraction to your advantage and visualize what you want! Under this flowing mashup, your intuition may be borderline psychic. Read the reports and check the data, but then follow your gut.

November 19, 3:57 pm ET

TAURUS FULL MOON
(Lunar Eclipse)

Show us the money! The full moon in fiscal and security-seeking Taurus would be powerful enough on its own. But in a game-changing lunar eclipse, it could bring big opportunity to shift (and increase!) the way you save, spend and earn. Ready to do away with a longtime bad habit and start fresh? This eclipse can give you the courage and resources to release what no longer serves you.

FRI

19

Venus-Uranus trine

With Venus making an extended run through Capricorn, love turns super serious—and the holiday season pressure to pair up only adds more Yule logs to that fire. Today, frisky Uranus adds a twist of much-needed spontaneity to your personal life. Looking for romance? Tech-friendly Uranus could help you connect through dating apps, a video chat "date" or some other virtual means.

SAT

20

Mercury-Jupiter square

Easy does it! It'll be easy to over-promise under today's wildly optimistic mashup of chatty Mercury and cocky Jupiter. But it's important that you crunch the numbers and make sure you can follow through. You can't afford to mislead a key client, partner or collaborator. Don't believe everything you hear today, either. As exciting as an opportunity sounds, it's highly likely you don't have the full story. Listen with enthusiasm then dive into due diligence!

WED

24

Mercury in Sagittarius through December 13

Dream it, do it! As the messenger planet jets through Sagittarius for the next three weeks, you'll be able to articulate some of your grandest dreams. Corral your crew for some blue-sky brainstorming and big-picture visioning. Have you made your 2022 plans yet? This period is perfect for identifying the exciting goals you want to pursue in the coming year. Caution: This can be a big talk, little action transit. Some people will be blowing hot air, but excitement could fizzle as quickly as it sizzled. Luckily, there will be no shortage of adventurous opportunities to explore. Next!

November 21
Sagittarius Season Begins

The worldly adventurer of the horoscope wheel, Sagittarius energy inspires us to dream big, chase the impossible and take fearless risks.

Sagittarius Crystals

by MizChartreuse

Affirmations

I am the light of the world.

I activate my regeneration.

I aim toward seeing higher truth.

I observe the power of self-awareness.

I ascend to spiritual maturity and healing.

I trust each experience is for my highest good.

I see the bigger picture.

I am worthy because I exist.

I perceive with the mind of the divine.

I am at one with the universe.

I decode beyond the veil of binary limitations.

I activate and practice my gifts in service to the world.

PYRITE

Invokes feelings of cheer; stimulates digestive and immune systems; helps you to see the big picture

LAPIS LAZULI

Encourages self-awareness and expression; activates the body's elimination processes

November 27
Third Quarter Moon in Virgo

MON

29

Mars-Neptune trine

Trust your hunches! Insistent Mars in psychic Scorpio is harmoniously connected with tuned-in Neptune, which is parked in intuitive Pisces. Serendipities, coincidences and "signs" are practically announcing themselves in bold neon lights today. Don't dismiss these directives from the universe!

Sexy Mars and fantasy-spinning Neptune connect in emo water signs, sparking a mind-body-soul connection. Couples could find the perfect balance of lust and trust, as compassionate Neptune softens the red planet's raw intensity. Single? A sultry person with a strong spiritual side will be more appealing than the sparklepony with sheer animal magnetism.

To find out how each Hotspot date will specifically impact your zodiac sign, read your Daily Horoscope at **Astrostyle.com**

https://www.astrostyle.com/horoscopes/daily

The AstroTwins' 2021 Horoscope   462

Sagittarius Season *Journaling*

How do I define abundance?

_____
_____
_____
_____

I feel comfortable taking risks in these areas of life:

_____
_____
_____
_____

I would like to be more adventurous in these ways:

_____
_____
_____
_____

My favorite travel companions are:

_____
_____
_____
_____

How much is "enough" for me with money, love, etc?

_____
_____
_____
_____

december

Don't even think about slipping off for the holidays early! (Unless, of course, you've got a fabulous vacation planned.) The month begins with a solar eclipse in worldly Sagittarius, a boon for entrepreneurs and adventurers alike. Love planet Venus turns retrograde mid-month, and the year's third and final Saturn-Uranus square arrives on Christmas Eve. Lucky Jupiter returns to compassionate and creative Pisces right before the calendar turns. Here's to a fantasy-fueled NYE. Champagne, anyone?

DECEMBER 2021

SUN	MON	TUES	WED	THUR	FRI	SAT
			1	2	3	4 Solar Eclipse
5	6	7	8	9	10	11
12	13	14	15	16	17	18 ♊
19	20	21 ♑ Capricorn Season Starts	22	23	24	25
26	27	28	29	30	31	

Key:

HOTSPOT LOVE HOTSPOT

Third Quarter New Moon First Quarter Full Moon

WED
1

Neptune Direct in Pisces

Hazy Neptune ends its confusing annual retrograde through Pisces, which began June 25. There'll be no more wondering who's got your back and which members of the flock are actually wolves parading as sheep. Have you felt adrift from your purpose? Add some soul to your goals. Tap into your creative right brain (and the divine flow) with journaling, meditation or visualization exercises.

December 4, 2:42 am ET

SAGITTARIUS NEW MOON
(Solar Eclipse)

The year's only new moon in visionary Sagittarius is also a solar eclipse! Get ready for a bold entry into uncharted terrain or to take a supersized leap of faith. Multiply your adventurous and boundary-expanding ideas by (at least) ten. As the final eclipse in the Gemini/Sagittarius series that began mid-2020, this is your lunar "last call" to take advantage of these optimistic moonbeams. Don't overthink— go for it!

The AstroTwins' 2021 Horoscope　　　467

TUES
7

Mercury-Neptune square

Your left and right brain hemispheres battle for supremacy as analytical Mercury squares off with intuitive Neptune. You could feel conflicted about which is the right course of action. And with both planets in mutable signs, every option may seem as valid as the next. Try expert Suzy Welch's 10-10-10 rule for decision-making. Reflect on how the results of your actions could unfold in ten minutes, ten months and ten years. You'll be surprised by the insight!

WED
8

Mars-Jupiter square

You can't always be on the same page with everyone, but today a small disagreement could flame into a shouting match as hotheaded Mars squares over-the-top Jupiter. Are you being overly optimistic or trying to force your agenda? Tunnel vision mixed with stubborn willfulness will make a combustible cocktail today.

December 10
First Quarter Moon in Pisces

FRI
11

Venus-Pluto meetup

Things could get deep without much warning today as Venus makes its first of two scintillating summits with potent Pluto this month. As they commune in future-focused Capricorn, couples could make permanent plans for the long haul. Single or newly dating? Your mind could be on whether or not a certain match can go the distance. This cosmic combo may stir up a powerful sexual attraction, possibly with someone who feels like a soulmate, too. Don't leap to conclusions, but enjoy an opportunity to test those lusty waters!

SAT
12

Sun-Neptune square

Hit pause and take stock of how realistic your ambitious ideas are. While you don't want to limit yourself, hazy Neptune's clash with the confident Sun can obscure facts or draw in people who don't keep their word. Err on the side of caution, but watch out for a paranoid streak. You don't want to start flinging unfounded accusations. Inspect before you project!

SUN

13

Mars in Sagittarius through January 24, 2022

With self-determining Mars blazing through go-getter Sagittarius, ambitions take flight as the calendar turns. It's been a long year and this surge of much-needed optimism buoys your adventurous plans for 2022. Over the holidays, find ways to get active with outdoor sports or heart-pumping movement in nature, even if you have to bundle up. (Snowboarding, snowshoes, a winter hike?) Mars in entrepreneurial, wisdom-seeking Sagittarius can spark ideas for an indie business or a teaching project. Deep dive into online courses or metaphysical study instead of binging on mindless movies or sleeping the days away. Start those inspiration engines!

The sky's the limit as lusty Mars races through adventurous and worldly Sagittarius. Go boldly where you've never been before, whether that means giving someone wildly different than your usual "type" a chance, or taking a dream trip with your partner.

Mercury in Capricorn through January 2, 2022

Plan, strategize, negotiate like a #Boss! Communicator Mercury in stoic Capricorn helps us set emotions aside and think through everything with objectivity and precision. Cut the fluff and keep it simple. Sometimes, the first answer is the best one. Over the holidays, you could get a jump-start on your 2022 resolutions, as the responsible Capricorn influence will have your mind on the future.

Decmber 18, 11:35 pm ET

GEMINI FULL MOON

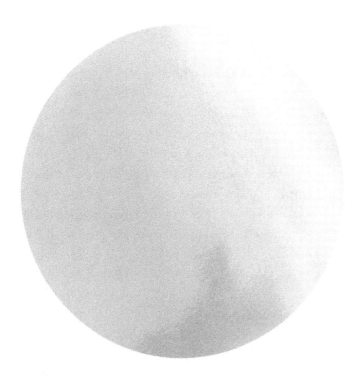

Keep your devices charged and powered on! This once-
a-year full moon in communicative Gemini could bring
the news you've been waiting for all year. If you've got a
big announcement to make, press "post" and get the buzz
going. It's a great time to commune with kindred spirits or
to find that "other half" who perfectly complements you in
business, friendship or possibly even love. The Gemini vibe
is more lighthearted than lusty, but there's plenty of room for
playful flirtation under this frisky full moon!

The AstroTwins' 2021 Horoscope   471

SUN
19

Chiron retrograde ends

Healing comet Chiron, which has been powered down since July 15, moves ahead in self-determined Aries. It's time to start using your voice and making confident choices on your own behalf. No more sacrificing and enabling—your needs count as much as everyone else's!

Venus retrograde through January 29, 2022

Romantic plans: interrupted? The love planet makes a six-week backspin through Capricorn, disrupting the flow in relationships and triggering arguments. An ex could resurface, perhaps someone you once had a serious commitment with. Is it worth a second chance? Explore with caution and take your time. Couples might find that their long-term goals don't overlap. Can you still make this work or is it a dealbreaker? This relationship review period, which happens every 18 months, is your time to step back and really consider that.

MON
20

Mercury-Uranus trine

People are powering down for the holidays, but don't squander this spark of celestial genius! Take advantage of clever Mercury and innovative Uranus teamed up in grounded earth signs and lay out your brilliant plan. You'll win supporters with your clear thinking, especially if you can articulate the payoff in fast, simple terms.

Capricorn Season Begins

The measured master planner of the horoscope family, Capricorn energy teaches us the power of structure, delayed gratification and setting goals for the long haul.

FRI

24

Saturn-Uranus square

The third and final faceoff of authoritarian Saturn and rebellious Uranus shows up on Christmas Eve, disrupting anything too stuffy or traditional. Remain flexible and try things in a new way. But don't let mutinous disruptors overturn all your plans either! Look back to the first two squares on February 17 and June 14 for clues of what may come to a grand finale today.

SAT

25

Venus-Pluto meetup

This month's second mashup of affectionate Venus and potent Pluto brings emotions (and attractions) to a boil. Get ready for a repeat performance of their December 11 tryst, only this time, Venus is retrograde. Beware a "love bomber," especially if it's someone from your past. The temptation to leap into a lusty encounter will be strong, and you're likely to act on raw attraction alone. Think twice (or thrice) before you jump into the deep end of this emotion ocean!

December 26
Third Quarter Moon in Libra

Capricorn Crystals
by MizChartreuse

Affirmations

I am unlimited in all aspects of growth.

I enjoy the process of self-development.

I trust that slow and steady wins the race.

I use my skills in service for humanity at large.

I empower myself to continue the mountain climb.

I improve with age and gain more wisdom over time.

I work to cultivate my own inner sanctum of security.

I am protected as a child of spirit.

I am diligent in building toward the bigger picture.

I enjoy romance and love in its purest form.

I appreciate the beauty and magic in life.

I see the bird's eye view beyond the horizon.

I trust the process of the magic of life's unfolding.

I am safe in my vulnerability and emotional transparency.

ONYX

Mastering your future,
grounding and balance,
clearning mental & emotional
stress, restoring realistic vision

GALENA

Harmony, detoxification,
healing childhood wounds, past
life regression work, revealing
the root cause of our fears

TUES

28

Jupiter in Pisces through December 20, 2022

Expansive Jupiter starts its second visit to Pisces this year, staying for an extended trip. Global consciousness will shift toward healing, creativity and the arts. Truth-teller Jupiter in illusory Pisces could expose a few scandals, but it will also make our shared humanity a topic of open conversation. As the famous recovery saying goes, you're only as sick as your secrets.

WED

29

Mercury-Venus meetup

As expressive Mercury and love planet Venus unite in sensible Capricorn, you'll have the ability to talk about your feelings without gushing or overwhelming anyone. Is it time to have "the talk" about your shared future? This could be a good moment to do that, right before the calendar turns. Better to clear the air today than during a champagne-fueled crying jag on NYE, in case you needed an incentive!

THUR

30

Mercury-Pluto meetup

Get an early start on that 2022 vision board or list of New Year's intentions! Today's clear-headed combo of strategic Pluto and messenger Mercury in master-planner Capricorn sharpens your focus and reveals a near-prophetic vision for your next big chapter.

To find out how each Hotspot date will specifically impact your zodiac sign, read your Daily Horoscope at **Astrostyle.com**

https://www.astrostyle.com/horoscopes/daily

Capricorn Season *Journaling*

One thing I'd like to master in this lifetime is:

_____
_____
_____
_____

If I could learn from any teacher or expert, it would be:

_____
_____
_____
_____

I need structure in order to succeed with these activities:

_____
_____
_____
_____

Unstructured flow is what I need with these activities:

_____
_____
_____
_____

Which activities are zapping my time? How can I fix this?

_____
_____
_____
_____

2021
NUMEROLOGY

The 5 Universal Year

Freedom. Risk-Taking. Adventure.
2021 Numerology calls for dramatic changes.

How to Calculate the Universal Year:

In Numerology, each calendar year adds up to a single-digit number, which holds a unique energetic influence and imprint. It's called the Universal Year. This means that everyone on the planet will experience the energy of a particular number during the entire year, from January 1 until December 31.

> Add the individual numbers of the current year together, like this:
>
> $2021 = 2 + 0 + 2 + 1 = 5$
>
> 2021 is a 5 Universal Year.

Whether or not you make New Year's resolutions, most of us intuitively feel a profound energy shift whenever the calendar turns. In Numerology, that transition is a big deal: It marks the passage into a new Universal Year.

This affects the collective atmosphere of the world for a 12-month period! You can think of the Universal Year as the state or country you're driving through on your yearly "road trip," and each number comes with its own unique resonance.

In Numerology, the number 5 represents the energy of instability. Change is its key mandate. The emphasis during a 5 Universal Year is pushing boundaries, exploration and new ideas—embarked upon with an adventurous and fearless spirit. To make the most of a 5 Universal Year, expect the unexpected!

The Universal 5 vibe is volatile, yet exciting—and that should come as no surprise given the turbulent state of our world. But unlike the heavy and hardworking

4 energy of 2020 (more on that in a minute), a 5 Universal Year invites us to explore the true meaning of freedom. How do we collectively secure a sense of sovereignty while also handling our mundane responsibilities? In 2021, we'll all have to strike that balance.

For example, we can't have financial freedom unless we earn money, invest wisely and plan effectively. Taking this responsible route earns us the financial resources to live on our own terms—a strong 5 desire.

Some people say that good health is freedom. We can't continuously indulge in excessive behaviors if we also want to experience physical strength and mobility. How can we bring discipline to our diets and routines in order to experience a vibrant mind, body and spirit?

Under the Numerology of 2021, outmoded lifestyles and beliefs will dramatically shift. While there will be continued uncertainty, the 5 Universal Year will also bring progress and impactful change. Unlike last year, rocking the boat and making waves are essential now. No more clinging to the past. Welcome the vivacious energy of a new era—as the 5 brings our passion alive!

Where We're Coming From:
About 2020 and the 4 Universal Year

Before we go further into what 2021 holds, it's helpful to understand where we're coming from. The new decade began with a 4 Universal Year, which is historically a tough time that demands hard work and hustle.

In Numerology, the responsible 4 carries the energy of long-term goal setting. Because of this, 2020 was a no-frills year that required us to update systems and firm up foundations. Between the global pandemic, shutdowns of schools and businesses, and economic turbulence (in an election cycle no less), the 4 Universal Year tested our character in extreme ways.

Last year's Numerology asked us to:
• Investigate the very foundation of our lives.
• Diligently work at setting longer-range goals for the future.
• Do the practical research to formulate a sustainable plan for the future.
• Systematically implement a new mission statement.

- Tenaciously move through limiting situations and circumstances.
- Hold ourselves and our leaders accountable.
- Come to terms with old ancestral infractions or wounding.

By now, you might feel like there's not enough sage in the world to clear out the apocalyptic energy of 2020! But you might also look back and see how much character you've built from all of 2020's endurance tests.

Now, 2021 offers a new focal point for our collective consciousness—the point of emphasis for the entire planet. Here's how to build upon the hard work of the 4 Year and welcome the 5—with all its courage, chaos and charisma.

How to Thrive in the 5 Universal Year

Be curious. Get out of your head and into the world! The 5 is fun, social, and gregarious. This is a year where we'll ache to stretch our wings and embrace new visions for our collective future. Magic happens when we open our minds and question long-held beliefs. That doesn't mean falling into lockstep with any movement. The 5 Universal Year mandates critical thinking and asks that we be open to changing our minds.

Don't think about it—do it! The 5 is the number of experience. This is a year for "doing"! The Numerology of 2021 wants us to experiment, not just talk or think about ideas. We're collectively learning to embrace radical change and adapt to new circumstances. Unconventional approaches will be favored in 2021. We can't simply skim the surface and drift aimlessly from one day to the next. Amid great uncertainty, we must test, try, and participate in a variety of potential solutions before settling on the approach or approaches that hold the most promise.

Focus singularly instead of multitasking. The 5 Universal Year offers a plethora of bright-and-shiny distractions that will compete for our attention. While the emphasis is on exploring new things, you don't have to try them all at once! A little "single-tasking" will help temper 2021's frenetic and chaotic pace. Question everything, but don't throw the baby out with the bathwater. Be sure you fully test any new system before you implement it. Something may sound great, but that doesn't mean it's sustainable.

Embrace uncertainty. Who doesn't rely on some level of control in their lives? And with so many things to legitimately worry about, the impulse to seek stability and certainty is understandable. But here's the deal: During a 5 Universal Year, a new reality is gestating.

You could think of 2021 as a "bridge year" between idea and implementation, when we get everything out into the open in vivid technicolor truth.

The 5 is a reservoir of ideas, so let them flow—and know that it may take until 2022, a more grounded 6 Universal Year, before systemic shifts take root.

Don't forget to dance during the revolution. With so much solemn news in the headlines, we can easily skip the essential "nutrient" that gets us through anything: Fun! But the 5 Universal Year brings out a friskiness that can't be contained. After a year of quarantine and isolation, with limited physical touch and social activity, many people are starved for pleasure. While we may not be able to get the party started to the raucous levels preferred by the 5, finding ways to celebrate is a must. The only caveat? Hedonism and excess are also hallmarks of the 5 Universal Year, as well as a certain self-centeredness. We don't want to end up with a collective hangover—or worse, interminable shutdowns and pandemic problems—from flouting the rules. Go ahead and "do you," but don't encroach on other people's freedom and rights in the process.

Distinguish between freedom and escapism. During a 5 Universal Year, we come face-to-face with our fears of being confined. The frenzied pursuit of joie de vivre can also be a means to avoid our problems. The fact that life doesn't always give us sunshine and rainbows is a truth that nobody wants to think about—especially after the depressing events of 2020. Will we be able to recover from a global economic crisis? How will we move forward dismantling racist, sexist, and discriminatory systems and replace them with something equitable? What is the future of travel, work environments, social gatherings, artistic venues, and all of the other aspects of what was formerly considered normal?

One of the key features of the 5 Universal Year involves staring down our deepest fears and seeing how we handle our desire for freedom. Are we running away from something that haunts us…or toward something that inspires us?

This could be a helpful metric: Are we scattering our energy in a million directions—or are we willing to do the work to make our grand visions a reality? The difficulty is that the energy of the 5 can feel like the Tasmanian Devil from the vintage Looney Tunes cartoon! There's a lack of discipline and order. Impulsiveness can lead to actions that we soon regret. We might choose to bypass the hard questions and stir up drama, using decoys to camouflage serious issues—or our own personal issues.

The Big Picture

Overall, the 5 Universal Year demands change on a radical level. We may begin 2021 collectively feeling stuck, tethered and restricted. Our mission, all year long, is to solve this riddle: How can we obtain the personal liberties we desire without taking away the liberties of others?

The "personality" of the 5 is that of an instigator and disruptor—with the higher purpose of shedding the old and moving into a contemporary and inclusive new way of being. Consensus is the foundation. Adaptability is mandatory. Solid direction is key.

This is a time to learn the true meaning of freedom as it applies to everyone on the planet. The highest expression of the energy of the 5 is to be open to new possibilities and have the fortitude to take a new direction with focused commitment and follow-through—even when that likely means a bit of personal sacrifice. It's a year to actively expand into the unknown. Put on your seatbelt and get ready for a wild ride in 2021! ✳

FELICIA BENDER
THE PRACTICAL NUMEROLOGIST

Felicia Bender, Ph.D.—The Practical Numerologist— is the author of *Redesign Your Life: Using Numerology to Create the Wildly Optimal You* and *Master Numbers 11, 22, 33: The Ultimate Guide*. She earned a doctorate in theater from the University of Missouri–Columbia. Felicia is passionate about writing, counseling, teaching, and presenting ways to use numerology, spirituality and intuition to understand ourselves and others on a deep level—to validate our life purpose and to develop tools to understand how to trust our own intuitive language. She is a contributor to elephantjournal.com, numerologist.com, and other media. Felicia's the resident numerologist for AstroStyle.com and you can find her at FeliciaBender.com.

2021

YEAR OF THE
METAL OX

The AstroTwins' 2021 Horoscope   484

2021 YEAR OF THE METAL OX

February 12, 2021 – February 1, 2022

Downsizing, simplifying and creating systems—with an industrious push—will restore our resilience in this tide-turning Ox lunar year.

Carrying a heavy load? After a historically disruptive year (to put it mildly), even the most enlightened among us are probably dragging some baggage into 2021. Enter the strong, determined Metal Ox! This powerful draft animal is the Chinese zodiac ruler of 2021, here to help us shoulder the burden.

On a fundamental level, the Ox's role reminds us of the value of a hard day's work. Is there sweat on your brow? Have you plowed every inch of the metaphoric field? In 2020, the shrewd Metal Rat allowed people to cut corners, embellish the truth and sneak around in the dark. Not in 2021! Under the Metal Ox's watch, success must be earned with good old-fashioned integrity.

Too much "lather, rinse, repeat" won't cut muster, though. The Metal element lends strategy to the Ox's game, upgrading any basic B.S. like a master engineer. How can we improve existing processes so that we're working smarter, not harder? Along with all the planetary transits pushing for this (Jupiter and Saturn in Aquarius, Uranus in Taurus), the Metal Ox can help us revamp failing systems so that everyone gets fed, not just a privileged few. The Metal element is sharp, cutting through any outdated or overhyped "sludge" and making way for improved processes. Since Metal is connected to infrastructures, we may revamp entire industries—which, in an Ox year, could be associated with food production, groceries, labor, security and home.

Exodus to…suburbia? As people flee pandemic-wracked cities in search of fresh air and green space, we expect a continuation of 2020's real estate trends.

According to reports, searches for suburban homes jumped 13 percent in the middle of last year, with Millennials gaining interest in this (currently) more affordable housing market. The traditional Ox thrives in quiet, open spaces. However, the refined Metal element makes proximity to arts, cutting-edge industry and culture a priority as well. Bedroom communities may see a boon in 2021, as well as cities where larger houses with yards are still available. Well, as long as there's a Whole Foods, yoga studio and twee home décor shop near the downtown strip…

So, uh, what about all those high-rise apartments that were built pre-COVID? Because 2021 is a Metal year, there could be interesting developments for these steel and glass constructions. Under the pragmatic Ox's influence, rooftops may become shared gardens that provide food for tenants. A set number of units could be earmarked as affordable housing for people whose jobs were affected by the economic crisis. Some buildings may even adopt a modified barter system, allowing skilled tenants to trade work hours for rent. Hey, who couldn't use an on-site IT whiz in their complex these days?

Homesteading might gain popularity in 2021, with a savvy Metal year twist. Always wanted to grow your own vegetables, gather up fresh eggs from the coop or churn butter a la Laura Ingalls Wilder? The Ox is 100 percent with that plan! With Metal's refinement, however, the standards could get even more Portlandia. Think: grass-fed, free-range, non-GMO, heirloom and organic everything. Metal years are great for money moves. We expect a boon for the cannabis industry—more CBD-infused everything, coming to a grocer's freezer near you!

A "back to the land" movement might even gain popularity, perhaps following the model of the original Israeli kibbutz, where people lived, farmed and raised families collectively. Our own father grew up in an agricultural community like this where he gained specialized skills in fruit trees and chickens, all while living in a dorm-like situation with other kids his age. With Jupiter and Saturn in collaborative, idealistic Aquarius this year, we're sure to see all kinds of utopian experiments spring up.

Oxen are yoked together in pairs—then grouped together further in twosomes. That makes 2021 a potent year for figuring out new ways to cooperate and collaborate. Essential workers continue to be the heroes of the year, but people

The AstroTwins' 2021 Horoscope   486

who can both hustle and innovate will rule the world. How cool and composed can you be? That refreshing attitude will win the day in 2021—a huge relief after weathering the showboating Earth Dog, the hedonistic Earth Pig and the cunning Metal Rat—all since 2018. But it may also be hard to know what people are thinking or to read their steely energy this year. The downside? Unyielding, sharp and even quietly destructive people could gain command.

Sometimes, we need to shut off our brains for serenity's sake. The best way to do this in a Metal Ox year? Lean in to routine. Repetitive tasks can be a form of moving meditation. Seek solace in doing the same things over and over, like reconciling your finances, working out at the same time each day, gardening, cooking or any domestic work (the Ox loves home life). Just make sure there is some sort of purpose. Knit scarves for holiday gifts, make a large-scale macramé piece as bedroom décor.

Equally important? Knowing when to stop! The tireless Ox can keep running, even when there's barely any steam left. This is a year where workaholic tendencies can really creep in, especially if there's promise of some Metal year coin. Lean in to the strategic and infrastructure-based vibes and create org charts, workflow plans, budgets and schedules. Delegate instead of DIY-ing everything. Sure, we might be able to handle it all, but that can sidetrack us from the higher-earning tasks that benefit the entire pack. No need to be anyone's beast of burden!

If you work at a desk, physical exercise is more important than ever. Once again, having a set routine is advised, making it a goal to incrementally build strength and endurance. Weight training or kettlebell workouts can be effective during a Metal Ox year, as well as any exercise you can do in the fresh air. Since Metal is associated with the lungs, improve yours with cardio (all the more important as we grapple with the coronavirus) and experiment with eating foods that are rich in mineral content: nuts, legumes, dark leafy greens, fish, avocados, beef and lamb, to name a few. Filter your drinking water and get your iron levels checked if your energy dips.

Socially, Ox energy tends to be quiet and contained—certainly in contrast to the last two years of the neighborly Pig and communal Rat. Oxen hate small talk and aren't big into group activities, which will make social distancing easier for however long it continues to be the mandate. Staying close to home will be easier during the Ox year, a time when gathering with family and loyal friends may be everyone's preference.

Since Ox years are not for slackers, get into hobbies and crafts that involve Metal objects. Invest in that great set of kitchen knives or copper-bottomed pans. Tinker under the hood of a car, do needlecrafts or garden with tools. Weld, solder jewelry, try making fashions that are apropos for the Metal Ox year by adding studs, buckles, chains and other bling to utilitarian pieces. Speaking of styles, be on the lookout for those oversized Dickies coats and trucker caps of the early 1990s, or lumberjack trends with a farmland twist: suspenders, coveralls, utility belts and so on. Hats and hairstyles with horns might even make a debut!

If you network, be selective. We're not saying Metal energy is snobbish, but it is refined and discerning. Inflexibility can cause conflict among people, so we'll all have to work a little harder to bend and compromise. But hey, it's also a relief to know where you stand with folks. And after 2020's media circus, the Metal Ox's demand for truth and integrity will be oh-so-refreshing. Under this zodiac influence, people prefer to make decisions based on careful research rather than sensationalized stories or "fake news." If trust isn't restored this year, at least it will be improved. Traditional media outlets may be asked to back up their claims with legitimate reporting. In 2021, those fact checkers might finally have the last laugh!

As the economy continues to struggle post-pandemic, follow the metal—literally! During the passage of the indomitable Chinese Metal Ox, interest in precious metals will be white-hot given the global state of uncertainty. We see that shiny, appreciating trend continuing for the foreseeable future as many savvy investors will continue to reallocate their weaker stock positions into "safe haven" assets like gold and silver in order to hedge against the titanic forces imperiling the economy. That metallic view also includes the hardest currency on the planet, Bitcoin, which is likely to see a stampede of investors as governments continue to print fiat currencies to vertiginous, hyper-inflationary levels.

And Astrostyle is not alone in this view. Numerous financial analysts predict a bull run for both precious metals and Bitcoin extending for the next decade. But expect much volatility in the months and years ahead given the unstable nature of the global markets. If you do buy gold, silver or BTC, you might want to make like the tenacious Ox and play the long game—"buy and hold"—while covering your bases with a diversified plan. Having cash on hand for the short-term seems wise during a year ruled by the battle-tested, old-school Metal Ox.

Even our loose change is getting harder to come by. During the 2020 Metal Rat year, minting shortages disrupted the production of coins in the U.S.A.. We may see more of that in the second of two consecutive Metal-ruled years. As we write this, the International Monetary Fund (IMF) is calling for a Bretton Woods-style monetary summit to reset the global economy, the likes of which haven't happened since 1944.

When it comes to love, the Year of the Metal Ox makes everyone hella picky. But hey, if you're going to be "yoked" together, selecting the right mate takes on more gravitas. Conversations about the future could get serious fast—to the detriment of flirting. We might hit the brakes on fast-moving romances when the Ox year begins on February 12, 2021. Just be mindful not to go from casual curiosity to instant marriage, even if you're sure you've found your happily-ever-after mate. And with the perfectionistic Metal energy afoot, make room for people's humanity. We can't be refined and glamorous 24/7, after all! (That said, the burping and snorting can also go.)

If you're already attached, this is a year to create clear agreements and improve your conflict resolution skills. Make a point of breaking up stale routines. Take on a bigger household project if funds are available, perhaps putting in a second bathroom or creating the garden of your dreams. As tempted as you'll be to DIY this, work with the pros for the heavy lifting. When the terrestrial Ox plays groundskeeper and rules the skies, it's all about a solid team effort! ✳

The AstroTwins' 2021 Horoscope   489

The Aquarian Technocalypse

The Years 2020 and 2021 are a prelude to events that will usher in a new period of human civilization.

I n the coming decade, we will witness the convergence of many cycles, secular and non-secular, ancient and contemporary in orientation. The period is circumscribed by generational astrology, with the outer planets Uranus, Neptune and Pluto returning to key positions they occupied during pivotal points in American history, echoing watershed events of our past, including the founding of the United States more than two centuries ago.

The years 2020 and 2021 are a prelude to major transformations in our social, economic and political ecologies. The disruptions we've endured to this point will begin to coalesce into a meaningful narrative, albeit a challenging one, in the winter of 2022. Governments and economies around the globe will reorganize, ushering a new epoch of human civilization that will coincide with Pluto's reign in Aquarius between 2023 and 2044—what we have termed the Aquarian Technocalypse.

. . . .

To support our planetary thesis, we look to two major transits of early 2022:

Neptune: As the transiting Sun ingresses into Pisces on February 18, 2022, transcendent Neptune will arrive at 22° Pisces, beginning its opposition to the USA's natal Neptune, which is at 22° Virgo. A Neptune opposition occurs only once every 165 years.

Pluto: Two days later, on February 20, 2022 (2/20/22), under a 2°02′ Pisces Sun, the planet of prophecy, power and transformation will return to 27°33′ Capricorn for the first time in 246 years. Pluto will reach its exact "home" degree in the birth chart of the United States, dated July 4, 1776. This will mark America's first "Pluto return."

On 2/22/22, both Neptune and Pluto will be at 22° positions.

America's Pluto Return: Secrets Revealed, Transformation Ahead

Beginning on February 20, 2022, the United States will enter its historic Pluto return, as the cosmic alchemist makes a homecoming at 27°33' Capricorn for the first time since the country's birth on July 4, 1776.

Thirteen months later, on March 23, 2023, Pluto will enter Aquarius for the first time since 1797, the year that George Washington, who was born on 2/22, made democratic history by transferring his presidency to John Adams, earning the adulation of many world leaders. (When told that Washington would honor the new Constitution rather than rule interminably, King George III of Britain said, "Then he shall be the greatest man in the world.")

This Pluto homecoming is a decisive moment for the entire planet, not just the United States, as the world's major powers grapple with the unleashing of revolutionary forces. Pluto's looming presence has been exhuming buried truths for at least a decade, the revelation of which Astrostyle highlighted in our *2020 Horoscope Guide*—most notably our much-touted Black Swan economic prediction, where we correctly foretold 2020's calamitous financial deterioration.

With that heavy prediction tucked under our wing, we forged ahead, sensitive to the global tumult emerging from the Saturn-Pluto conjunction of January 12, 2020. The fallout is still underway at the time of this writing, with twin economic and viral pandemics, both in their respective early stages.

The United States has its roots in many Plutonian secrets. It's well-documented that several of the Founding Fathers, including George Washington and Benjamin Franklin, were members of the Freemasons, a philosophic organization embedded in the construction of the nation and its cities and landmarks, many of which, like the Washington Monument obelisk, directly reflecting the architecture of ancient Egypt.

Some believe that Benjamin Franklin chose July 4, 1776, as the ratification date for the United States *Declaration of Independence* because of its favorable planetary alignments. One of America's preeminent astrologers, Franklin has his natal Sun at 27° Capricorn, an exact conjunction with the U.S.A.'s natal Pluto. (The fact that Pluto wasn't officially discovered until 1930 only reinforces its occulted influence on the country's origins).

Published annually from 1732-58, Franklin's *Poor Richard's Almanack* contained a detailed astrological ephemeris (calendar) that tracked monthly moon phases and motions of the known planets, along with predictions based on their astral interactions—the Colonial American equivalent of a daily horoscope.

In his *Almanack*, Benjamin Franklin championed astrology and called to task those who denounced it:

"Courteous Reader: Astrology is one of the most ancient Sciences, had in high Esteem of old, by the Wise and Great. Formerly, no Prince would make War or Peace, nor any General fight a Battle, in short, no important Affair was taken without first consulting an Astrologer, who examined the Aspects and Configurations of the heavenly bodies, and mark'd the lucky hour. Now the noble Art (more Shame to the Age we live in!) is dwindled into contempt; the Great neglect us, Empires make Leagues, and Parliaments Laws, without advising with us; and scarce any other Use is made of our learned Labors."

Synastry (Comparison) Chart of the U.S.A. Natal Chart and February 22, 2022

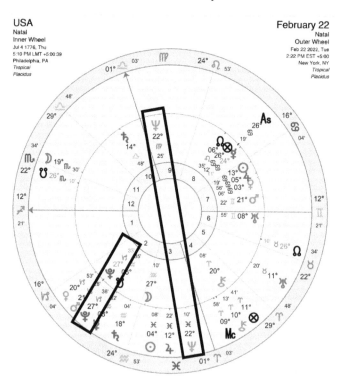

USA
Natal
Inner Wheel
Jul 4 1776, Thu
5:10 PM LMT +5:00:39
Philadelphia, PA
Tropical
Placidus

February 22
Natal
Outer Wheel
Feb 22 2022, Tue
2:22 PM EST +5:00
New York, NY
Tropical
Placidus

Pluto In Aquarius: The Separation of Money and State

With Pluto entering Aquarius in 2023 again, we predict that the next great global political revolution will be the attempt to separate money from the state, a demand that will gain traction throughout Pluto's long transit. Enigmatic Pluto will herald changes to technology, industry and economy that will span over at least the next two decades, especially as the tiny powerhouse transits the final degrees of Capricorn and enters the Aquarian realm.

On March 23, 2023 (3/23/23), Pluto will move into Aquarius until 2044, its first visit to the Water Bearer's domain since 1778-98, which was a 20-year period of explosive growth for both the Industrial Revolution and the Age of Enlightenment. The origin of our monetary system has roots in Pluto's last visit to Capricorn and Aquarius, an era that encompassed both the American and French Revolutions.

History demonstrates that major changes to our financial systems, at a fundamental level, parallel the cycles of the outer planets, which are drivers of progress and innovation. The takeaway? Money and government are both forms of human technology, subject to evolution—and technology always disrupts.

This truism is evident throughout civilization, from the harnessing of fire to the creation of the wheel and the birth of every alphabet. Each of these inventions emancipated humankind, leading us to our next great age or cycle, just as a silicon chip or satellite signal is doing today. We are a technological species, magicians of the material realm.

The infinite creation/destruction cycle that's embedded in Pluto's primordial nature will become more evident as this planet moves into innovative Aquarius. When Pluto couples with the power of Uranus, we'll reach a full understanding of *techne*, the ancient Greek philosophic term that is the prefix of technology.

Felt by many scholars to precede observational science and its methodology, *techne* refers to a survival-based urge to create or make something new (Uranus), which is often accompanied by the destruction of what came before it (Pluto). *Techne* is the fundamental impulse that drove the American colonists to emancipate themselves from Britain with the creation of their own sovereign laws and currency. It's the same spirit of radical individualism now fueling the global Information Age.

In 1792, while Pluto was last in Aquarius, the United States dollar became the nation's standard unit of currency. Prior to this, the colonists issued the "continental," paper money intended to unyoke them from the British monetary system. To offset their war debts and finance the building of the nation, the colonists used the vanguard technology of their time—the printing press—to produce continentals. While this allowed them to break away from the tyranny of King George III, the unchecked printing of notes, exacerbated by British counterfeiting, drove up inflation and debased the continental until it became essentially worthless. This cycle of creation/destruction necessitated the birth of a new Federal currency, the dollar—and is no doubt why the U.S. Constitution explicitly defines the difference between money (gold/silver) and currency.

> ## "We predict the next great global political revolution will be the attempt to separate money from the state."

As the French Enlightenment philosopher Voltaire warned, "Paper money eventually returns to its intrinsic value: zero." Today, the U.S. Federal Reserve is debasing the U.S. dollar—the world's reserve currency—by "printing to infinity" in an effort to keep the debt-addled American economy afloat.

It is generally agreed among economists that the U.S. dollar has exhausted its utility and value. Since no government-issued fiat currency in human history has ever survived debasement, we find ourselves once again in need of monetary innovation, rooted in the spirit of *techne*.

The timely movements of the outer planets are again present as we reconfigure our political and monetary systems. Starting in 2024, technological Uranus (the ruler of Aquarius), will travel in a close trine (120-degree angle of activation) to Pluto for the rest of the decade, accelerating when Uranus enters quicksilver Gemini in 2025. A quintessential example of *techne's* evolutionary thrust is the emergence of Bitcoin and its distributed ledger known as the blockchain, which reimagines the advantages of Gutenberg's printing press (Uranus) and the enduring power of precious metal (Pluto) into the next iteration of money via cryptography (Pluto). Wholly technological, Bitcoin carries the torch of *techne* into the contemporary Aquarian epoch.

At this writing, Bitcoin, whose creator is still unknown, is poised to disrupt the world's fiat currencies. Given the presence of Uranus and Pluto, we may want to entertain the possibility that a breakaway intelligence group, rather than a single person (the enigmatic Satoshi Nakamoto), is the creator of Bitcoin. Perhaps the return of Pluto to Aquarius will unveil this cryptographic entity.

Neptune, The Fourth Turning & The Cross of Ixion

It's not just Pluto portending great changes in early 2022. Numinous Neptune is also part of this story. Neptune rules divine revelation, but this planet has a lesser-known association with war and catastrophe, including natural disasters such as earthquakes, tsunamis and storms. In mythology, Neptune carries a three-pronged trident, a weapon given to him by his brother Pluto, which granted him authority over the oceans.

On February 18, 2022, Neptune will begin a trek through 22° Pisces, making an exact opposition to Neptune in the United States' natal chart (which is at 22° Virgo). This aspect only occurs every 165 years. Neptune was last at 22° Pisces in the late 1850s, a pivotal time in the nation's prelude to Civil War.

We might look at generational researchers Lewis and Howe's book *The Fourth Turning* to understand Neptune's cyclical nature and how it expresses throughout history. (These are the authors who coined the term "millennial.")

According to their theory, generations shift every 22 years (for example, we now divide into Boomers, Gen X, Millennials and Gen Z). These generations are grouped into four "turnings" that last for 80-90 years each, which coincide with half of a Neptune cycle. The major themes of these larger cycles repeat every 80-90 years—or what Lewis and Howe call a *saeculum*, Latin for "a natural century" and roughly the span of a well-lived human life. (Long before books like the *Fourth Turning* created cycles in which to understand human history, this observational role was, and continues to be, the province of the ancient art of astrology.)

As stated, Neptune takes 83 years to complete half a cycle around the zodiac wheel. Uranus takes 84 years to complete a full revolution, encompassing a "turning." If we begin counting with the founding of the United States in 1776, while Neptune was at 22° Virgo, we observe Neptune's first American *saeculum* completing in 1859, right before the Civil War began, when Neptune first reached 22° Pisces.

The next 83-year *saeculum*, and Neptune's first return to 22° Virgo since the founding of the U.S.A., began in 1939. Once again, major upheaval ensued: World War II officially began on September 1, 1939, with Neptune at precisely 22° Virgo.

As we approach Neptune's second 22° visit to Pisces in the history of the United States (in February 2022), we look back to the start of the Civil War, which began in 1861, as Neptune exited Pisces to begin its quest through Aries. In 2025,

Neptune will repeat this cycle. Given the total nature of the sky, is a new type of civil conflict upon us—perhaps one that is both digital and algorithmic, not simply an overt demonstration of military or physical force?

To answer this profound question, one that we take great caution in advancing, we must acknowledge and consider the promethean forces of high technology impacting every sphere of human endeavor, including our monetary system. To wit: Uranus will complete an American *saeculum* on July 27, 2027 (7/27/27), returning to 8°55' Gemini, where it's also positioned in the U.S.A.'s 1776 birth chart. Historical markers of conflict are present again: Uranus was at 9°20' Gemini when the Civil War began, and again at 9°20' Gemini on D-Day (June 6, 1944), when the Allied Forces liberated Europe with the largest invasion in military history, codenamed Operation Overlord.

History shows us that major economic shifts often correlate with war, if not exclusively so. The American Revolution, the U.S. Civil War and World War II all ushered in new monetary systems: the birth of the U.S. dollar, the National Currency Act and the Bretton Woods system, respectively. As Neptune, Uranus and Pluto all return to placements that coincided with prior wars and the emergence of these new financial orderings, their transits support our planetary thesis that upheaval is highly probable and will birth the next monetary system during this decade. As we are now in the high-tech era known as the Fourth Industrial Revolution, the constellating spirit of *techne* will be palpable, whether its representation is found in Bitcoin or another digital currency that Neptune's fourth *saeculum* has yet to reveal.

A clue to that revelation can be obtained by casting our vision across Neptune's great ocean to the nascent financial superpower of China, where we discover a cosmic harbinger of the Aquarian Technocalypse. The birth date of modern China and its currency, the Chinese renminbi (yuan), is October 1, 1949, and features a natal chart conjunction of the Sun (7°), Mercury (13°) and Neptune (14°) in Libra. Incredibly, these three planets form a climactic "cardinal cross" with the U.S.A.'s natal Sun (13° Cancer) and Saturn (14° Libra), and the natal Suns of the U.S. dollar (13° Aries) and Bitcoin (13° Capricorn), a burning wheel of Ixion for each nation-state.

In astrology the Sun represents the drive to define and preserve one's identity, whether person or nation—the solar ego. This rare and intractable four-way solar cross contains inordinate power, profound in its implications. Given the configuration between the U.S.A., China and their currencies, we have named this solar configuration the "Cross of Ixion," a vexing new aspect with a fitting astronomical reference: a glowing red trans-Neptunian plutino (discovered in Chile on May 22, 2001) named for the mythical Ixion, who was struck by Zeus' lightning bolt for his ceaseless intemperance then bound to a burning solar wheel condemned to turn for eternity.

The cardinal Cross of Ixion and the natal chart of the U.S.A.

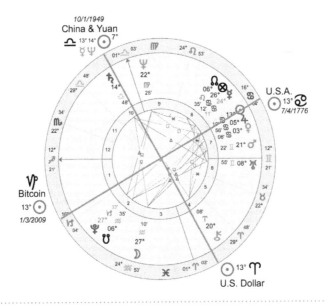

The Power of Two ♒

In the ancient divination system of numerology, 22 is a master number. It adds up to four, a number that displays itself prominently in astrology and prophecy, in both Eastern and Western practices. With 2/22/22 being a pivotal date, and prophetic Neptune reaching 22° Pisces, it's clear that the numbers hold a message. In other traditions, 22 is also prevalent: There are 22 Major Arcana in the Tarot and 22 letters in the Hebrew alphabet. In Biblical scripture, 22 is the number of Revelation.

How will we set the foundation for U.S.A. 2.0 amid such typhonic forces? Since the moment before us demands our attention in so many unknown and challenging ways, perhaps we are best served by learning from those bright stars that have preceded us, as we peer into the vast amphora of the Aquarian future-time. Embracing uncertainty, complexity and human diversity may ultimately liberate individuals and society alike.

As the transcendent Enlightenment-era mathematician and author of the world's first computational algorithm, Sagittarius Ada Lovelace, stated so memorably, "I never am really satisfied that I understand anything; because, understand it well as I may, my comprehension can only be an infinitesimal fraction of all I want to understand about the many connections and relations which occur to me..." ✳

Co-authored by Matthew Swann, October 2020

OPHIRA & TALI EDUT
THE ASTROTWINS

Dubbed the "astrologers to the stars," identical twin sisters Ophira and Tali Edut, known as the AstroTwins, are professional astrologers who reach millions worldwide through their spot-on predictions. Through their website, Astrostyle.com, Ophira and Tali help "bring the stars down to earth" with their unique, lifestyle-based approach to astrology.

They are the official astrologers for *ELLE* Magazine, Monster.com and MindBodyGreen.com. The AstroTwins have been featured by major media such as the *Good Morning America*, the *New York Times* and *People* and they've collaborated with major brands including Coach, Vogue, Nordstrom, Revlon, H&M, Urban Outfitters, Ted Baker and 1Hotels.

The sisters have read charts for celebrities including Beyoncé, Stevie Wonder, Emma Roberts, Karlie Kloss, Elizabeth Gilbert and Sting. They have appeared on Bravo's *The Real Housewives of New Jersey*, doing on-air readings for the cast. They have authored numerous print books, including *Love Zodiac, Shoestrology* and *Momstrology* (their #1 Amazon best-selling astrological parenting guide) and a series of self-published books, including their popular annual horoscope guides. ✳

VISIT THE ASTROTWINS AT WWW.ASTROSTYLE.COM
FOLLOW US EVERYWHERE @ASTROTWINS